Gender and Language Research Methodologies

Edited by

Kate Harrington
The New School, New York

Lia Litosseliti
City University, London

Helen Sauntson
University of Birmingham

and

Jane Sunderland
Lancaster University

First published in 2008 by
PALGRAVE MACMILLAN
Houndmills, Basingstoke, Hampshire RG21 6XS and
175 Fifth Avenue, New York, N.Y. 10010
Companies and representatives throughout the world.

PALGRAVE MACMILLAN is the global academic imprint of the Palgrave
Macmillan division of St. Martin's Press, LLC and of Palgrave Macmillan Ltd.
Macmillan® is a registered trademark in the United States, United Kingdom
and other countries. Palgrave is a registered trademark in the European
Union and other countries.

ISBN-13: 978–0–230–55068–1 hardback
ISBN-13: 0–230–55068–1 hardback
ISBN-13: 978–0–230–55069–8 paperback
ISBN-10: 0–230–55069–X paperback

This book is printed on paper suitable for recycling and made from fully
managed and sustained forest sources. Logging, pulping and manufacturing
processes are expected to conform to the environmental regulations of
the country of origin.

A catalogue record for this book is available from the British Library.

A catalog record for this book is available from the Library of Congress.

10 9 8 7 6 5 4 3 2 1
17 16 15 14 13 12 11 10 09 08

Printed and bound in Great Britain by
CPI Antony Rowe, Chippenham and Eastbourne

Contents

Part 3   Conversation Analysis

Part 4   Discursive Psychology

Part 5   Critical Discourse Analysis

Part 6   Feminist Post-Structuralist Discourse Analysis

Part 7   Queer Theory

List of Tables and Figures

Tables

Figures

Notes on Contributors

Julieta Ojeda Alba is Associate Professor of American Literature at the University of La Rioja, Spain. In addition to her interest and publications in Applied Linguistics, she has also published translations of American Literature works such as Nathaniel Hawthorne's *Fanshawe: A Tale*, and studies in American Literature and culture such as 'Representaciones de la mujer en la música tradicional y country norteamericana', in Vigara and Jiménez (eds.).

Paul Baker is a Senior Lecturer in the Department of Linguistics and English Language at Lancaster University, UK. His research interests are language and gender/sexuality, critical discourse analysis and corpus linguistics. He has recently published *Using Corpora in Discourse Analysis* and is the commissioning editor for the journal *Corpora*.

Judith Baxter is a Lecturer in Applied Linguistics at Reading University, UK. She has written many articles and books, the most recent being *Speaking Out: The Female Voice in Public Contexts* and *Positioning Gender in Discourse: A Feminist Methodology*.

Harold Andrés Castañeda-Peña teaches 'Gender, language and identity' in the School of Language and Communication at Pontificia Universidad Javeriana, Colombia. He has authored preschool language learning materials. His main research interests include issues of gender identity, bilingualism and information literacy. He is currently working on a book about children's discourses of gender, using a feminist and post-structuralist discourse analysis approach, in educational contexts where English is taught as a foreign language.

Rosa Mª Jiménez Catalán is Associate Professor of Applied Linguistics at the University of La Rioja, Spain. Her current research interests include the analysis of the effect of the gender factor in foreign language learning and cross-linguistic analysis of gender in English and Spanish. Some of her publications in this connection are 'Sex differences in L2 "Vocabulary learning strategies"' in the *International Journal of Applied Linguistics* (2003), and 'Semantic derogation in female/male examples of animal metaphor', in the *Journal of Pragmatics* (co-authored with Almudena Fontecha, 2003).

Nigel Edley is a Senior Lecturer in the School of Arts and Humanities at Nottingham Trent University, UK. His interests are around Discursive Psychology and social constructionism as they pertain to, and help make sense of, the production of men and masculinities. He is the author of many articles in journals such as *Feminism & Psychology, British Journal of Social Psychology* and, most recently, *Sex Roles.*

Kate Harrington is a Consultant for the New School in New York, USA. Her main teaching and research interests are gender and language, the history of English, conversational narrative and reported dialogue.

Anna Kristina Hultgren is working towards her DPhil at the English Faculty, University of Oxford, UK. Her research interests include sociolinguistics and language and gender.

Laurel D. Kamada, Professor at Aomori Akenohoshi College in Japan, has published in such areas as Gender and Ethnic Studies and Marginalised (hybrid and gendered) Identities in Japan and has drawn on various discourse analytic approaches including Feminist Poststructuralist Discourse Analysis, Discursive Psychology and Critical Discourse Analysis. She is currently working on a book about gender and hybrid identities of adolescent mixed-ethnicity girls in Japan, referred to as 'half'.

Celia Kitzinger is Professor of Gender, Sexuality and Conversation Analysis and Director of the Feminist Conversation Analysis Unit at the University of York, UK. She has published nine books and more than 150 articles on issues relevant to gender, language and sexuality. She is currently analysing more than 350 calls to a helpline for women in crisis after childbirth, and working with midwives to improve counselling in this area.

Veronika Koller is a Lecturer in English Language at Lancaster University, UK. She is the author of *Metaphor and Gender in Business Media Discourse: A Critical Cognitive Study.*

Konstantia Kosetzi holds a PhD in Linguistics from Lancaster University, UK (2007). Her PhD thesis is a Critical Discourse Analysis study of a Greek TV series, *Schedon Pote*, where she analyses women's representations in terms of gender roles and sexual practices in the 'text', and viewers' responses, all in relation to women's position in Greek urban society. Her academic interests are related to the fields of CDA, Gender and Language Studies and the media, within which her publications also fall.

William L. Leap is Professor of Anthropology at American University, Washington DC, USA. His recent publications examine the politics of language, race/ethnicity, sexuality and citizenship in US and South African settings.

Lia Litosseliti is a Senior Lecturer in Linguistics at City University, London, UK. Her research interests are in the areas of gender and language, discourse analysis, and research issues and methodologies. She is the author of *Gender and Language: Theory and Practice* (2006) and *Using Focus Groups in Research*

(2003), co-editor of *Gender Identity and Discourse Analysis* (2002), and editor of *Research Methods in Linguistics* (forthcoming).

Janet Maybin is a Senior Lecturer in Language and Communication at the Open University, UK. She has written extensively for Open University courses on language, literacy and learning, and also researches and writes on children's and adults' informal language and literacy practices. She originally trained as a social anthropologist. She is the author of *Children's Voices: Talk, Knowledge and Identity*.

Louise Mullany is a Lecturer in Sociolinguistics at the University of Nottingham, UK. Her research primarily focuses on language and gender in business, media and medical settings. She has published in a range of international journals and edited collections on gender and professional discourse, and has recently co-edited *The Routledge Companion to Sociolinguistics*. She is author of *Gendered Discourse in the Professional Workplace*.

Pia Pichler is a Lecturer in Linguistics at Goldsmiths College, University of London, UK. Her research interests include discourse and conversation analysis, sociolinguistics, language and gender/identity and feminist linguistics.

Helen Sauntson is a Lecturer in English Language at Birmingham University, UK. Her main teaching and research interests are in the areas of discourse analysis, language, gender and sexuality and language in education. She is author, with Liz Morrish, of *New Perspectives on Language and Sexual Identity*, and co-editor, with Sakis Kyratzis, of *Language, Sexualities and Desires: Cross-Cultural Perspectives*.

Elizabeth Stokoe is Reader in Social Interaction in the Department of Social Sciences at Loughborough University, UK. Her current research interests are in conversation analysis and ethnomethodology more broadly; gender and interaction, neighbour disputes and speed-dating. She recently published *Discourse and Identity* (2006), with Bethan Benwell, and has completed an edited collection entitled *Conversation and Gender* (forthcoming), with Susan Speer. She is working on two further books on gender in interaction and speed-dating.

Jane Sunderland is a Senior Lecturer at Lancaster University, UK. She teaches 'Gender and Language' at postgraduate level and co-ordinates a 'Thesis and Coursework' PhD programme. Her most recent books are *Language and Gender: An Advanced Resource Book* (2006) and *Gendered Discourses* (2004).

Joan Swann works in the Centre for Language and Communications at the Open University, UK. Her main research interests are in sociolinguistics, particularly language and gender, and gender in education.

Margaret Wetherell is Professor of Social Psychology at the Open University, UK, and Director of the ESRC Identities and Social Action Programme. Her research has focused on developing theory and methods for discourse analysis in social psychology and has included empirical work on masculine identities, 'race' and ethnicity and, recently, discursive democracy and citizens' councils. She is the co-author of *Citizens at the Centre* (Policy Press), *Men in Perspective* (Prentice Hall) and *Discourse and Social Psychology* (Sage), among other books, and co-editor of *Discourse Theory and Practice* (Sage), *Discourse as Data* (Sage) and *Analyzing Race Talk* (Cambridge University Press).

Ruth Wodak is Professor of Discourse Studies, Lancaster University, UK, and was previously Professor of Applied Linguistics in the University of Vienna. She holds multiple visiting professorships (Stanford, Georgetown, Minneapolis, Uppsala, UEA) and in 2008–9 will hold the Karen Hesselgren Chair of the Swedish Parliament. She is co-editor of the *Journal of Language and Politics* and *Critical Discourse Analysis* and has many book publications on the application of Critical Discourse Analysis.

1
Current Research Methodologies in Gender and Language Study: Key Issues

Jane Sunderland and Lia Litosseliti

Gender and language, best seen as a topic or field, is investigated *through* an increasing range and diversity of theoretical and methodological approaches. To explore this characteristic of the field, the editors of this book[1] organised a British Association of Applied Linguistics/Cambridge University Press Seminar entitled 'Theoretical and Methodological Approaches to Gender and Language Study', which took place at Birmingham University, UK, in November 2005. We planned both the Seminar and this book with a very broad notion of 'approach' in mind, but as something chosen in a principled way, which then has implications for, and is manifested methodologically in, the researcher's choice of research questions, data, data selection/collection/generation, analysis and interpretation. *Approach*, then, spans theory and research practice.

In the recent *Handbook of Language and Gender* (Holmes and Meyerhoff, 2003), the contributors draw on ethnography, grammatical analyses, discourse-based analyses, 'discourse-historical' critical discourse analysis, conversation analysis, linguistic anthropology, text analysis, discursive psychology and 'pragmatic eclecticism'. This diversity is testimony to the richness of the highly interdisciplinary gender and language field. Few of the contributors, however, address approach explicitly. Three exceptions are Susan Philips, Jack Sidnell and Joan Swann. Philips claims that discourse analysis *'allows for* empirical documentation of the production of gender ideologies, and *can reveal in detail* how these ideologies are grounded and ordered in discourse' (2003: 272; our italics). Sidnell notes that by *'wedding the close analysis of talk-in-interaction with ethnography, it is possible to examine* the manner in which the settings of everyday life, and the relevance of them to the participants' gender, are constructed and managed through practices of talk-in-interaction' (2003: 345; our italics). Claims about what an approach *allows for, can reveal* and makes *possible* suggest that there are also certain things particular approaches cannot do, are less well-equipped to do, or can do together (see below). And Swann's 'pragmatic eclecticism' explicitly acknowledges 'the possibilities and limitations of all methodological choices' (2003: 630).

Despite this reticence in the *Handbook*, approach is *important*: as gender and language researchers, we need to be alert to the risk of becoming entrenched in our approaches, or taking them for granted. In publications, we need to declare our interest in the research – not only 'which questions are asked or not asked' but also 'which methods of analysis are followed and why' (Litosseliti, 2006a: 151). Accordingly, *Gender and Language Research Methodologies* has *approach* as its organising principle.

*   *   *

Historically, there has always been diversity of approach within language and gender study, even before today's theoretical complexities. Otto Jespersen (1922) can retrospectively be seen as using 'native speaker intuition' in his chapter 'The woman'. Mary Haas (1944), in her anthropological study of women's and men's speech in Koasati, a Native American language, followed a more empirical approach; this anthropological tradition has shaped present-day ethnographies. Gender and language use was later addressed, more substantially, by variationist sociolinguistics, with gender – or, rather, biological sex – having the status of an independent variable (Labov, 1990, 1966; Cheshire, 1982; Milroy, 1980; Gal, 1978; Trudgill, 1972).

The 'parallel' strand of work, gender as part of linguistic code (e.g., Corbett, 1991) was, in the 1970s and 1980s, addressed from a critical (if at times rather determinist) feminist perspective with a focus on (non-)sexist language (Spender, 1980); more recently, this has been documented as feminist-inspired language change (e.g., Hellinger and Bußmann, 2001; Pauwels, 1998). A major early player in the 'sexist language' debate (and in gender and language study more generally) was Robin Lakoff. Her monograph *Language and Woman's Place* (1975) is now routinely acknowledged as valiant and productive, if flawed (being a pioneer carries a price). Lakoff's own methodological approach was the Chomskyan one of native speaker intuition, or 'introspection', which she took pains to document ('I have examined my own speech, and that of my acquaintances, and have used my own intuitions in analysing it' (1975: 4)) and defend:

> any procedure is at some point introspective: the gatherer must analyze his [sic!] data, after all. Then, one necessarily selects a subgroup of the population to work with: is the educated, white, middle-class group that the writer of the book identifies with less worthy of study than any other? And finally, there is the purely pragmatic issue: random conversation must go on for quite some time, and the recorder must be exceedingly

lucky anyway, in order to produce evidence of any particular hypothesis, for example, that there is sexism in language...

(1975: 4–5)

Lakoff is right about 'any procedure [being] at some point introspective', or at least subjective – a point made also by feminist and critical linguists, that is, *no* approach is, can or even should be objective. However, her other arguments are more problematic. Of course we can investigate the talk of 'educated, white, middle-class' women – as long as we do not pretend that they are more widely representative. And, though sexist language may indeed be absent on a given stretch of tape, this is less true of gender tendencies in language use, actually Lakoff's greater area of concern.

'Introspection' was not taken up in subsequent gender and language study, giving way to different forms of empiricism,[2] with a focus on small-scale social interactions. These studies sometimes went under the name of 'Conversation analysis' (see Stokoe, this volume) or 'Interactional sociolinguistics'. Feminist-informed work included projects on interruption (West and Zimmerman, 1983; Zimmerman and West, 1975), verbosity, questions and back-channelling (Fishman, 1983). Like their sociolinguistic variationist predecessors, these studies were essentially comparative (men *vis á vis* women, i.e., focusing on gender *differences*). Social constructionism and *discourse* were still in the very early stages of development.[3]

The theoretical approach to gender in much of this work was based on the critical, feminist notion of 'male dominance' – of men, over women, through language. 'Dominance' was a child of its (political) time – the Women's Liberation Movement of the 1970s was in full swing. 'Dominance' did not, however, fit a well-established variationist paradigm, and soon took second place to the much less critical '(cultural) difference' approach. Cameron writes:

The gradual ascendancy of difference over dominance was almost inevitable given the ideology of twentieth-century linguistics, especially its anthropological and sociological variants. Difference, and not inequality, is what the framework of structural linguistics is designed to deal with.

(1995a: 35)

'(Cultural) difference' saw variation in the talk of women and men as the result of their being members, from an early age, of different 'linguistic sub-cultures' (Gumperz, 1982; Maltz and Borker, 1980). This suggested that gendered talk needed to be understood via study of single- as well as mixed-sex groups, which prompted investigation and positive re-evaluation of women's talk (e.g., Tannen, 1990; Coates, 1989), and, later, investigation of men's talk (e.g., Coates, 2003; Johnson and Meinhof, 1997). Such work highlighted the importance of examining conversational style in context, particularly speakers' own 'speech communities'.

The '(male) dominance' and '(cultural) difference' approaches had much in common. Both *compared* women and men, as members of two social groups. The common focus was very much private talk, small groups, and the *who* and *how* of communication. Work on public talk, on *what* was said, and on written texts was relatively rare.

This changed with the advent of social constructionism. Hitherto, the impetus behind much gender and language study had been either to uncover inequality in mixed-sex talk (given a feminist mandate to show how language use systematically disadvantaged women), or to celebrate the strengths of all-women talk. The underlying (unstated) assumption had tended to be that language use was somehow a reflection of gender. Social constructionism, however, entailed the very different notion of language use as *constructing* gender.

As regards gender itself, 'dominance' and 'difference' studies tended to see gender as sets of 'differential tendencies' between women and men, boys and girls (i.e., the *who* (speaker sex) and *how* of talk). And 'differential tendencies' is still the current 'popular' understanding of gender. Social constructionism, broadly defined, however, sees gender as:

- the active/interactive/negotiated construction of gender, including self-positioning
- linguistic dealings *with* (individual/groups of) women, men, boys and girls, e.g., how they are addressed, what is said *to* them
- what is said and written *about* gender differential tendencies, similarities and diversity, including what is said and written *about* (individual/groups of) women, men, boys and girls

Social constructionist perspectives thus de-emphasise gendered speakers (and writers) as agents, focusing rather on *what* is communicated *by, to* and *about* women, men, boys and girls.

The post-structuralist thinking associated with social constructionism allowed gender, *inter alia*, to be seen as not fixed but something interpreted – hence *talked and written about* (as well as enacted). Accordingly, any gender differentiation constructed *in* talk or writing may be more significant socially than any stylistic or interactional 'differential tendencies' in language use (see Krøløkke and Sørensen, 2006: 106; Cameron, 1997b).

Most gender and language study today broadly encompasses social constructionist meanings of *gender* together with a nuanced version of 'differential tendencies'. Its (post-structuralist) concerns are (see Cameron, 2005a, b):

- diversity (e.g., class, ethnicity, and their interaction with gender; multiple masculinities/femininities; differences among 'women' and among 'men')
- gender being 'performed' (see below) in an ongoing way, allowing for *agency*; performance being achieved partly through language (which is

therefore *constitutive*); power being 'done' rather than something speakers 'have'

- 'local' or 'contingent' explanations for gendered language patterns and the importance of specific contexts (see below).

Post-structuralism in its different forms has over the last 25 years turned much gender and language study – and much social scientific thinking – on its head. The associated notion of *performativity* (Butler, 1990), which has its roots in linguistics and language philosophy, allows gender to be seen as performed in part through the 'embodied reiteration' of particular linguistic acts. *Performance*, however, has other origins (e.g., Goffman, 1974) and is used more widely in the gender and language field. We now read frequently about gender being *performed*, but also *constructed, accomplished, achieved, enacted* and *effected*.

'Local' or in-context explanations for gendered language patterns have increasingly been theorised in terms of *Communities of Practice* (CofPs) (Lave and Wenger, 1991): groups of people 'who come together around mutual engagement in an endeavour', when 'ways of doing things, ways of talking, beliefs, values, power relations – in short, practices – emerge' (Eckert and McConnell-Ginet, 1992: 464). We participate in multiple CofPs, for example as members of a family, students in a classroom, employees in a workplace, members of a political party or other group. Gender identities (see Benwell and Stokoe, 2006; Litosseliti and Sunderland, 2002) are arguably produced, reproduced and contested through such participation, in particular through *differentially* gendered engagement (see Holmes and Meyerhoff, 1999, for a discussion). The CofP notion allows us to 'distinguish between speakers' assumed gendered behaviour and the range of identities available in the gendered communities that speakers inhabit' (Litosseliti, 2006a: 66). For instance, co-operative interactional patterns are not 'natural' to (or even socially predictable in) women, but rather reflect and are shaped by the gendered CofPs in which women participate (see Ostermann, 2003, for an example).

About this book

The book is organised in seven sections, representing an important selection of the current major methodological approaches to gender and language study. Each section includes a chapter laying out the foundations of an approach, followed by an illustrative chapter or chapters. Emphasised is the approach itself – its rationale and implementation, with empirical studies acting in an illustrative capacity. Our seven approaches are (1) sociolinguistics and ethnography, (2) corpus linguistics, (3) conversation analysis (CA), (4) discursive psychology, (5) critical discourse analysis (CDA), (6) feminist post-structuralist discourse analysis (FPDA) and (7) queer theory. These may be combined in current research practice in interesting and productive ways. Some (but not all) may act in the service of others. Needless to say, these seven approaches do not constitute a comprehensive (or neat) typology.

Part 1 Sociolinguistics and ethnography

Sociolinguistics has a long history and a wide scope. Now much broader than its original variationist paradigm, sociolinguistics is no longer concerned only with large-scale surveys, comparisons and unproblematised notions of gender. Many modern approaches to gender and language can now thus be described as sociolinguistic. Some pre-feminist 'gender differences' work carried out within this variationist paradigm (see Labov, 1966, and Trudgill, 1972), produced findings of relevance to the later feminist project. The importance of situating gender in context was shown by Susan Gal (1978) in her study of gender and bilingualism in Oberwart (on the Austrian-Hungarian border). Similarly, social context in the form of social network was key to Lesley Milroy's 1980 finding that a group of women in one Belfast community produced more particular vernacular forms than did their husbands (in contrast to Labov and Trudgill's findings).

These 'landmark' sociolinguistic studies are discussed by **Joan Swann** and **Janet Maybin** in Chapter 2. In an overview of sociolinguistic approaches to gender and language, they trace the movement away from broadly quantitative variationist approaches towards more local, contextualised, qualitative explorations of gender as intersecting with other social identities, including race, class and sexuality, and note the emergence of Communities of Practice approaches.

The subsequent chapters in Part 1, by **Anna Kristina Hultgren, Louise Mullany** and **Pia Pichler**, illustrate different sociolinguistic methodologies – correlational sociolinguistics, ethnographic/interactional sociolinguistics and linguistic ethnography, respectively. In Chapter 3, Hultgren evaluates contemporary quantitative investigations of sex differences in language use, emphasising the benefits of combining quantitative (correlational) and qualitative (ethnographic) approaches, and using her research on call centres to highlight the strengths of correlational methodologies. Mullany, in Chapter 4, explores the use of a qualitative paradigm – interactional sociolinguistics – in workplace contexts. In Chapter 5, Pichler looks at the use of linguistic ethnography and the ethnographic principle of engaging participants in the research process, and considers what can be gained from enabling participants to provide an 'insider' perspective on linguistic data.

Part 2 Corpus linguistics

Dealing with frequencies and probabilities in its analyses of corpora of up to several million words, corpus linguistics is ideally placed to investigate whether a particular word or phrase is used more by men or women. It thus has the potential to make claims which other approaches cannot. Corpus linguistics however can also show how women and men are differentially constructed, or 'positioned', in the way they refer to themselves or are referenced by others. Janet Holmes and Robert Sigley (2002), for example, used corpora to look at the use of *girl/boy* in a New Zealand workplace. Corpus linguistics faces a particular challenge in the current *qualitative* gender and language climate. However, the textual environment in corpus studies can be wide and diverse. Secondly, frequencies do not determine interpretations – and corpus linguistics has been used to identify and interpret contesting gendered discourses (e.g., Baker, 2005). Thirdly, corpus linguistics can support and complement small-scale qualitative studies. Swann includes corpus linguistics in her discussion of 'pragmatic eclecticism', referring to 'the use of quantitative (e.g., corpus-based) approaches to complement an analysis of more contextualised examples' (2003: 630).

In the first chapter, **Paul Baker** gives an overview of the potential of corpus methodologies and argues against the idea that a corpus approach sacrifices depth for breadth. In an analysis of the terms *bachelor* and *spinster* in the British National Corpus, he shows in Chapter 6 that while the former collocates with positive words such as *eligible* and the latter is constructed as unattractive and lonely, the corpus also reveals a conflicting *feminist* discourse surrounding spinsters.

The following two chapters show the benefits of researchers constructing their own corpora. **Kate Harrington** shows in Chapter 7 how combining quantitative corpus techniques with qualitative analysis facilitates an understanding of how and why reported dialogue use appears to be gendered. Using a corpus of conversational talk, she demonstrates how transparency ensures that individual variation is not hidden by a generalised use of statistics that may exaggerate gender differentiation. With their own corpus of learner English, in Chapter 8 **Rosa Jiménez Catalán** and **Julieta Ojeda** Alba explore the written English of Spanish primary school girls and boys.

Part 3   Conversation analysis

Conversation analysis (CA), developing out of ethnomethodology and linguistics, is concerned with the sequential organisation of naturally-occurring talk (everyday conversations or institutional talk), and with the accomplishment of social action in talk. As such, it is 'well-positioned to consider the constructed nature of gender in talk' (Kroløkke and Sørensen, 2006: 49). In its microanalysis of talk-in-interaction, CA empirically identifies recurrent, structural characteristics – namely patterns such as turn-taking, interruptions and repairs. CA aims to:

> take singular sequences of conversation and tear them apart in such a way as to find rules, techniques, procedures, methods, maxims…that can be used to generate the orderly features we find in the conversations we examine. The point is, then, to come back to the singular things we

observe in a singular sequence, with some rules that handle those singular features, and also, necessarily, handle lots of other events.

(Sacks, 1984: 413)

Some early (1970s) work on gender and conversational interaction (e.g., Fishman, 1983) drew upon CA (problematically, given the prior identification of gender as a variable) to reveal male dominance in everyday conversation (see also Kitzinger, and Stokoe, this volume). However, in analysing gender only when speakers explicitly orient to it, and rejecting 'prior variables' or analyst agendas such as gender and feminism, orthodox CA can be seen as problematic for feminist and gender study (there has been a long-running debate about claims for gender in a localised stretch of talk (e.g., Schegloff, 1998, 1997; Wetherell, 1998; and see p. 12)). In the late 1990s, CA was reclaimed by and for gender and language study (e.g., Speer, 2005; Stokoe and Smithson, 2001; Kitzinger, 2000 and this volume).

Celia Kitzinger introduces CA in Chapter 9 and explores its relevance and value for feminist research on gender and sexuality as well as for the broader issues of power and oppression in everyday interaction. She focuses on 'interruption', of concern to gender and language researchers and conversation analysts alike. Kitzinger argues that CA offers a 'systematic and contextually sensitive analytic method grounded in co-interactants' *own* practices and actions' (p. 136) that can help us understand where and how gender is achieved in the ordinary practices of talk.

Elizabeth Stokoe then demonstrates in Chapter 10 how the topic of 'gender' can be studied via its categorial reference and sequential organisation in talk-in-interaction – for example, by looking at the way members' categories (such as *girls/women, fellas/men, secretary*) are put to use in the same kinds of sequential environments, doing the same kinds of actions. Stokoe suggests that this allows us to see 'how everyday notions of gender are taken up, reformulated, repaired, or resisted, in turns of talk that accomplish conversational action' (p. 139). She concludes with a discussion of the theoretical upshot of analysing gender from an ethnomethodological/CA perspective, particularly in relation to social constructionism.

Part 4   Discursive psychology

'Discursive psychology' originated with Edwards and Potter (1992; see also 2001), who were concerned to unpack and critique social, developmental and cognitive psychology (both topics and methods). This challenge to mainstream psychology entailed a radical shift – from seeing psychological states as being *behind* talk, to their being deployed and handled *in* talk.

Since the mid-1990s, discursive psychology has taken two different directions (Benwell and Stokoe, 2006; McIlvenny, 2002), the original branch maintaining its focus on the study of psychological phenomena as constructed, attended to and organised in talk as social action (e.g., Edwards,

2005; Potter and Hepburn, 2007). However, its increasingly close relationship to CA led to the emergence of a new branch: 'critical discursive psychology' (cf. Edley and Wetherell, 1999), which is more closely related to post-structuralism and critical discourse analysis, drawing both on the Foucauldian notion of *discourses*, and the comparable notion of *interpretative repertoires* (Edley, 2001; Potter and Wetherell, 1987).

In Chapter 11, **Nigel Edley** and **Margaret Wetherell** identify a particular challenge for discursive psychology, that is, to fruitfully combine analytical principles from both branches – in the face of critics who maintain that macro-analysis of discourse patterns works at the expense of micro-analysis of the interactional context of talk (Wooffitt, 2005). They claim that an expanded and integrative discursive psychology that assumes a broad understanding of constructionism and aims to work across both the micro and the macro would in principle combine a focus on 'how speakers construct (and use) gender categories and how they are constructed – as gendered beings – by those very categories' (p. 166).

A related synthetic approach is taken by **Laurel Kamada** in Chapter 12, who examines how six Japanese-Caucasian girls in Japan construct and combine their multi-ethnic and gendered 'embodied' identities, within and across a range of discourses. In framing her work within the integrative trajectory of discursive psychology, as well as incorporating analytic tools from Feminist Post-Structuralist Discourse Analysis (FPDA), Kamada's 'multi-perspective' approach sheds light on the discursive work involved in the girls' negotiation of gendered and ethnic identities, and on their sense of their 'lived-body-selves' – how they speak together, and enact the 'body work' of friendship.

Part 5   Critical discourse analysis (CDA)

Discourse analysis grew out of an awareness of the importance of language *beyond the sentence*, and of context. When discourse analysis becomes *critical* discourse analysis is debatable. CDA *per se* has very particular epistemological roots – including critical linguistics, with its Marxist underpinnings, and critical theory of the Frankfurt School. Kroløkke and Sørensen pay tribute to Norman Fairclough for seeing critical theory as a theory of *discourse*: 'one may say that Fairclough combined discourse theory with sociolinguistics and created CDA' (2006: 52). CDA also identifies and analyses the workings of (often gendered) *discourses*, ways of seeing or representing the world which 'systematically form the objects of which they speak' (Fairclough, 2003; Foucault, 1972: 49), that is, are constitutive of social structures.

There is not just one, monolithic CDA (see Wodak and Meyer, 2001), but several, which together constitute a 'programme' (Weiss and Wodak, 2003). All CDA shares a focus on ideology and power (and its contestation), and goals of working towards progressive social change, challenging assumptions and, more recently, opening up new possibilities through different readings of linguistic, discoursal and social products and processes (i.e., texts, and the production and consumption of texts; Fairclough, 1992). All CDA considers both discursive and non-discursive practices, and assumes a dialectical relationship between discourse and the social, that is, that discourse shapes but is also shaped by some form of material reality (a position rejected by post-structuralist writers).

Though there have been studies of gender using CDA (see Kosetzi, this volume), CDA has been accused of downplaying both gender concerns and feminist approaches to language study (e.g., Cameron, 1998b). One question is whether CDA's conventional focus on social class, hierarchy and power relations, and on the 'dominant' and 'dominated', *enables* it to deal fully with gender. Some gender and language analysts self-identify as CDA analysts; others do not, though their work may well be feminist (hence 'critical') (see also Wodak, 1997; Kotthoff and Wodak, 1997). And there is now a collection devoted to 'feminist critical discourse analysis' – Michelle Lazar's *Feminist Critical Discourse Analysis: Gender, Power, and Ideology in Discourse* (2005) (see also Walsh, 2001).

The CDA section starts with Chapter 13 by **Ruth Wodak**, who discusses feminist CDA and illustrates its combination with her 'discourse-historical' approach to CDA with a case study of migrant identities – one crucial principle of CDA being a focus on a problem and not on a linguistic unit *per se*. The analysis is both macro and micro, addressing the all-important (different levels of) context. **Veronika Koller** then shows in Chapter 14 how CDA can combine with cognitive semantics through a study of the representation of businesswomen in a business magazine and a lesbian magazine, and also engages with notions of discursive psychology. Chapter 15, by **Konstantia Kosetzi**, applies Faircloughian CDA to Greek TV fictional texts, and considers the special challenges of fiction for CDA.

Part 6   Feminist post-structuralist discourse analysis (FPDA)

With roots in post-structuralism and feminism, and sharing some similarities with both CDA and CA, *feminist post-structuralist discourse analysis* (FPDA) (Baxter, 2002a, b, 2003) also 'responds' to both (it is informed by broad social issues *and* includes very detailed analysis of talk). Important here is the post-structuralist notion of 'positioning' (of oneself and others, in discourse); individuals can also (as in CDA and 'critical' discursive psychology) be seen as *multiply* positioned. Having a degree of *agency*, manifested in different linguistic forms, they have the potential not only to *recognise* how and through which discourses they are being 'positioned', but also to *take up* particular subject positions, and to *resist* positionings. FPDA thus rejects the notion of individuals being 'at the mercy of these competing discourses' (Baxter, 2003: 31). A degree of agency does not entail, however, what Baxter describes as a 'liberal-humanist conception of the free individual in control of their destiny': the range of possible subject positions for women remains limited.

Discourses are important to FPDA (as well as to CDA). Often 'competing', they are what shifting/fluctuating power relations are 'constantly negotiated through' (Baxter, 2002b: 831). And shifts in power are a key concern of FPDA, which accordingly allows for dynamism in all exchanges. A woman may be (simultaneously) positioned as powerful within one discourse and powerless within another (e.g., as an employee but as someone whose labour is essential). FPDA is also about encouraging textual interplay (between different, related texts within a very specific social context) for its own sake, so that the possibility of new meanings, richer understandings and alternative insights into gender identities may emerge.

Part 4 is introduced, appropriately, by FPDA's originator, **Judith Baxter**. Baxter in Chapter 16 carefully compares FPDA and CDA, identifying commonalities (including 'the discursive construction of subjectivity' (p. 245)) and teasing out differences. FPDA, she claims, may *supplement* CDA by focusing on those instances of power which may be too fleeting or unusually manifested for conventional CDA to deal with. **Harold Andrés Castañeda Peña** in Chapter 17 documents his own FPDA study of Colombian preschool children in a lesson on English personal pronouns. His analyses show how these children 'live between and within shifting versions of masculinities and femininities' (p. 268).

Part 7   Queer theory

A key principle of queer theory is the destabilising of what appears 'natural' and stable. Queer theory takes 'normality' as its primary object of investigation and works to continually problematise taken-for-granted, socially sanctioned notions of gender and heteronormativity (see also Sunderland, 2006; and Bucholtz, 1999b).

Queer refers to that which is not aligned with any particular identity and resists categorisation; *queer theory* is post-structuralist in that it sees gender and sexualities as performed – through repeated, 'citational' discursive acts (e.g., Butler, 1990). Butler's significant work on performativity provides a theoretical framework in which gender and sexual (and other) identities are *brought into being* by a series of such acts.

In Chapter 18, **Helen Sauntson** reviews key principles and developments in queer theory which are particularly relevant to gender, sexuality and language. She also identifies tensions, most notably the problem of retaining a commitment to a political and emancipatory agenda while, at the same time, resisting notions of 'identity' as fixed, stable and inevitable. Sauntson focuses upon Bucholtz and Hall's (2004) 'tactics of intersubjectivity' analytical framework, which offers a methodology influenced by both queer and feminist theories. **William Leap**, in Chapter 19, focuses on different discursive constructions of gay masculinity, using an oral narrative of a gay man in South Africa. Leap explores how masculine gender/sexual identities are produced in relation to particular material conditions. He considers the value of 'not naming the subject' (e.g., as *woman*) for queer theory, and gender and language study alike.

* * *

Our claim is that gender and language study can only *benefit* from access to this range of approaches,[4] as 'each [method], in its own way, helps uncover the gender issues at stake in communication' (Krøløkke and Sørensen, 2006: 47). Rather than asking which is the most appropriate approach for gender and language study, we argue that more productive is the 'value-adding' question of 'What is each approach *particularly well-equipped* to achieve? What are its *affordances*?' – as well as 'What are its limitations?'

When it comes to identifying an approach for a given research project, some may decide on a topic of interest, research questions and data – and then on the approach. However, this is to see approach as a *tool*. Rather, we see an approach as *conceptual*, with theoretical and epistemological underpinnings as well as *methodological* ones. Some see conversation analysis as inadequate for understanding human social interaction in general, and gendered interaction in particular; others feel similarly about critical discourse analysis. Ontological considerations (Mason, 2002), including those of researcher affiliation and commitment to a particular approach (to which the researcher is then 'accountable'), may thus also influence the choice of approach. If you self-identify ontologically and epistemologically as a discursive psychologist, for example, then your chosen data will probably be a recording and transcript of naturally-occurring or elicited talk. If you see yourself as a *critical* discursive psychologist, your analysis may focus on *discourses* (whereas if you are a discursive psychologist who aligns herself with conversation analysis, it almost certainly will not).

Approach, therefore, is not simply a matter of 'what works best' or even 'goodness of fit'. The extended debate in *Discourse and Society* over the definition of 'context' and the (in)appropriacy of CA for (feminist) gender and language study (initiated by Schegloff (1997) and Wetherell (1998)) has included defences of CA by feminist scholars of gender and language, including Stokoe and Smithson (2001), Kitzinger (2000), Speer (1999) and Stokoe (1998). The debate has hinged on the question of when gender is, or can be claimed to be, relevant to a given stretch of talk. To illustrate: a critical discourse analyst who uses her knowledge of society and gender relations to identify gender as relevant may be challenged by a conversation analyst who sees no evidence of its consequentiality, that is, when *participants* manifestly 'orient' to gender (the classical CA 'warrant' for claiming that gender is 'relevant').

Combining approaches

These days it is not uncommon to use more than one approach for a piece of research, a 'deliberate recombination of methods' (Kroløkke and Sørensen, 2006: 61). Indeed, this is precisely what research students are frequently encouraged to do, perhaps to demonstrate their methodological contribution to the field. Combining approaches is in principle feasible, as Holmes and Meyerhoff exemplify in the *Handbook of Language and Gender*:

> Meyerhoff...demonstrates, in her discussion of *sore* in Bislama, that variationist approaches are not inconsistent with detailed ethnographic sociolinguistic description, and a social constructionist focus on the emergent nature of gender.
>
> (2003: 12)

But can Approach A always go with Approach B, in a pick-and-mix sort of way? Might some approaches be particularly compatible and others incompatible? Must some always serve or supplement others? And can a researcher achieve accountability to more than one method?

Feminist post-structuralist discourse analysis is (at least on the surface) relatively straightforward here. Baxter emphasises that FPDA *is* a 'supplementary' approach: it looks at 'the continuously fluctuating ways in which speakers, within any discursive context, are positioned as powerful or powerless by competing social and institutional discourses' which is 'an aspect of spoken interaction perhaps overlooked by CA and CDA' (2003: 44).

Of course, conversation analysts and critical discourse analysts may wish to contest Baxter's premise that they may overlook fluctuating positionings. And neither CA nor CDA are static entities. Baxter's real point is, however, the desirability of 'supplementarity' (Derrida, 1976) more widely:

> to convey the built-in dependencies and oppositions of any one theoretical paradigm with any other. In other words, each theoretical approach should be seen as both necessary to and *yet simultaneously threatening to* the identities of the others.
>
> (2003: 43, our italics; see also
> Chouliaraki and Fairclough, 1999)

This representational 'nexus' of approaches constitutes a reminder of the epistemological complexity, organic nature and, indeed, dynamism of the modern research endeavour, as well as its potential tensions. It also points to the need for researcher reflexivity (see below) – already characteristic of critical research.

Critical discourse analysis has conventionally been 'served' by textual analysis, often using argumentation theory, Halliday's systemic-functional grammar (2004), van Leeuwen's critical notions of social actors/action (e.g., 1996) and, more recently, ethnography (e.g., Wodak, 1996). The discursive-historical (Wodak), socio-cognitive (van Dijk), and different Faircloughian (e.g., 1995a,b, 2001b) branches of CDA draw on different grammars as they see fit. And imaginative and flexible CDA studies do indeed also draw on conversation analysis, discursive psychology, corpus linguistics, pragmatics or sociolinguistics, as well as FPDA. However, supplementarity is not automatically a theoretically valid way forward – a relationship may not be reciprocal. Whereas CDA might draw on CA, for example, it is harder to imagine the reverse (neither CA nor the CA branch of discursive psychology entertains the notion of *discourses*). And, given their different intellectual roots, FPDA and CDA are not comfortably compatible, so whereas a CDA practitioner who sees discourse as working *dialectically* (i.e., shaped by as well as shaping material events), might be willing for FPDA to *supplement* it, she might reject CDA 'serving' FPDA given the latter's anti-materialist stance.

'Warrants' for gender, approaches to gender and notions of gender

Questions that all approaches to gender and language study have to address are: what counts as gender? how is it to be theorised? with what 'warrant' can the analyst claim that gender is relevant in a stretch of talk or written text? We have already seen the classical CA warrant of 'participants' orientations as evident in the text' (see Swann, 2002: 49). But what constitutes an 'orientation'? Schegloff's (1997) famous example is a speaker's ironic use of 'Ladies last' when passing butter at a dinner table: that is, a feature *made visible or audible* in an interaction. However, Kitzinger (2000) contests this, observing that to wait for an explicit 'gender orientation' would be 'unbearably limiting' (see also Stokoe and Smithson, 2001).

Swann (2002: 50–8) identifies six other 'warrants' for gender, as follows:

Quantitative and/or general patterns (derived from correlational studies of language use, large (computerised) corpora or other systematic comparison between the language of different social groups).   In large-scale variationist sociolinguistic studies and corpus linguistics, quantitative procedures may establish statistical significance of the relationship between gender and another variable – but not causality, or even whether gender is the real issue.

Indirect reliance on quantitative/general patterns.   Small-scale, 'interactional sociolinguistic' studies may draw on previous, larger scale studies, and either then map their findings and claims onto them, or contest previously identified general patterns (or their interpretations, or methodology).

Speakers'/participants' solicited interpretations.   This warrant, irrelevant to CA and unacceptable to the CA branch of discursive psychology, *is* relevant to its critical branch, data for which is characteristically, intentionally, interview transcripts. Solicited interpretations are also important in ethnographic approaches and, often, CDA. Such data requires an epistemological position not only that non-naturally-occurring data constitutes *good* data but also an acceptance that solicited interpretations constitute reported understandings (not 'mined facts'). While understandings may bear little relation to 'facts', they are *nevertheless* interesting in their own right. Use of solicited interpretations also entails taking on board co-construction, that is, that interviewees' responses will be tailored to the questioner (as in any 'conversation').

Analysts' theoretical positions. While CA espouses the ideal of *minimising* the analyst's theoretical position, and proponents would claim that CA (being concerned with *speakers'* orientations) can come close to this, all interpretations are arguably *influenced* by analysts' theoretical positions – on both gender and language. Some approaches are, however, particularly explicit about this. The position of FPDA is self-evident, and critical discourse analysts often put their cards on the table from the start. Doing this, however, risks accusations of tailoring interpretation to the theory, and CDA has been a target of critique here (e.g., Widdowson, 1995; but see response by Wodak, 2006).

Analysts' intuitions. As we saw earlier, Lakoff (1975) vigorously – but problematically – justified her reliance on introspection. However, analysts' intuitions play a role in most linguistic (and other) research, including the attribution of meanings or functions to utterances (Swann, 2002, see p. 58) – and intuitions are not unrelated to informed insights and, indeed, theoretical positions (see above).

Speakers are female, male (or whatever). This last, 'atheoretical' warrant is characteristic of past gender and language study, and of current popular discourse (e.g., a piece of behaviour is attributed to gender ('that's a man thing') when there is no basis for this). Clearly, because members of a social group do X, this does not in itself make X explicable by that group membership: it needs to be established whether gender (say) is *relevant* to analysis of the data in question or whether it is more important that the individuals concerned are, say, (in some sense) powerless (cf. O'Barr and Atkins, 1980) or members of a certain CofP or social network (e.g., Milroy, 1980). Arguably, however, elements of this warrant remain in most language and gender research (see Stokoe, this volume), and Swann herself comments: 'Despite the current emphasis on context and performativity, I do not think language and gender researchers actually do dispense with gender as an *a priori* explanatory category – and probably they cannot' (2002: 60).

Table 1.1 overleaf suggests a relationship between these seven warrants, the approaches illustrated (or referred to) in this book, and notions of gender (see p. 4).

Table 1.1   Relationships between 'warrants' and approaches to, and notions of, gender

	Warrants for gender (from Swann, 2002)	Possible associated approach(es)	Notions of gender
1	Quantitative and/or general patterns	• Large scale variationist sociolinguistic studies • Corpus linguistics	• 'differential tendencies' between women and men, boys and girls (as regards language use)
2	Indirect reliance on quantitative/general patterns	• Small-scale, 'interactional sociolinguistic' work which draws on and maps findings onto claims of larger-scale studies	
3	Participants' orientations as evident in the text	• Conversation Analysis (CA) • Feminist Poststructuralist Discourse Analysis (FPDA)	• linguistic dealings *with* (individual, and groups of) women, men, boys and girls, e.g. how they are addressed, what is said *to* them and what they say *about* gender
4	Speakers'/Participants' solicited interpretations	• Discursive psychology • FPDA • CDA	• what is said and written about gender differences/tendencies, similarities and diversity
5	Analysts' theoretical positions	• CDA • FPDA • Queer Theory (at least)	• potentially any
6	Analysts' intuitions	• Introspection	
7	Speakers are female, male (or whatever)	• Popular discourse (mainly)	• 'differential tendencies' between women and men, boys and girls (as regards language use)

Interpretation and feminism

The current emphasis on qualitative methodologies across the social sciences, moving away from *positivistic* paradigms of research towards more *interpretative* (e.g., discourse analysis, ethnography) and *critical* ones, has helped illuminate the fluidity and complexity of (gendered) meaning. However, all gender and language researchers, including those working within a qualitative paradigm (see Hultgren, this volume), need to explore a range of interpretations. This raises the question of the role of the analyst and her theoretical and political alignments (see also p. 12).

Given that CDA explicitly goes beyond the text to identify relationships between language and wider social and political workings, CDA analysts routinely engage with and acknowledge their role in the research process (which includes drawing on their own critical/feminist interpretative insights, perhaps as members of the relevant community). Such reflexivity is also key to FPDA and critical discursive psychology. In contrast, interpretation in conventional CA is very differently based on the sequential intersubjectivity constructed between *participants* as they display their understanding of prior and subsequent actions (but see Stokoe, and Kitzinger, this volume).

So what of the role of feminism? Starting with what is now called the 'Second Wave' of the Women's (Liberation) Movement, blossoming in the 1970s, feminism has influenced gender and language work considerably (work culminating in the new *Gender and Language* journal in 2007). Feminism has influenced specific perspectives and epistemological approaches (the '(male) dominance' approach prevalent in the 1970s; feminist critical discourse analysis (Lazar, 2005); Feminist post-structuralist discourse analysis (Baxter, 2002a, b, 2003); feminist conversation analysis (Kitzinger, 2000; Speer, 1999)), but *most* gender and language study can be described as broadly feminist, in its questioning of androcentrism and 'objective' or 'universal' truths, and in its commitment to the promotion of progressive gender relations.

Litosseliti summarises three key principles of feminist research as:

1. Characterized by self-reflection, self-reflexivity, even conscious partiality.
2. Done by researchers who 'locate themselves within, rather than outside the research topic and the participants'.
3. 'Informed by feminist politics'.

(2006a: 151–2)

The first point refutes the idea that facts can be divorced from values or that impartiality is possible. Such reflexivity facilitates the monitoring of feminist work, in part to ensure that it does not inadvertently perpetuate rather than subvert the inequalities it tries to address. The second pertains to research on (sometime) marginal or oppressed individuals and groups, and power relations between researcher and those researched: scholarship 'which does not transform those it studies into objects but preserves in its analytic procedures the presence of the subject as actor and experiencer' (Smith, 1981: 1). The possibility of participants' perspectives actually taking *precedence* over those of an 'expert' researcher is much debated (see Sarangi and Roberts 1999; deFrancisco, 1997; Cameron et al., 1992). That, in reality, the researcher's perspective will typically prevail within (feminist) academic publishing is an irony acknowledged by, *inter alia*, FPDA (Baxter, 2003).

The third point, feminist research as *informed by* feminist politics, extends to empower*ment* (see De Francisco, 1997), that is, *contributing* to feminist politics (see also Sunderland, 2004). Feminist linguistics accordingly, explicitly, 'aims to draw connections between gender-related linguistic phenomena and gender inequality or discrimination' (Litosseliti, 2006a: 152). We acknowledge that it is, however, harder to facilitate empowerment, than to identify and demystify areas of gender inequality.

This book lacks the scope to discuss feminism but we stress that its meaning is not self-evident. FPDA, for example, because it rejects absolutes (including absolute power), and, indeed, 'grand narratives', rejects any feminism which is omnirelevant or entails a ubiquity of powerlessness and disadvantage for women (women *may* be powerless and disadvantaged, but this depends on time, place and other contextual features). As regards any feminism/approach relationship, we need to distinguish between theory and *application* (see Gill, 1995): discourse analysis, say, can be used in the interests of misogyny as well as feminism.

The necessity to resist categorical thinking and 'grand narratives', and at the same time maintain a broad political and progressive perspective (see Cameron, 2006; Litosseliti, 2006b; Philips, 2003), was emphasised by several contributors at the fourth International Gender and Language Association conference (2006). The current diversity of gender and language methodological approaches, and indeed – perhaps in particular – the creative tensions between them, are to be welcomed in the facilitation of this. We hope this book will encourage both debate and innovative, creative feminist practice here.

Notes

1 With Carmen Caldas-Coulthard.

2 In contrast, many related disciplines, including gender, cultural and media studies, do *not* rely on empiricism (see Bucholtz, 1999b).

3 Although West and Zimmerman (1983) anticipated what was to come with their notion of 'doing' power and gender in face-to-face interaction.

4 One omission from our approaches is Pragmatics. Deborah Cameron (1998a, 2005b), proposes a 'Pragmatic turn' for discourse analysis, informed by relevance theory, i.e., conversational participants infer meaning from what is relevant *to them*, including a set of background assumptions. This gets round the dilemma of the analyst either looking at what participants may or may not be explicitly orienting to (as in CA), or being accused of imposing her own interpretations on the data.

Part 1

Sociolinguistics and Ethnography

2
Sociolinguistic and Ethnographic Approaches to Language and Gender

Joan Swann and Janet Maybin

Sociolinguistics An orientation to the study of language that stresses the inter-relationship between language and social life, rather than focusing narrowly on language structure.

(Swann et al., 2004: 287)

As a tradition of enquiry, sociolinguistics is characterised by considerable breadth and heterogeneity. Sociolinguistics foregrounds diversity and change in language in particular social contexts, but within this rather general orientation it encompasses a range of areas of study – contemporary variation and change; language choice in multilingual contexts; the socially and culturally oriented study of language-in-interaction; applied concerns such as language policy and planning – and a range of methodologies, both quantitative and qualitative.

Sociolinguistics does not, therefore, represent a single, unified approach to the study of language and gender, either in terms of the types of language use, or language practices that provide a focus for research, or the methodology brought to bear on the interpretation and analysis of linguistic data. A great deal of research, particularly within the 'variationist' tradition, has been quantitative, identifying systematic differences between groups of speakers in their realisation of certain linguistic variables. There has also, however, been a strong qualitative tradition, associated particularly with the analysis of spoken interaction. Qualitative, interactional sociolinguistics may be combined with an ethnographic approach – this has been a continuing thread within the field and seems to offer a particular potential, in relation to addressing the intersection of language use with social and cultural processes. ('Interactional' studies may, however, also be quantitative – an example is Hultgren's study in Chapter 3.)

As in some other disciplinary areas in the social sciences, the study of language and gender within sociolinguistics has seen a theoretical and methodological shift since its beginnings in the 1970s. At a general level, this shift can be seen as running from an earlier focus on gender differences in language to a more contemporary preoccupation with the contextualised performance of gender. Research carried out in the 1970s and 1980s was concerned, in the main, with the identification of differences between women and men as social groups. A well-known finding in variationist studies (in this case studies of sociolinguistic patterns more generally, not just of language and gender) was that women tended to use more standard, or prestige linguistic features than men from the same social background. This finding is associated with Labov's classic study of language use in New York City (Labov, 1966) but was also identified in other studies carried out in (mainly) Western contexts. Some later studies discovered more complex patterns – for example, differences in the use of certain linguistic features being associated with speakers' lifestyles, social networks and other factors indirectly related to gender, and not just with gender *per se*. Milroy's (1980/1987) research on three working-class communities in Belfast, for instance, found the expected pattern of gender differentiation, with women using more prestige features and men more vernacular features. This general finding, however, concealed differences between the communities. The use of local vernacular forms of language was associated primarily with speakers' integration into the local community, and patterns of integration differed between women and men in the three communities depending on factors such as work, family and friendship ties. In one community where young women had strong community ties, the expected sociolinguistic patterns were reversed, with young women using more vernacular features than young men.

Studies of spoken interaction focused, similarly, on gender differences – in this case differences in interactional style. Lakoff's (1975) characterisation of 'women's language' – features such as 'empty' adjectives, question intonation in statement contexts, tag questions and hedges that, in combination, were said to indicate uncertainty and a lack of authority, and to be associated with women's relative powerlessness – gave rise to a spate of empirical studies, producing rather equivocal results in terms of the meanings of such features and their association with female speakers (on tag questions see, for instance, Cameron, McAlinden and O'Leary, 1988; Holmes, 1984). Other work focused more closely on aspects of conversation management. Two often-cited findings were that women provided more interactional support than men (e.g. Fishman, 1978); and that men interrupted women more than vice versa (e.g., West and Zimmerman, 1983; Zimmerman and West, 1975). On the basis of several studies of conversation management, some researchers have come to see women's speech as relatively co-operative and men's speech as relatively competitive. Like early variationist studies, then, interactional studies gave rise to generalisations about gendered language use (women's language, powerless language, co-operative vs. competitive language). In this latter case however there was also a focus on the potential for unequal interactional outcomes, female speakers often being seen as giving away power in mixed-sex contexts. (For reviews, see Coates, 2004; Graddol and Swann, 1989.) Interpretations of specific differences have always been the subject of debate. Sociolinguistic interpretations of women's use of standard linguistic features have in particular been hotly contested, and there have been debates about the meanings attributed to different features of spoken interaction (see Coates, 2004; Cameron, 1992; Graddol and Swann, 1989). But the broader theoretical and methodological shift referred to above goes beyond such local disputes, by questioning the models of 'gender' and 'language' on which much earlier research was based. Over the past 10–15 years, and in line with developments in gender theory and queer theory (e.g., Butler, 1990/1999), both gender and language have been reconceptualised, with the field undergoing what has been seen as a 'postmodern turn' (Cameron, 2005a). Gender has come to be seen not as a prior category that affects how people speak, but as a contextualised achievement brought into being in particular contexts. The focus is on how aspects of gender are produced as salient, represented and given meaning and significance within everyday life across various cultural and social settings.

Gender is also seen not so much as an independent category, but rather as intricately embedded in other social divisions: race, class, age, sexuality and so on, all of which are in turn embedded within – and (re-)produced by – structures of power, authority and social inequality. There is greater emphasis on the complex and highly contextualised nature of language meaning – on how certain ways of speaking may be drawn on to particular effect in particular contexts, sometimes ironically, playfully or subversively. Contemporary research often questions generalisations about 'women's' or 'men's' speech, and indeed interpretations based on broad distinctions such as that between co-operative and competitive talk.

The methodological consequences of this shift can be seen in a move away from comparative, often quantitative studies of gendered differentiation in language towards more local, qualitative explorations of gender, with limited scope for, and limited interest in, the establishment of generalisations. Thus, for instance, Barrett (1999) studied the language of African-American drag queens, focusing on how, in their performances, they adopt stereotypical 'white women's' language but also code-switch between this and other varieties to index variously their identities as drag queens, African-Americans and gay men. Similarly, Hall (1995) studied the language of telephone sex workers – women (and one man) who create a fantasy persona for the sexual gratification of male callers. She found that this is achieved by the adoption of a stereotypically feminine speaking style that has much in common with the kind of powerless language associated with female speakers in earlier studies – although in this case the women are deliberately manipulating a gendered style, and Hall argues that they felt in control of the interaction. The attribution of powerlessness, then, is at least open to question in this context. (For further discussion and examples, see Holmes and Meyerhoff (2003) and Litosseliti and Sunderland (2002)).

While reflected in a number of empirical studies, this is not simply a shift in research practices. It is also a *rhetorical* shift – a way of accounting for current research preoccupations. It is a story of the field, and like all stories has been neatened up a little. For instance, earlier comparative studies of gender differences always identified *tendencies* within particular sociocultural contexts – exceptions to any general patterns were acknowledged, and sometimes explored, as in Milroy's work on social networks. Earlier research, like more contemporary studies, was also often concerned with the local construction of gender as a social category – for example, with the adoption of certain linguistic variables seen as indexing gender, or aspects of gender, directly or indirectly – although the complexity of this process was not foregrounded as in much contemporary research.

Nor does the story map evenly on to all traditions of enquiry. Ethnographic research, for instance, with its commitment to prolonged participative observation and the establishment of insider meanings and interpretations, has always paid close attention to the ways in which relationships between language and gender are played out within the context of beliefs and values in particular cultural contexts. Linguistic anthropological studies in the 1970s and 1980s did tend to invoke gender as a prior category. Thus Keenan (1974) found that women speakers in a Malagasy community appeared to break the general norm of the indirect, tactful speech style used and valued by men. In her classic study of language shift across three generations in Oberwart, a Hungarian-German bilingual community in Austria, Gal (1979) also identified gender contrasts, with young women leading a shift towards the increasing use of German. However, both researchers drew on substantial ethnographic evidence to provide a socially and culturally informed account of gendered language practices. Keenan's understanding of Malagasy everyday encounters (where men might use women to do their confronting for them), ritual speech-making practices (from which women were barred) and men and women's own accounts and explanations of the differences between them, enabled her to challenge Western assumptions about the gendering of confrontation and indirectness in talk. Gal's systematic observation and ethnographic interviews, together with an analysis of the community's broader sociopolitical context, helped her explain young women's greater preference for German. She was able to demonstrate the association of German with modern urbanism, which appeared to offer an escape from 'dirty farm work' in Hungarian-speaking peasant families where women's tasks, unlike men's, had not been eased by mechanisation. It was the gendered experience of changing socioeconomic practices and opportunities and the modern connotations of German that prompted the youngest women's language choice, which contributed to the overall shift in the community towards German.

However, while cultural and social context has always been foregrounded in ethnographic research, there have also been shifts in this tradition which to some extent parallel the broader postmodern shift in sociolinguistic studies of language and gender referred to above. The growth of urban ethnography, multi-sited ethnography and ethnography 'at home' has been accompanied by its application within unstable, mixed and hybrid cultural contexts where beliefs and meanings may be contested by different social groups. For instance, Besnier (2003), in his anthropological study of *fakaleitī*, transgendered males in Tonga who are said to 'act like women' and who pepper their conversations with English (associated in Tonga with cosmopolitanism and modernity), echoes Gal in his focus on gendered social groups' differing investment in tradition and modernity and associated language behaviours and ideologies. However, Besnier foregrounds the potentially heterogeneous nature of gender as a social category and the way in which language practices may emerge as a site of struggle over power and inequality. He suggests that the use of English by *fakaleitī*, who tend to be poor with minimal knowledge of the language, does not necessarily increase their prestige and worldliness, but may paradoxically lead to further marginalisation in the still mainly monolingual local Tongan society.

More recently in British sociolinguistics, the term 'linguistic ethnography' has been used to refer to theoretical and methodological developments which draw on established traditions of the ethnography of communication in anthropology (Hymes, 1974) and interactional sociolinguistics (Gumperz, 1982), but orientate also towards post-structuralist theory and interpretative approaches in anthropology, applied linguistics and sociology. Combining linguistics with ethnography, it is argued, brings together a powerfully precise formalist framework from linguistics with the commitment within ethnography to particularity and participation, holistic accounts of social practice and openness to reinterpretations over time (Rampton, Tusting et al., 2004). Combining ethnography and linguistics suggests ways of exploring the mutually constitutive relationship between language and the social world, including the dynamics of gender, to produce culturally and socially sensitive linguistic or discourse analysis of local communicative practices. Rather than producing traditional full-blown anthropological ethnographies, linguistic ethnographers in Britain have tended to employ an 'ethnographic perspective' (Green and Bloome, 1997) in 'topic-orientated' studies (Hymes, 1996: 5), which can include a discussion of gender and communicative practice (e.g., Maybin, 2006).

As a result of the theoretical and methodological developments outlined above, studies that appeal to a highly contextualised, performative model of gender have become mainstream within sociolinguistics, but still they face a number of challenges:

1. The focus on the local, contextualised playing out of gender plays down, and sometimes explicitly rejects, earlier assumptions about gender as a prior category – something that speakers *have*, rather than what they *do*.

However, gender is clearly not done afresh in each interaction. Speakers necessarily bring with them a 'gendered potential' – the sedimentation of accrued prior experience, of prior genderings – and this may be drawn on (performed, renegotiated, contested, subverted or of course ignored) in response to particular interactional contingencies. In this sense, gender may legitimately be seen as both a prior category (something that one has) *and* a contextualised practice (something one does, that bolsters, subverts, etc. the category).

2. In order to interpret an interaction in terms of gender, that is, to see the relevance of gender within an interaction, researchers themselves must have some prior conception of this. In practice, contemporary 'local' research is often framed by, and thus dependent upon, patterns identified in earlier research, even when it seeks to qualify these. For instance, both Barrett and Hall (above) drew on prior conceptions of 'women's language' in their studies (whilst acknowledging the ideological status of this concept).

3. A particular challenge for researchers working with complex models of identity and identification is how to untangle the maze of interconnections between the aspects of language and gender in which they are interested, and other multiple dimensions of people's social practice.

4. A focus on the particularities of specific interactions may lead researchers to miss broader connections with other contexts. Alongside these particularities there will also be continuities with others; such continuities form the stuff of general, even quantifiable patterns that may, in principle, be identified in research.

5. It is also debatable how far research on situated language use does actually restrict itself to local relevance. Researchers usually wish to do more than address isolated and disconnected particularities. There is a danger, however, in moving towards more generalisable claims without adequate methodological warrants.

Some researchers have argued for a broader range of warrants for gender, underpinned by a broader range of methodological choices. Such choices might include, say, the quantitative documentation of broad, general patterns along with more qualitative exploration of local practices that both contribute and form exceptions to such patterns (see Swann, 2002). In a survey of language use in New Zealand, Holmes (1996) draws on quantitative methodology to establish patterns across different social groups, but also examines speakers' language choices in particular interactions. Holmes argues that general patterns (the association of certain features with certain groups) allow her to be more confident about attributing meanings to speakers' contextualised linguistic choices. Quantitative examination of intergroup differences may, then, complement qualitative approaches within the same study, or it may contribute to a backdrop of general claims that inform more local, qualitative research.

Eckert (2000, 1989) draws on qualitative and quantitative methods somewhat differently, combining ethnographic participant observation, recording and informal interviewing of American high school teenagers together with sociolinguistic study of language variation in their recorded talk. She employs a performative frame and the heuristic notion of 'communities of practice' (Eckert and McConnell-Ginet, 1995) in order to explain how teenagers 'act out' subcultural identities of 'jock' or 'burnout', and argues that this identification contributes to their construction of gender and class identities. Eckert's detailed analysis of sociolinguistic variation at the level of phonology and grammar enables her to make quantitative claims about differences between social groups, and about language change, thus providing an additional warrant for her qualitative findings. While neither Holmes nor Eckert use a broader anthropological analysis to warrant their findings in local sites, their research claims are strengthened through 'cross-warranting' between quantitative and qualitative methods.

The issues discussed above have relevance both for the broader field of language and gender and for sociolinguistics more widely. Some of the most exciting ideas on social categories, and speaker identity, have been developed in relation to gender and sexuality and these are able both to inform and challenge other areas of sociolinguistics.

The three chapters that follow in this section are located within, and in various ways respond to, such contemporary debates, each representing particular methodological choices and research stances. Hultgren's chapter is an attempt to reinstate the quantitative investigation of sex differences within language and gender research. While she acknowledges the value of integrating quantitative and qualitative approaches – her own research combines quantitative investigation with ethnographic methods – her focus here is a robust defence of quantification. Hultgren draws a broad distinction between quantitative studies that take gender as a pre-discursive category, termed 'correlational sociolinguistics', and more performatively oriented traditions (including conversation analysis, discursive psychology, critical discourse analysis and feminist post-structuralist discourse analysis), which she groups under the heading of 'gender in discourse' approaches. Hultgren identifies and responds to criticisms that have been levelled at correlational research. She points up what she sees as the strengths of quantitative methodology, appealing to values that have been rejected by many language and gender researchers (objectivity, reliability, generalisability, replicability) as well as acknowledging limitations of the approach. She also includes a brief illustration from her own research on telephone call centres. Hultgren's stance is valuable precisely in that it contrasts with, and provides a useful counter to, some contemporary orthodoxies. She also contributes to debates about the potential depoliticisation of language and gender research within postmodern approaches, pointing to the benefits of quantitative evidence ('numbers count') in pursuing a feminist political agenda.

Hultgren refers to the need to reflect the concerns of research participants, and this is a major focus of Mullany in Chapter 4. Like Hultgren, Mullany is sympathetic to the possibilities of integrating quantitative and qualitative approaches, although in her own research practical constraints contributed to her selection of a qualitative paradigm, combining interactional sociolinguistics with ethnography. Mullany investigates discourse in workplace contexts: given the significant part these play in most people's lives, she argues, institutions such as workplaces constitute an important site for language and gender research. However, particularly for researchers committed to the full involvement of research participants, institutional concerns are likely to effect research at all levels, from design through the conduct of research to outcomes and dissemination. For Mullany, this gives rise to a number of tensions, including issues of access, negotiating company expectations (e.g., a company wanting the research to produce positive findings) and discrepancies between commercial and research timescales. Mullany's chapter provides a detailed reflexive account of the possibilities and constraints associated with applied sociolinguistic research on language and gender.

The final chapter in this section, by Pichler, focuses on everyday informal interaction rather than institutional/workplace discourse, but Pichler shares with Mullany and Hultgren a concern with the relationship between researcher and researched. Pichler adopts a linguistic ethnographic approach in Chapter 5, and focuses on the methodological status of ethnographic interviews with research participants. She looks at the negotiation of gender, ethnicity and religion in the self-recorded friendship talk of British Bangladeshi teenage girls, and in subsequent interactions between herself and one of her participants whom she consulted about aspects of the friendship talk. It is common in interactional sociolinguistics and ethnography to take tapes and transcripts back to participants to gain an 'insider' perspective on the data. Pichler explores the status of such researcher/participant consultations, questioning whether they can be treated as providing 'facts' that aid in the interpretation of primary interactional data or whether they should, themselves, be subject to analysis as interactions. Pichler's own analyses, from a range of complementary perspectives, demonstrate the possibility of creating a mutually informing dialogue between the two datasets.

While a number of themes run through these three chapters, they also cover a diverse range of interests and perspectives. In combination, they both draw on, and pose challenges for, contemporary sociolinguistic and ethnographic approaches to the study of language and gender.

3
Reconstructing the Sex Dichotomy in Language and Gender Research: Some Advantages of Using Correlational Sociolinguistics[1]

Anna Kristina Hultgren

Introduction

This chapter discusses the method of 'correlational sociolinguistics'. For the purpose of the chapter, I define this as a strand of research within the field of language and gender that (1) takes binary sex as a legitimate starting point for analysis, and (2) relies on quantification to identify general patterns of variation between male and female speakers. Whilst such methods are still prominent within variationist sociolinguistics, they have virtually been abandoned within language and gender research. This chapter is essentially a discussion of the advantages of using correlational sociolinguistics in relation to some of the other approaches explored in this volume. Rather than a demonstration of application and use; it is about the 'whys' and not the 'hows' of correlational sociolinguistics.

In the 1990s, influenced by postmodern thinking, scholars in the field of language and gender set out to part company with their field's early practitioners and move away from an interest in male-female differences in discourse style (Swann and Maybin, Chapter 2). The move was motivated by a recognition that a dichotomous conceptualisation of gender is too simplistic and that focusing on and quantifying differences between men and women actually risks perpetuating such differences (Bing and Bergvall, 1996; Crawford, 1995; Cameron, 1992). The criticism was aimed equally at scholars who believe that women are disadvantaged because their speech style lacks something in relation to a male norm (the 'deficit' model, often associated with Lakoff, 1975), those who see women's speech style as 'different but equal' or even superior to that of men (the '(cultural) difference' approach advocated by Coates, 2003, 1996; Holmes, 1995; Tannen, 1993; Maltz and Borker, 1982) and those who emphasise societal power inequalities between the sexes and see these played out in conversational interaction (the '(male) dominance' approach associated with Fishman, 1983; Zimmerman and West, 1975).[2] Where researchers rely on quantification to investigate male-female differences in speech (not all do; Tannen (1993) is a case in point), I bunch them together and take them to exemplify the use of a correlational sociolinguistics approach. Though correlational sociolinguistics, in the definition proposed here, shares its binary and quantitative premises with variationist sociolinguistics, as pioneered by Labov (1966, 1963), it is not co-extensive with it. The interest of variationists lies primarily in phonology and linguistic change, but correlational sociolinguistics can be used also to study variation on the level of discourse and interaction, which is how I have used it in my own work.

Today, with a few notable exceptions (e.g., Eckert, 2000; Holmes, 1995), correlational sociolinguistics is hardly ever used in language and gender study. Indeed, the method is often draped in discourse describing it as antiquated and obsolete: 'By refusing to allow oversimplification and by asking *new* questions, we can abandon the *tired* and repressive *old* dichotomy' (Bing and Bergvall, 1996: 24, my emphasis) and 'The focus of this book is not the unproductive and *conservative* idea of 'gender differences'' (Sunderland and Litosseliti, 2002: 1–2, my emphasis). Correlational sociolinguistics has been almost entirely abandoned in favour of small-scale, qualitative studies: as Swann remarks, 'there does seem to have been a shift towards more localised studies' and 'far less reliance is placed on quantifiable and/or general patterns' (2002: 59).

In this chapter, I propose a reintroduction of correlational sociolinguistics into the field of language and gender on the grounds that there is much to be gained from an eclectic and inclusive research climate (Hammersley, 2003). Swann argues that 'a pragmatic combination of methods and approaches, along with an acknowledgement of their possibilities and limitations, might allow us to focus on different aspects of the relationship between language and gender, or have a wider range of things to say about it' (2002: 62). I do not intend correlational sociolinguistics to *supplant* more fluid and dynamic approaches to gender, nor, indeed, would I want to commit myself to using only correlational sociolinguistics. I do not share the view of scholars who argue in favour of accountability to a certain method, but rather align myself with those who aim to problematise 'linguistic orthodoxies' (Billig, 2000: 292) and 'an unquestioning and overrespectful adherence to methods of discourse analysis' (Baxter, 2003: 3). This is not least because there may be cases in which methodological and ethical accountability conflict, for example, when participants' demands for and/or entitlement to know the practical value of a research study would require certain compromises on the part of methodology (see Mullany in Chapter 4).

Correlational sociolinguistics

In this section, I suggest two defining criteria to delimit correlational sociolinguistics in relation to the other main approaches represented in this volume. The first characteristic is that it explicitly acknowledges that binary sex[3] exists *prediscursively* as a potential (though not necessarily relevant) analytical category. This is in contrast to both postmodernist-inspired ideas (represented in this volume by feminist post-structuralist discourse analysis and, to some extent, discursive psychology[4]) and ethnomethodological approaches (represented by conversation analysis) which assert that gender does not have any reality, or at least no consequences for linguistic behaviour that are worth studying, outside of its 'doing'.[5] To ethnomethodologists, 'gender is not a set of traits, nor a variable, nor a role, but the product of social doings of some sort' (West and Zimmerman, 1987: 129); to postmodernists it is '[not] a stable identity or locus of agency from which various acts follow' (Butler, 1990: 179). Though postmodernists and ethnomethodologists have long debated the exact locus of such 'doings of gender', and the respective balance between speakers' agency and structural constraints, in common is a denial of gender as having any prediscursive reality. Gender rather comes into being when we talk about it, whether this is in the conversation at hand (as conversation analysts posit) or as part of grander discursive structures in a Foucauldian sense (as postmodernists contend). In the following, I refer to such approaches collectively as 'gender in discourse' approaches.[6]

A second defining characteristic of correlational sociolinguistics is its preoccupation with identifying general patterns of language use and relying on quantifications to support these. Recognising the possibility that the sex of a speaker may (or may not; correlational sociolinguistics is unbiased in this respect) have a bearing on the speech that s/he produces, a correlational sociolinguist will look for distributional patterns in the occurrences of linguistic variables and correlate these with speaker demographics and contextual factors. Linguistic variables may be phonological, grammatical, lexical or interactional; speaker demographics may include sex, age, ethnicity and education; and contextual factors include topic, setting, task or activity. It is the strict reliance on quantification and statistical tests which most clearly differentiates correlational sociolinguistics from qualitative and ethnographic approaches (including those used by Mullany in Chapter 4 and Pichler in Chapter 5). The reliance on quantification and generalisations, however, is shared with corpus linguistics (Baker, Chapter 6; Harrington, Chapter 7; Jiménez Catalán and Ojeda Alba, Chapter 8) as well as with other sociolinguists (e.g. Eckert, 2000; Holmes, 1995).

Before I describe the benefits of correlational sociolinguistics, I want to scrutinise the criticism that has been levelled against it and argue that subsequent approaches do not seem to have provided a better alternative.

Criticism and defence

Criticism of correlational sociolinguistics tends to centre around two interrelated issues. First, it is suggested that the prediscursive category 'sex' should not be taken as the starting point for analysis (McElhinny, 1998; Bing and Bergvall, 1996); second, it is argued that the interest in men and women as separate groups in correlational sociolinguistics does not allow for variation within the categories or similarities between them (Eckert and McConnell-Ginet, 1992). If these criticisms have led to more research being conducted on individuals who do not fit into one of the two categories 'man' or 'woman', such as *kotis* (a sexual minority in India whose exaggerated femininity marks them as a distinct gender) (Nagar, 2005), *hijras* (often described as Indian eunuchs) (Hall and O'Donovan, 1996), *fakaleitī* (transgendered males in Tonga) (Besnier, 2003) and *travestis* (male prostitutes in Brazil who live as women) (Kulick, 1998), this is of course welcome. There is also a growing body of studies focusing on individuals who, at least initially, seem to fit into one of the traditional bi-polar categories yet display linguistic behaviour that departs from this (on men doing femininity see, e.g., Hall, 1995; on women doing masculinity see e.g. McElhinny, 1995).

Nonetheless, the suggestion not to take sex as the starting point for analysis has proven difficult to live up to in reality and a large proportion of studies undertaken in language and gender research does, albeit implicitly, start out with assumptions about whether their informants are women or men. One example among many is Christie (2002), who sets out to compare male and female MPs' discourse strategies in debates in the British parliament encouraged by a belief that 'differential access to and use of these resources will affect the impact that women as a group are able to have on political decision-making'. Christie describes her approach (a 'Community of Practice' framework (Eckert and McConnell-Ginet, 1992; Lave and Wenger, 1991)) as one that 'conceptualises gender as an aspect of identity that is achieved through language use rather than an attribute that precedes and in some way determines language use'. Gender, in other words, is not a given.

If gender is not a given, however, then why should we expect *a priori* that women 'as a group' will experience certain problems in parliament? To say that gender is 'achieved through language use' is, in my view, not compatible with starting out from the prediscursive categories 'man' and 'woman'. Of course, adherents of 'gender in discourse' approaches might object that the behaviour they are studying is not so much linked to the categories 'female' and 'male' as to the gendered expectations that these categories produce, but, even so, studying the way gendered expectations affect *women* does not solely, as is purported, locate gender in discourse but also in a material and binary reality.[7]

An overwhelming proportion of studies undertaken in 'gender in discourse' approaches still take sex as their starting point; correlational sociolinguistics differs from these approaches in that it explicitly acknowledges this assumption. Therefore, the theoretical steering away from 'essentialism' to social constructionism is not consistently reflected in practice and it has certainly not led us to discard the old binary categories 'men' and 'women' – and may even have led us to conceal them under a smokescreen of postmodern rhetoric. Holmes and Meyerhoff, in the introduction to their *Handbook of Language and Gender*, acknowledge the discrepancy between what is theorised and what is done and doable in practice in the field:

> If we truly believed a radical version of the anti-essentialism that has recently become an axiom of the field, then we would put away our pens, our tape-recorders, and our notebooks, and the field of language and gender research would disappear. There would be no meaning to a handbook of language and gender because gender would have become such an idiosyncratic quality that it would be non-existent as a category across individuals.
>
> (2003: 10)

The second point of criticism that has been levelled against correlational sociolinguistics is the attendant risk of overgeneralising the speech behaviour of men and women and disregarding intra-group variation. We should not assume, in other words, that a female speaker of a certain nationality, ethnicity, age, social stratum, education, profession, for example, would speak the same way as a female speaker with another of these identities. This is a valid point: different aspects of identity are interwoven and to tease them apart is difficult and perhaps undesirable. Yet if the object under study is indeed a diverse community, a quantitative approach could in fact turn out to provide a valuable resource. It is possible within most statistical software packages, provided the sample is large enough, to take account of interaction between different variables, which will allow the researcher to establish whether, say, the salience of 'ethnicity' for speech production overrides 'sex' within a certain community. So although there may have been a tendency in past correlational sociolinguistic work to overstate in simplistic terms differences between the sexes, the charge that quantitative approaches cannot take account of the complexity of gender is not an inherent flaw. Indeed, more recent work undertaken within the quantitative paradigm has discovered more complex patterns, relating linguistic variables not to speakers' sex but to their lifestyles and social networks (Swann and Maybin, Chapter 2). Accounting for complexity, then, is not unattainable in correlational sociolinguistics.

The charge that correlational sociolinguistics is simplistic is often accompanied by a fear of reifying stereotypes about men and women. It is worth questioning, however, whether more localised, smaller scale studies necessarily solve the problem of perpetuating stereotypes. Indeed, as Eckert and McConnell-Ginet (2003) (among others) have pointed out, there is an omnipresent risk when analysing language and gender of being victim to the 'hall of mirrors' effect. In other words, we read into the data an interpretation of what we expect to be gendered behaviour. Cameron tells of a student who set out to record and analyse a sequence of casual conversation among five men, himself and four of his fraternity friends, in order to investigate whether generalisations about men's speech – for example that it centres on topics such as sports and sexual conquest – were borne out empirically. He reported that they were and gave his paper the title 'Wine, women, and sports'. Though this was not an inaccurate interpretation, Cameron reports that it was partial: 'shaped by expectations that caused some things to leap out of the record as "significant" while other things went unremarked'. She argues that

> Analysis is never done without preconceptions, we can never be absolutely non-selective in our observations, and where the object of observation and analysis has to do with gender it is extraordinarily difficult to subdue certain expectations.
>
> (1997b: 270)

People in general (and analysts are not exempt from this) tend to read anything everyone does through gender lenses, that is, gender is as much in the interpretation as in the production of discourse (see also Cameron, 1998a). Kessler and McKenna (1978) argue that once one person has decided on whether another is male or female, almost anything that person does will be read as being consistent with his or her sex. Possible gender-incongruent features (e.g., a low-pitched voice in a female) will be understood as deviations from that person's perceived sex (e.g., 'a husky-voiced female' (1978: 128)). I argue below that correlational sociolinguistics provides a researcher-independent resource for circumventing such culturally loaded readings, and deciding, on a less biased basis, which pieces of the data can be considered salient in terms of sex and which not.

Strengths of correlational sociolinguistics

Having questioned whether 'gender in discourse' approaches have, in fact, delivered on their promise, I now turn to the main strengths of correlational sociolinguistics. First, it strives to reduce researcher interference in the data; secondly, its reliance on quantification means that it has the capacity not only to report on sex differences but also on the absence of such differences; lastly, it is not as guilty as 'gender in discourse' approaches of theorising in a void. I discuss each of these below.

Reducing researcher interference

In the introductory chapter to their edited collection *Gender Identity and Discourse Analysis*, Sunderland and Litosseliti preview the volume with:

> The collection [thus] reflects the shift from 'differences' to discourse and the associated discoursal shaping of gendered identities and relations. Where

gender differences are explored, this is done with a view to challenging existing 'givens' and the generalisability of empirical findings.

(2002: 1–2)

In contrast to this, correlational sociolinguistics does not set out 'with a view' to do anything. The fact that it starts out from the categories 'woman' and 'man' is not to say that it sets out to find differences. Granted, there may have been a tendency in past work undertaken within a quantitative paradigm to overstate differences and disregard similarities, but this potential danger of correlational sociolinguistics is also, I would argue, its strength, a point I return to below.

The criterion for reducing researcher interference in correlational sociolinguistics is quantification. This, of course, is not without its problems and the questions a correlational sociolinguist is confronted with include: 'How large is a difference between a group of male and a group of female speakers supposed to be in order to count as a reportable research finding?', 'Is the difference attributable to a single or a few extreme deviant cases from an otherwise fairly homogeneous sample?' and 'If no differences are found, can I conclude this with certainty or is it because my sample size is too small?' In contrast to 'gender in discourse' approaches, which do not provide any researcher independent answers to these questions, correlational sociolinguistics does suggest ways to accommodate them. Significance tests can be used for measuring whether an apparent difference is truly a difference or rather a chance pattern generated by random variation; speaker identity can be controlled for so that it becomes clear whether a single individual is responsible for an apparent pattern; and 'power analyses' can be used to identify whether a negative result is truly negative or the function of a too-small sample size.

Postmodernists in particular have challenged claims to objectivity arguing that they too carry their own ontological and epistemological baggage. To say that something has a probability value of 0.05, that is, that there is a 5 per cent possibility that something could have happened by chance, is to postmodernists simply playing with an arbitrary number. I suggest, however, that the way to think about this is less in terms of number crunching and more in terms of 'common sense' (a notion, of course, that has also been problematised). However, just as few people would want to bet a fortune on a tossed coin coming up heads six times in a row, so too can statistics provide a resource for common sense thinking by drawing on our intuitive knowledge that reliability increases with sample size. If these resources provided by statistics are properly adhered to, it is difficult for those who criticise correlational sociolinguistics to argue that differences are exaggerated and similarities overlooked.

Even though postmodernists' charge that nothing is objective is readily conceded, I suggest that correlational sociolinguists' claim to objectivity extends not so much to ideology as to methodological practices. Where correlational sociolinguistics does not escape its ideological bias (in that it feeds into an ideology of 'assumed gender difference'), it does aim to reduce methodological bias in its strict and consistent procedures for how to code data. In correlational sociolinguistics, it should be possible to justify why you have coded the data in the way you have and, more importantly, to communicate this justification to a wider audience. In discourse analysis it is often not possible for readers to trace the analyst's moves from data to interpretation and hence much interpretation remains clandestine.

Relevant here is the notion of objectivity, which it is useful to discuss in relation to conversation analysis. Despite their differences, conversation analysis and correlational sociolinguistics share an interest in objectivity and in reducing researcher 'interference' in data. It is a given of conversation analysis that analysts should discard sociological assumptions and not import their own categories onto the data unless these are also 'oriented to' or 'made relevant' by speakers in interaction (Stokoe, this volume). Conversation analysis, like correlational sociolinguistics, is an empirical, data-driven approach and analytic claims should be demonstrable. This is a fair point. But this raises the question of whether issues in talk can be identified as relevant to the participants unless they are *already* relevant for the analyst; a possibility conversation analysts would not so much dispute as say that the problem here is *access* (for a debate, see, e.g., Weatherall, 2000; Billig, 1999; Wetherell, 1998; Schegloff, 1997).

In fact, conversation analysts' allegiance to sociological agnosticism seems to be difficult to stand by in analysis in practice. Here, Billig (1999) argues that even though conversation analysis claims to be unbiased by not making any assumptions prior to analysis, analysts do precisely this in the simple act of labelling speakers in a transcript. Billig refers to a data extract in which Schegloff (1997) labels the speakers 'Tony' and 'Marsha' and argues that this *is* pre-interpreting the data in that first names suggest a certain degree of informality. They are also (though Billig does not mention this explicitly) gender-marked names. Schegloff justifies referring to the speakers as 'Marsha' and 'Tony' thus: '[t]his is how they address one another (and they do in the data I examined, even if not in the particular segment I analysed) and how they generally refer to one another' (1999: 566). If categories outside the data that are accessible to the reader can be invoked and justified by 'this is how they address each other', then surely a case could also be made for the corre-lational sociolinguistic position that sex may be relevant even when speakers do not invoke these categories in the data under analysis. After all, 'she', 'he', 'man', 'woman', 'girl', 'boy' are also how we 'generally refer to one another'.

The power of numbers

In contrast to other conversation analysts, Kitzinger (this volume) explicitly relies on the extra-discursive categories 'man' and 'woman'. Studying a classic conversation analytic topic, turn-taking, she explores differences between male and female speakers in their use of interruptions. Her study complements research that has focused on male conversational dominance by showing that women also interrupt. Because conversation analysts do not go beyond the interaction under analysis, however, we become none the wiser with regards to male and female speakers' general patterns of usage. I suggest that as a *supplement* to a fine-grained conversation analysis, we need methods to document reliable patterns of systematic differences between male and female speakers.

Another advantage of correlational sociolinguistics is its capacity to convincingly and reliably document the *non-existence* of sex differences, provided that the statistical 'power', calculated on the basis of sample size, is strong enough. This is in contrast to 'gender in discourse' approaches, which are arguably able only to point out (albeit often important) isolated exceptions to general patterns identified in earlier studies. The problem with this is that few would deny the existence of exceptions to a general pattern and thus, in this respect, the scholarly contribution of such studies is arguably limited. Moreover, there is a potential political backlash inherent in such studies in that the step from pointing out exceptions to the rule to arguing that 'there is no sex inequality in British politics; anyone can succeed, just look at Margaret Thatcher' is worryingly small. Certainly, correlational sociolinguistics will not report non-existence of sex differences unless this is statistically warranted.

Grounding theory in reality

A further problem with the 'gender in discourse' position, and particularly the view that there is no prediscursive gendered reality, is that this fails to resonate with most people outside academia. Bourdieu (1998), speaking about the 'family', notes that even though it is socially constructed, it still exists in that it is 'collectively recognised'. The same case can be made for sex. In Swedish newspapers, there are recurring and vigorous debates between gender researchers on the one hand and the general public and journalists on the other. The debates revolve around beliefs that feminists disavow difference and want everyone to be the same, which is a scary prospect to most people. While this says something about the power of the status quo and the 'naturalisation' of the male/female dichotomy, it also says something about the division between gender theoreticians on the one hand and the general public on the other. As Bourdieu comments:

Homo scholasticus or homo academicus is someone who is paid to play seriously; placed outside the urgency of a practical situation and oblivious to the ends which are immanent in it, he or she earnestly busies herself with problems that serious people ignore – actively or passively.

(1990: 381)

Bourdieu's point is that academics, whom he calls 'the scholastic point of view', run the risk of theorising in a void, bracketing the motives or rationality, whether conscious or unconscious, of the agents being studied. If we as scholars have an ambition that our work should benefit the community we are studying, a view widely accepted by feminist researchers (see, e.g., Holmes and Meyerhoff (2003) and Cameron and colleagues (1992)) and which may be particularly pertinent to researchers obligated by a *quid pro quo* relationship with research gatekeepers (e.g., Mullany, this volume), it is worth thinking about the relationship between our theories and the concerns of those who participate in our study.

The binary reality of call centres

I will now briefly illustrate the correlational sociolinguistic method drawing on data from call centres – one British and one Danish. In call centres, agents' interaction with customers tends to be highly regulated and guided either by full-blown scripts or by documents outlining core moves that the agent must perform (Cameron, 2000b; Taylor and Bain, 1999). Just over two-thirds of the workforce in British and Danish call centres are women (El-Salanti, Wiegman and Sørensen 2004; Holman and Wood, 2002) (though this varies with the specialisation of the call centre (Belt, 2002)). It has been suggested that sex imbalances in workplaces become 'naturalised', that is, that the 'overrepresented' sex is perceived as better at the job (Leidner, 1993). Moreover, the speech style required of call centre agents and codified in scripts and staff training material alludes to features of what Lakoff described as 'women's language' in 1975 (Cameron, 2000b): smiling, using 'expressive' intonation, creating rapport and empathy, deploying minimal responses and asking questions. Though these features may not be accurate empirical representations of how women speak, Cameron, drawing on Ochs's (1992) notion of 'indirect indexicality', argues that they may be stereotypically associated with female speakers through an intervening variable, such as the quality of caring or showing deference. When I interviewed call centre managers responsible for recruitment, they generally believed that women were better suited for the job than men.

Adherents of 'gender in discourse' frameworks do not deny the power of stereotypes, but do warn against taking such stereotypes as the basis of research. I would argue, however, that there is still work to be done to empirically test the accuracy of stereotypes, including those described above. The call centre industry is characterised by a high staff turnover and absenteeism, low pay and often stressful work conditions; staff have little autonomy and a high workload (Deery, Iverson and Walsh, 2004; Taylor et al., 2002). If women are over-recruited to the industry because they are regarded as 'naturally' suited for this type of job, or because those who recruit to the industry perceive their speech style as a valuable resource (Belt, 2002; Cameron, 2000a, b), this may perpetuate a gender order in which women occupy the least prestigious positions in society.

To test the accuracy of such stereotypes, I decided to use correlational sociolinguistics because its unabashedly binary starting point seemed to resonate with the tenet of the industry. Moreover, I needed a method that had the potential to convincingly invalidate stereotypes by reliably documenting the *non-existence* of sex differences. Lastly, in the event that these stereotypes did turn out to be empirically founded, I needed the evidence to be as rigorous and objective as possible in order to avoid accusations of inaccurately reifying stereotypes. Of course, such accusations do not necessarily disappear by invoking statistics but – a point I shall return to – documenting sex differences need not betray a feminist cause.

Contrary to my expectations, I found statistically (or near statistically) significant differences between male and female agents' use of the prescribed linguistic rules in both countries (see Table 3.1).

While the use of the majority of these linguistic rules does not correlate with sex, but with contextual variables such as call type and activity, the statistically significant sex differences that *were* found invariably point in the same direction. Female agents use more of the prescribed features than their male colleagues irrespective of whether the rule specifically prescribes a stereotypically 'feminine' ideal (such as creating rapport by using the customer's name) or whether it is a norm not conventionally associated with gender (such as greeting the customer in the correct way). This pattern holds

Table 3.1   Male and female call centre agents' average adherence to linguistic rules

Linguistic rule (call centre location)	Agent sex		Statistical test (Mann-Whitney U)
	Female	Male	
Use correct greeting (UK)	43.7%	8.5%	$p = 0.000$
Use customer's name twice (UK)	39.7%	17.8%	$p = 0.021$
Acknowledge customer's problem (UK)	34.4%	18.8%	$p = 0.150$
Use phrase 'welcome to call back' (UK)	25.0%	5.4%	$p = 0.020$
Acknowledge customer's problem (DK)	21.4%	6.0%	$p = 0.033$
Elicit permission to enter sales stage (DK)	5.7%	.0%	$p = 0.095$

regardless of whether the call centre is located in Britain or in Denmark, and has been reported also by Orr (2006).

One possible interpretation of these findings is that women, given their inferior position in society as a whole, must work harder than men to prove their worth (see Eckert (1998) and Eckert and McConnell-Ginet (2003, 1995)). This theory seeks to generalise not in terms of 'women are like this and men are like that' but in terms of institutionalised gender inequalities, which position women and men differentially *vis-à-vis* the available linguistic resources.[8] More succinctly, '*the difference arises in a context of unequal gender relations*' (Cameron, 1996: 44, emphasis in original).

In the light of these findings, it seems that there may be an empirical warrant for maintaining the sex dichotomy as a theoretical construct within language and gender research. Politically, this may be viewed as a sort of 'strategic essentialism' (Spivak, 1985) whereby members of a marginalised group benefit from highlighting similarities and downplaying differences among them for the purpose of social action.[9] As Cameron puts it, '[w]hile the shift away from naïve and essentialist conceptions of gender among sociolinguistics is unequivocally welcome, it need not – and on the balance of the evidence, should not – entail deconstructing gender dualism out of existence' (Cameron, 1998b: 955).

Concluding remarks

Like any method, correlational sociolinguistics has limitations; these need to be acknowledged. Correlational sociolinguistics is just that – correlational. It is up to the researcher to make sense of the observed or non-observed patterns (just as it is in 'gender in discourse' approaches).

Cameron (1990) and Romaine (1984) point out that patterns of correlation must be linked to an adequate social theory. Moreover, correlational sociolinguists need to take into account the possibility that there may be some other variable in between sex and language that explains a certain pattern. Ochs, for instance, points out that a linguistic form, such as a tag question, can be associated equally with female speakers ('indirect indexicality') and with 'stances such as hesitancy, and social acts such as confirmation checks' (1992: 340) ('direct indexicality'). I argue that correlational sociolinguistics nevertheless provides a powerful tool to supplement other methods currently used in language and gender. With its feet firmly grounded in the gender dualism that continues to be valid for most people, it approaches stereotypes with objective ambitions to test their empirical accuracy.

Proponents of 'gender in discourse' approaches have had legitimate and understandable reasons for criticising correlational sociolinguistics. Such paradigmatic shifts, however, can sometimes be accompanied by a risk of throwing the baby out with the bathwater. Like Swann (2002) and others, I feel that it may be time to let correlational sociolinguistics out of the dog-house: '[w]e will make greater progress if we seek to accommodate insights from a variety of sources, rather than dismissing, in a blinkered and unreflecting manner, results from currently unfashionable paradigms' (Holmes and Meyerhoff, 2003: 16).

Notes

1 I gratefully acknowledge the editors and Jakob Bro-Jørgensen, Deborah Cameron, Janet Maybin, Lucinda McDonald and Joan Swann for their insightful comments on previous versions of this chapter. Any errors and omissions are, of course, my own. Special thanks also go to Bernhard Magnusson for keeping me updated on the Swedish gender scene as it unfolds in the media. The chapter is the result of work funded by the Danish Ministry of Science, Technology and Innovation.

2 This criticism was also levelled against the lengthy tradition of social psychologists empirically testing the accuracy of Lakoff's (1975) claims; e.g., that women use more tag questions, hedges and hypercorrect grammar, and against those neurologists who documented brain differences in men and women.

3 Here, I use 'sex' to refer to the, admittedly not always perspicuous, binary variable with the two variants 'man' and 'woman', and reserve 'gender' to refer to something non-binary (Greenwood, 1996). In reality, however, the *sex/gender* distinction often turns out not to be tenable (Freed, 2004; Butler, 1990). Moreover, no one has ever said how a researcher can approach embodied persons without treating them as sexed/gendered (Cameron, personal communication).

4 Discursive psychology is dually and differentially influenced by postmodernism/post-structuralism and ethnomethodology (see, e.g., the range of different approaches in Wilkinson and Kitzinger, 1995); but arguably increasingly by the latter (see Edley and Wetherell, Chapter 11).

5 I am arguably simplifying matters somewhat as the approaches mentioned are not internally unified. They differ, for instance, in the extent to which they explicitly or implicitly recognise 'sex' as a prediscursive category.

6 Although the 'Community of Practice' approach (Eckert and McConnell-Ginet, 1992; Lave and Wenger, 1991) also emphasises the 'doing of gender', it is less radical in its anti-essentialism than, e.g., Butler's followers, and therefore I do not include it under the collective label 'gender in discourse'. Indeed, Eckert (1989, 2000), being a variationist sociolinguist, does not shy away from generalising and indeed relies on sex-based (as well as, importantly, other social categorisations, such as class, age and race) classifications.

7 Christie does comment on the uneasy tension between the two frameworks: '[In adopting a "Community of Practice" framework] it is not my intention to entirely dismiss the sociolinguistic assumption that gender can function as an aspect of structure in that it can act as a determinant of linguistic variation. To an extent therefore I am working with, and attempting to reconcile, two sometime[s] conflicting models of gender' (2002). Contrary to Christie, however, I question whether these two models can be reconciled.

8 Of course, since correlational sociolinguistics provides patterns and not explanations, we can ask whether the female agents unwittingly adopt these linguistic features or whether they deliberately use them as strategies to compensate for their lesser power. Given the intense surveillance in the call centre environment, which means that agents may be deprived of bonuses if they do not adhere to the linguistic rules, the latter explanation is not unlikely.

9 There is always a risk that evidence of gender differences will be misused: Finch argues that it is difficult for feminists to ensure that their findings 'will not be used ultimately against the collective interests of women' (1984: 83). On the other hand, Hammersley and Atkinson (1995) ask whether such concerns should outweigh the value of scientific knowledge or the public's right to know.

4
Negotiating Methodologies: Making Language and Gender Relevant in the Professional Workplace

Louise Mullany

Introduction[1]

This chapter explores the complexities of selecting methodological approaches when conducting a qualitative sociolinguistic study of language and gender in the workplace through a reflexive account of research that I conducted within two professional organisations. My investigation followed an ethnographic, interactional sociolinguistic approach. I define 'ethnographic' in accordance with Swann and Maybin's (this volume) description of the most typical ethnographic research within sociolinguistics, following Green and Bloome (1997): I utilise classic ethnographic tools, including participant observation and interviews, and take what is termed an *ethnographic perspective*, using my own insider knowledge to assess social and linguistic practices. However, whilst the fieldwork took place over a period of six months, it did not entail extremely lengthy periods of immersion in a culture, the approach more traditionally associated with linguistic anthropology/ ethnography.

I have been firmly committed to producing findings that are of practical relevance to those being studied in my research on gender and language in the professions. However, in order for sociolinguistic analysis to be of real practical relevance and overall political value, there needs to be careful negotiation between the researcher and the researched (Cameron, 2000b; Cameron, Frazer et al., 1992), and this complex process has a significant impact upon the selection and implementation of research methodologies. Roberts and Sarangi (2003) have argued that the relationship between the researcher and the researched can be a fruitful topic of study in itself (see also Pichler, Chapter 5). As opposed to just being mentioned as a by-product of research, the question of how studies can be of practical relevance to the researched can be thoroughly explored if the relationship itself becomes the central topic. By conducting a reflexive examination of my own processes of negotiation with the researched, including a focus on the problems that arose and suggested solutions, my aim is for this chapter to be of practical use to other researchers investigating language in institutional contexts.

Before moving on to examine the processes that I engaged in with the researched in professional workplaces, I will consider the overall value of conducting sociolinguistic research of practical relevance to those being studied, as well as emphasising the importance of investigating language and gender in professional settings. Recent methodological trends within feminist sociolinguistics will be referred to in order to highlight how a project such as this one can be assessed in the light of current paradigms.

The importance of practical relevance

Holmes and Meyerhoff (2003) make the crucial point that, despite the recent trend away from essentialised notions of gender within language and gender research, it is clear that gender as a social category is still highly prevalent in wider society, and very often it is essentialised, stereotypical gender categories which are perceived to exist. These inaccurate, overgeneralised categories reify gender differences and can have a direct, negative impact upon people's daily lives. As a consequence, there is a real need for language and gender research to make itself more relevant to those outside of the academic world, as convincingly argued by Freed (2003). Holmes and Meyerhoff urge researchers to be 'directed by the needs and interests of the communities of speakers studied' (2003: 10), instead of simply satisfying 'academic appetites'. Therefore, instead of creating knowledge for knowledge's sake, they encourage academics to think very carefully when selecting areas of investigation, coming to final decisions through negotiation with those being researched in order to find out what would be of use to them. Holmes and Meyerhoff go so far as to question the overall logic and purpose of engaging in academic research *not* based upon such principles, using workplace employment practices as one example of a worthwhile, societal concern which warrants investigation:

> There seems little point to our academic interests if they do not at some stage articulate with real-world concerns and enable us or our readers to identify, for example, certain employment practices as unfair and ill-informed, based more on stereotypes and prejudice than they are on people's actual behavior in the real world. At some point, our research has to be able to travel out of the academy in order to draw attention to and challenge unquestioned practices that reify certain behaviors as being morally, or aesthetically, better than others.
>
> (Holmes and Meyerhoff, 2003: 14)

Feminist language and gender research has always been political in the broadest sense, through its commitment to gender equality. However, Philips (2003: 266) argues that 'there has been a loss of a broader practical political perspective' within recent research which needs to be rectifed. In the words of Holmes and Meyerhoff (2003: 14), academic research needs to be a form of 'social activism', following examples such as Cameron (2003), Talbot (2003) and Holmes and Stubbe (2003a,b).

Holmes and Meyerhoff (2003) make a further point in relation to research funding. They argue that increasingly academics are being called into account in terms of the research they produce, in that more and more frequently academic work is held accountable in terms of what it gives back to the community that funds it in the first place (indirectly through taxation and/or more directly from particular funding bodies). All this suggests that academics have a responsibility to conduct research which is directly orientated towards the political needs of the communities being studied.

However, there is a range of tensions here, and academic responsibility is far from straightforward when put into practice. For example, academic research which has wider political relevance outside of the immediate community of people being studied may be at odds with the aims and needs of the researched. It is possible too that individuals *within* communities will have different and perhaps incompatible needs. Those being researched may have a heterogeneous set of political needs, particularly in institutions where power roles, as well as differing social identities, can result in a range of different and often conflicting political positions. Furthermore, the community may have aims that researchers feel uncomfortable with, perhaps conflicting with researchers' own political positioning. The negotiation process is thus extremely complex, and academics are frequently faced with a number of dilemmas.

The workplace as a sociolinguistic research site

Drawing on Gal (1991), McElhinny (2003) argues that it is crucial for the language of social institutions, including the workplace, to be investigated in sociolinguistics and linguistic anthropology in order to reveal hidden power structures and to contribute to the understanding of specific social problems including unequal pay, the sexual division of labour, and differences in training and promotion opportunities. Ehrlich (2003: 648) also points to Gal (1991) to argue that, because we spend most of our time interacting within institutions, the value of focusing on language and gender within informal settings is limited. From a practical perspective, data within informal spheres is also far more accessible than data in formal, institutional settings where researcher access is often tricky. However, just because data is difficult to come by does not mean that investigators should give up on such potential research sites, and Sarangi and Roberts warn that researchers should 'fight against the temptation to collect what is easily collectable' (1999: 40–1).

There has in fact in recent years been a noticeable move within language and gender research from the private to the public sphere, including the workplace (see Baxter, 2006a; Holmes, 2006; Mullany and Litosseliti, 2006). (This transition is not limited to sociolinguistic enquiry: similar trends can be seen in critical discourse analysis (Koller, Chapter 14 in this volume, 2004b; Wodak, Chapter 13 in this volume, 2003; Walsh, 2001), and feminist post-structuralist discourse analysis (Baxter, 2006b; 2003).)

Methodological transitions

The 1990s was a time of great change within language and gender research: the new prevalence of the conceptualisation of gender as a fluid and dynamic social construct led to methodological transitions within feminist sociolinguistics. Instead of following traditional, quantitative sociolinguistic methods which catalogue different linguistic tendencies between females and males (e.g., Holmes, 1995), qualitative, ethnographic research became the preferred methodological approach, with a focus on how gender identity is enacted or 'performed' (Butler, 1990) through language within specific localised settings. However, whilst Holmes and Meyerhoff (2003) acknowledge the current dominance of qualitative methodological approaches, they also highlight the benefits of *integrating* quantitative and qualitative approaches, for example, using overall general patterns identified by quantitative methods to inform the fine-grained qualitative analysis that takes place at a more local level (see also Swann and Maybin, this volume). Calls for language and gender studies not to reject quantitative, correlational sociolinguistic approaches have also emerged (Hultgren, this volume).

Whilst I adopt a qualitative, ethnographic approach, I am not averse to using quantitative methods or a combined approach. However, the research *setting* often shapes the methods that a researcher is able to employ, especially with naturally-occurring data. It quickly became clear with my study that a quantitative, survey approach examining language and gender in a variety of businesses would not be possible due to the immense difficulties in gaining access to professional workplaces. Such practical constraints illustrate how choice of methodological approach cannot be simply based upon commitment to a particular research paradigm (Tashakkori and Teddie, 1998).

I now critically examine the processes that I adopted in order to access, establish and maintain relationships with the researched, and detail the resultant methodological approaches adopted as a consequence of careful negotiation in two professional organisations.

Gaining access

My overall intended purpose as a workplace researcher was to examine the role that language can play in maintaining gender inequalities within organisations. The rationale was that this would have wider political relevance, as well as being of value to the specific managers taking part in the research. The starting point for selecting potential companies was primarily based upon logistics, the initial aim being to gain access to businesses based within a reasonable travelling distance (50 miles). As I expected that workplaces would be resistant to the presence of a fieldworker (see Sarangi and Roberts, 1999), I did not attempt to design the study any further in terms of, for example, the type of managerial professionals who would provide the data, or what size the workplaces would be in terms of number of employees.

I approached the personnel managers of companies as a first point of contact, as they most often play gatekeeping roles in terms of granting access (Bargiela-Chiappini and Harris, 1997). Personnel departments of various professional organisations from a variety of different occupational sectors were contacted. I decided to approach females at middle/senior management levels within personnel, following the rationale that female professionals would be more sympathetic to a project on gender, perceiving it as relevant to their own lives and careers. I also thought that a potentially fruitful starting point would be organisations who already had some contact with academia in the past and thus who, in theory at least, may be more open to participating in academic research. A list of personnel managers/directors who had participated in recruitment open days provided an initial contact list, and I managed to get one organisation on board here.

There are a number of crucially important issues surrounding the initial point of contact between the researcher and the researched within institutional settings. Sarangi and Roberts argue that 'researchers may encounter barriers at the earliest stages if they present themselves through discourses that are seen as threatening, obfuscating or irrelevant' (1999: 42). It was therefore essential that the professionals I approached could clearly comprehend what I was trying to achieve in my research, be assured that I was not posing a threat to them or their company, and, most importantly, could see how the research process could be of potential practical relevance to them.

As a first point of contact with organisations, I produced a written project outline. This aimed to be accessible to a non-academic audience, and the potential practical relevance that the project could have was directly signalled. Managers were informed that the project would focus on professional communication in the workplace with the potential aim of investigating the impact this may have on the 'glass ceiling' (Morrison, White and van Velsor, 1987), the invisible barrier preventing women breaking through into the higher echelons of power in the workplace. By foregrounding the glass ceiling, a pre-existing, widespread problem of which professionals would already be aware, the intention was to highlight how academic research could potentially be of practical use. In addition to signalling practical relevance, I assured confidentiality in order to convince organisations to take part.

The project outline was followed by a telephone call a few days later to see if the personnel manager was interested. If agreement was reached, I planned to arrange a face-to-face meeting. It quickly became evident that projections of the difficulties that would be encountered in attempting to collect data within this institutional setting were well-founded. The vast majority of responses were that, although the project sounded interesting, those contacted were too busy, or their concerns about ethical issues were too great, particularly in relation to confidentiality.

Another problem was in relation to the presentation of my own identity as an academic researcher. Being a linguist located within an English department turned out to be a noticeable barrier. Contacts were often puzzled as to why anyone within English would want to look at the language of organisations, and potential participants were lost as a consequence of this confusion. This problem points towards more general preconceptions that people outside of academia hold as to who belongs where within a university, and what the legitimate institutional identity is for researchers who wish to investigate language within professional spheres. I return to this point later.

In order to broaden the pool of potential organisations, I decided to also approach male personnel managers/directors, as my preconception that female managers would be more interested and willing did not appear to have been borne out in practice. Indeed, the second company that agreed to take part in the study had a male personnel manager. Both organisations were corporate businesses based in the same UK county.

Negotiating a multi-method approach

The negotiation process of research aims and demands really got underway within the initial face-to-face meeting, leading to the establishment of parameters within which an agreed set of methods could be implemented once the research 'proper' began. As I had approached the businesses and not the other way round, there was an expectation for me to inform personnel managers of what I thought I could do for them, and give them details about potential practical implications in order for them to be able to reach a decision. I thus informed them, in layperson's terms, of the methodological approaches that could be taken in order to investigate the negotiated research question(s), and the benefits that my research could have for the company. The practical issue of lack of access to more than two companies, combined with the theoretical and methodological shifts that had taken place during the 1990s and my wish to conduct an in-depth investigation of the role that language can play in maintaining gender inequalities, meant that I hoped to take an ethnographic approach to data collection.

There was clear interest in gender and communicative strategies and the issue of the glass ceiling from the two organisations that agreed to face-to-face meetings. Following a joint process of negotiation, I agreed with the personnel representatives that I would investigate how the language women and men managers use in workplace interactions, in conjunction with the language used to represent and evaluate women and men in their workplaces, may impact upon women's inability to break through the glass ceiling. I introduced the key components of an interactional sociolinguistic, ethnographic study that would investigate workplace communication and the glass ceiling in non-obfuscating, non-technical language.

In order to conduct a legitimate sociolinguistic study, it was crucial that the personnel gatekeepers granted me permission to audio-record spoken discourse within the organisations. Audio-recording was selected as the least obtrusive form (see Mullany, 2007). Reassurances regarding research ethics and confidentiality played a key role here. The personnel representative was assured that copies of all recordings made could be requested at any time and any audio-recorded material that participants were unhappy with would be deleted immediately on request. Initial agreement was reached with both organisations that I would be allowed to enter the workplace as a participant observer to shadow managers, attend and audio-record meetings and conduct recorded interviews.

Neither company agreed to allow me to audio-record informal encounters, perceiving this as an invasion of privacy which could potentially lead to hostility surrounding my presence, thus making it difficult for me to establish good relationships with employees. It was, however, agreed that field-notes could be used for informal encounters on two conditions. The first was that all employees were informed that my participant observations would be logged during shadowing, and the second was that I did not produce any written notes whilst the encounters were taking place, to minimise distracting managers in their daily routines. These fieldnotes proved to be an invaluable source of ethnographic information.

One difficulty in using the personnel department as my initial point of contact was that employees may think that I was working on 'behalf' of personnel, and thus potentially 'spying' on them. (I referred earlier to the heterogeneity of political needs that may exist within an organization.) I hoped, however, that employees in all parts of the company could see how gender and equal opportunities were relevant to their everyday working lives, as opposed to being something that I was investigating on behalf of personnel. If this issue was raised, I made it clear that I had no 'official' relationship with personnel. I also emphasised that the reports and feedback I produced were for everyone who had taken part. However, as well as being gatekeepers, personnel departments within businesses are also responsible for the implementation of equal opportunities policies and company training programmes. Thus, despite potential drawbacks, their role in the research was integral.

The personnel departments in both organisations agreed that I could initially spend a full week with them and then return to the companies for day visits to continue observing, recording and conducting interviews. As an entry point into both companies it was agreed that it would be useful for me to go through the same induction process as new employees. This turned out to be an extremely beneficial way to begin my participant observation. It enabled me to gain insight into company culture by being immediately exposed to the company's official metadiscourse. Once initial access had taken place, and as I began to establish relationships with managers in the company, I hoped that more opportunities would open up in terms of meeting new informants.

Although my relationship with the two companies developed along different lines, I ended up with the same multi-method approach: audio-recording meetings and interviews, writing fieldnotes to record my participant observations during shadowing and informal talk, and gathering written documents as additional ethnographic information. It was agreed that I would feedback my observations on workplace practices and give practical suggestions and solutions via a written report, as well as offering presentations and one-to-one feedback to all managers who took part in the research.

Drawing on the work of Bourdieu (1993), Sally Candlin (2003: 389) argues that a key access-related issue within institutional research sites is the need to develop 'an understanding of the habitus of practitioners'. I aimed to pick up the 'habitus' of the workplace professionals that I was shadowing and observing with a view to utilising this information in order to make the study of key relevance to the managers themselves. Candlin points to a need for prolonged contact with the site, but this is easier to achieve if the researcher is a 'complete' participant observer (Duranti, 1997: 99) who already belongs to the community being researched before the project begins. However, if the researcher is an outsider with fairly restricted access, as I was, this is more difficult.

In the second organisation, once the initial agreements about access had been finalised, the male personnel manager officially handed my case over to one of his female subordinates, on the principle that she would find my project more 'applicable'. However, he still played an active and influential role in the research process (see below). My key female informant maintained control over the choice of people I shadowed, the meetings I attended and the people I interviewed by producing written daily schedules. This organisation was therefore rather strict about my movements within the company. In contrast, my key informant in the first organisation took a far more distant role once I had completed the initial induction. I was presented with a list of email addresses for all managers in the company, and given free reign to contact anyone on this list and make arrangements directly with them. There was thus far less control in terms of who I approached and observed, the meetings that I attended and the interviews I conducted. Without an official schedule, I could independently negotiate access to individuals within the organisation. I used the people that I had been introduced to at meetings as future points of contact, as well as my initial contacts, to get others within the business interested and involved. I thus had much more control over the data that I gained in the first company, whereas the second company seemed to want me to develop a particular 'picture' of the organisation, and tried to 'police' my movements accordingly. It was obviously important to bear these factors in mind when analysing the data.

The negotiated, multi-method, ethnographic approach enabled the sociolinguistic analysis to take place from a range of integrated perspectives. My participant observation (observing/shadowing managers, recording meetings, conducting interviews, utilising the information provided in written documents) enabled a wealth of ethnographic background information to be utilised to inform the interactional analysis of managers' discourse, enriching and enhancing the resultant interpretation (see Sarangi and Roberts, 1999).

In all, the discourse of 45 different managers (22 females and 23 males) was observed in six different communities of practice (see Mullany, 2007). I observed both companies for approximately one month's working hours in total. After spending the initial week within both organizations, I re-entered them on at least 15 different occasions over a period of six months. The meeting data analysis is based on eight hours of audio-recording, and is informed by a range of background ethnographic data.

The analysis highlighted the important influence that communities of practice play on the linguistic strategies that managers use. Whilst managers' speech varied depending upon the community of practice in which they were interacting, in both companies, women and men managers were observed using similar interactional styles in the specific context of business meetings. In contrast to older sociolinguistic studies, which argued that workplace speech norms are 'masculine' due to a tradition of greater historical male dominance (Kendall and Tannen, 1997; Coates, 1995), in these communities of practice both women and men managers used a range of speech styles stereotypically associated with femininity (see Mullany, 2007). This accords with Cameron's (2003, 2000b) observations of the feminisation of public discourse in workplaces, and may be indicative of changing linguistic and social practices. However, women and men managers showed themselves to be adept at changing speech styles to suit the specific circumstances of their interactions within particular communities of practice, and on occasions, could be witnessed using stereotypically masculine styles.

To explore these findings further, the meeting data analysis was interpreted as part of an overall 'gendered discourses' framework, following a Foucauldian-influenced definition of discourse (Sunderland, 2004; Mills, 1997) in order to interrogate wider power structures both within the organisations and within society as a whole. The interview data illuminated managers' attitudes to, and evaluations of, language and gender issues. The interview analysis highlighted a range of gendered discourses, maintained by and carrying gender ideologies, which were serving to place women at a disadvantage in the workplace. These deeply embedded discourses highlight a number of reasons why the 'glass ceiling' is still in place, and suggest reasons why women experience other forms of workplace discrimination including unequal pay and sexual harassment (see Mullany, 2007). As Cameron (2003) points out, such transitions in workplace linguistic practices have not straightforwardly resulted in empowerment of women. The evidence from my study overwhelmingly demonstrates that women and men are still evaluated very differently, often based upon inaccurate stereotypes of biological essentialism, resulting in women still continuing to fall victim to the 'double bind' (Lakoff, 2003). Alternatively, if men use speech strategies stereotypically associated with a feminine speech style, they are viewed positively, perceived as being sensitive, astute managers.

In summary, the ethnographic approach enabled a multilayered analysis of these two workplaces to be produced, taking the investigation much further than just focusing on interactional strategies. It also incorporates such findings within an overarching analysis of the broader gendered discourses that exist within the wider 'institutional order' (Sarangi and Roberts, 1999: 1).

Researcher identities and roles

The presentation of my own identity(ies), and the role(s) that those within the workplaces perceived me to have, raised a number of interesting and important issues. On occasion, participants would ask for my 'expert' opinion. Sarangi and Candlin (2003: 280) refer to this as the reversal of the 'actor-audience' roles, which happens within 'a consultative model of workplace research'. Whilst I was not in any official sense a 'consultant', my identity and roles were often perceived in this way. However, as Sarangi and Candlin also point out, once you are perceived as an 'expert', pressure is exerted upon you to perform like one. Whilst I was happy to give general background information on language and gender within the professional workplace, it was very difficult to give the kind of 'expert' advice and guidance that some managers were requesting before I had conducted any analysis or even completed the data collection. This relates to the recurrent problem with timescales. Often participants would request feedback immediately after a meeting had taken place, or directly after shadowing had been completed (aptly referred to as demands for 'hot' feedback (Sarangi and Candlin, 2003: 277)). Attempting to explain how a transcription process takes place in order to produce a thorough linguistic analysis does not sit well with the fast-moving world of business, and this was a source of frustration for some managers. Another recurring problem was managers' desires to compare themselves directly with managers in competing companies. I obviously could not oblige here due to my commitment to protect the anonymity of other organisations, without even beginning to get into the difficulties of attempting to get a range of organisations from within a similar sector to agree to take part. I also experienced unexpected difficulties with my own role as researcher within the second company. When talking on my own for the first time with the male personnel manager who had granted me access, he informed me that, although they had decided to allow me into their organisation, they were happy with how things were in relation to gender. In particular, they were satisfied with their equal opportunities policies, and my research should reflect this and not 'rock the boat'. Therefore, before I had even begun to analyse data from a linguistic perspective within this organisation, I was being told what my results should be when feeding back to the company. The overt control that this company was exerting upon the research made more sense when I was told this.

The process of negotiating research questions and producing research findings that could be of practical relevance thus appeared somewhat artificial in this case: I had basically been told that my presence within the company was acceptable on the understanding that I gave them the results they wanted, regardless of any that I might produce as a result of my own linguistic analyses. I got the strong sense that the people I had been selected to spend time with had been hand-picked and would be firm advocates of the company. Interestingly, however, this did not always turn out to be the case, particularly within some interview encounters, with certain women employees being very critical of the organisation's handling of gender issues, as well as directly raising the manner in which they felt they were negatively perceived as women managers. This problem highlights the deep complexities involved when negotiating research on language and gender within the workplace, and in the dissemination of findings. The methods used for dissemination will now be further explored.

Dissemination

I produced written reports which conveyed the findings in an accessible register, without any technical linguistic terminology. I drew attention to key issues and gave practical suggestions for changing attitudes towards how women and men are evaluated differently. With the first company, I indeed felt obliged to produce a report that didn't 'rock the boat', although I *did* make (rhetorically careful) reference to problems raised, particularly those that hamper women's career progression (see Mullany, 2007).

Overall, the time-consuming nature of the transcription and analysis process affected the relationships that I had established with both organisations. Whilst the findings were received with much interest, by the time the analysis had been completed, it seemed that the importance of the project from the perspective of the companies had dwindled somewhat. (Two key employees who had taken part had in fact left by the time I had produced a written report.) Whilst both companies expressed their interest and gratitude, I was unable to monitor if my research had been of any real applied use. As Mullany and Litosseliti point out, 'it is not easy to see (and much less to control) which components of academic research are taken on board in organizations, and which research findings are used to shape their policies and practices' (2006: 143).

The advent of new technologies that enable transcripts to be produced quickly and easily would no doubt improve the turnaround time for dissemination based on linguistic findings. Formalising the consultancy role could also potentially be used as a means of efficiently providing workplace feedback – if funding comes from within the company. However, becoming an official consultant in this sense opens up a whole range of ethical issues for academics, as well as making the aim of producing research that can be of practical use to those outside the companies very difficult (though see Baxter, 2003 for an example of an academic working in conjunction with official business consultants). Another suggestion is collaborative, interdisciplinary research, by large research teams, to cover a wide range of issues from different perspectives and to enable a quicker turn around in terms of being able to disseminate findings to the researched. Candlin's (2003) suggestions for the collaborative writing of research findings by practitioners and academics is an excellent one; this also suggests a real need for interdisciplinary research (see Roberts and Sarangi, 2003). A related point, and one which would also help overcome the problem highlighted earlier in terms of our own institutional identities being at odds with popular expectations, is to establish interdisciplinary research centres which can provide both an institutional authority and alternative institutional identity to one's own university department.

Ground-breaking publications such as Holmes (2003a, b) and Holmes and Major (2003) show that turning academic research into practically relevant, practitioner publications can succeed. Indeed, the large body of work that has been produced by Holmes and her research colleagues in New Zealand workplaces (see Holmes and Stubbe, 2003b) is also an excellent model of how team research can be successfully produced. In terms of dissemination within academia, my project was relevant to journals outside my own field, including professional, practitioner journals. However, pressure from our own universities in terms of producing publications for the Research Assessment Exercise (RAE) within the United Kingdom,[2] and equivalent pressure in other countries, can influence where we decide to publish. Furthermore, Candlin (2003) argues that traditional hierarchies within academic publications dictate both where scholars decide to publish and what audiences are reached as a consequence; a range of confrontational issues need to be addressed if academia is ever to contribute properly to wider social expectations and professional practice.

Conclusion

By producing a detailed account of the development of the relationship between the researcher and the researched, I have emphasised and hopefully illuminated the complex processes of methodological negotiation that take place when conducting research within the public sphere of the workplace. A fluid approach is required, which, in order to work effectively, requires a good deal of flexibility and accommodation to each others' needs. The reflexive account that I have produced has drawn attention to a number of problems that arose when attempting to conduct research of this nature. Some potential solutions to these problems have been suggested, and it is the overall intention that the issues raised here will be of practical use to others conducting research in institutional contexts.

Notes

1 I am indebted to Joan Swann, Janet Maybin and Helen Sauntson for their insightful comments on an earlier version of this chapter. Many thanks are also due to my workplace informants who made this research possible.

2 Whilst this chapter was being written, the British Government decided that the Research Assessment Exercise (RAE) would be disbanded after the 2008 exercise. Current plans to assess academic research instead by metrics testing, based in part upon the perceived prestige of specific journals and publishing houses, would seem, however, only to exacerbate this problem.

5
Gender, Ethnicity and Religion in Spontaneous Talk and Ethnographic-Style Interviews: Balancing Perspectives of Researcher and Researched

Pia Pichler

Introduction

In this chapter I explore the potential insights that can be offered into the study of language and gender by complementing spontaneous conversational data with ethnographic-style interviews. I shall demonstrate that the use of interviews in combination with spontaneous talk can create a dialogue between researcher and researched, which not only reveals and reflects the 'tacit and articulated understandings of the participants in whatever processes and activities are being studied', but also increases the researcher's reflexivity about her 'own cultural and interpretive capacities' which play a significant role in the analysis and interpretation of linguistic and social practice (Rampton, Tusting et al., 2004: 2, 3). This emphasis on participants' perspectives as well as on the researcher's awareness of their own locatedness in sociocultural space, and, I would add, in a specific discipline of research, are central concerns of (linguistic) ethnography, whose potential contribution to language and gender studies I explore in this chapter.

In this chapter I compare my findings from the self-recorded spontaneous talk of one group of British Bangladeshi girls with extracts from ethnographic-style interviews which I carried out more than a year later with one of the girls from the group. In my analysis of these data I am particularly interested in additional, and at times seemingly contradictory, perspectives and interpretations gained from comparing these two sources.

Interviews have always been key to ethnography, due to their potential to capture perspectives of, and give a voice to, participants (Hammersley, 2006: 9; see also Spradley, 1979). Nevertheless, the validity of interview data has been a matter of debate among language-oriented ethnographers, especially when interview are used as primary data rather than in combination with participant observation. Besnier aligns himself with Kulick (1999: 615) in describing 'an analysis of talk produced in the context of ethnographic interviews [as] both limited and limiting' (2003: 288). However, Besnier does not dismiss the use of ethnographic interviews altogether, arguing for ethnographers to take a reflexive, critical stance to their own position in interviews, and echoing Saville-Troike's (2003: 99–100) view that interviews can be valuable, if only as a 'supplement to observation and participation'. Other ethnographers, however, see the role of interviews as more central, arguing that 'there are distinct advantages in combining participant observation with interviews; in particular, the data from each can be used to illuminate the other' (Hammersley and Atkinson, 1995: 131; see also Hammersley, 2006).

Ethnographic or ethnographic-oriented research in language and gender which relies heavily on interview data includes Eckert's (1989) study of 'jocks and burnouts' in a Californian high school, and Sunderland's (1995) UK study of classroom interaction of 11–12 year-olds. However, in common with other existing ethnographic research on language and gender, neither foregrounds the question of how to approach interview data. This question is central to my chapter, which considers whether the ethnographic (-style) interview should be conceptualised as a technique to obtain the interviewee's 'report on another reality' which the researcher would otherwise be unable to access (Silverman, 2001: 111), or as a 'local accomplishment' (Silverman, 2001: 104), in which participants actively and collaboratively construct knowledge and meaning (Holstein and Gubrium, 1997: 114). A mid-position, taken by Miller and Glassner (1997: 99), is to see the ethnographic (-style) interview as a display of cultural knowledge by the interviewees: a possible balancing of the externalist and internalist perspectives of the other two approaches. I will demonstrate these different approaches using several extracts from my own ethnographic-style interviews, identifying methodological issues and potential insights of each approach.

Data: spontaneous talk and ethnographic-style interviews

This chapter focuses on a group of five 15–16 year-old British Bangladeshi girls who took part in my comparative study of the interplay between gender, ethnicity and social class (Pichler, forthcoming). I started by collecting spontaneous conversational data, self-recorded by the girls during their lunch-breaks at school. In this chapter, however, I foreground the ethnographic-style interviews, which I had originally intended to play a minor, supporting role in my analysis of the spontaneous conversational data.

Although my study was not planned as strictly ethnographic research, as I did not engage in any long-term participant observation, I sought to encourage interaction between the girls and myself right from the beginning.

The closest and most fruitful relationship with one of the girls developed more than a year after completing the collection of spontaneous conversational data. Hennah and I spent many hours together translating and transcribing the Sylheti utterances in the talk of her friendship group. These sessions soon turned into informal interviews,[1] which I used initially to clarify points that I had discovered in the first stages of transcribing and analysing my data. I asked Hennah about individual members of the group, about norms and practices within the group, and about aspects of the girls' (sociocultural) backgrounds, which I, as an outsider, did not have access to. Moreover, the one-year gap between the collection of the spontaneous data and my collaboration with Hennah also meant that I was able to provide feedback on my findings, an opportunity which is frequently unavailable to researchers due to the time-consuming process of linguistic transcription and analysis (see Mullany, this volume). These feedback sessions allowed me to check my own understanding of the girls' discursive practices against that of an insider in the group, who increasingly also adopted the role of data analyst. Thus, Hennah provided me with her own interpretations of some of my material and interpretations, volunteering additional information about the group, the girls' families and communities. It is essential to acknowledge that Hennah's views and positions may or may not have been representative of the entire group. Nevertheless, hers is a more 'insider' view than my own and I argue with Larson that this dialogue between (the perspectives of) researcher and researched 'makes understanding of the life world and lived realities of others possible' (1997: 459).

In the course of this collaboration I got to know Hennah's family and we developed the type of friendly and close relationship which is the aim of many ethnographic researchers. I met up with her for five five-hour sessions in her house to work on the transcript, another time to have lunch with her and her friends, and on one further occasion I was smuggled into her college. The relationship continues to this day.

Despite these intense researcher-researched interactions, I hesitate to use the label 'ethnographic interview', as I believe this would wrongly suggest full alignment with an ethnographic research design. Moreover, I felt that the concept of 'ethnographic interview' would not capture the multi-purpose nature of these sessions, including translation, transcription, conversation and 'interviews' with (requests for) clarification and feedback from both researcher and researched, and I therefore adopt the term 'ethnographic-style interview' (from Roberts, Cooke et al., 2005).

Situating my research in ethnographic methodologies

Ethnographically oriented research, including my own, tends to focus on local, situated language use and discourse practices, adopting a micro-perspective to cultural analysis (Rampton, Tusting et al., 2004: 6; Silverman, 2001: 56). However, despite claims to investigate 'a number of different levels/dimensions of sociocultural organisation/process at the same time', ethnographers have been criticized for 'neglecting larger-scale social and historical processes and systems' (Rampton, Tusting et al., 2004: 2, 15; but see Hammersley, 2006; Blommaert, Collins et al., 2003; Miller, 1997 on combining micro and macro perspectives). My own chapter foregrounds the intersection and negotiation of gender, ethnicity and religion in ethnographic-style interviews and in situated friendship talk, but I also argue for the extension of the analytic focus beyond the local context of the speech event to other contexts, data sources and even disciplines, to gain a fuller understanding of the complexity of sociocultural norms and practices.

My decision to carry out interviews after listening to the girls' spontaneous talk on tape was motivated by one of the most established concerns of ethnographic research: the perspective of the researched (Rampton, Tusting et al., 2004: 2; Silverman, 2001: 46). My observation of, and interaction with, the girls was not sufficiently in-depth or long term for my work to be considered fully ethnographic. However, the conversational and the interview data, in addition to other sources – (non-participant) observation, questionnaires and group interviews – provided a variety of ethnographic tools and data sources, which allowed me to adopt what Green and Bloome (1997) define as an ethnographic perspective.

Linked to the focus on the research subjects' own understanding of their cultural practices is ethnographers' rejection of *a priori* hypotheses combined with an openness to their data, and to unanticipated concepts and categories which are generated in the course of analysis (Rampton, Tusting et al., 2004: 2, 5; Hammersley and Atkinson, 1995: 205–14). Much current ethnographic work, influenced by ethnomethodological and conversation analytic procedures and constructionist theorisations of discourse and identity, is critical of research which draws on pre-established social categories like 'male', 'Londoner' and 'doctor' (Rampton, Tusting et al., 2004: 6). These methodological and theoretical developments in ethnography have also lent themselves to performative and contextualised models of gender which have dominated the last decade of academic research (see Swann and Maybin, this volume). My own chapter approaches the issue of '*a-priori* categories' from a reflexive, ethnographic perspective by discussing the similarities and discrepancies between the categories that are considered relevant by researcher and researched in spontaneous and in interview data.

Introducing the spontaneous talk: an overview

In this section I briefly introduce two significant findings from my analysis of the girls' spontaneous talk before re-examining these findings in relation to my interview data. My discourse analytic study of the girls' spontaneous talk sought to integrate a micro-linguistic perspective with a critical investigation of discourses (as language reflecting and shaping sociocultural norms and practices) and the girls' linguistic negotiation of, and positioning in relation to, these discourses in their talk. Firstly, I found that the girls' positioning in the group was influenced by discourses which revealed both British and Bangladeshi cultural norms (Pichler, forthcoming, 2006a). Secondly, the girls had devised linguistic strategies such as teasing and boasting which allowed them to switch between, renegotiate and synthesise these discourses and cultural norms, which, I argued, allowed the girls to construct hybrid British Asian identities (Pichler, 2007, 2006b). For example, the girls used teasing in their talk about boys to switch between a Bangladeshi discourse which views pre-marital dating critically and a second, pro-dating discourse, which I found in both my British working-class groups, and which positions dating as the norm (and frequently a pressure) for adolescents within their peer group. Thus, in their spontaneous talk the girls' teasing functioned as a strategy to reconcile opposing culture specific discourses on problematic topics such as dating, boyfriends, love and sex (see Pichler, 2006a, 2006b), and therefore to accomplish hybrid identities by constructing themselves both as British working class and as Muslim Bangladeshi.

Talking about topics associated with heterosexual relationships appeared to be problematic for the girls in part because it associated them with boys and men, which, I argue, was a threat to the girls' good reputation, particularly if there was a risk of them being observed by a member of their own Bangladeshi 'community', as the following extract from my transcriptions[2] of the girls' spontaneous talk shows:

Extract 1   'Kissing in the street'

001	Rahima	(but-) oh Go:d {embarrassed/amused} I just get so **embarrassed**=
002	Ardiana	=**that** is fu*nny* [*Rahima*: (I really-)] though kissing somebody
003	Ardiana	on the street everyone *watching* [*Dilshana*: innit] you
004	Rahima	{disgusted}ugh that is so (-) %stupid I find it%
005	Ardiana	(-) it's ALRIGHT *if you're* [*Rahima*: (yeah but-)]
006	Ardiana	kissing someone in front of a **white** person right

This extract is part of a longer conversation initiated by Rahima who previously asked the others whether they 'find it weird when you're kissing someone in the street'. Although Ardiana first adopts a resistant position, which is framed playfully as a boast (lines 2–3), her switch back from a playful into a serious frame (Bateson, 1987/1972; Goffman, 1974) in lines 5–6 also reveals her acknowledgement that it can be problematic to kiss somebody in the street. The extract points to the group's awareness of a dominant code of conduct for girls which is associated with 'non-white' people. My own interpretation of this extract links this dominant code of conduct to cultural norms associated with the girls' Bangladeshi ethnicity (for a detailed discussion, see Pichler 2006a).

My understanding of concepts like 'cultural norms' and 'culture' has been influenced by cross-disciplinary theories and research on cultural hybridity, including Brah's (1996: 234) definition of culture as a 'process' and as 'semiotic space with infinite class, caste, gender, ethnic or other inflections' (ibid.: 246). However, as Bauman (1997: 209) notes, dominant and essentialist notions of culture(s), equated with discrete and homogeneous ethnic (and, I should add, religious) groups, remain relevant aspects in a critical examination of culture as a process, as they 'form ... part of the discursive competence of citizens from "ethnic minorities" themselves, and continue ... to function as one element in the negotiation of difference'. In the current chapter, I deal with these 'dominant' and 'demotic' (i.e., alternative) discourses of culture (ibid.: 209) by contrasting the categories invoked in my informant Hennah's self-identifications with those ascribed by myself, the researcher.

Interpreting interview data: a question of methodology

In our ethnographic-style interviews Hennah frequently speaks about the need for girls to avoid contact with boys. However, she links these dominant norms about mixed-sex interaction not to ethnic but to religious inflections of culture, emphasising the significance of the category 'religion' for her identity:

Extract 2   'Our religion is really strict – Part 1'[3]

```
010   H:   we are Muslims (-) there is not much
011        (.) difference but *there* [P: yeah] is a lot
012        do you get me *.hh* [P: yeah] (>and dyknow<)
013        Christians allow their children to go out and
014        everything and my parents like .hh they prefer
015        to b- be like (-) the same as the old religion
016        [P: yeah yeah] like (xxxx) things were like in olden
017        times [P: yeah] but because of k- society and all
018        the changes [P: = yeah] you can't really stick to it
019        [P: yeah *yeah*] *but* they try as hard as they can
```

This extract provides an initial example of Hennah's emphasis on her religious identity, in which she attributes her parents' objections to their children 'going out' to religious practices rather than ethnic customs. The relevance of this distinction, which I adopt for this chapter, is also emphasised in critical research on multiculturalism (Mirza, 2006) and in the anthropological and sociological work of Asian Muslim feminists on hybridity (Ahmad, 2003; Shain, 2003). This provided me with a significant interdisciplinary basis for my own linguistic work (Pichler, forthcoming, 2007) but, again, did not tend to foreground the question of how to approach interview data (see Archer, 2002, for an exception).

The question I want to ask is how to treat Hennah's claims about the significance of religion and the hardship of diverging cultural practices and how to resolve any discrepancies between her and my perspectives which emerged in the course of the ethnographic-style interviews. The answer, I argue, to a significant extent depends on the purpose of the interview, and on the methodological and theoretical approach a researcher takes to their data. A positivist approach to interviews (usually based on a highly standardised and structured format) would seek to establish whether Hennah's claims can be seen as 'true or false' reports on reality, aiming to gather factual information independent of the interview context (see Silverman, 2001: 88–90, 110–13). However, discourse analytic research influenced by constructionist theory tends to treat interviews as 'social encounter[s] in which knowledge is constructed', highlighting the significance of the interview context and viewing interviews as *interactions* between interviewers and interviewees (Miller and Glassner, 1997: 114; but see also Silverman, 2001: 95–113; Holstein and Gubrium, 1997; Hammersley and Atkinson, 1995). This constructionist perspective has dominated research which relies on interviews as the primary source of data; as, for example, Wetherell's (1998) discursive psychological investigation of the positioning of young white British men, or Archer's feminist (2002) research with young British Muslims in the field of education and policy studies. This constructionist influence on interviews has not, however, gone unchallenged in ethnographic research, which has frequently used interviews as a *secondary* source of data to gain insight into informants' accounts of, and perspectives on, social worlds which go well beyond the immediate context of the interview (Hammersley, 2006: 9).

The remainder of this chapter foregrounds the question of how researchers may approach interviews on the basis of three extracts from my own data.

Interview as display of cultural knowledge

If we approach interviews as techniques to generate ethnographic information about our informants and their perspectives on and knowledge of a reality outside the interview context, without aligning ourselves with a strictly positivist stance, we might choose to focus on what Miller and Glassner (1997) call 'cultural stories'. The following extract illustrates this approach:

Extract 3   'Our religion is really strict – Part 3'[3]

061   H: because like you (know > when I) say <
062   like (.) I wanna go out something like *that*

```
063        [P: yeah] and I can't do it because (.) (obviously)
064        I have to wear a scarf and then I have to (.)
065        think about erm cause when I- in *our* [P: mm]
066        religion yeah you are supposed to be really
067        strict yeah you are not supposed to go next to
068        your (.) even your dad when you're (not) older
069        th- erm about the age of fifteen or stuff like
070        *that* [P: right] (>you're not supposed to go<)
071        next to your dad or your brother .hh and when
072        I go outside there's loads of guys [P: there's loads
073        of guys] yeah (.) and even in college you know
074        *(xxxxxx)*
075    P:  [and even] if you don't go look*ing* [H: yeah]
076        for them they are still *there* [H: yeah]
077    H:  {amused/embarrassed}they're still the*re* [P: yeah]
078        and sometimes if there is a religious person
079        around you they assume that you're
080        {amused/embarrassed} looking for it [P: yeah yeah]
081        *d'you* get me [P: yeah] and it's really hard
```

As in many other instances of our interview-encounters, Hennah identifies religion as the most central category to explain the practices of her own group, and, by extension, her community: 'in our religion you are supposed to be really strict' (lines 65–67). Thus, Hennah explains her claims about strict gender segregation for girls who reach mid/late adolescence not by ethnic customs but by religious norms, re-emphasising the difficulty of coping with a situation like this: 'it's really hard' (line 81).

Rather than providing 'objective facts' which can be verified or falsified, cultural stories present dominant cultural knowledge, tapping into (frequently stereotypical) cultural narratives which participants draw on to make sense of their experience. The concept of 'cultural stories' is therefore not dissimilar to the ethnomethodological concept of 'membership categories' (Sacks, 1992; see also Silverman, 2001: 101–4; Stokoe and Smithson, 2001) or the concept of 'interpretative repertoire', defined as 'a culturally familiar and habitual line of argument comprised of recognizable themes, commonplaces and probes' (Wetherell, 1998: 400) and employed by discursive psychologists in their analysis of 'locally managed positions in actual interaction' (ibid.: 401).

In the light of this approach, the question in relation to the above example is not if Hennah's explanation in the interview is more 'true' or 'false' than my findings based on the conversational data. Instead, one needs to approach her explanation as revealing a 'cultural story' about gender segregation for religious reasons. This cultural story reveals categories that are relevant to the participant (religion; gender), which *complement* rather than contradict my own understanding of the girls' cultural practices. Ethnographers are suspicious of using pre-established categories, especially if they suggest essentialist identities or groups (e.g., gender, ethnicity, religion). However, it is very clear from this interview data that if ethnographers take seriously their own aim to 'comprehend the tacit *and articulated* understandings of the participants in whatever processes and activities are being studied' (Rampton, Tusting et al, 2004: 2, my emphasis), they cannot easily dismiss the significance of these categories as resources for their informants' self-identification. I do not advocate a return to a naturalist ethnography which has as its aim the largely uncritical '*description* of cultures' (Hammersely and Atkinson, 1995: 3–16). However, I believe that a critical and self-reflexive approach to ethnographic interviews can offer valuable insights into the participants' own understanding of norms and practices in their group which may not have emerged in the researcher's observation or analysis of spontaneous, situated interaction.

Interview as local accomplishment

Although the above focus on 'cultural stories' also shows some influence of a social constructionist perspective by framing the informant's accounts as stories rather than facts, the contstructionist perspective is much more pronounced in conversation analytic studies of interviews. Conversation Analysis (CA) has linked the ethnomethodological concern about participants' displays of their own understanding of everyday interaction to an exploration of conversational turn-taking (Sacks, Schegloff and Jefferson, 1974; Sacks, 1992). Thus, CA research foregrounds the sequential analysis of interviews as co-constructed events between their participants (interviewer and interviewees), frequently replacing the traditional focus of interviews on the 'what' with a focus on the 'how' (Silverman, 2001: 101, but see Holstein and Gubrium, 1997, for an exception).

Ethnographic studies of linguistic micro-phenomena have been influenced by this conversation analytical emphasis on sequential, interactional processes in their own investigation of spontaneous conversational talk (Rampton, Tusting et al., 2004: 7). A focus on the sequential organisation of my interaction with Hennah would foreground the collaborative processes of researcher and researched 'doing' an ethnographic-style interview, examining question-answer pairs, reformulations, minimal responses, mirroring and joint constructions. For the purpose of this chapter, a sequential analysis can make a significant contribution to the investigation of the collaborative processes of constructing meaning and knowledge in interviews, especially when it is paired with an analytic focus on discourses and subject positions (see also Wetherell, 1998) and with the ethnographic concern for a 'reflexive' analysis of the role of the researcher, which encourages a critical assessment of the researcher's own 'cultural and interpretive capacities' (Rampton, Tusting et al., 2004: 3).

Extract 4   'Our religion is really strict – Part 2'

```
031   H:   it's really hard cause you know/ .hh when I when we
032        go to school *like* [P: yeah] if you are like (.) we are eating
033        food ye*ah* [P: yeah] they aks you to shut your mouth and eat (.)
034        y*eah* [P: *yeah* yeah] and when I come home my dad
035        goes {amused voice} 'let some air get into your mouth'
036        you /know [P: yeah yeah *yeah*] *do* you get me [P: yeah]
037        and (-) [P: yeah] you know them (.) they don't mind if
038        they talk with their mouth full [P: yeah yeah *yeah
039        yeah*] *do you* get me and when i- if you go to
040        school they think it's *rude*
041   P:                              [so that]'s differen- I mean
042        that's [H: yeah] the thing (.) [H: yeah] *that* they are
043        being (xxxxxx)
044   H:   if you can adapt to them [P: yeah] if you can
045        adapt to them when you go to the (.) location
046        you adapt to it (-) [P: OK *brilliant*] *that's fine*
047        /yeah (.) so that's *(fine)* [P: *xxxxxxx* xxxxxx]
048        if you can't adapt to it I (.) {amused} I suggest
049        you stick to the one that (-) don't get you in trouble
050        [P: yeah (.) yeah] = do you get me [P: yeah right] otherwise
051        (-) I think (.) I find it fine because I like doing
052        different [P: yeah] things yeah {laughing quietly}every
053        time [P: yeah yeah] do you get me [P: yeah yeah] so I
054        ada- *adjust* [P: brilliant] (to those things) (-)
055        *(same thing)*
056   P:   [so basically] you just do both *(I mean)* [H: yeah]
057        depending on the situa/tion [H: yeah] and is there ever
058        any time when you think you can't do both (-) you know
```

In line 31, Hennah turns away from her earlier emphasis on religion and provides a different example from her cultural life to demonstrate the hardship she associates with being both English and Bengali: rules of decorum. After my reformulation in lines 41–43, which highlights differences in table manners rather than the difficulties involved in balancing them, Hennah signals her awareness of context- or culture-specific norms and the ability of individuals to switch between them in different domains. This meta-knowledge about situational 'code-switching' earns an enthusiastic response from me in line 46: 'OK brilliant'. My enthusiasm could also be the trigger for Hennah's sudden switch from stressing the difficulty of a situation like this (line 31) to claiming 'I find it fine because I like doing different things every time' (line 51). This, in turn, encourages me to reformulate Hennah's account to fit my own interpretation of the spontaneous conversational data of her group (lines 56–58). My reformulation 'so basically you just do both' emphasises Hennah's familiarity with both codes, and her ability to switch between them, rather than the difficulties and the hardship that Hennah had associated with this code-switching earlier (line 31).

Approaching my ethnographic style interviews as co-constructed events with myself as a participant thus allows me to reflect on my own cultural and interpretive capacities. These appear to be motivated by my linguistically grounded postmodern understanding of flexible and multiple identities, which encourages me to celebrate the girls' abilities to switch between different culture-specific discourses (see also Puwar's 2003 critique of postmodern celebrations of young Asian femininities). This reflexivity about my own stance as a researcher also encouraged me to acknowledge the limitations of my conversational, situated data, as the following section shows.

Interviews as reports on other social realities

Whereas my analysis of the conversational data focused on how the girls managed to switch between or synthesise culture-specific discourses (Pichler, 2007, 2006b), there are several instances during the interview when Hennah tends to take a more critical stance to what I perceived as her bicultural or hybrid status, highlighting the hardship of balancing two different sets of norms. In the final extract I approach this discrepancy from a macro- rather than a micro-perspective.

Extract 5   'Torn between two cultures'

```
001   P:   the thing is I I do not you know from from like
002        looking at this [H: yeah] I do not think that it's:
003        like true: .hhh ah: how a lot of like sociologists
004        have said {slightly mock dramatic}'oh you know like
005        .hh erm: .hh it's so: difficult and people:
006        and and (.) you know like (.) girls .hh they are
007        completely torn between the two cultures'4
008        [H: {outbreath?}] *I* think that you lot are doing
009   P:   really well *you know with the two* [H: {laughs}]
010        with the two (-) I mean *don't you /think* [H: no nono]
011   H:   nonono .hh you know this yeah [P: yeah] this i- we'r (-)
012        there's so much teasing there yeah [P: yeah yeah]
013        that it makes it look like but it it isn't honest to God
```

014   *{almost staccato}*it is not **like** cause if you look [P: yeah]
015   at Dilshana Ardiana yeah [P: yeah] look at the mess they're in
016   (-) and look at Rahima [P: yeah] .hhh if it was erm: (-)
017   if it was OK they wouldn't be torn now (-) do you get me
018   because .hhh [P: yeah] %her parents are really (angry)%
019   they **know** that she's going out with someone .hh but
020   she won't tell them .hh w*ho it* [yeah] is or who erm when
021   he's gonna come for her (like) for good and stuff like that
022   and they aks her *{authoritarian}* 'tell him to come to you
023   for good cause (-) I don't like what people are saying to me'
024   (-) [P: yeah *yeah*] *d'you* get me [P: yeah] and erm:
025   *{laughing}*Ardiana she's in aboad (sic.) [P: ye*ah*] *and*
026   Shashima she's already **married**

In this extract Hennah objects to my assessment of the girls 'doing well' (lines 8–9) and my challenge of the 'torn between cultures' metaphor (line 7). Hennah points out that several of her friends, including Dilshana, are 'in a mess' (line 15): Ardiana abroad (in Bangladesh amongst speculations that she would be married off) and another friend, Shashima, already having been married off (after her parents' discovery that she was dating) (lines 25–26). Interestingly, Hennah also challenges my interpretation of the relevance of teasing for the group (which I had told her about previously), positioning it as a strategy to cover up difficulties (line 12), rather than as a strategy to resolve difficulties and synthesise different cultural discourses and norms, as I had suggested on the basis of the girls' spontaneous talk. Thus, in the extract above Hennah argues that some of the girls in the group are in fact torn 'between two cultures' (Watson, 1977), rather than stressing their bicultural or hybrid identities, clearly positioning the different norms on dating and marriage as incompatible and adopting a rather essentialist definition of culture.

Rather than approaching this discrepancy between my own interpretations and those of Hennah from a conversation analytic or from a strong constructionist perspective (as in the section above), in this section I address the relationship between ethnography and macro-perspectives and therefore look at the relevance of interviews beyond their immediate context. For this purpose I consider whether Hennah's challenge of my interpretation above suggests that there is a 'reality' of the girls' heterosexual relationships which is much more difficult to manage than my spontaneous conversational data suggest. Here, we should ask whether a focus on conversational micro-phenomena attributes too much emphasis to participants' agency (see Rampton, Tusting et al., 2004: 15). However, this is not only an issue for ethnography, but also for other qualitative approaches to language and identity which take a post-modern/post-structural or strong constructionist stance towards their situated interactional data (Sealey, 2005; McElhinny, 2003). McElhinny highlights the relevance of this question for language and gender research:

> It is worth considering why post-structuralist models of gender have been so readily embraced by sociolinguists and linguistic anthropologists working on gender. Our very subject matter – language – may lend itself to an ability to focus on gender and the social construction of 'sex'. People's ability to adapt language readily and rapidly from situation to situation, addressee to addressee, may accord people an unusual degree of agency and flexibility in their construction of themselves in a way that other forms of cultural and actual capital can and do not (e.g. body hexus, occupational opportunities).
>
> (McElhinny, 2003: 26–7)

Hennah's claims about the girls' difficulties in balancing religious and other cultural norms in relation to marriage and dating could thus suggest that my conversational data does not sufficiently capture the girls' experience outside the context of their friendship talk (see also Hammersley, 2006). In the cultural field (Bourdieu, 1991) of the girls' wider community, gender norms about heterosexual relationships may be much less flexible than the diverse and shifting discursive positions analysts might identify in the girls' spontaneous conversations.

Conclusion

This chapter demonstrates that the use of ethnographic-style interviews *in addition to* spontaneous conversational data can be revealing for an investigation of the interplay between discourse and cultural norms and practices, inflected with gender, ethnicity and religion. Above all, this combination of data sources seems very well-suited for a multi-dimensional investigation of participants' own understanding of the practices and categories that they consider relevant, encouraging a reflexive and critical exploration of the perspectives and positions of both researcher and researched. Ambiguities which arise out of this combination should not be seen as an unfortunate challenge to validity, but instead as holding particular interest for language and gender researchers taking an ethnographic perspective as they can capture the complexities of situated everyday practice on the one hand, and highlight the limitations of an exclusive focus on local conversational data on the other.

I argued above that the question of how to treat these ambiguities will depend on whether we understand interviews as local accomplishments, as displays of cultural knowledge or as reports on other social realities. As shown above, all three approaches to interviews can yield important insights, and I would argue, are valid, if not equally weighted. The weighting of the individual approach, I suggest, depends above all on the purpose of the interview, which, in turn will be linked to the aim and methodology of each research project.

Whereas Silverman (2001: 113) expresses a degree of scepticism towards attempts to bridge the different approaches to interviews, my own position on such bridging is less critical. In recent years ethnographic studies of language and gender have arguably been better equipped to deal with interviews as local accomplishments due to their focus on situated microphenomena. By contrast, I believe that this 'micro-ethnographic' perspective should be integrated into a more 'holistic' approach to ethnography, which aims to 'locate what is studied in the context of wider society' (Hammersley, 2006: 6). Thus, I believe it is important to continue asking what relevance interview data have outside the immediate context of the ethnographic (-style) interview, and therefore to look beyond one source of data and even one discipline of research. My own research from this group of British Bangladeshi girls aims to create a multi-perspective approach not only by investigating the relationship between discourse and cultural norms and practices in two sources of data, but also by drawing on sociological and anthropological data dealing with young 'Asian' femininities. Ethnographic studies of language and gender (and ethnicity) on a local, micro-linguistic level are likely to benefit from a contextualising of their findings in their wider social background and in an interdisciplinary framework of research.

Acknowledgements

I would like to thank all the girls who participated in my study. I am particularly grateful to my in-group informant 'Hennah' for her insightful comments and challenges, and for her enthusiasm about this project.

Notes

1 In this paper I draw a distinction between interviews and spontaneous speech although I am aware that the boundaries between the two can be fuzzy, especially in the case of informal ethnographic(-style) interviews (Hammersley and Atkinson, 1995: 139; Holstein and Gubrium, 1997: 126).

2 Transcription conventions are as follows:

When another speaker inserts a minimal response or short utterances into the turn of the current speaker this minimal response is marked by square brackets [...]. The onset and offset of simultaneous speech is marked by stars *....* . For example:

H: about the age of fifteen or stuff like *that* [P: right]

H (the informant) is speaking and P (the researcher) produces a minimal response 'right', which overlaps with the informant's 'that':

or

H: they talk with their mouth full [P: yeah yeah *yeah
H: yeah*] *do you* get me and when i- if you go to school

H (the informant) is speaking and P (the researcher) is inserting minimal support. The first two instances of 'yeah' are not uttered simultaneously, but the second two are uttered at the same time as the informant's 'do you'.

Further Conventions:

H:	Hennah (in-group informant)
P:	Pia (researcher)
{laughter}	non verbal information
<u>xxxxxx</u>*{laughing}*	paralinguistic information qualifying underlined utterance
(xxxxxxxx)	inaudible material
(......)	doubt about accuracy of transcription
'......'	speaker quotes/uses words of others
CAPITALS	increased volume
%......%	decreased volume
bold print	speaker emphasis
>...<	faster speed of utterance delivery
/	rising intonation
yeah:::::	lengthened sound
-	incomplete word or utterance
=	latching on
(.)	micropause
(-)	pause shorter than one second
(1); (2)	timed pauses (longer than one second)
.hhh; hhh	in-breath; out-breath

3   This stretch of talk is from a longer interaction, which I entitled 'Our religion is really strict'. I present several extracts from this interaction (Parts 1–3).

4   I offer my apologies to 'sociologist' colleagues for this generalisation, drawing on an outdated source (Watson, 1977), and aiming to elicit a critical response from my informant in this moment of the interview.

Part 2
Corpus Linguistics

6
'Eligible' Bachelors and 'Frustrated' Spinsters: Corpus Linguistics, Gender and Language

Paul Baker

Introduction

For the past couple of decades corpus linguistics has sat somewhat uncomfortably on the sidelines of language and gender research. As Swann points out, in her examination of language and gender studies: 'On the whole...there does seem to have been a shift towards more localised studies' and 'far less reliance is placed on quantifiable and/or general patterns' (2002: 59).

Why is this the case? Older approaches to research in the social sciences, which used quantification in order to distinguish, say, male and female differences in language use, have more recently been regarded as essentialist. It has also been argued that these approaches help to reify norms which contribute towards the social regulation of language itself (see Hacking, 1990) and act as ways of controlling and predicting populations (Buchanan, 1992). Other researchers (e.g., Cicourel, 1964) have criticised quantitative researchers for fixing meanings in ways that suit their preconceptions.

Language and gender research has therefore increasingly made use of methods relying on the postmodern conceptualisation of there being no such thing as an 'objective' position, while actively looking at ways to challenge existing hegemonies, by focusing on smaller scale texts, such as narratives in interviews or qualitative analyses of conversations.

Corpus linguistics methodology, which rose to prominence with the advent of powerful personal computers towards the end of the 1980s, appears to have much in common with older sociolinguistic models of statistical variation and sampling. But by the time it had become a viable option for language and gender research, the epistemological shift towards postmodernism in general, and post-structuralism in particular, had already occurred, and corpus linguistics' grounding in quantification has not made

73

it attractive to social scientists. Both McEnery and Wilson (1996) and Biber, Conrad and Reppen (1998) note that the amount of corpus-based research in discourse analysis has been relatively small.

However, corpus linguistics arguably has a great deal of untapped potential to offer the field of language and gender. This chapter and the two which follow demonstrate how corpus techniques can be fruitfully applied to a range of 'gendered' data, including general English, spoken conversations and learner English. This first chapter in the corpus linguistics section presents an overview of the corpus research that has *already* been carried out on language and gender with examples of the ways that corpus linguistics can be gainfully utilised in language and gender research, along with a few notes of caution (because it is not sensible to be overly evangelising, even about a methodology that one recommends).

Defining corpus linguistics

According to McEnery and Wilson (1996: 1), *corpus linguistics* is 'the study of language based on examples of real life language use'. However, unlike purely qualitative approaches to research, corpus linguistics utilises bodies of electronically encoded text, implementing a more quantitative method-ology, for example by using frequency information about occurrences of particular linguistic phenomena. However, as Biber (1998: 4) points out, corpus-based research actually depends on quantitative *and* qualitative techniques: 'Association patterns represent quantitative relations, measuring the extent to which features and variants are associated with contextual factors. However, functional (qualitative) interpretation is also an essential step in any corpus-based analysis.'

Corpora are generally large (consisting of thousands or millions of words), representative samples of a particular type of naturally occurring language, so can therefore be used as a standard reference against which claims about language can be measured. The fact that they are encoded electronically means that complex calculations can be carried out on large amounts of text, revealing linguistic patterns and frequency information that would otherwise take days or months to uncover accurately by hand, and which may run counter to intuition.

Electronic corpora are often annotated with additional linguistic infor-mation, the most common being 'part of speech' information (e.g., whether a word is a noun or a verb), which allows large-scale grammatical analyses to be carried out. Other types of information can be encoded within corpus data – for example, in spoken corpora (containing transcripts of dialogue), information about the sex, age, socio-economic group and region of speaker can be encoded into individual utterances. As the following section describes, this allows for linguistic comparisons to be made about different types of speakers.

Analysing difference

Language corpora have been used in combination with speaker-annotated data to investigate usage. Two wide-scale studies which have considered gendered speech styles in reference corpora (large corpora collected in order to be representative of a particular variety of language) are Rayson, Leech and Hodges (1997) and Schmid and Fauth (2003).

Rayson and colleagues (1997) examined the spoken section (about 10 million words) of the British National Corpus (BNC). On the whole, the female speakers tended to take more turns and talk for longer than male speakers. Looking at words which occurred statistically most often, they reported that males used more taboo words (*fucking, fuck, shit, hell, crap*) and numbers (*one, two, three, four, hundred*), and made more use of more colloquial language (*guy, quid, mate*) and informal interjections (*yeah, okay, right, ah, aye*). On the other hand, females used more first person pronouns (*I, me, my, mine*) and family terms (*mother, father, sister, brother*). Finally, males used more common nouns, while females favoured personal pronouns, verbs and proper nouns (although this only related to personal names like *Jim* – males used more proper nouns referring to geographical places like *London*). To an extent, therefore, Rayson and colleagues' research confirms Tannen's (1991: 76–7) 'difference' hypothesis that male speech is more 'factual' and concerned with reporting information, whereas female speech is more interactive and concerned with establishing and maintaining relationships (the male 'report' vs. female 'rapport' distinction).

Schmid and Fauth (2003) identified 45 linguistic features from various grammatical domains and retrieved their occurrences from within same-sex conversations taken from the International Corpus of English (ICE). Four features correlated with female speech: use of third person pronouns, indefinite pronouns, predicative adjectives and intensive adverbs. Male speech was characterised by use of definite articles, nominalisations and noun phrase postmodifications realised by *of-* prepositional phrases (e.g., [N the needs [P of [N our clients N]P]N]). Their analysis allowed them to predict the gender of speakers in same-sex conversations with a probability of 88.10 per cent for females and 85.80 per cent for males.

So corpora are useful for helping to confirm or refute theories of gendered language use, by allowing researchers to identify trends within a wider population, rather than simply making claims based around introspection or the examination of a limited number of speakers. However, as Rayson, Leech and Hodges (1997) point out, care needs to be taken with the *interpretation* of results – and one finding which corpus-based approaches almost always reveal is that differences are rarely absolute but more often based on gradients. Male speakers may use more taboo words, but these words are by no means absent from female speech, indeed, for some taboo words, including *bitch* and *shit*, females are the more frequent users in the BNC.

'Difference' models of gender and language tend to background the existence of similarity – creating the somewhat erroneous notion of two gendered 'species' of language user (cf. *Men are from Mars, Women are from Venus*), and corpus linguistics research can help to rein in this view. The following chapters by Jiménez Catalán and Ojeda Alba and by Harrington also examine differences between male and female language users. Catalán and Alba, using a small corpus of learner English, found that on average female students produced longer compositions as well as overall gender differences in the type of vocabulary used. Harrington also notes that, combined with a closer qualitative analysis, corpus linguistics techniques can appear to show evidence for gender differences, but at the level of individual speakers – and that such differences should not be over-generalised.

The delineation and analysis of gendered speech 'styles' helps us to understand some ways in which men and women characteristically tend to use language, and awareness of such phenomena can be applied to a wide range of areas – for example, performative uses of language, sexual identity and desire, construction of hegemonic masculinities and femininities, group dynamics and speech styles in educational contexts such as L2 language settings. However, I turn now to an approach within corpus linguistics which focuses not so much on differences in language use, but on the ways in which corpora can be used to uncover gendered discourses in society.

Analysing discourses

One of the most important ways that discourses are circulated and strengthened in society is by language use, and a task of discourse analysis is to uncover *how* language is employed, often in quite subtle ways, to reveal these discourses and their workings. Corpora contain thousands or millions of words of text and are therefore resources which can be used to identify values, beliefs, attitudes and discourses. Because of the sheer size of a corpus, we can collect evidence of linguistic patterns and trends that reveal something about societies or 'identity groups', in a way that wouldn't be possible had we only examined a small sample of text.

A single word or phrase might just suggest the existence of a discourse. But other than relying on our intuition, or (often faulty) cognitive biases (e.g., Mynatt, Doherty and Tweney, 1977; Kahneman and Tversky, 1973), it can sometimes be difficult to ascertain whether such a discourse is hegemonic, mainstream, resistant or marginal. It is only by collecting numerous supporting examples of similar linguistic phenomena, that we can start to witness the cumulative contribution of specific linguistic items to a given discourse.

Stubbs observes how 'Repeated patterns show that evaluative meanings are not merely personal and idiosyncratic, but widely shared in a discourse community. A word, phrase or construction may trigger a cultural stereotype' (2001: 215). Hoey (2005) refers to this as *lexical priming*, that is, words are 'primed' for use in discourse due to the *cumulative* effects of our encounters with language. This focus on the incremental effect of language is something we also find in critical discourse analysis studies:

> The hidden power of media discourse and the capacity of...power-holders to exercise this power depend on systematic tendencies in news reporting and other media activities. A single text on its own is quite insignificant: the effects of media power are cumulative, working through the repetition of particular ways of handling causality and agency, particular ways of positioning the reader, and so forth.
>
> (Fairclough,1989: 54)

And this is where corpora are useful. An association between two words, occurring repetitively in naturally occurring language, is much better evidence of a discourse than if we just have a single case to report.

Thus, we can use frequency or related concepts in order to uncover these cumulative effects of language. The concept of *collocation* is useful here – the tendency of words to co-occur in patterns. A noun like *bank* collocates at different times with other nouns that help us to understand its meaning, like *river*, *blood* and *piggy*, but also with articles like *the* and *a*, which suggests evidence for grammatical patterns. Two concepts related to collocation are semantic prosody and, importantly, discourse prosody. Semantic prosody (Louw, 1993; Sinclair, 1991) is the tendency for words to collocate with sets of semantic classes, for example, the word *man* co-occurs with adjectives to do with age (*young*, *old*, *middle-aged*) and appearance (*tall*, *handsome*, *stocky*, *bearded*). Discourse prosody (Stubbs, 2001: 65) is the tendency for words or phrases to collocate with sets of words which express attitudes. Stubbs shows, for example, how the words *happen* and *cause* tend to occur in connection with words and phrases which describe negative events. Hoey (2005: 163) argues that these lexical primings are two-way: words have particular prosodies due to the fact that writers or speakers intend to express themselves in a particular way; writers choose certain words in order to take advantage of a discourse prosody, at the same time reinforcing that prosody. There is a close relationship between semantic prosody and discourse prosody – with the example of the semantic prosodies of *man* above, certain types of men may be labelled with the 'semantic class' of appearance words that are more negative in meaning (*ugly*, *fat*, *bald*), which would in fact be suggestive of a discourse prosody.

Corpora can thus be used to examine gendered terms in a reference corpus, in order to identify the range of patterns of collocation and prosodies surrounding them, which may point to ways in which identities are constructed in everyday language use. For example, in an analysis of frequencies and collocations of the terms *girl(s)* and *boy(s)* in five corpora of British English, Sigley and Holmes (2002) concluded that adult females are linguistically constructed as immature, with emphasis on appearance, dependence, domesticity and submissiveness. Romaine (2001) examined supposedly male and female sets of terms in the British National Corpus, identifying differences in usage and frequency – for example, *lady of the house* is not matched in meaning by the equivalent *gentleman of the house*, while *man of the world* is more frequent than *woman of the world*. She also pointed out that *Mr* occurred more than *Mrs*, *Ms* and *Miss* taken together, while *chairman* and *spokesman* continue to be prevailing titles. Biber and colleagues (1999: 312–16) similarly report that 'male words' tend to occur more frequently than 'female words': in the Longman Spoken and Written English Corpus there are 620 nouns ending in *–man* and only 38 which end in *-woman*.

Stubbs's (1996) analysis of the ways that gender is constructed within two of Robert Baden-Powell's speeches to boys and girls highlights the fact that ideological issues can be present even around a fairly innocuous word like *happy*: Baden-Powell (the founder of the Boy Scouts Association) instructed girls to make other people happy whereas boys were simply instructed to live happy lives. Varga (2005) looked at the terms *sex* and *gender* in the Brown family of corpora (which enables the examination of diachronic variation – 1960s vs. 1990s English; and of synchronic variation – British vs. American English). The term *gender* was virtually absent in the 1960s corpora, while in the 1990s corpora both terms had multiple and overlapping uses (e.g., *sex* as an act vs. *sex* as biological difference. She also found evidence to suggest that British and American writers employed different terms to refer to the same concept – British writers would talk about *sex differences* whereas American writers tended to use *gender differences*.

In order to illustrate in more detail how corpora can be used to identify discourses in society, I turn now to my own study of the 100-million-word British National Corpus (using the web-based corpus tool BNCWeb), to elucidate gendered discourses surrounding the concept of 'unmarried people'.

Bachelors and spinsters

Although the words *bachelor* and *spinster* are dictionary 'equivalents', both referring to people who have never been married, the way they are used in real life, and the associations that they carry, are somewhat different. In the British National Corpus *bachelor(s)* occurs 506 times in total, *spinster(s)* only 176 times. While these frequencies in themselves are potentially interesting (we could ask whether other male terms occur more frequently than their female equivalents and, if so, what this suggests about men in society), I want to look more closely at collocations and discourse prosodies surrounding

Table 6.1 Collocates (log-log) of *bachelor(s)* and *spinster(s)*

bachelor(s)	eligible, button, degree, Gilbey, males, education, elderly, lonely, arts, brother, science, confirmed, status, son, flat, life, living, James, old, days, party
spinster(s)	elderly, widows, sisters, three

these words. Table 6.1 shows the main collocates of the two terms and their plurals. Collocates were calculated using the log-log statistic (Kilgarriff and Tugwell, 2001), and only collocates which had a log-log score of over five were considered (in order to both achieve a reasonable level of collocational saliency and to limit the number of collocates considered to a manageable amount).

Most obviously, *bachelor* has more collocates than *spinster*. This is partly due to the fact that *bachelor* occurs more frequently in the corpus, as shown by the following collocates: *degree, education, science, arts*. Where *bachelor* occurs with these collocates, they all relate to a university qualification (e.g., *Bachelor of Arts*). Here the meaning of *bachelor* (a type of degree) is different to the meaning we are concerned with (a man who has not married). Should we therefore discount these collocates because *bachelor* is a homonym and clearly 'Bachelor of Arts' does not imply an unmarried man? Although this may seem like a good idea, Löbner (2002: 44) states that actual homonyms are rare and accidental phenomena. Polysemy, two words having the same spelling *and* inter-related meanings, is much more common. Here I need to step outside the corpus for a moment and consider other types of historical information.

The term *Bachelors Degree* can be traced back to the thirteenth century, to the University of Paris which used a system established under Pope Gregory IX. Historically, *bachelor* has also meant a young monk, someone belonging to the lowest stage of knighthood, or younger member of a trade guild. It has variously referred to young men at the beginning of their careers. Although *bachelor* now means 'unmarried man', it is not difficult to see how this meaning is related to the early meaning of a young person (in the past almost certainly male) studying for a preliminary degree. So while the collocates of *bachelor* associated with university education no longer have the same association with *bachelor* as an unmarried man, the two meanings are perhaps due to historical polysemy rather than being accidental homonyms. It is notable that there are no collocates of *spinster* which suggest a university education; historically it is a male term.

As there isn't space to examine all the *bachelor* collocates here (see Baker, 2006 for a more complete analysis), I will focus on the more illustrative ones. For the examples below, I use concordance tables – which present instances of the word *bachelor* and *spinster* in context, quoting a few words either side of each case in the corpus. This helps us to understand the ways that that the words are used. Let us take one collocate of *bachelor*: *eligible*. Table 6.2 gives a sample of concordance lines of these two words as they occur together.

Even without the concordance table, we probably could have reached the conclusion that the collocation *bachelor + eligible* exists because bachelors are often described as eligible: a somewhat positive representation, eligibility for marriage implying that a bachelor must be attractive. However, it could have been the case that most of the co-occurrences of *eligible* and *bachelor* in the corpus were to do with people writing about bachelors *not* being eligible, or bachelors looking for eligible brides. It is always worth carrying out a concordance check before reaching a conclusion regarding the relationship between two collocates.

Another collocate, *days*, is less easy to make sense of. The concordance in Table 6.3 illustrates its use in connection to the word *bachelor*.

Table 6.3 shows that the relationship between the two collocates always occurs in descriptions of someone's 'bachelor days'. However, we can go

Table 6.2   Concordance of *eligible* and *bachelor*

1	llue my freelance status. The	**eligible**	bachelor	.' Kelly thought she detected a trace
2	s with mock suspicion.' The	**eligible**	bachelor	on the pull?'
3	e must have been an	**eligible** enough	bachelor	: the son of a fairly prosperous artis
4	, formerly tennis' most	**eligible**	bachelor	, married long time girlfriend An
5	o longer the country's most	**eligible**	bachelor	-- he became engaged over the wee
6	as the industry's most	**eligible**	bachelor	.We couldn't help but notice he ha
7	at Steven was regarded as an	**eligible**	bachelor	, but we didn't think that marriage w
8	ld regard him, I think, as an	**eligible**	bachelor	. Highly eligible, if it comes to that.

Table 6.3   Concordance of *days* and *bachelor*

1	ipes that my husband attempted in his bachelor	**days.** 225g/8 oz haricot beans 2 × 1
2	d been Charles's girlfriend during his bachelor	**days** and in Diana's mind his contin
3	n and Queen Mother. Certainly in his bachelor	**days** Johnnie Spencer was the catch
4	new life, and keep in memory of his bachelor	**days** and the friends he has left beh
5	is party for me. May he enjoy happy bachelor	**days,** but not too many, before he re
6	her future, in memory of our happy bachelor	**days** together. The girls bringing in
7	nted), perhaps with a memento of her bachelor	**days,** such as a cassette by her favo

further than this by looking for discourse prosodies. Lines 5 and 6 refer to 'happy bachelor days', whereas lines 4 and 6 refer to 'memories' of bachelor days. With line 7 there is 'a memento' of bachelor days, again suggesting that they are worth remembering. So *bachelor days* could be characterised as containing a discourse prosody of happy memories – again, a positive representation of unmarried men (although there is also an implication, particularly regarding the references to memories – that these bachelors were youthful).

Interestingly, line 7 includes the phrase *her bachelor days*. Here, *bachelor* refers to a woman, suggesting that the fine gender distinction between *bachelor* and *spinster* is not absolute. This leads us to consider a further benefit of a corpus: we are likely to be presented with cases of language use which may not been considered. We not only see larger trends and patterns, but we also have evidence of exceptions, rare cases, minority positions and resistant or marginal discourses that may have been missed had a smaller sample been used. A corpus is helpful in revealing what is *infrequent* as well as what is frequent.

To illustrate this in more detail, I now examine some of the cases of *spinster* in the British National Corpus. On the whole, the collocates of *bachelor* tend to suggest a positive discourse prosody (the exception being occasional characterisations as *elderly*, with its associations of loneliness and eccentricity). However, when a similar analysis of *spinster* is performed, a different picture results. As well as having strong collocates like *elderly* and *widows*, Table 6.4 shows some of the other ways that spinsters are referred to. Most of the words in bold are not strictly speaking collocates, as they occur too infrequently with *spinster* in order to have a log-log score of five or more. But, taken together, they constitute a strongly negative discourse prosody.

Table 6.4 reveals terms that characterise spinsters as *elderly, atrocious, frustrated, dried-up, lonely* and *sex-starved*. The discursive implication from the concordance is that these spinsters are unmarried because they are unattractive and that they are likely to be unhappy or bitter about this. On the other hand, *bachelor(s)* does not have this unattractiveness connotation. In contrast, *bachelors* are more likely to be characterised as attractive, hence the word *eligible*, and references to *happy bachelor days*.

However, one interesting point is the last line, in the reference to the 'cruel stereotype of the sex-starved spinster'. Although this still accesses (and recycles) the common discourse position, it acknowledges that this *is* a stereotype. An examination of other concordance lines in the corpus reveals that this is not an isolated case (see Table 6.5). Although there were only a small number in the corpus overall (ten in total), taken together the lines represent a resistant 'critical discourse of spinsterhood'.

Table 6.4   Discourse prosody (1) of *spinster* (sample)

1	esign. I outlined an **elderly atrocious**	spinster	and established her in Lamb House.
2	AN **ELDERLY**	spinster	froze to death on Christmas Day, an
3	Miss Symes, a seemingly **frustrated**	spinster	if ever there was one, have it to ex
4	s the good hearted and **love-starved**	spinster	. Peter's Friends (15) opens in
5	It was one of the rituals of this **lonely**	spinster	's life that every day she would take
6	wise elder, set against the **dried-up**	spinster	, the interfering granny, the miser, t
7	but not the standard **over-made-up**	spinster	secretary. She looked very positive
8	Miss Weeton was a **waspish**	spinster	, but the picture is not wholly unkin
9	in all my life,' sighs the **whey-faced**	spinster	, and Williams is wryly sympathetic
10	ly cruel stereotype of the **sex-starved**	spinster	fantasising about rape. At the clima

Table 6.5   Discourse prosody of *spinster* (2)

1	men and the **stereotype** of the elderly	spinster	, in part reflect cohort effects; future
2	y **cruel stereotype** of the sex-starved	spinster	fantasising about rape.
3	eighteenth century the **stereotypical**	spinster	was ' ... one to be despised, pitied, a
4	sfactory alternative, for the life of the	spinster	is often **portrayed** in stark terms.
5	paraging **word** for lesbians, and with	spinster	, less disparaging but still pretty ne
6	I think 'housewife' is like	spinster	and 'spinster' is a **terrible label** to
7	ers were, in the **language of the day,**	spinster	-- mainly former teachers or civil s
8		Spinsters	are **still despised and mocked.**
9	To be a	spinster	is **not quite the abnormality it was**
10	Here, too, **the word**	spinster	**evokes** an ugly, lonely woman who

In Table 6.5, people talk *about* the stereotype, referring to the 'language of the day', and describing how the word *spinster* is a label. This is a more feminist discourse position, commenting on and challenging the discourse in Table 6.4. A reference corpus like the BNC can thus be useful in elucidating a range of discourses, which can sometimes run counter to expectations. (At this stage in the analysis we would need to step outside the corpus again in order to provide explanations for our results – linking the presence of the different gendered discourses identified to (changing) social positions of men and women in society.)

Conclusion

Hopefully, this chapter has revealed how corpora can be used to provide not just evidence for gender differences and similarities in language use, but also for gendered discourses constituted in everyday language. As a methodological tool, corpora have a great deal to offer language and gender research. However, that is not to say that corpora are equally applicable to every area of gender research. I conclude this chapter by referring to some limitations.

Firstly, corpora tend to contain transcriptions of written or spoken language. During transcription, texts may lose a great deal that is relevant. So it would be difficult to use a corpus to analyse, say, gestures during a spoken conversation or the use of visuals or layout in a newspaper text (unless such aspects were also encoded into the corpus). Additionally, a corpus contains somewhat decontextualised examples of language use, so more work would need to be carried out in order to uncover information relating to the processes of production and consumption of individual texts. Would a newspaper text read by millions of people have more 'power' in terms of shaping discourse(s), than a personal letter? Different texts in a reference corpus may not always be 'equal' in the sense of their original audiences and genres in the BNC. The discourse of the 'elderly, sex-starved spinster' tended to be found in fiction (novels), whereas in newspaper texts spinsters tended to be represented as victims of crime. The oppositional discourse, which characterised the other discourses of spinsters as 'stereotypical', tended to occur in social science texts. These genres are not going to be consumed in equal numbers or by the same groups of people and this is likely to impact the influence of the discourses they carry.

There are three further limitations. First, a corpus is a self-contained entity. It is unlikely to tell us much about the socio-historical contexts of the texts, or the linguistic histories of the particular words we are examining (with *bachelor*, it was necessary to step outside the corpus to discover the etymology of the word). Second, corpus analysis tends to focus on presence – it can be difficult to analyse *absence* in a corpus, as researchers may not know what to look for. For example, there may be other words which refer to unmarried people (e.g., *bachelorette*) and, unless they are known in advance, their absence in a corpus may go unnoticed. Third, while a computer is extremely useful for laying out linguistic patterns, it is not particularly good at making sense of them. Computers can only take researchers so far: they present a set of relatively unbiased results, but it is still up to human researchers to analyse and interpret them.

It should, however, be noted that many of those criticisms also hold true for other methodological approaches to the study of language and gender. They should not therefore preclude us from considering corpus-based analyses of gender and language, rather, they ought to make us aware of what *is* possible, as well as what is unlikely, so that individual researchers can make informed decisions about when it is appropriate to utilise corpus techniques. As I wrote at the beginning of this chapter, corpus-based approaches have sat uncomfortably on the sidelines of language and gender research for some time. I hope that this chapter and the two which follow it will show that they can in fact make a valuable contribution.

7
Perpetuating Difference? Corpus Linguistics and the Gendering of Reported Dialogue

Kate Harrington

Introduction

Reported dialogue is an important part of everyday speech. It has been analysed as a means of negotiating social identities (e.g., Hamilton, 1998; Schiffrin, 1996) and, in particular, as a way of negotiating power and solidarity (e.g., Buttny and Williams, 2000; Carranza, 1999). The amount and type of reporting frames[1] used by a speaker are important indicators of what they want to achieve in a conversation or, at least, sensitive indicators of their conversational context (Segall, 2005).

Gender has consistently been shown to be relevant to the ways in which speakers use reported dialogue. Tannen (1989: 148) has observed that, when speaking to friends, women include more details of social happenings, such as conversations and social events, than men, and she identifies reported dialogue as one such social detail. This is arguably supported by Holmes who observes that women are more likely to include 'implicit' or 'embedded' evaluation in their narratives while men are more likely to make 'points' explicitly (1997a: 284).

Further analysis bears out these opinions. Johnstone (1990, 1993) showed that men and women from Fort Wayne, in 'Middle America', told stories about different things. Women were more likely to tell personal stories about community success or personal failure where the protagonist could be either male or female. By contrast, men's stories were more likely to involve a male protagonist and a contest in which he was successful. They also told stories in different ways, women including more personal detail and, of particular relevance to this study, using more reported dialogue than men.

Studies of reported dialogue have also linked age with gender, particularly in younger speakers. Tannen (1989) and Romaine and Lange (1991) have suggested that the use of *be like* is a 'college age' use, the latter adding that it is also perceived as 'feminine'. More recent studies in the United States and Canada have confirmed that *be like* is more prevalent among (younger) females, who appear to be leading a 'change in progress' (D'Arcy, 2004; Tagliamonte and D'Arcy, 2004; Tagliamonte and Hudson, 1999).

Reported dialogue in general, and the newer quotative of *be like* in particular, is also increasing (Tagliamonte and D'Arcy, 2004), and has in fact become something of a contemporary gender stereotype. However, a speaker's subjective assessment of usage is unreliable: Bythe and colleagues (1990: 224) found that although *be like* was perceived as a 'female marker', it was actually used more by men. Even in my own study, one of the male participants specifically mentioned to me that he disliked people using *be like* and that he never used it himself – although his actual usage, in one of his conversations, showed him using the frame more than most of the other speakers in the corpus.

Such stereotypes are reinforced by popular literature. In Zadie Smith's *White Teeth*, the Whitbread prize-winning novel of 2000, one (minor) character is developed mostly through her own speech which incorporates the conventional use of *like* as a preposition, its informal use as a discourse marker and its newer use as a quotative:

> Once you know the restriction enzyme for a particular, **like**, bit of DNA, you can switch anything on or off, **like** a bloody stereo. That's what they're doing to those poor mice … Not to mention, **like**, the pathogenic, i.e. *disease*-producing, organisms they've got sitting in Petri dishes all over the place. I mean I'm a politics student and I'm **like**: what are they creating? … And then they're planting cancers in poor creatures; **like**, who are you to mess with the make-up of a mouse?
>
> (Smith, 2000: 417–18; bold mine)

Such apparently prototypical speech here constructs the character of 'female student'. As with the more traditional 'gender difference' stereotypes, it is (again) a female who is singled out as the different 'other', females being popularly perceived as using *more*, rather than males as using *less*.

My study therefore examines the reality of this gender stereotype and, most crucially, shows how the quantitative corpus methodologies used to assess the amount of reported dialogue usage can actually perpetuate stereotypes in the face of a contrary, or at least more complex, reality.

Methodology

In keeping with much of the research on reported dialogue (e.g., Stenström, Andersen and Hasund, 2002; Johnstone, 1990), this study used tape recordings of naturally occurring, informal conversations of pairs or groups of friends (in nearly all cases). All but one group of speakers came from, or had lived for some time in, the South East of England, and all were broadly middle class.

In total there were 34 speakers (17 female, 17 male), in 14 conversations (8 dyads and 6 triads), totalling just over 11 hours of talk or, in more conventional corpus terms, just under 200,000 words. Groups and speakers were evenly split into all-female, all-male and mixed sex groups and, although most groups contained speakers of roughly the same age, across the set there was an age range of 9 to 63. As conversations naturally varied in length they were made comparable by adjusting the number of quotative frame tokens present to per 100 minutes.

Like Jiménez Catalán and Ojeda Alba (Chapter 8), constructing my own corpus, rather than using an already established one such as the BNC, enabled greater in-depth knowledge of my speakers and their situations. In order to understand the way reported dialogue works as a feature of social negotiation, this was of key importance. This methodological set-up was therefore to assess how much, and in what ways, the more overt objectivism of the quantitative analysis related to, or could compliment, the qualitative analysis.

Reported dialogue as 'characteristic' of female speech?

Initial qualitative analysis of the data could appear to provide evidence in support of the traditional perception of gender-differentiated reported dialogue use. For example, the corpus contained examples of females addressing topics such as making a fool of oneself, the personal politics of relationships, religion, the body and illness, against examples from the males' talk which was more likely to be dominated by work and details of electronic equipment. This is represented in the two examples below. Example 1 comes from an all-female dyad in which Sally (aged 27) and Laura (aged 23) are chatting at Sally's flat:

Example 1   Embarrassing yourself on an answerphone

Laura: I'll never listen to an answerphone message though from er . I rang Pete up one night 'cos we- we were off to the Ballroom and I'd bought this new dress very excited . and er it got to about midnight and . Jo and I were there and we were *'Pete hasn't turned up yet' 'well where the hell is he?'* so I decided to give him a ring and left a message on his answerphone and then came out of the- the phone bit and he was there he'd just arrived sort of thing so blah blah and we went home and then next morning. I listened to the answer phone message . *'Pete where are you it's Laura!'*
Sally 1:   [laugh]

Laura: [laugh] like this and I sounded like a five-year-old and I was **like** *'oh my God'*

Sally 1:   no yeah me too!

Laura's story is about how she embarrassed herself by leaving a humiliating message on her boyfriend's answering machine, which prompts Sally's agreement, and is then followed by a short discussion about the topic (not shown).

The story itself is, in many respects, very mundane. But the purpose of the story is more than just relating an experience. It is about two people affirming friendship through sharing an interest in social situations and, in particular, an interest in the language that defines that situation. Rather than any more remarkable exchanges, such personal details and incidents are what constitute everyday life. It is important for Sally and Laura to affirm each other and their friendship through sharing these very everyday details and incidents. ǀ share everyday nurtday things too!!!

One of these details is the reported dialogue itself. Laura uses it to highlight the key events in the story: first her exasperated exchange with Sally about where her boyfriend was, then her child-like message to him, and then her horrified reaction. All these could have been described without using reported dialogue, but, by recreating the human voice, she is making the situation more vividly 'real' and providing a more concrete example which Sally can effectively relive with her. The story would not be as interesting or make precisely the same point without reported dialogue.

By contrast, some talk is not particularly personal and so is not likely to feature reported dialogue (see Segall, 2005). An example of this can be seen below where, in one of the male dyads, Chris (aged 27) is talking to Geoff (aged 33) over lunch in an informal restaurant:

Example 2   'My PC spec'

Chris 1:   I've got . something that's way over the . basic . bottom range . system and I have to . run this at such low spec

Geoff: that's right

Chris 1:   mean I bought the latest version of (? word) Links the golf game

Geoff: yeah

Chris 1:   and . um . it runs much better now that I've got the G-force

Geoff: yeah

Chris 1:   it's much happier but I still have to have the- I mean I can- it's really odd actually . it must be the difference between . resolution and . picture quality because I have to have the graphics quality on kinda h- there's a slider and I have to have it half way down the slide out but I can run it in one o two four by seven six eight

Geoff: right .
Chris 1:   although I have to run it on sixteen bit textures
Geoff: yeah I mean it's a whole mixture of things isn't it really?

In contrast to the example from the female dyad, there is nothing overtly personal about this exchange about computers. However, it is still a way of doing friendship through sharing – instead of sharing feelings about a situation, the speakers are sharing knowledge. It provides a good counter-example of how reported dialogue is characteristically rooted in an interest in the personal, and how without that element topics are likely to be presented without extra voices.

That this second type of talk is clearly different does not mean that males and females consistently talk differently, but it does demonstrate how the overall emphasis of themes within talk can be perceived as different. Such examples suggest that both women and men do friendship by sharing, but females might *tend* to do this *more through personal details* as a way of building collaborative opinion and males might *tend* to do this *more through information exchange* and with more emphasis on individual opinion. This would be supported by previous research. For example, Johnstone (1990, 1993) found women used more reported dialogue than men including talking about the act of speaking as part of the important detail in talk. Tannen (1989) also suggests that reported dialogue is just another 'detail' in social interaction. Therefore, it appears that women may use more reported dialogue due to their greater attention to social detail in their talk.

However, although such (subjectively) selected examples may suggest gendered trends, they can also lead to construction of apparently stark binary categories. Generalisations about social and gendered behaviour lack an adequate (objective) perspective about how *often* something may in reality happen – or, more significantly, why such examples may *appear* so representative.

Quantative analysis as misleading evidence

One obvious way to interrogate the 'reality' of this perceived gender differentiation is to look at 'the numbers', often perceived as more 'objective'. The traditional (qualitative) view might seem, at first glance, to be supported by quantitative statistics. Certainly, totals for reported dialogue across gender appear to support the view that females use much more reported dialogue than males.

Figure 7.1 overleaf shows that, within their dyads, females used 50 per cent more reported dialogue than males with a total of 536 frames against 357. The results for triads of males and females are proportionally similar to the results for dyads, but there are important differences in the actual *number* of reports per individual.

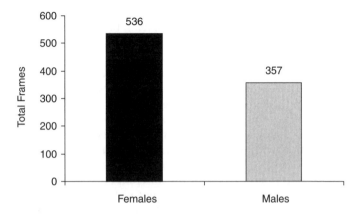

Figure 7.1   Total number of reporting frames across gender (dyads)

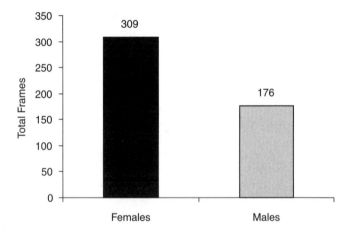

Figure 7.2   Total number of reporting frames across gender (triads)

Figure 7.2 shows that results for triads are similar to dyads. Females still used much more reported dialogue than males regardless of group size – here, almost twice as much, with a total of 309 frames for females against 176 for males. However, while the gender differentiation presented in these figures might appear consistent and marked, it should not be ignored that reported dialogue was still consistently present in the talk of *all* recorded speakers.

These results also show that, although usually unmentioned, group *size* should always be taken into consideration when looking at statistics for reported dialogue. It is for this reason that I have separated the results for dyads and triads. While a similar amount of reported dialogue is used *per group* in conversations of two and three speakers, with an average total use of 112 frames for dyads and 106 frames for triads per 100 minutes, per *individual* speaker there was more of a difference with an average of 56 frames per speaker in dyads and of only 40 frames per speaker in a group of three speakers. The amount of reported dialogue used by individual speakers is thus relative to the number of other speakers in the group.

Two important points are therefore raised by these generalised 'totals'. First, although there does appear to be a consistent gender contrast, this does *not* present reported dialogue as the sole preserve of females over males. Neither is such a consistent pattern an *explanation*, so important questions remain about *why* such a pattern exists, and how representative such generalised statistics can be of (male/female) individual speakers. The answer to this lies in a more detailed assessment of both qualitative and quantitative analysis (as shown below). Second, as a key point of methodology, different size groups need to be analysed separately in order to accurately characterise quantitative usage – the number of individuals within a group will affect the amount of speech a given individual uses, so proper quantitative comparisons can only be made with equal sized groups.

Beyond generalisation – qualitative analysis

The generalised qualitative and quantitative results above, while not inaccurate, are certainly misleading, if not flawed. Qualitatively, such analysis can pretend that sensitivity and the importance of 'people' as a topic is the domain of females (rather than males); quantitatively, because generalised figures are easily interpretable to stand for what is 'typical' without adequate analysis of individual, within-group variation or the local, situated reasons for such patterns.

It is clear from my corpus that most conversations include at least some topics connected to people, and so some report of personal interaction or reaction. In discussing hedges, Coates (1996) underlines how important it is not simply to correlate the number of hedges with the variables 'masculine' and 'feminine', but to take into account where the hedges are used – the topic being discussed and therefore the role of the hedge in the interaction. Hedging occurs when sensitive topics are under discussion, so if one group discusses more 'sensitive' topics than another,then it is likely that they will also use a greater number of hedges. The use of reported dialogue to 'distance' the reporter from the reported opinions or situation (and so appear to lessen their personal responsibility) is a form of hedge (Segall, 2005). Therefore greater use of reported dialogue will correspond with more personal or sensitive topics.

This is supported by other research which identifies a connection between reported dialogue and sensitivity of topic. For example, Beach (2000) shows how two American males created reported speech in the guise of uneducated Southern males in order to express sexist opinions which otherwise may have been too obviously unacceptable. Romaine and Lange (1991: 228) similarly acknowledge the quotative importance of indirectness where *be like* can be seen as reducing commitment both to what was said *and*, on the part of the speaker, to the exact way in which it is presented. As such, *be like* serves to express an opinion but with greatly reduced speaker responsibility. It is therefore interesting that *like* in this new quotative form is perceived as a characteristic of 'female' speech (Romaine and Lange, 1991: 255). Socially sensitive topics, associated with females, are more likely to be dealt with through devices which enable reduced commitment – of which *be like* is a good example.

Importantly, however, and unsurprisingly, there are also similarities between the reported dialogue use of males and females. Female conversations are less likely to include lengthy information exchange but when they do, they do not use reported dialogue. Similarly, the males in my corpus often included much that is personal and everyday, and, when they did, used more reported dialogue.

Qualitative evidence for this effect of genre (here, conversational context) can be seen in two examples of Colin's (age 34) talk in a conversation one evening at home with his wife Becky (aged 36). The couple have temporarily moved to Manchester and Colin is complaining about how he finds that music is played more often in shops and other public places than in London. In Example 3, when he is complaining about the music in the gym, he does not use any reported dialogue:

Example 3   'The music there just makes me want to get up and leave'

....

1   *Becky 1*:
    Colin: no . I just- it just annoys me the way that- the- there's this

....

2   *Becky 1*:
    Colin: assumption that [1 sec] it's a gym therefore you've got to listen

....

3   *Becky 1*:
    Colin: to that kind of music but . y'know it's like no other music

....

4   *Becky 1*:
    Colin: can make you feel excited or give you . y'know give you the

....

....

5   *Becky 1:*   mm
      Colin: um the energy that you   that you need to do the exercise

....

6   *Becky 1:*
      Colin: which is stupid because I mean loads of music makes me feel

....

7   *Becky 1:*
      Colin: like getting up and dancing but none of it they play in fact

....

8   *Becky 1:*
      Colin: most of the music there just makes me want to get up and leave

....

9   *Becky 1:* yeah
      Colin: and the worst thing- it wouldn't be so bad if it was-

....

10 *Becky 1:*
      Colin: if there were more variety . but as I say it's the same . limited

....

11 *Becky 1:*
      Colin: number - really limited number of songs it really is I would say

....

12 *Becky 1:*
      Colin: no more than . at a generous estimate about twelve to fifteen

....

13 *Becky 1:*   mm
      Colin: different songs they play   and it's just in rotation and the g-

....

14 *Becky 1:*
      Colin: and that's just because they pick up the radio stations and the

....

15 *Becky 1:*   mhm
      Colin: stations only play those songs   and it's just y'know

....

16 *Becky 1:*
      Colin: it's - it's just like anyone if- if you're just listening to music you

....

17 *Becky 1:*   yes .
      Colin: don't like all the time it just drive you mad

....

This is very much about Colin's perspective and his opinions. As a result Becky listens, but is clearly not actively engaged in the subject as can be seen by her role of supportive listener, and her sounds of 'mm', 'yeah' and 'mhm'.

A contrast is found in a virtually identical topic just a minute later. Here Colin is talking about how he doesn't like the music that is played in the supermarket, but this time he does not just give his own perspective and opinions, rather, instead, also shares personal details:

Example 4 'The one decent thing they played'

....

1 *Becky1:*
   Colin: one decent thing they played oh no they played Let it- no was

....

2 *Becky1:*
   Colin: it? they played 'Hey Jude' once as well while I was there but

....

3 *Becky1:*
   Colin: they kept interrupting it with that *'Debbie can you come to the*

....

4 *Becky1:* |[laugh...
   Colin: *till one please'* |that really [?word] it that really annoyed me .

....

5 *Becky1:* ....]   ah dear . that's funny
   Colin: I [?2 words] not have bothered

....

6 *Becky1:*
   Colin: I wanted to go and find Debbie and drag her to till one or just .

....

7 *Becky1:*   =*'get your butt over there!'*
   Colin: just to shut up =

....

By including the personal elements and, in particular, the reported dialogue, Colin appears to involve his listener more in the conversation: Becky laughs and even contributes her own supportive report in stave 7 to echo Colin in staves 3–4. Unlike his solo complaint about the music in the gym, his complaint about music in the supermarket leads him to include more personal detail. This prompts a more collaborative style of talk with Becky joining in, so that the experience is shared.

Another speaker, Chris, is a particularly notable example of a male who does not fit rigidly into gender dichotomies about reported dialogue. Although his talk includes many 'information exchanges', as in Example 2 above, he also includes a lot of talk which centres on the personal, more, in fact, than most females in the corpus. However, like the other males, and unlike some of the females, he never engages in stories about personal failure or embarrassment and always presents himself in a positive light – a gender tendency also found by Johnstone (1990). He does, though, show great interest in social behaviour and conversations: characteristic of talk that contains a greater *amount* of reported dialogue.

However, it would be simplistic to say that the *topic* dictates whether or not reported dialogue is used. Arguably, it is rather the way in which the speaker chooses to construct themself within the social context of the conversation – it is whether or not there is social interest and a social point. In the two examples above, Colin shows that although superficially he is talking about the same topic of 'I don't like music in shops', there is a different point to each story with a different effect on the participation of his conversational partner. Similarly, Chris's conversation about his computer (Example 1) could easily have included reported dialogue to demonstrate his reactions to the problems but it doesn't because the personal element of the issue is not the point, rather, the information exchange is. Similarly, Laura (Example 2) could easily have described her embarrassing phone message story without any reporting, but that would not have prompted the shared laughter and empathy with Sally, and would ultimately have removed the point of the telling.

The amount of reported dialogue in conversations corresponds to the amount of personal detail a speaker presents in the interests of encouraging a shared social outlook. The more of this type of personal detail, the more reported dialogue (Segall, 2005). In this study, all speakers use some, but, as the more detailed quantitative analysis shows (below), the greater personal emphasis in *some* of the female conversations in this corpus meant that, as a group, they risk being characterised as typically using more reported dialogue than the males.

Beyond generalisation – quantitative analysis

Quantitative analysis can provide key evidence for understanding actual language use, but this is also crucially dependent on the way in which the numbers generated by raw data are presented. These need to be processed in some way for the sake of clarity, and usually this is done by generalised totals as shown above, as 'tokens per 1000 words' (e.g., Stenström, Andersen and Hasund, 2002) or even as 'normalized distribution per 5,000 words' (e.g., Levey, 2003). However, it is the more detailed analysis *within* this labyrinth of numbers that reveals how individual speakers behave behind such generalised statistical accounts. And there is a potential contradiction here.

Females might use more reported dialogue than males overall, but analysis of the individual frames used (such as 'she *said*', 'he *thought*' or 'I *was like*') begins to show that the picture is complex with much individual variation – simply concluding 'gender differences' from total or mean figures does not give an accurate picture. Any generalised figure will show greater female use of reported dialogue (recall Figures 7.1 and 7.2, above). To use such figures alone implies that all females typically use much more of every frame than all males, and this is misleading.

The reality is instead that females present a much larger *range* of individual variation in the number of each frame they use than males. This range was largely consistent across all frames: the lower end of the range was usually comparable with males, but at the higher end, some females use many more frames. An example of this characteristic range pattern can be seen in Table 7.1 below when looking at indirect speech:

Table 7.1   The range of indirect speech found in female and male dyads[2]

Female	Indirect Speech	Male	Indirect Speech
Laura	2	Bill	0
Becky 1	3	John	2
Sally 1	5	Steve 1	3
Meg	**9**	**Geoff**	**6**
Becky 2	**10**	**Alan**	**9**
Penny 1	14	Paul	12
Mary	18	Colin	13
Kate 1	24	Chris 1	14

Within their dyads, females had a range of 2 to 24 and males 0 to 14. Using totals, means or even medians (highlighted in bold above) cannot represent both the few larger female scores at the top end *as well as* the minimal differences seen when comparing most individual male and female reporting use. A standard deviation calculation can take account of this spread from the mean, in this case 7.67 for the females, 5.4 for the males. However, these numbers have to be interpreted, for example by the reader of a research report, and this does begin to explain the often cited difference – dependent on the few and not representative of the many.

This initial gender similarity at the lower end of the range and then the relatively steady rise that is more marked in females presents even more of a statistical problem when a frame is less frequently used. Table 7.2 overleaf shows again how this pattern can affect the accuracy of *any* generalised figure (such as a total, mean or median) when looking at the more sporadic distribution of non-conventional frames (predominantly *go* and *be like*).[3]

Median values (in bold) might suggest that non-conventional frames were used roughly the same amount across males and females (1 for females and

Table 7.2 The range of non-conventional frames found in female and male dyads

Female	Non-Conventional	Male	Non-Conventional
Becky 2	0	Bill	0
Meg	0	Alan	0
Mary	0	Paul	0
Kate 1	**0**	**Geoff**	**1**
Becky 1	**2**	**Steve 1**	**2**
Sally 1	5	Chris 1	2
Laura	12	John	2
Penny 1	20	Colin	3

1.5 for males). Table 7.2 shows that this is not however a true reflection of actual usage as some females (e.g., notably Laura and Penny) use far more non-conventional frames. The female range increase is much more marked than that of the males with a range span of 20 against 3, despite *most* females using the same, or similar, amounts to the males of between 0 and 2, reflected in a standard deviation of 7.4 for the females and 1.16 for the males. It is therefore not typical for females to use more than males but it is certainly more likely that a few will, particularly those in their late teens and early twenties. As a result, grouping individuals together can give some idea about patterns, but can also disguise interesting individual variation.

Speakers in triads have been shown (above) to use far less reported dialogue than groups of two speakers (and also, interestingly, to produce more individual variation). But they still demonstrate a similar gendered pattern. Again, there is an initial similarity at the lower end of the range while at the higher end some females produce much more.

Tables 7.3 and 7.4 contain the ranges for both indirect speech and non-conventional frames for triads to make the patterns easily comparable with those presented for dyads.

Table 7.3 overleaf shows that in triads females had a range of 0 to 20 (standard deviation 6.46) and males 0 to 16 (standard deviation 5.15). This is only slightly closer than for dyads, with a female span of 2 less and males 2 more (although the highest male result of 16 is rather anomalous compared to the steep, but slightly more consistent, rise of the females after the median point (in bold)). The same pattern can again be seen in the non-conventional range.

Median values might suggest that non-conventional frames were used in roughly similar amounts across males and females (0 for males and only 2 for females). Table 7.4 overleaf shows, however, that this is not the whole truth. Again, females used far more, with a range of 0–8 which starts to rise

Table 7.3 The range of indirect speech frames found in female and male triads

Female	Indirect Speech	Male	Indirect Speech
Penny 3	0	Rob	0
Sonia	0	Tom	0
Sally 2	2	Tim	0
Imogen	3	Matt	2
Kate 2	**3**	**Brian**	**4**
Maria	4	Chris 2	5
Fiona	8	Chris 3	7
Sophie	11	Steve 3	7
Penny 2	20	Steve 2	16

Table 7.4 The range of non-conventional frames found in female and male triads

Female	Non-Conventional	Male	Non-Conventional
Fiona	0	Steve 2	0
Maria	0	Steve 3	0
Imogen	0	Rob	0
Kate 2	1	Chris 2	0
Sonia	**2**	**Matt**	**0**
Sophie	5	Brian	0
Sally 2	6	Tom	0
Penny 3	7	Tim	1
Penny 2	8	Chris 3	9

just before the median point (standard deviation 3.27). The male range was 0–9 but, as this was only contributed by two speakers, cannot be judged as a true pattern: it is certainly not a gradual increase where Tim uses 1 frame and Chris 3 uses 9 (standard deviation 2.98).

These detailed quantitative figures support qualitative analysis suggesting how, in both dyads and triads, all speakers engage in personal details, but that *some* females do so more often and in more ways than males. As a consequence, these females are more likely to use a greater amount and variety of reporting frames than males. Like males, females can use talk that lacks reported dialogue because it lacks personal detail and, like males, they can discuss personal topics that include, for example, recreating a past conversation. But *some* females are *also* involved in more 'confessional' talk about embarrassment, failure or just why they don't understand something.

Detailed quantitative figures also showed how within this recurring pattern, there were some minor gender differences in frames preference. The 'confessional' talk of some females was more likely to involve 'direct thought' reports to convey personal insecurity or non-understanding, often in contrast to other speakers, as a way of (humorous) bonding. It was also more likely to involve non-conventional frames in younger female speakers as a vivid but less face-threatening way of dealing with more sensitive topics in a way that encourages collaboration often, again, through humour. Conversely, males in my study did not usually show as much variety as some of these females because they did not explicitly include the same confessional type of talk. However, a few did use more zero frame reports (where there is no reporting verb present) than females as a way of presenting a humorous contribution and mimicking a past or hypothetical opinion or reaction, and some used more indirect thought frames as a way of (re)creating greater personal distance.

There may be a relationship between the variety of frames a speaker uses and the number of different identities that speaker is trying to negotiate and understand, and this may be gendered:

> So wide a variation observed in the speech behaviour of many women can be interpreted as a response to the often conflicting demands of their various roles (Moonwomon, 1989: 244) ... From this perspective, women's identity is signalled not so much by the choice of particular linguistic variants which contrast with those preferred by men, but rather by the ways in which women are often required to use language to construct a much wider range of social identities and express a wider range of social roles than men.
>
> (Holmes, 1997b: 199)

More variety of reported dialogue thus arguably relates to the negotiation of a greater variety of social identities: the 'domestic' person, the 'emotional' person, the 'friend', the 'successful career person'. It might be typically 'feminine' to have more social roles than males, but in my data both males and females show that such stereotyping is far from accurate. *All* speakers experience identity restrictions and all have multiple identities, but *some* speakers constructed more identities than others.

Interestingly, the only overt comment on 'doing gender' in my data, is in the following extract about masculinity, as constructed between two males:

Example 5   Men don't read manuals

Chris: Kate's just got one of those tiny little Siemens ones with-
Geoff: oh that are- that are about that big=
Chris: =it's tiny . with WAP services

> *Geoff*:   oh yeah
> *Chris*:   it is pretty cool […]and we've been having these endless discussions because she wants me to have the same phone as her
> *Geoff*:   why?
> *Chris*:   um on the basis that she won't read the manual and I will which means that-
> *Geoff*:   **you're a man you don't read manuals**
> *Chris*:   oh I do
> *Geoff*:   [laugh]
> *Chris*:   only for the mobile phone I don't read it for anything else
> *Geoff*:   ahhh

Geoff's challenge to Chris that 'you're a man you don't read manuals' is ultimately accepted. It is not clear why manual-reading should be a means of constructing gender, but what it does highlight is that masculinity is, in this instance, being represented as *restrictive*. The idea that men, particularly in all-male groups, construct their identity through talk about what they are *not* has been analysed in relation to talk about not being a woman or not being gay (e.g., Gough and Edwards, 1998; Cameron, 1997a). Geoff's comment is not specifically constructing the 'heterosexual man' against the 'other', but it still draws on the idea that there is a particular way of (not) being masculine. Interestingly, after recording the conversation Geoff said to me that he hoped he was 'male' enough – the only speaker in my corpus to voice such a concern and the only speaker also to overtly mention gender construction in their recorded talk.

In conversation, the constraints on masculine identities may therefore be different to the constraints on feminine identities. Masculine identities in my corpus are more restricted by what topics are deemed socially acceptable, as Geoff suggests in the example above and as discussed in Cameron (1997b) and Gough and Edwards (1998). However, Holmes (1997b: 199 above) suggests that females are 'required' to develop a wide range of femininities because of social demands on them: (some) females may talk about a greater variety of topics but this wider variety arises from social pressure (and is also, arguably, a constraint).

Qualitative analysis points to a correlation between topic and the amount and variety of reported dialogue. The wider variety of different identity constructions may be signalled by the greater amount and variety of reported dialogue used; the more restricted identities present in male (and many female) conversations may be signalled by less and less varied reported dialogue usage.

The stereotypes which exist for females' active use of *more* of certain reported dialogue frames, such as *be like*, than males, are in part supported and in part contradicted by the quantitative analysis. Tables 7.1–7.4 above show that this female stereotype of a wider variety of reported dialogue (and, arguably, wider variety of identities) is not a true reflection of actual talk. Females use more reported dialogue frames *overall* than males because, at least in my corpus, *some* of them negotiated more (personal) topics and therefore constructed a wider range of social identities than their male counterparts. Most of the females, however, did not demonstrate this variety and at least the lower half of the female range was usually the same, or similar, to the male range. It was only in the upper half of the range that differences were usually found.

Ironically, it would be easier to stereotype masculinity in the light of these males' generally more restricted use of topic (and, arguably, identities). 'Feminine' reported dialogue would then still appear negatively evaluated because of its connections with stereotypically feminine 'sensitive' topics. However, the reality is that, among my sample, individual reported dialogue use overlaps to such an extent that although some generalisations are possible, the popular gendered stereotypes are misleading about the variety of identities often created by each speaker, and the commonplace similarities that exist between male and female use of reported dialogue.

Conclusion

The use of intersecting qualitative and quantitative methodologies here suggests that a speaker's use of reported dialogue has more to do with individual social context than with gender as a social category. However, it also shows how gender can, on occasion, be relevant to that social context for some speakers, with the usages of a few (female) speakers posing something of a challenge to generalisations from statistics and/or commanding an exaggerated gendered presence in selected examples.

Corpus linguistics methodologies are certainly of great value in language and gender research. However, future analysis must take care with how raw data of counted tokens is translated into meaningful patterns. In particular, the value of using generalised figures can be as misleading as the subjectively selected examples of 'representative' (male and female) talk. The combination of quantitative and qualitative methods can contribute complimentary perspectives: qualitative analysis helping us understand the local motivations behind certain language use, how and why it is used the way it is; and careful use of quantitative evidence in understanding the prevalence of such use within larger social groups.

Notes

1 The reporting 'frame' is the reporting verb such as *said, thought* or *be like.*
2 Some speakers were recorded in more than one group. For example, because 'Becky' was recorded in two different conversations, she appears as 'Becky 1' and 'Becky 2'. This was useful for any comparisons across the same speaker to see whether their use was more or less consistent across conversations.

3   The 'non-conventional' category contains the frames *go* and *be like* which are not found in standard grammar textbooks. These frames are commonly associated with a less formal style. My data shows that a subdivision into speech and thought is not possible for these non-conventional reports as not only can they be either, but they can also represent a report of perception or even be ambiguous. There were only a couple of instances of non-conventional reports that were not *go* or *be like*.

Transcription conventions

Symbol	Meaning
.	Pause of less than 1 second
(1 sec) (2 secs)	Pause of 1 second, 2 seconds etc
[laugh] [sigh]	Background sounds relevant to conversation
(?word) (?3 words)	Unclear speech
-	Sharp cut-off of word, usually as a false start or when interrupted
?	Intonation signalling a question
!	Intonation signalling an exclamation
=	Where one speaker's utterance runs on from another speaker without a gap
|	Where two or more people start speaking at the same time
Italics	Pronunciation different from speaker's norm e.g. mimicry.
<u>Underlining</u>	Highlights the reported dialogue
Bold	Highlights the reporting frame

8

The English Vocabulary of Girls and Boys: Evidence from a Quantitative Study

Rosa Mª Jiménez Catalán and Julieta Ojeda Alba

Introduction

Corpus linguistics has particular applications to second language acquisition. Here, we report on a study which aimed to provide a profile of the vocabulary produced by Spanish primary school girls and boys learning English as a foreign language (EFL). We looked at: (1) the number of words produced in compositions written by fourth-year male and female students; and (2) the characteristics of these words. Our objective was to build a corpus of girls' and boys' writing and apply quantitative analyses to determine differences and similarities. We explored the advantages and disadvantages of using a quantitative methodological approach to investigate the relationship between gender and the productive vocabulary of EFL learners.

Our study is thus linked to the field of learner corpus research as well as to gender and language education. Within the latter, it is particularly related to studies of the influence of gender on the learning of English as a *second or foreign* language. Three well-known corpora are the Hong Kong University of Science and Technology Corpus (HKUST), the Longman Learners' Corpus (LLC), and the International Corpus of Learner English (ICLE) (Granger, 1996). These corpora provide data on English language learners with various mother tongues, enabling us to study written texts. Our study differs from other research on learner corpora as: (1) it is smaller and more modest in scope; (2) we focus specifically on vocabulary; (3) our corpus only contains Spanish informants; and (4) our subjects are primary school learners of EFL.

The relatively few studies that have examined second/foreign language learning with respect to gender point to female students' advantages, in terms of achievement, attitudes and motivation towards foreign language learning (see Sunderland, 2000a, for an overview). A similar gender tendency has been observed regarding vocabulary learning. When investigating usage of vocabulary learning strategies by 581 Spanish and Basque primary, secondary and university students of EFL, Jiménez Catalán (2003) found that female students used a greater number and a wider range of vocabulary strategies than males.

An earlier study of students' choices of social discussion topics for the English classroom (Jiménez Catalán, 1997) showed different *social preferences* of female and male students. Here, a checklist made up of 56 words drawn from an analysis of the main news items found in Spanish newspapers during a one-month period was given to a sample of 898 Spanish students learning English in junior and high schools. Each word referred to a different social issue and students were asked to tick those that they were interested in. The top ten words chosen by female and male students were, in descending order:

Girls	Boys
AIDS	AIDS
Racism	Racism
Child abuse	Damage to nature
Rape	Drugs
Damage to nature	War
War	Freedom
Freedom	Anti-militarism
Drugs	Unemployment
Love	Terrorism
Death	Pollution

While the same six words appeared in both groups' 'top ten', female students appeared more interested in 'child abuse', 'rape', 'love' and 'death' while their male counterparts selected 'anti-militarism', 'unemployment', 'terrorism' and 'pollution'. Lastly, in a qualitative analysis of the openings and closings used in informal letters by Spanish primary students in their English class (Jiménez Catalán and Ojeda Alba, forthcoming), subtle differences between girls and boys were observed: girls tended to use conventions as reflected in openings and closings more frequently; they also asked more questions and showed more concern for their addressees. These findings about gender and vocabulary in EFL education bear a close relation to findings on girls' and boys' achievements in *first* language education (Swann, 1992), which provide evidence for different preferences of girls and boys in their writing: boys say they prefer factual writing, girls say imaginative writing and fiction.

Our study fills a gap in learner corpus studies as well as in gender and language education. Learner corpus studies have mainly focused on older learners, mostly university students; there is little research on secondary school students, and hardly any on primary school students. Concerning gender and language education studies, most have dealt with English as a native language, have focused on oral language, and have analysed the data qualitatively rather than quantitatively. Regarding gender and foreign language learning, a small amount of research exists on gender and vocabulary in L2. Given the great number of students that learn English as a second or a foreign language in school contexts all over the world, we believe that there is a need to investigate whether the same gender tendencies reported in English as a first language classrooms also appear in EFL learning contexts.

Methodology

Participants

The corpus for this study consists of 271 essays written by ten-year-old fourth-year students (average age 10.4) of EFL from four Spanish primary schools; 152 were boys and 119 girls. To minimise the influence of social factors on their English performance, care was taken to select groups that shared similar socio-economic background, school location, language teaching approach and amount of language instruction. The sample of students was homogeneous for age, background and language level. The four schools were located in middle-class areas of Logroño, in the North of Spain. At the time of data collection, the students had received about 420 hours of English instruction, been introduced to reading and writing in English, and were taught English broadly with a communicative approach.

Data collection

During the school year 2003–4, students were given the following writing task:

> Imagine that you are going to live with an English family in Oxford for a month. The family's name is *Mr and Mrs Edwards* and they have a son and a daughter: *Peter* and *Helen*. Write a letter to them in English: introduce yourself, and tell them about your town, your school, your hobbies and any other thing of interest that you might like to add.

The students' age and language level were considered in the selection of this topic, and its adequacy confirmed in a pre-testing session with students of same age and educational level from a school not participating in the study. Our participants received oral instructions in Spanish before performing the task. The time assigned was 30 minutes. Dictionaries and other kinds of help were not allowed.

The compositions were collected and encoded electronically as separate files (after manual typing rather than electronic scanning). The corpus of essays was edited to correct spelling mistakes, then subjected to a frequency analyses by means of the textual analysis program *Wordsmith Tools* (Scott, 1996).

Results

Quantitative analysis shows the existence of both gender similarities and differences concerning word frequencies, word class distribution and the top 50 content words.

Word frequencies

Following Richards and Schmidt (2002: 567), we use the term *type* as a class of linguistic item, *token* as actual examples or number of occurrences of a type, and *Type–Token Ratio* as 'a measure of the ratio of different words to the total number of words in a text'.

Our data show that male students as a group produced a total of 12,184 word tokens, and 5651 word types, whereas female students as a group produced a total of 10,530 tokens, and 4905 word types. The means of word tokens per composition were 80.16 (sd 57.00) for males and 88.49 for females (sd 49.50), whereas the mean for word types was 37.18 (sd 20.99) and 41.22 (sd 19.36) respectively. Finally, the average type–token ratio per composition was 52.35 for males and 50.37 for females. The differences between the male and female samples were assessed for statistical significance by the non-parametric Mann-Whitney test. Table 8.1 gives the values of this analysis.

The difference in tokens is statistically significant. From the mean ranks it can be seen that the females produce a higher quantity of *tokens*. The difference in *types* is almost but not quite significant at the 5 per cent level, and again females produce a higher number. The difference in type–token ratio is non-significant, but the differences in the lengths of individual compositions also have an effect on the type–token ratio, so that the comparison is not altogether reliable.

Table 8.1 Type–token ratio differences between male and female students

	Tokens	Types	Type-token ratio
Male Mean ranks	126.71	127.89	142.49
Female Mean ranks	147.87	146.36	127.71
Values	$U = 7631.500$	$U = 7811.000$	$U = 8057.500$
	$z = 2.206$	$z = 1.926$	$z = 1.541$
	$p = 0.027$	$p = 0.054$	$p = 0.123$

Word class distribution

The total numbers of word types produced by male and female students, 5651 and 4905 respectively, were obtained by totalling the types evident in each composition. Out of the totals, by means of WordSmith Tools, we edited the alphabetical list of types for female students and the alphabetical list of types for male students to find the unique types (those only used by females or only used by males) in each subcorpus. The result was as follows: females as a group produced 509 unique content word types, and 38 unique grammatical word types; males produced 578 unique content word types and 47 unique grammatical word types. In this section, we focus on unique content word types.

Content words have stable lexical meanings and are usually compared to grammatical words whose function is to express grammatical relationships (Crystal, 1992). The classification of content words into word classes enables a deeper analysis of the data that give us a glimpse of what students may have intended. Traditionally, four word classes are distinguished within content words: noun, lexical verb, adjective, and adverb (Crystal 1992). Table 8.2 shows the class of content words most frequently used by female and male students is *nouns*, followed (at a great distance) by adjectives, verbs and, finally, adverbs. The ratio of content words into word classes is similar for both groups; differences are observed in each category concerning the number of content words produced by female and male students.

The distribution of content words according to sex is also shown in Table 8.2. The percentages stand for all the nouns, adjectives, verbs or adverbs taken together. The figures in square brackets represent the frequencies expected on the basis of the null hypothesis that there is no association between sex and word class.

Boys, as a group, produced 59 unique nouns (types), 7 adjectives (types) and 3 verbs (types) more than girls. The difference is not great in numerical terms (particularly as far as verbs and adverbs are concerned, and taking into account that there are more boys than girls); nevertheless, it suggests that these boys used a slightly greater number of unique content words than

Table 8.2 Distribution of content words according to sex

	Nouns	Adjectives	Verbs	Adverbs	Total
Words produced only by boys	166 (30.7%) [159.0]	23 (28.2%) [27.7]	13 (21.3%) [18.0]	11 (68.7%) [8.3]	213
Words produced only by girls	107 (19.8%)) [107.5]	16 (17.0%) [18.7]	10 (16.3%) [12.2]	11 (68.7%) [5.6]	144
Words produced by both boys and girls	266 (49.3%) [272.5]	55 (58.5%) [47.5]	38 (62.2%) [30.8]	6 (37.0%) [14.2]	365

girls. A chi-square test on the values in Table 8.2 gives a value of 17.1 (df = 6), p = 0.0089, which confirms clear differences in the use of nouns, adjectives, verbs and adverbs by these female and male students. There is a very significant association (p < 0.01) between the two variables. If we compare the observed frequencies with those expected under the null hypothesis of no association between variables, it can be seen that:

- More nouns than expected are produced only by boys, and fewer nouns than expected by both sexes
- Fewer adjectives and verbs than expected are produced only by boys or only girls, and more by both sexes
- More adverbs than expected are produced by only boys or only girls, and fewer by both sexes

From the assumption of no association between variables, it appears that the girls and boys share their use of adjectives and verbs more than their use of nouns and adverbs, and that boys produce more unique nouns than expected.

The top 50 content words

Table 8.3 shows two frequency lists, each list containing the top 50 words for male and female students alongside their percentages in descending order of frequency.

There are shared tendencies between the two lists. On the one hand, most words can be classified into the same word classes: nouns, verbs, adjectives, and adverbs. Interestingly, each category shows almost identical distributions in girls' and boys' percentages. An exception is the case of adjectives, where eight adjectives occur among the boys' top 50 words, in comparison to 13 in the girls' top list. Among the latter, eight adjectives appear in the two lists: 'favourite', 'big', 'one' 'small', 'two', 'old', 'nine' and 'beautiful'. The remaining five are exclusive to the females' top 50 list: 'brown', 'blue', 'English', 'tall', and 'green'. Nouns form the most numerous category, followed by adjectives, verbs, and adverbs.

Among the verbs, 'is' (functioning as a lexical verb), occupies the first position in both girls' and boys' top lists. To determine whether verbs such as 'be', 'do' or 'have' were used as lexical or auxiliary verbs, we made use of the concordancing tool in WordSmith Tools. This provided us with all the occurrences of any given word in its context within the sentence, and allowed us to obtain useful insights into students' use of verbs. One finding was that these fourth-year primary school students do not use 'be' or 'have' as auxiliary verbs, but that 'do' is used in this way.

A second common tendency shown in these girls' and boys' 'top 50' lists concerns the arrangement of content words into similar semantic fields. Among them, we find kinship names, sports and hobbies, numbers, animals,

Table 8.3 Boys' and girls' 50 most frequent words

	Boys			Girls		
Position	Word	%	Position	Word	%	
1	is	7.14	1	is	7.43	
2	like	2.56	2	name	1.92	
3	have	1.72	3	like	1.84	
4	name	1.70	4	have	1.36	
5	play	1.39	5	favourite	1.18	
6	favourite	1.35	6	big	1.15	
7	big	1.31	7	school	1.00	
8	school	1.28	8	play	0.97	
9	football	0.96	9	father	0.76	
10	very	0.80	10	mother	0.64	
11	father	0.72	11	one	0.62	
12	one	0.70	12	brother	0.60	
13	small	0.65	13	friend	0.60	
14	house	0.56	14	very	0.56	
15	friend	0.51	15	house	0.55	
16	brother	0.51	16	old	0.51	
17	basketball	0.50	17	small	0.49	
18	two	0.50	18	sister	0.49	
19	live	0.44	19	football	0.46	
20	mother	0.44	20	brown	0.45	
21	old	0.44	21	family	0.45	
22	year	0.44	22	live	0.43	
23	dog	0.39	23	two	0.43	
24	sister	0.39	24	year	0.42	
25	tennis	0.38	25	classroom	0.36	
26	nine	0.36	26	dog	0.34	
27	go	0.34	27	nine	0.33	
28	family	0.33	28	go	0.32	
29	spaghetti	0.27	29	teacher	0.31	
30	sport	0.25	30	swim	0.30	
31	animal	0.25	31	colour	0.25	
32	beautiful	0.25	32	music	0.25	
33	bedroom	0.23	33	animal	0.24	
34	car	0.23	34	blue	0.23	
35	teacher	0.23	35	city	0.23	
36	book	0.22	36	eyes	0.23	
37	fish	0.22	37	hair	0.23	
38	game	0.20	38	basketball	0.22	
39	boy	0.20	39	beautiful	0.22	
40	cat	0.19	40	cat	0.22	
41	lot	0.19	41	Mrs.	0.22	
42	station	0.19	42	spaghetti	0.22	
43	three	0.19	43	maths	0.20	
44	computer	0.18	44	Mr	0.20	
45	bathroom	0.17	45	English	0.19	
46	swim	0.16	46	tall	0.19	
47	birthday	0.15	47	book	0.18	
48	food	0.15	48	mum	0.18	
49	Mr	0.15	49	bedroom	0.17	
50	read	0.14	50	green	0.17	

classroom objects and activities, the house, food, parts of the body, and colours. However, although semantic fields are shared, remarkable gender differences emerge when we look at the two lists closely. Concerning sports and hobbies, we find occurrences of 'football' and 'basketball' considerably lower in the girls' list. With regard to the semantic field of numbers, male students use a wider variety of number terms than do female students. Salient differences between the two groups are also found in kinship and colours. Given the importance of these data for gender research, we now address each of these semantic fields below.

Kinship terms

Girls mention family (and friendship) terms more frequently than boys, as shown in Table 8.4.

This tendency is only reversed when we go beyond the top 50 to the overall ranking, with terms such as 'uncle', 'grandfather', 'granddad', 'grand-mother' and 'granny', in which higher percentages are shown in the list for males than in that for females. Nevertheless, care should be taken in the interpretation of these results since these terms are not found among the most frequent of each group and variations in the percentages are so small as to be almost meaningless.

Colours

Colour names do not appear in the boys' top 50 list but they do in the girls' list. No fewer than four terms are found: 'brown' (60) (0.45 per cent), 'colour' (34) (0.25 per cent), 'blue' (31) (0.23 per cent) and 'green' (23) (0.17 per cent). This does not mean that male students do not use these terms: they do, although not as frequently as female students, as revealed by the following boys' percentages: 'brown' (14) (0.10 per cent), 'colour' (17) (0.12 per cent), 'blue' (11) (0.08 per cent), 'green' (11) (0.08 per cent). In addition to these adjectives, both male and female students use 'black', 'orange', 'red', 'yellow', 'purple', 'grey', 'pink' and 'blond'. These colour terms are not as frequent as

Table 8.4 Ranks of kinship terms for girls and boys

Word	Rank for girls	Rank for boys
father	9th	11th
mother	10th	20th
brother	12th	16th
sister	18th	24th
family	21st	28th
friend	13th	15th

Table 8.5 Differential uses of colour terms by boys and girls

Word	% for girls	% for boys
black	0.16	0.13
purple	0.05	0.01
grey	0.04	0.01
pink	0.03	0.01
blond	0.02	0.01
orange	0.13	0.13
yellow	0.09	0.09

the ones appearing in the top 50 content words, in most cases are either used equally by the two sexes *or* used more frequently by female students, as shown by the comparative percentages in Table 8.5.

Both female and male students use colour terms to describe their eyes, hair, home, school and favourite colours. They also employ them to describe their family, including, in one case, the cat's family, and to report their favourite colours.

Shared and non-shared vocabulary

Using the top 50 content words as a point of reference in the comparison of girls' and boys' vocabularies, we note that 36 of the words in the boys' top 50 list are also in the girls' top 50 list, and 38 of the words in the girls' top 50 list are also present in the boys' top 50 list. However, as Table 8.3 reveals, several words are not shared by the two groups: 'bathroom', 'birthday', 'boy', 'car', 'computer', 'fish', 'food', 'game', 'lot', 'station', 'three', 'tennis', 'sport', 'read', are present in the boys' top 50 list but not in the girls'. Conversely, 'blue', 'brown', 'classroom', 'city', 'colour', 'eyes', 'English', 'green', 'hair', 'maths', 'Mrs' 'mum', 'music', and 'tall', occur in the girls' top 50 but not in the boys'.

Discussion

The results of our study reveal both similarities and differences. About half of the words are present in the vocabulary of each sex: 266 nouns out of a total of 539 (49.3 per cent) , 55 adjectives out of 94 (58.5 per cent) , 38 verbs out of 61 (62.2 per cent) , and 6 adverbs out of a total of 11 (54.5 per cent). There are also common tendencies regarding the word classes used, as both male and female students produced more nouns and verbs than adjectives or adverbs. Likewise, and as expected because of the topic and the type of composition, the content words used by male and female students make reference to their daily lives and fall into predictable semantic fields such as: sports and hobbies, animals, food and drink, classroom objects, home appliances, professions, places, family and relations, garments and musical instruments.

Our results also point to differences in the means of word tokens and word types of female and male students' compositions. Taking into account the individual means, girls make use of a statistically significant greater number of tokens and a near significant greater number of types than boys – an indication that (these) girls have a more varied vocabulary and are more prolific in writing. A significantly higher mean in word tokens and word types may be related to a wider range of lexical representations. The fact that, on an individual level, girls employ a higher number of tokens and types than boys suggests that they may be better positioned to perform successfully in communicative interactions in English, at least with regard to informal letter writing. More generally, a higher productive vocabulary has important educational implications: research on the acquisition of a second/foreign language has supplied evidence of the positive relation between vocabulary size and success in reading comprehension (Grabe and Stoller, 1997; Laufer, 1997), quality of writing (Muncie, 2002), and the achievement of good marks in the target language (Meara, 1996). The results of the present study corroborate those obtained in previous vocabulary research in EFL, that is, the higher the number of words known, the higher the degree in reading comprehension and writing performance, and the higher the chances of achieving good marks.

Clear differential patterns are found in the top 50 content words produced by each sex in the assigned composition task. As far as males' and females' means are concerned, our results do not support the folk-linguistic belief that women's vocabulary is less extensive than men's, as claimed by Otto Jespersen and later by Robin Lakoff, but do corroborate some lexical differential patterns put forward by empirical sociolinguistic research (see Harrington, this volume; Rayson, Leech and Hodges, 1997; Holmes, 1995; Coates, 1993).

The study conducted by Rayson, Leech and Hodges provided empirical evidence of a male preference for common nouns and females' orientation towards family terms. Our results support this since male students used more nouns than female students, and, in contrast, female students mention more family terms than male students. Our results are also in line with the differential patterns observed in gender and language education research; for example, in the investigation conducted by Norah Arnold (1990), different choices of topics for writing were found for UK female and male pupils. Results from research in sociolinguistics, language and education and the learning of EFL suggest that some slight gender differences may be relatively consistent across different contexts. Likewise, gender-differential patterns are observed in (these) 10-year-old learners of EFL and point to differential gender identities in even young learners of English. What is particularly revealing is not the different vocabulary frequencies on the part of females and males but the presence, among the top 50 words, of vocabulary which is *exclusive* to each group.

The quantitative methodology followed in our study has provided us with lists of words. These are meaningless without interpretation. Our cultural perception tells us that girls and boys are following the roles traditionally 'assigned' to them on the basis of their sex and according to predominant values current in Western society. Coates (1993: 144) notes that 'Girls and boys learn during childhood to identify with one group or the other. They demonstrate their membership of the group by their use of gender-appropriate behaviour, and this includes gender-appropriate *linguistic* behaviour'. The results of the present study seem to point in this direction: it seems as if 'proper' behaviour for girls should be to display an orientation to others (see Rayson, Leech and Hodges, 1997); here, this may be revealed by their greater use of family terms. Girls also may be more familiar with colours and home decoration (del-Teso-Craviotto, in press). For Lakoff (1975), colour discrimination is more relevant for women than for men. While Lakoff's claim has been widely challenged, our study reveals that this is indeed the case for these 10-year-old learners. Our hypothesis is that this is part of learning gendered social behaviour for females and as such it is reflected in their foreign language use.

In the same vein, gendered social behaviour for males seems to include use of a high percentage of terms related to sports and numbers. These topics appear to be mediating males' identity as suggested by their (personally observed) predominance in most males' conversations, particularly as far as football or basketball is concerned – although an increasing number of women (at least Spanish women) are becoming more fond of these sports, and even practising them regularly in school and community centres. It is also true that some men are becoming more clothes-conscious and interested in home decoration, but in both cases, those women and men are still in the minority.

Are these word choices due to students' age and/or the topic and type (or genre) of the composition task? Nichols (1983), writing on South Carolina Black communities, and Milroy (1980) on working-class communities in Belfast, provide evidence of different linguistic behaviours according to age. Referring to the use of Standard English, Montgomery (1986: 154) claims that: 'the speech of older and younger women is more different from each other than it is from men'. It may be the case that gender differences in vocabulary choice in EFL change with age. Litosseliti (2006a) notes that some tasks and topics may be female-oriented, and partially explain girls' superiority in foreign languages. It may be the case that both the letter writing task and the topic somehow suited girls more than boys. However, at present we can only identify similarities and differences in the vocabulary of girls and boys as far as informal letter FL writing is concerned.

The use of a corpus-based methodological approach goes hand in hand with the use of quantitative measures in conjunction with electronic tools. These have enabled us to order, count, and make sense of the thousands of tokens and types contained in the 271 compositions which constitute this 'small' corpus. The application of descriptive and inferential statistics to the data has allowed the identification of raw frequencies and percentages, means, standard deviations, and values of significance, which in turn has provided empirical evidence of differences and similarities within these Spanish learners of English in the context of fourt- grade primary Spanish education.

We hope this chapter has demonstrated the potential of a corpus-based analysis to the study of language and gender. However, quantitative measures do not give us the whole picture. The total number of tokens and types as well as their means gives us information about males and females as groups but hides individual variation: some students may produce a high number of tokens and types while others may not be so productive. In our corpus we have found such extreme differences. For instance, regarding the male sub-corpus, Student 8 produced 113 tokens and 53 types whereas Student 182 produced only 3 tokens and 3 types. Exactly the same happened with the female sub-corpus, where Student 70 produced 174 tokens and 75 types and Student 145 only 8 and 7, respectively. The standard deviation measure already acknowledged the existence of diversity among the students, but it was by carrying out an individual quantitative analysis of *each* composition that we became fully aware of such disparity; had we not done so, these enormous differences among individual students would have gone unnoticed and undocumented. Therefore, as well as focusing on differences and similarities between males and females, it is also important to take into consideration the fact that there will always be considerable variation *among* different males and *among* different females.

In our study we used WordSmith Tools to organise the vocabulary pro-duced by students in alphabetical and frequency orders as well as in their contexts of use. This has proved extremely useful for counting tokens and identifying the most frequent word types appearing in the compositions of each sex. Thanks to it, we have been able to compare girls' and boys' vocab-ularies in a systematic, replicable way. However, care should be taken in the editing of the data since WordSmith Tools does not 'understand' languages: it counts as tokens any word separated in space from another word, whether is it written in English or in Spanish, and whether it is an incorrectly spelt or a nonsensical word. In order to obtain a real picture of learners' productive vocabulary we had to edit the compositions one by one, deleting everything that was not 'real' English and correcting spellings at the input stage. Had we not done so, the total number of tokens and types would have been different. Extreme care is necessary in the handling of these instruments and considerable thought about what quantitative measures really do and do not tell us, otherwise it is very easy to arrive at incorrect conclusions regarding gender and language use.

Acknowledgements

This study has been carried out under the auspices of a research project funded by the Spanish 'Ministerio de Ciencia y Tecnología', Grant nº BFF 2003-04009 and by 'Ministerio de Educación y Ciencia' and 'FEDER', Grant nº HUM 2006-09775-C02-02/FILO.
We would like to thank Paul Baker, Kate Harrington and Jane Sunderland for their positive criticisms, and insightful comments on this chapter. Thanks also to Professor Christopher Butler for his invaluable assistance in the statistical analysis and helpful comments on the data. Any remaining errors are solely our responsibility. Finally, we would like to express our gratitude to Soraya Moreno Espinosa for her generous help with WordSmith Tools.

Part 3
Conversation Analysis

9

Conversation Analysis: Technical Matters for Gender Research

Celia Kitzinger

Introducing conversation analysis

Conversation analysis (CA) is a theoretically and methodologically distinctive approach to the study of social life, developed in the late 1960s and early 1970s by Harvey Sacks in collaboration with Emanuel Schegloff and Gail Jefferson. For Sacks, talk-in-interaction was simply one site of human interaction that could be studied for what it revealed about the production of social order. Talk as such is not given any *principled* primacy in CA: the key interest of CA is in talk not as *language*, but in talk as *action*: that is, in what people *do* with talk. CA 'describes methods persons use in doing social life' (Sacks, quoted in Psathas, 1995: 53).

The methodology of CA was shaped by the availability to Sacks of tape-recorded calls to a suicide prevention centre, which provided its earliest dataset:

> It was not from any large interest in language or from some theoretical formulation of what should be studied that I started with tape-recorded conversation, but simply because I could get my hands on it, and I could study it again and again, and also consequentially, because others could look at what I had studied and make of it what they could, if, for example, they wanted to be able to disagree with me.
>
> (Sacks, quoted in Heritage, 1984: 235)

Conversation analysts work with *actual instances* of talk-in-interaction (not role-play, intuition, recollection or idealisation). The analytic procedure depends upon the repeated inspection of recorded naturalistic data (either ordinary everyday conversation, or institutional talk in settings such as courts, classrooms or doctors' surgeries). It focuses upon the organised, recurrent, *structural features* of talk-in-interaction. CA is defined by a cumulative body of empirical research that describes the basic characteristics of talk-in-interaction. It develops technical specifications of the recurrent patterns, structures and practices that constitute key interactional phenomena.

These include, centrally, sequence organisation and preference structure (e.g., Schegloff, 2006); turn-taking and turn-design (e.g., Sacks, Schegloff and Jefferson, 1974); repair and error correction (e.g., Schegloff, Jefferson and Sacks, 1977); storytelling (e.g., Sacks, 1972); word selection, person reference and membership categorisation (e.g., Schegloff, 1996a; Sacks and Schegloff, 1979); and the overall structural organisation of interaction (e.g., Jefferson, 1980). This reliance on, and contribution to, a set of cumulative empirically derived, technical specifications of interactional phenomena is an important part of what differentiates CA from other methods of analysing talk in interaction, including discourse analysis and discursive psychology (see Kitzinger, 2006a for further discussion). The foundational discoveries of 'pure' CA consist of rigorous and systematic contributions to understanding conversational norms and they provide the empirical infrastructure for 'applied' CA – such as research using CA in the study of gender and sexuality.

Conversation analysis and feminist research

As a long-time feminist researcher, who has used a range of qualitative and quantitative methods in analysing talk, I am committed to understanding how sexist and heterosexist presumptions are threaded through the ordinary practices of talk and interaction that, cumulatively, constitute an oppressive social order – a commitment shared by other feminist researchers now drawing on conversation analysis in their work (see Stokoe, Chapter 10). Conversation analysis offers a powerful and rigorous method for exposing the mundane oppressions of everyday life.

This chapter explores the value of CA for feminist research, for research on issues of gender and sexuality, and – more generally – for any research concerned with power and oppression as they are produced and reproduced in human interaction. Critics of CA (e.g. Lakoff, 2003; Billig, 1999; Wetherell, 1998) have proposed that, because of its attention to the fine detail of talk, independent of speaker characteristics, CA is not well-suited to the feminist agenda of understanding power and oppression. As I have shown elsewhere (Kitzinger, 2000), these critiques incorporate various 'misunderstandings or misreadings' of CA (Schegloff, 1999: 559). In this chapter I do not address these critiques directly nor engage in theoretical argument with them, but rather aim to show how some of the technical tools that define CA as a discipline can be deployed within a feminist framework.

There is now a body of classic feminist work on gender which draws on CA. This includes research on interruptions in cross-sex conversations (e.g., West, 1979; Zimmerman and West, 1975) and on girls' talk (e.g., Goodwin, 1990). In addition, in the last five years or so, there has been a dramatic increase in CA and CA-influenced research on gender and sexuality by feminists and other critical researchers: see, for example, Stokoe (2000, this volume); Speer (2005); Tainio (2003); Weatherall (2002); and several contributions to the collections edited by McIlvenny (2002) and Stokoe and Weatherall (2002). The major focus of my own recent work has been the use of conversation analysis to understand how heteronormativity is produced and reinforced in everyday interactions – in conversations between heterosexual friends and family members (Kitzinger, 2005a), calls to a doctor's surgery (Kitzinger, 2005b), and lesbians' contacts with a wide range of service providers including plumbers, insurance salespeople and a dentist's receptionist (Land and Kitzinger, 2005). In this chapter I explore what conversation analysis can contribute to our understanding of gender and interruption.

Gender and interruption

I have chosen 'interruption' to illustrate the value of CA for feminist research because this topic has been of interest both to gender researchers and to conversation analysts. For gender researchers, ever since Zimmerman and West (1975) famously claimed that women are disproportionately interrupted by men and that these interruptions are displays of dominance and control, interruption has been a recurrent concern: 'no other conversational behavior (except possibly the overall amount of participation) has received as much attention as the interruption' (Okamo, Rashotte and Smith-Lovin, 2002: 38). The extensive body of research on gender differences here consists of contradictory and, ultimately, inconclusive findings. Although some research has supported Zimmerman and West's claim (e.g., DeFrancisco, 1991; Fishman, 1978), other research points to the intersection of gender with other variables such as status hierarchy (Eakins and Eakins, 1978) or expertise (Leet-Pellegrini, 1980). Some researchers have suggested that speaking at the same time as another is not necessarily gendered but can index a 'high involvement' style characteristic of some ethnic groupings, such as New York Jews, irrespective of gender (Tannen, 1994), and that overlapping talk can be supportive (Coates, 1996). Beattie (1981) found that, in university tutorials, females interrupted males as much as the reverse, and the feminist researcher Deborah Cameron similarly noted that in her data samples, women interrupted more, disagreed more and back-channelled less. She comments: 'Conversation is a highly contextualised phenomenon and to generalise about it on the basis of so gross a variable as speaker sex is unwise' (Cameron, 1995a: 42). Overviewing research in the area, Aries (1996) concludes that the pervasive focus on gender difference in speech styles is an example of 'the fundamental attribution error', that is, an instance of the human tendency to attribute behaviour to personal characteristics rather than social context. In other words, any differences in 'male' and 'female' speech are related not to gender *per se* but to differences in power, social roles and context.

One of the earliest classic foundational texts of the field of conversation analysis (Sacks, Schegloff and Jefferson, 1974) deals with turn-taking in conversation. 'Interruption' can be understood as what happens when someone violates normative turn-taking practices, so in order to understand interruption as an interactional phenomenon, we need first to understand how participants orient to turn-taking in conversation. Their key finding is that overwhelmingly, participants speak one at a time and conversation is demonstrably organised through a system of turn-taking. Co-interactants track their own talk and that of their co-conversationalist(s) in the course of its production, using syntax, prosody and pragmatics as resources to project when a turn is coming to possible completion. A next speaker may legitimately start to speak at a place where a turn at talk is possibly complete (a 'transition relevance place'). This is typically at the end of any one of the units (sentences, clauses, phrases, lexical items) out of which a turn can (in any given context) be constructed (see Sacks, Schegloff and Jefferson 1974, for a detailed exposition of turn constructional units.) A key finding of conversation analytic research – indeed, one of those that underpin the turn-taking model upon which conversation analysis is based – is that a great deal of overlapping talk is caused by next-speaker start up at a place where a turn could, indeed, have been possibly complete but – as it turns out – is not. For example (bold typeface highlights the overlapping speech):

Extract 1

```
001   A:   What's yer name again please   [sir,
002   B:                                   [F.T. Galloway.
                                            (from Sacks, Schegloff and
                                                   Jefferson, 1974: 708)
```

Extract 2

```
001   A:   Uh you been down here before [havenche.
002   B:                                [Yeh.
                                            (from Sacks, Schegloff and
                                                   Jefferson, 1974: 707)
```

In both instances, Speaker A has produced as part of their turn what the authors term 'optional elements' – the address term 'sir' (Extract 1), the tag question 'haven't you' (Extract 2). In both instances Speaker B started up at a point at which it was projectable that the prior turn would be complete and that their turn would be launched in the clear without either a gap or an overlap. Because of the 'optional' element included in the prior turn, this turned out to be a misprojection. Brief and unproblematic instances of overlap like these are very common in conversation and they are characteristically resolved by one speaker stopping talking a few syllables (or beats) into the overlap (Schegloff, 2001, 2000). They are not exercises of power or attempts to dominate the conversation, but a by-product of the operation of the turn-taking system. As one of the authors of the classic turn-taking paper has subsequently expressed it: 'Looking at talk which might well be characterised as someone starting up "interruptively", that is, in the midst of another's utterance, I found again and again that the places at which such talk started were perfectly reasonable "completion" points' (Jefferson, 1986: 153). These conversation analysts concur that most overlap in conversation results because a recipient reasonably, and with good warrant, treats some current utterance as complete and starts to talk, while at the same time a current speaker, perfectly within her rights, keeps talking. In other words, it is 'accidental' – a product of co-interactants' orientations to turn-taking rules and not a flagrant violation of them. Conversation analysts distinguish, therefore, between overlapping talk (which is simply a description of two or more persons in the same conversation talking concurrently) and interruption (or 'interjacent' overlap, Jefferson, 1986) in which the overlapping talk is analysably produced in violation of turn-taking rules. In a discussion of the claimed link between interruption and gender, Schegloff raises various concerns about research in this area, including in particular the need for 'full technical exploration of the aspects of interaction being accounted for and the micro-level mechanisms that are involved in their production' (1987: 215).

Gender researchers do routinely commonly cite conversation analytic research on turn-taking as informing their enterprise, and Zimmerman and West's (1975) early research was framed as a conversation analytic study. Unfortunately, however, in many of these studies, the Sacks and colleagues (1974) turn-taking model seems to have been operationalised in a very mechanical way: 'interruptions occur when speaker A cuts off more than one word of speaker B's unit-type' (Esposito, 1969, cited in Tannen, 1994: 57); or 'all vocalization where, while one subject was speaking, the other subject uttered at least two consecutive identifiable words or at least three syllables of a single word' (Leffler et al., 1982: 156, cited in Tannen, 1994: 570). From a conversation analytic perspective these are crude and innaccurate notions of 'interruption' that ignore what is being said and why, the projectability of the utterance under way, and the nature of the interaction between the people concerned. Reading through the literature, it is apparent that few, if any, gender-related studies have used the insights of conversation analysis in analysing interactions involving overlapping talk. In the rest of this chapter I will use 'interruption' as a case study for displaying what the technical discoveries of conversation analysis can offer to researchers interested in language and gender.

Overlapping talk and interruption

Confronting the contradictory findings of research on gender differences in interruption, the question of definition has become an increasing concern.

Following from Zimmerman and West (1975), most researchers do make a distinction between 'overlap' (an error in projecting where a speaker is planning to end their turn, as in Extracts 1 and 2, and an 'interruption' (a start-up at a point in a speaker's talk where it cannot possibly be complete). However, it is apparent from the data displayed in support of this distinction that in practice these two concepts are confusingly and inconsistently applied. Furthermore, recent work has posited two different definitions of 'interruption' (as distinct from 'overlap'), one of which is attributed to Zimmerman and West (1975) and sometimes referred to as a 'conversation analytic' or a 'purely syntactic' definition (though contemporary conversation analysis is very far from being 'purely syntactic'!); the other of which is attributed to Murray (1985) and is sometimes referred to as a 'context sensitive' or 'cultural' definition (which implies, rather oddly and counter to the facts, that conversation analysis is *not* 'context sensitive' or not interested in displays of 'culture'). Since both of these claimed disparate definitions embody features of what I understand by a conversation analytic approach to interruption, and since both have features that depart from it, I do not intend to assess their merits and demerits here (see Okamoto, Rashotte and Smith-Lovin, 2002, for such an assessment – although, in my terms, a problematic one). Instead, I will use my own understanding of conversation analysis to point to some of the methodological problems that beset existing work on interruption, and to suggest ways forward for gender and language researchers.

To begin with, here are a couple of instances of overlapping talk that previous gender researchers have coded as 'interruptions' but which, from a conversation analytic perspective, are – as far as one can tell from the tiny fragments of data and minimal analysis presented – entirely legitimate start-ups by second speakers. Extract 3 comes from research investigating gender differences in interruption (with a 'no difference' finding). The researcher claims that this 'simple interruption' occurs when the first speaker's turn is left incomplete.

Extract 3

```
001  A:   ... so he (.) he gives the impression that he
002       wasn't able to train them up. [Now
003  B:                                 [He didn't try hard
004       enough heh heh heh
```
                                        (from Beattie, 1983: 115)

It seems clear enough, however, that Speaker A has reached the possible end of a turn after completing the sentence that ends with 'train them up' – and it is only after the end of this unit of talk (and not before) that Speaker B starts up. Starting to speak after 'that' (in line 1) or after 'wasn't' (in line 2) might well have qualified as violating turn-taking rules – as an 'interruption', but beginning to talk after the end of someone's sentence is not normally violative. Indeed, the classic conversation analytic model of turn-taking is rooted in the observation that, in ordinary conversation, people frequently and normatively start to speak at the end of their co-conversationalist's sentence thereby displaying that (in the absence of any special arrangements to the contrary, such as story telling, list construction, etc.) a sentence is one complete unit out of which a turn can be constructed ('a turn constructional unit', or TCU).

Extract 4 (below) is also not a clear instance of 'interruption', although it differs from Extract 3 in that Speaker A *is* part way through a sentence when C starts to speak:

Extract 4

```
055  A:  Yeah he doesn't remember that [he was standing there
056  C:                                 ['cause they told him
057      that he had been shot.
```

(from Okamoto, Rashotte and
Smith-Lovin, 2002: 45)

The authors present this data as exemplifying an instance of 'interruption' as they understand the term within what they call 'the West-Zimmerman coding scheme': 'Speaker C interrupts Speaker A in mid-sentence, five syllables away from a possible turn-transition point' (ibid.: 44). But notice that 'he doesn't remember' is a perfectly good sentence. So is 'he doesn't remember that'. We do not know (because the authors do not show us) what A and C are talking about, or what immediately prior turn C's alleged 'interruption' is responsive to – but suppose that C had just said (for example) 'They said he was standing there', so that A is confirming 'yeah' and then adding an account of why the person being talked about hadn't also reported 'standing there'. This would make either 'he doesn't remember' or 'he doesn't remember that' possibly complete, and C's turn therefore *not* interruptive. In other words, for a recipient of A's talk who is tracking the production of her turn 'in real time', a start-up after 'that' may well be targeting a possible transition relevant place. A recipient who hears the turn in the course of its production, turn-so-far by turn-so-far, may not know – as we do, because we can see it on the page – that A 'intends' to continue at this point. This is not, for a conversation analyst, a clear instance of 'interruption' – but unfortunately it is displayed by the authors to exemplify the kind of data coded *as* 'interruption' by 'the coder trained in the West-Zimmerman technique'.

Conversation analytic knowledge about turn-taking and sequencing rules and, in particular, about the projectability of turn constructional units, enables us to analyse the onset of overlapping talk as either violative (interruptive) or as a rule-governed misprojection. This kind of analysis would enable us not only to address the question as to whether men (or some men, or particular types of men in particular types of setting) disproportionately interrupt women, but also to explore the interactional motivations and consequences of interruptions and their reverberations for the conversation as a whole.

Unlike the extracts displayed above, the following extracts are taken from those classic conversation analytic data sets to which I have direct personal access and which illustrate the most common types of overlapping talk I have discovered. I have searched for instances of overlapping talk (which is pervasively present) and then sought to determine which of these are also 'interruptive', that is, they violate normative turn-taking practices in that speaker start-up is not at a possible transition relevance place. On the basis of this preliminary analysis, I have no evidence whatsoever that males launch interruptive talk more often than females, or disproportionately when in interaction with female speakers.

I have listened to all of these conversations and transcribed them (using a transcription notation originally developed – and recently updated – by Gail Jefferson, 2005; see key at the end of this chapter) so as to preserve fine-grained details such as in-breaths, sound stretches, and (timed) pauses, and other characteristics of the timing and delivery of the talk.[1] This is necessary because CA research has shown that such apparently tiny and insignificant details of the talk are oriented to by participants in conversations: that is, they systematically affect what they do next, and how. If, as analysts, we want to understand how people do things in and through talk, then we need to attend to their talk at the same level of detail as they do.

The most common occasion for overlapping talk seems to be when the incoming speaker misprojects where a prior speaker means to complete their turn, either because they have built into the design of their turn some kind of 'optional' elements (Extracts 5–8) or because they add on to a turn constructional unit that is already brought to grammatical, pragmatic and intonational completion some increment, thereby reopening a turn that seemed to its recipient already to be complete (Extracts 9 and 10). Neither of these qualifies as 'interruption' in the sense of a violation of turn-taking procedures. Rather they are accidental by-products of interactants using normative turn-taking practices to try to launch their turns at appropriate places – neither overlapping the prior talk, nor leaving a gap. For example, in Extract 5, taken from the closing moments of a telephone conversation, a man (Donny) starts up his turn in overlap with a woman (Marsha) who is completing hers. (Sound files of this and many of the following extracts are available on my web page: www.york.ac.uk/depts/soci/s_kitz.html.)

Extract 5

027   Don: Okay? =

```
028  Mar:  = Okay    [#Don# ]
029  Don:             [Thanks] a lot. = Bye-.
030  Mar:  Bye:.
```

(Stalled)

This is not an 'interruption' in that (as in the talk displayed in Extracts 1 and 2), Marsha has added an 'optional' element to her turn (the address term 'Don') which Donny could not have predicted: 'okay' would have been sufficient for Marsha's whole turn on its own (indeed, 'okay' *was* a turn on its own in the immediately preceding talk, line 27). So, Donny is not interrupting Marsha.

In Extract 6, a man (Tony) starts up his turn in overlap with a woman (Marsha again) who is completing hers – but again, this is not 'interruption'. The conversation (also analysed along parallel lines in Schegloff, 1997) is between the now separated/divorced parents of a teenage son whose car has been vandalised. He had planned to drive back home to his father's house but is flying instead (see Extract 12), and Marsha has just told Tony about what has happened:

Extract 6

```
039  Ton:  That really makes me ma:d.
040        (0.2)
041  Mar:  .hhh Oh it's disgusti[ng ez a matter a'f]a:ct.
042  Ton:                       [P o o r    J o e y.]
```

(STOLEN)

Having been informed of the theft by Marsha (data not shown), Tony assesses it as something that makes him angry (line 39) and Marsha expresses similar views ('it's disgusting') – while also claiming (via the 'oh', see Heritage and Raymond, 2005) to have arrived at this conclusion independently and not simply to be agreeing with Tony. She continues past possible completion (she *could* have been done after 'Oh it's disgusting') with what is (syntactically) an 'optional' element. Since Tony started up in terminal overlap with what was projectably a possible ending of Marsha's turn (with an aligning expression of sympathy for their son), he finds himself in overlap with her talk as it continues past possible completion. Again, this is not an interruption.

These kinds of misprojections are commonplace irrespective of the gender of the co-interactants. Extracts 7 and 8 show the same phenomenon between female interactants. In Extract 7 Emma asks her friend Nancy about her love life:

Extract 7

```
001  Emm:  Y'got any(b) frie:nd boyfrie:nds? or anything
```

002   [goin:g [steady'r:]
003   Nan: [Oh::: [↓h*ell n]*o.↓

(NB:II:2)

Emma's turn is possibly complete after 'boyfriends' but she extends it (perhaps because this is a somewhat delicate question given that Nancy is a middle-aged woman whose husband has recently left her) to add 'or anything' – a recompleter which adds nothing substantive to the meaning of the turn but extends the turn constructional unit to a new possible transition relevant place. Her question, 'You got any boyfriends or anything' is a sentential turn constructional unit that is possibly complete grammatically – and so Nancy starts to speak, only to find herself in overlap with Emma who is continuing to add more to her turn. Again, this is not interruption.

In Extract 8, Vera is explaining to her friend Jenny why her grandchildren didn't want any lunch;

Extract 8

001   Ver: They mucked intuh biscuits.=They had (.) quite
002   a lotta biscuits ['n c h   [e e: : : s e,]
003   Jen: [Oh: well   [thaht's it th]en [ye[s,]
004   Ver: [.h [a:]nd
005   e-she said that's enough ↓fo:r them.
006   Jen: M-hm::. They're bonny ki:ds [I   mus'   say]
007   Ver: [They are: lovely ch]il:dren=
008   Jen: =[Yeh,]
009   Ver: =[are'n]'t they. Yes I wz pleasantly surpri::zed becuz
010   I'd heard about James bein' such a devil.

(Rahman: B:2:14)

The overlapping talk at lines 2/3 and at lines 6/7 are both instances of misprojection. In the first of these, Jenny – the incoming speaker – treats Vera's talk as possibly complete after 'biscuits' – not unreasonably, given that 'they had quite a lotta biscuits' is a complete sentence and that Vera's immediately prior unit ended with the word 'biscuits'. In the second instance, Vera – the incoming speaker – treats Jenny's sentence 'They're bonny kids' (an assessment of Vera's grandchildren) as possibly complete, and asserts her own assessment of them as 'lovely children', but finds herself in overlap with Jenny's 'optional' element ('I must say'). These are not, then, instances of interruption – in the sense that neither Jenny nor Vera is flagrantly violating turn-taking rules and starting up at non-transition relevance places.

In Extract 9 a male speaker, Jon, who works for a bookstore, is dealing with an enquiry from a female speaker, Lesley, about the arrangements for mailing her book:

Extract 9

```
007   Les:   Well you'll send me a bill will you:? [Or what. ]
008   Jon:                                         [Well: if y]ou
009          c'd send th'cheque first it'd be helpful,
```
(Holt 2.2.1)

Lesley's turn constructional unit is complete after 'Well you'll send me a bill will you'; more than that, it is a question, making relevant some answer from Jon. At exactly the moment Jon starts to answer, Lesley starts to speak again, adding an increment ('or what.') to her already completed prior turn. In this instance, if anyone can be held 'accountable' for the overlap it is surely not Jon, who is starting to speak after Lesley has completed a unit of talk requiring a response from him.

In Extract 10, the same phenomenon (an increment added to a turn that has already been brought to completion) results in overlapping talk, but this time it is a male speaker who adds the increment. Mark and Karen are students commiserating about essays ('papers') they have to write for their various classes:

Extract 10

```
003   Mark:   nI've got a paper t'write after
004           (0.7)
005   Mark:   'haftuh wait until Friday.
006           (·)
007           t'see the last films.
008           (0.8)
009   Kar:    Y' [d n ever know I had a] paper due Wednesday, wouldju.
010   Mark:      [in that film class.    ]
011           (·)
012   Mark:   N[(h)o] hhh
```
(SN4)

At line 5, Mark reports that he will 'have to wait until Friday' – a unit that sounds complete (it is grammatically and pragmatically complete, and also prosodically complete, with the falling intonational contour that routinely signals the end of a unit of talk). After a short silence in which Karen declines to comment, Mark adds an increment to the already completed turn ('to see the last films'), extending his previous turn with this additional element, which works to bring Mark's talk to a second completion and place of transition relevance. After a prolonged gap (eight tenths of a second is a long silence in conversation), Karen starts to speak, reporting her own predicament with regard to essay deadlines, but finds herself to have started almost exactly in overlap with Mark. What Mark does in line 10 is distinctive in that he is not starting a new sentence or other new unit of talk. Instead, he builds his talk as a continuation of the unit that had been in progress eight-tenths of a second before – the unit that had already been closed and following which a protracted silence had ensued. In claiming not to have completed his prior turn, Mark produces Karen as an interruptor – in the sense that she is speaking in the middle of and in overlap with his ongoing sentence (now displayed as 'Have to wait til Friday to see the last films in that film class'). Of course, from Karen's perspective, she heard that Mark was done and waited eight-tenths of a second before launching her own turn, thereby organising her own talk with reference to normative turn-taking practices. This, then, is an instance in which overlapping talk is the consequence of the behaviour of the purported 'victim' of the interruption.

It should be apparent from Extracts 1–10 that a great deal of overlapping talk is *not* interruptive. Here, by way of contrast, are some of the – rare – instances in the data set at my disposal where speakers launch their turns at places that are *not* possibly transition relevant. In the first of these, Extract 11 below, the man (Hal) not only interrupts, but also labels his actions as 'interrupting you' (line 10). The speakers are negotiating how Lesley is to pay Hal for the tickets for the dance he has organised in the village hall, and that she and her husband plan to attend. It turns out she has some difficulty in arranging to see Hal to give him the money since she and her husband are currently entertaining foreign visitors. As this Extract opens, Lesley is accounting for her difficulty in getting the money to Hal:

Extract 11

```
001  Les:   ...it's just c'z these Italian: fellows come
002         ovah .hh [h an'
003  Hal:            [Oh ee Have th:ey.=
004  Les:   =iYe[:s
005  Hal:      [Yeh
006  Les:   hhh And so that's why we're [a bit-
007  Hal:                               [(But)-
008         (0.3)
009  Les:   .hh
010  Hal:   Ah- (0.2) Oh interruptin' you I wz gnna say
011         you could leave it.
```
                                              (Holt:SO88(II):1:3)

At line 7 Hal launches his turn at a place where Lesley's turn cannot possibly be complete. The turn-so-far is not grammatically complete, nor is it hearably intonationally complete, nor does it perform a recognisable action. On the basis of all three criteria, then, this is an interruption, and there is evidence that both Lesley and Hal hear it that way. Lesley (line 6) cuts off what she is saying, leaving her unit incomplete. Hal also cuts off his interruptive turn (line 7) and both wait for the other to continue (line 8) until Hal, labelling his action *as* 'interrupting you' (line 10) offers Lesley the opportunity to delay her payment to him. Although his turn is, then, interruptive, in the sense of not having been launched at a transition relevant place, it is not hostile or aggressive. On the contrary, Hal is cutting off Lesley's account for why she would find it difficult to pay him right away by claiming that there is no need for her to do so. The practice of interruption is here deployed to make an offer that will make Lesley's life easier: the interruption is doing something co-operative and affiliative, and from Lesley's point of view is surely a helpful interruption. This is overwhelmingly the case of interruptions in my corpora. Here are some more examples.

Extract 12 is taken from the call between the separated/divorced couple we met in Extract 5, Tony and Marsha, who here are continuing to talk about their son's problems in travelling on a standby flight from Marsha's home back to Tony's. Here again Tony's talk is launched in overlap with Marsha's but (unlike Extract 5), in this instance he launches it at a place where Marsha's turn cannot possibly be complete (after 'oh maybe he g-'):

Extract 12

```
001  Mar:  What time did'e get on the pla:ne.
002  Ton:  Uh::: (0.2) I: don't know exactly I think ih wz
003        arou:nd three uh'clock er something a'that sort.
004        (0.2)
005  Mar:  Oh: maybe he g    [ot s'm-
006  Ton:                    [He took it et fou:r. Gerda says.
                                              (MDE:60:1:3:1–2)
```

This interruption is also co-operative. In response to Marsha's enquiry about when their son boarded a plane, Tony reports not being sure and then gives an approximate answer ('around three o'clock or something of that sort'). At line 5 Marsha is apparently using this report as the basis for some speculation about what may have happened and it is this speculation, based on his (as it turns out erroneous) report, that Tony interrupts. Tony's new partner, Gerda, who has overheard his report of Joey's departure time, has apparently corrected him and he is relaying this correction ('four o'clock') to Marsha before she can develop a theory about Joey's flight based on incorrect information. The interruption is here used to implement a correction that has consequences for the turn Marsha is in the course of producing; it is thus clearly a co-operative action, and from Marsha's point of view, a helpful interruption.

Extract 13 also involves a man (Earl) interrupting a woman (Emma) in order to implement a co-operative action. Emma has phoned to speak to her friend Lottie, but it is Lottie's husband who has answered and it is apparent to her – as she later says – that the couple she is phoning 'have company' (i.e., people visiting them, presumably audible to her in the background, although the recording has not captured this). When Earl offers to call his wife to the phone ('you want to talk to Lottie?', line 2), Emma – who clearly *does* want to talk to Lottie (as it turns out she has exciting news to tell about events in her street) – demurs. After a short silence (line 3) and turn-initial delay (the 'uh' in line 4) she confirms that she did want to talk to Lottie but immediately follows this with a display of her realisation that Lottie is 'busy' (i.e., occupied with their guests) and launches a counter-offer – she'll call back later (line 4). This is the turn that is interrupted by Earl, and she doesn't complete it.

Extract 13

```
001  Emm:   How'r you:.
002  Ear:   Fine'ow'r you Emma yih wan'talk tih Lottie
003         (0.2)
004  Emm:   Uh ya:h WELL ↑LI [:STEN sh]e's busy I'll [call'e r  ]
005  Ear:                    [ He:re.  ]              [No: she]'s
006         right he:re waitaminit.
007         (0.3)
008  Ear:   Wayamin' hol' it.
009         (1.0)
010         ((receiver down))
011         (5.0)
012         ((receiver up))
013  Lot:   Ye:ah.
```

(NBIV:12)

Earl first overlaps Emma after she has confirmed that she wants to talk to Lottie and then, with 'WELL', indicates that she recognises there may be some problem with this. Earl's 'here' (line 5) is a first move to hand the phone over to his wife. Finding himself in overlap he waits until after Emma's next unit (until after 'Well listen she's busy') and then (with 'No', line 5) rejects the possibility it invokes that Lottie is not available to speak to Emma, finding himself again in overlap with Emma's offer to call back later. She abandons her unit (after 'I'll call her' where presumably what was projectable was something like 'I'll call her back later/tomorrow/some other time') and he persists with his unit, countering her 'she's busy' with his 'she's right here' and directing her to 'wait a minute' (lines 6 and 8) and to 'hold it' (line 8). Seven seconds later, Lottie speaks. These two women get to talk to each other in this call in part because a man interrupted one of them who was proposing to abandon the current attempt at conversation. From Emma's point of view, this interruption was implementing a helpful action.

In all three examples of interruption displayed thus far (Extracts 11, 12 and 13), the interruption is of a woman by a man but is done in order to implement some co-operative action – solving the interrupted speaker's difficulty (about when to pay for the dance tickets), making a correction relevant to the speculations of the interrupted speaker (about Joey's departure time), and fulfilling the interrupted speaker's wishes (to speak to friend). Interruptions are not always or definitionally co-operative – but in the corpora at my disposal there are very few unequivocally interruptive turns, and those that exist are overwhelmingly co-operative. It is also clear that women interrupt other women in this way, and also that women interrupt men. I will show one instance of each.

In Extract 14 one woman (Emma) interrupts another (Nancy): these are the Emma and Nancy we met in Extract 7 in which Nancy – a divorced/separated middle-aged woman – responded to Emma's question about whether she had any boyfriends with a dismissive 'oh hell no'. Extract 14 is a subsequent call from the same corpus – and there has been a significant development in Nancy's love life: she has met a 'real sweet guy' (line 13). Emma acknowledges and receipts the news with an enthusiastic 'wonderful' (line 14), following which Nancy continues to tell about the occasion of the meeting ('So we were sitting in'). This is the turn that Emma interrupts, loudly and emphatically, at a point where Nancy cannot be possibly done (after 'so we were' which projects, at least a verb to come, and – in this context – a more extended telling altogether).

Extract 14

```
013   Nan:   =He's jist a ri:l sweet GU *:y..h.t [.hhhhh
014   Emm:                                    [ WONder f*ul.
015   Nan:   So: we w'r [s*itting in]
016   Emm:              [YER LIFE]is CHANG [ing
017   Nan:                                 [EEYE::A:H
018          (0.2)
```
(NB:II:4:16)

Emma's interruption at line 16 is co-operative and affiliative in that it builds on her previous assessment of Nancy's good fortune and celebrates this.

Finally, women interrupt men, as is displayed in Extract 15, in which a male caller (Keith), who has called to speak to Lesley's daughter Katherine, is informed by Lesley that Katherine is not available (lines 2–3), receipts this information with an 'ah' (line 4) and, after a gap (line 5), starts a new turn of which only 'What' (presumably heading for 'what time will she be in') is produced before Lesley launches her interruptive talk. In this instance, unlike those we have examined so far, neither speaker drops out of overlap: both persist, despite the other's talk, to complete another unit of talk.

Extract 15

```
001   Kei:   This's Keith. C'n I speak to Kathrine plea [se.
002   Les:                                             [Oh Keith
003          she's not in at the moment.
004   Kei:   Ah.
005          (0.9)
006   Kei:   What- (.)   [D'y'know wh't time she ['ll be in.]
007   Les:               [Do you wan't'give me a  [m es s A]GE,
```
                                                            (Holt:1:4)

Starting at a place where Keith cannot be possibly complete, and persisting in overlap with him, Lesley is making an offer to convey a message to her daughter. Again, interruption is launched in the service of a co-operative action.

To sum up my findings in bringing a conversation analytic approach to bear on instances of overlapping talk in my own data corpora, then, it is apparent that instances of overlapping talk in either cross-sex or within-sex conversation are usually not 'interruptions', that is, most instances of overlap result from one person starting up at a transition relevant place – where it turns out that the first speaker did not mean to be finished. In some such instances, as we have seen, the first speaker had given every indication of having brought their unit of talk to possible completion: it was a syntactically complete unit, brought to intonational 'closing' completion, and performed a complete recognisable action in its sequential context. Overlap resulted when, testifying to this analysis of the prior talk as complete, the next speaker started up and found him/herself in overlap with the prior speaker who was adding an increment to their prior talk.

Although Murray (1988, 1985) constructs an argument that is highly critical of and oppositional to what he understands by 'conversation analysis', in fact conversation analysis is the method *par excellence* for providing concrete evidence of many of his own claims, including, for example, his contention that 'counting frequencies of simultaneous speech does not bear on whether women or men interrupt women or men more' (Murray, 1988: 115). Using conversation analysis, it is apparent that the two methods most commonly used by gender researchers in measuring interruption – counting instances of overlap as interruption if they fulfil some 'objective' criteria such as 'two or more syllables away from the end of a unit', and asking students (as 'cultural experts') to decide whether or not they count as overlaps (see Okamoto, Rashotte and Smith-Lovin 2002) – both seriously fail to capture the interactional import of overlapping talk. Finally, I showed that even turns at talk launched at *non*-transition relevance places are often affiliative and co-operative. Interruption is not always – or, in my data, very often – an act of domination or a bid for power. My data do not bear out the contention that 'interruptions are a critical measure of conversational dominance' (Kollock, Blumstein and Schwartz, 1985: 43).

What can conversation analysis offer research on gender and language?

This chapter has taken a topic of concern to many gender and language researchers – interruption – and begun to explore it from a conversation analytic perspective. I have not attempted to provide a comprehensive overview of all instances of overlap or interruption in my datasets, nor to quantify my findings (that would be a much bigger enterprise than can be attempted here), but to illustrate some of the ways in which research on interruption is complicated and enriched by conversation analysis.

My findings may be disappointing to those who hoped for a method that would finally and unequivocally establish interruption as one of men's methods for establishing power. On the basis of the evidence of my data, I don't think that's true: rather, it seems that 'the turn-taking rules themselves operate in terms of locally constructed discourse statuses rather than, for example, position in a social hierarchy' (Schegloff, 1992, 1987). Male power (as well as heterosexual power, white power, etc.) is certainly done through talk, and, if not primarily through interruption, then just *how* remains a worthy research topic. Focusing on the details of talk-in-interaction when interruption *is* what's being done, and being done to claim power, may also enable us to understand *how* power is being produced moment by moment in the course of interaction. Rather than simply counting how many times women (or men) are interrupted, we can begin to understand how interrupting is achieved and resisted in the course of real time power struggles as to who is to have the floor – as competing speakers raise their voices, hold firm despite another's bid to talk, or drop out (see Schegloff, 1987: 216).

Gender and language research has focused on a number of other features of talk traditionally seen as displaying gender differences (e.g., tag questions, topic proffers, 'back-channelling'), to all of which conversation analysis could be applied for a more nuanced and accurate understanding of their interactional import. There is, of course, the 'risk' that this kind of detailed analysis will *not* provide evidence of clear gender differences – in which case I think we will have learnt that these concepts, or the operational definitions that underpin them, are insufficient to capture how gender and power and oppression are done in talk.

Since Lakoff's (1975) pioneering suggestions – based largely on her own intuitions – about gendered speech differences, a large body of empirical research has been produced comparing men's and women's speech across variables: overall amount of speech produced, use of diminutives, civilities and polite forms, expletives, hesitations, repetitions, self-corrections, 'you know', tag questions, interruptions and so on – all variably (and inconsistently) applied across studies. Increasingly researchers have concluded that this is not a productive research focus and, like Freed and Greenwood, 'object to conclusions about speakers' general communicative style (or specific phonological characteristics) which are based on the examination of single linguistic variables, isolated from their full conversational and communicative contexts' (1996: 2).

Meanwhile, in the field of conversation analysis, researchers have developed sophisticated and detailed analyses relevant to all these purportedly gendered speech practices – analyses which set them firmly in their interactional contexts. For example, conversation analysts have explored how people set out to build long turns, how recipients of those turns display a willingness to listen to them (or not) and how speakers deal with the competition or heckling they may face in making demands for protracted turns (e.g., Schegloff, 2006). They have also explored the co-operative use of overlapping talk and co-operative entry into another's turn (Lerner, 2000, 1996); the different interactional uses of repetition in talk (e.g., Stivers, 2005; Schegloff, 1996b); the uses of tag questions (Heritage and Raymond, 2005) and repair and error correction (Schegloff, Jefferson, G. and Sacks, 1977). There is currently virtually no research that brings these key discoveries of conversation analysis to bear on the classic sociolinguistic questions of gender difference.

Moreover, if researchers in the field of gender and language research were to use conversation analytic methods in analysing naturalistic conversation, it is likely that the questions asked would quickly move beyond the preoccupation with *difference* to an exploration of how gender – or sexuality, or power, or oppression – is *produced and reproduced* in interaction (see Kitzinger, 2007, 2006a,b). What conversation analysis offers is a powerful, systematic and contextually sensitive analytic method grounded in co-interactants' *own* practices and actions. The mechanical (mis)application of the conversation analytic model of turn-taking, shorn of its connection to sequential and action analysis in the interests of quantifying gender differences, is unlikely to prove fruitful. The skilful application of conversation analysis – drawing on the full range of discoveries, including not only turn-taking but sequence organisation, repair, story-telling, word selection and so on – may enable us to better understand where and how gender is oriented to and achieved in talk.

Notes

1 I am grateful to Gail Jefferson and Emanuel Schegloff who had previously transcribed the data extracts used here. I used their transcripts as a basis for my own hearings of the audio data.

Transcription Key

[ ]	square brackets	overlapping talk
=	equals sign	no space between turns
(0.5)	time in round brackets	intervals within or between talk (measured in tenths of a second)
(.)	period in round brackets	discernable pause or gap, too short to measure
:::	colons	extension of preceding sound (the more colons, the greater the extension)
.	period	closing intonation (not necessarily the end of a sentence)
,	comma	continuing intonation (not necessarily between clauses of sentences)
?	question mark	rising intonation (not necessarily a question)
¿	inverted question mark	rising intonation weaker than that indicated by a question mark
!	exclamation mark	animated tone (not necessarily an exclamation)
-	dash	abrupt cut off of sound
here	underlining	emphasis
HERE	capitals	loud, relative to surrounding talk
HERE	underlining and capitals	very loud and emphatic, relative to surrounding talk
°here°	degree signs	soft, relative to surrounding talk
°°here°°	double degree signs	very soft, or whispered, relative to surrounding talk
>here<	'more than'/'less than' symbols	speeded up, relative to surrounding talk
<here>	'less than'/'more than' symbols	slowed down, relative to surrounding talk
<	'less than' symbol	rapid start to following talk
>	'greater than' symbol	slow ending to preceding talk
$	dollar sign	smile voice
hah		laughter
heh		laughter
hih		laughter
huh		laughter
(h)		laughter particle inserted into talk
hhh		audible outbreath (no. of 'h's indicates length)

.hhh		audible inbreath (no. of 'h's indicates length)
( )	empty round brackets	transcriber unable to hear words
(bring)	word(s) in round brackets	transcriber uncertain of hearing
((sniff))	word(s) in double round brackets	sounds or other material hard to transcribe; other comments by subscriber

10
Categories, Actions and Sequences: Formulating Gender in Talk-in-Interaction

Elizabeth Stokoe

Introduction

This chapter sets out a conversation analytic approach to the study of language and gender, and demonstrates how the topic of 'gender' can be studied empirically via its categorial reference in talk-in-interaction. I start with a short history of my location in the field, particularly in terms of my promotion of a shift from sociolinguistic studies of 'gender difference' to conversation and membership categorisation analytic studies of 'gender relevance' (Stokoe, 1998). I will then argue that, and show how, 'categorical' phenomena such as 'gender' can be studied as phenomena of sequential organisation using conversation analysis. I suggest that the analysis of members' categories in their sequential environment allows language and gender researchers to see how everyday notions of gender are taken up, reformulated, repaired or resisted, in turns of talk that accomplish conversational action; that is, how categories 'might be relevant for the doing of some activity' (Sacks, 1992, vol. 1: 597). The chapter concludes with a brief discussion of the theoretical upshot of analysing 'gender' from an ethnomethodological/ conversation analytic perspective, and what this means for debates and concerns about the 'reality' of gender.

From gender difference to gender relevance

I started out in the language and gender field during the early 1990s as a psychology PhD student. My topic was 'gender differences in university tutorial talk', and I was reading constructivist studies of cognitive development and interaction in school classrooms (e.g., Vygotsky, 1978; see also Norman, 1992). A basic premise of this work was that talking in small peer groups facilitates learning. However, a parallel literature was claiming to find that 'access' to this valuable resource of talk was unequal and, in particular, that because boys dominate mixed-sex group work, girls were not getting their fair share (e.g., Holden, 1993).

My initial interest, then, was in whether such a pattern would also be found in post-compulsory education settings (Stokoe, 1995). The limited evidence indeed suggested that, like boys in classrooms, adult male students dominated classroom proceedings, by, for example, taking more, and longer, turns at talk than female students (e.g., Kelly, 1991). However, analyses of my own data were throwing up problems. I had video-recorded 30 hours of small-group interactions in university tutorials, but was not finding evidence for women 'losing out' to men either in terms of the things that 'dominance' theorists had studied (e.g., number of turns, turn length, interruptions, unilateral topic shifts) or in terms of sociolinguistic features of talk (e.g., differential use of hedges, tag questions, 'collaborative' and 'competitive' features of talk) (for overviews, see Coates, 2004; James and Clarke, 1993; James and Drakich, 1993; and see Kitzinger, this volume, for a conversation analytic critique of interruption studies). I began to rethink the 'gender differences' agenda, with its imposition of 'gender' onto data that did not appear to be 'gendered' either in a quantifiable way or from the perspective of the participants themselves (Stokoe, 1997). At the same time, things were moving in the gender and language field. Many commentators were critical of so-called 'essentialising' studies of gender difference; instead arguing that gender should be studied as a 'social construction': an enactment, performance and product of discourse (e.g., Crawford, 1995).

However, the fact that I was not finding traditional 'male-female interaction' patterns did not mean that there was nothing interesting to be found in my corpus with regards to gender. Consider the extract below, which comes from a tutorial with graduate teacher-training students. The group has been discussing strategies for teaching pupils to write, but they have drifted off the topic and are discussing *a cappella* singing:

Extract 1

```
001  S:   No.=what's it called?
002            (1.0)
003  S:   Archipelago?
004            (0.2)
005  S:   >You know< where they sing in:: har:monies.
006            (1.4)
007  D:   ((shaking head)) Pa:ss.
008  P:   (I dunno)
009  J:   [((nodding head to P))
010  S:   [Archipelago.
011            (0.7)
012  D:   It's a choir
```

```
013              (0.5)
014   S:   Hhmm?
015   D:   Choir.
016              (0.5)
017   S:   .hhh n:o it's where you all start singin.=we used
018        to do that in De:von.
019              (0.5)
```

Pat

Dina

Joan

Sam produces 'f:our gi:rls'

```
020   S:  →Brilliant (1-) but I saw f:our gi:rls (0.4)
```

Sam looks away from other students on 'at um::'

```
021        →at um::
022              (0.2)
```

Sam rolls his eyes up on 'four wo:men'

```
023   S:   four wo:men (0.7) at um:: (1.0) >Por'obello Road
```

```
024        market.<
025            (0.7)
026   S:   They were incre::(h)dible.
027            (1.1)
```

Sam picks up his papers and gets up from his chair on 'S::tunning.'

```
028   S:   S::tunning.
```

(#1 UT-25[1])

My interest was in Sam's description of singers he saw at Portobello Road market in London (lines 23–28), which follows a discussion of candidate terms for 'a capella' singing ('archipelago?', 'choir'). Sam's first formulation is that he 'saw f:our gi:rls'. This is followed by a pause before he continues with the location part of his description: '(0.4) at um::'. He stops and reformulates his description as '(0.2) four wo:men'. He then returns to his description of the singers' location, recycling the words 'at um::' before eventually providing '>Por'obello Road market.<'.

This sequence provides an example of what conversation analysts call a 'self-initiated self repair' (on CA see Kitzinger, this volume; on the gender relevance of repaired person references see Stokoe, in press). Sam orients to the first category ('gi:rls') with his same-turn replacement category ('wo:men'), treating his word selection as the repairable item. Note also his embodied performance of the replacement repair, and the way his gestures, gaze and prosody work in aggregate with the talk to project trouble, orient to its source, and repair it. So, on 'f:our gi:rls', Sam's gaze is directed into the group towards his interlocutors (line 20). However, during the 0.4-second pause he begins to look away from his recipients, and is looking to his right as he says 'at um::' (line 21). As he produces the repair 'four wo:men', he swivels his eyes upwards in an exaggerated manner, explicitly orienting to his use of the first, problematic term 'gi:rls'. The other group members do not topicalise Sam's description or his subsequent assessments of the singers (lines 26, 28), and the sequence ends with Sam collecting some papers off the table before getting up from his chair and moving away from the group.

This switch between categories is one way 'into' studying how speakers orient to gender, produce it as a solid feature of the world, and invoke it as part of conversational action. We might go on to speculate that Sam's switch from 'girls' to 'women' is a recipient-designed management of his own identity. The category 'girls' belongs to a collection that includes 'women', 'ladies', 'females' and so on, and these are all partitions of the collection 'sex' (the other major partition being 'male') (Sacks, 1992, vol. 1: 590–1). As the transcript shows, Sam is the only 'male' in the group; his recipients are members of the other category in that collection. By orienting to, repairing and, crucially, *upgrading* his formulation of the singers from 'girls' to 'women', Sam pre-empts possible objections to his use of 'girls' in the context of this particular group and its gender composition (see also Edwards's (1998) discussion of the function of a husband's *downgraded* repair from 'woman' to 'girl' during marriage guidance counselling).

Here is another brief example, taken from an American telephone conversation between two friends.

Extract 2

```
001   Bee:   nYeeah, .hh This feller I have-(nn)/(iv-)'felluh'; this
002          ma:n. (0.2) t! 'hhh He ha::(s)- uff-eh-who-who I
003          have fer Linguistics [ is r e a l ]ly too much, 'hh  [ h=     ]
004   Ava:                        [Mm hm?]                        [Mm[hm,]
                                                                 (#2 TG, 6: 01–08)
```

This fragment provides another example of a replacement repair, also occurring in the midst of narrative description. Bee is launching a story about her linguistics tutor, and her turn includes several repair initiators and reformulations of the person being described. Her delivery of 'felluh' in a 'quotation voice' tells us what is to be repaired in her prior formulation 'This feller I have-', and 'ma:n.' is the replacement category.

These brief analytic snapshots demonstrate how the links between gender and language can be studied in a different way from identifying sociolinguistic and interactional features of talk and rushing to explain them in terms of gender-as-variable. As LeBaron argues:

> we should not ... say 'oh, look, here's a man and a woman talking; ... oh, we can make these conclusions about gendered communication'. But rather we should say, 'gender only becomes an issue when the participants themselves make it one and we can point to different things about that'.
> (1998; quoted in Tracy, 1998: 15)

This approach characterises the conversation analytic tradition of Sacks, Schegloff and Jefferson, a key feature of which is that any analysis of social categories like 'gender' is based in what participants do and say, rather in what analysts take to be relevant as a function of their hypotheses, research questions, politics or theory. One problem with studies that map sociolinguistic and interactional variables onto gender, and presume that gender explains their differential use, is that categories are not studied 'in the activities in which they're employed' (Sacks, 1992: 27). This means that analysts are in the business of *reproducing* rather than *studying* gendered 'facts' about the world, thereby reifying gender stereotypes and hierarchies. In contrast, the analytic task of CA is 'to analyze the workings of those categories, not to merely use them as they are used in the world' (Jefferson, 2004: 118). As Pels points out, it is in 'the routine conduct of everyday life we tend to *consider social facts as things* and behave towards them as such' (2000: 72).

From this perspective, then, in order to warrant an analytic claim that a particular category is relevant to any stretch of interaction, the analyst must be able to demonstrate that such identities are linked to specific actions. There are two key issues here for conversation analysts:

1. *The problem of relevance.* Given the indefinitely extendable number of ways any person may be categorised, which from a range of potential identities is relevant? The answer is to go by what is demonstrably relevant to participants 'at the moment that whatever we are trying to produce an account for occurs' (Schegloff, 1991: 50).
2. *The issue of procedural consequentiality.* If we can establish that a particular identity category is relevant, can we see that it is consequential for participants, in terms of its trajectory, content, character, or organisational procedures? Does it have 'determinate consequences for the talk?' (Heritage, 2005a: 111).

Returning to our two brief examples, we can see that the *problem of gender relevance* is solved by speakers' orientations to their category choices via the practices of repair and reformulation. However, it is less clear that, say, S's repair of 'girls' to 'women' has 'determinate consequences for the talk' – the other participants do not respond to it and S ends the sequence by walking away from the group.

However, consider another extract from my PhD data, in which four first-year psychology students are carrying out a collaborative writing activity. They have to produce descriptions of people in a series of photographs in a session on social cognition:

Extract 3

```
001   N:   D'you reckon she's an instructor then.
002             (0.2)
003   N:   Of some sort,
```

```
004  B:   →  Is somebody scribing. who's writin' it.=
005  N:      =Oh yhe:ah.
006             (0.8)
007  M:      Well you can't  [ r e a d m y]=
008  N:                      [She wants to do it.     ]
```

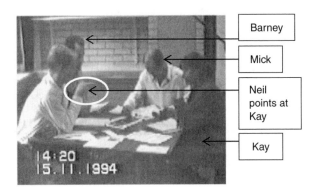

```
Barney
Mick
Neil points at Kay
Kay
```

```
009  M:      =writin' once I've [ wri:tten it.]
010  K:                         [.hehhhh     ]
011  N:   →  We:ll secretary an' female.
012             (0.3)
013  K:      .Hh heh heh heh
```

```
Kay picks up paper and pen
```

```
014             (0.4)
015  M:      It's uh::,
016  K:      Yeah: I'm wearing glasses I must be the secretary.=
```

017   B: =I think- (.) we're all agreed she's physical.
018   (0.2)
[...]
027   M: <u>M</u>ake a good start.
028   K: Heh heh heh .hhh (.) .hhh Okay what's her name.

Kay picks
up paper
and pen

029   (0.5)
[...]
104   K: Am I <u>wri</u>:ting (then.)
105   N: Yes: go on.
[...]
123   (0.3)
124   M: <<u>A</u>re you getting all this down.=Come on.
125   (1.6)
126   N: You've gotta learn this short hand before you get into
127   the- (0.4) the job market.
128   (0.7)

                                                        (#3 UT-23)

In order to meet the task demands, one member of the group must write down their ideas. Barney's question at the start of the sequence in Extract 3, 'is somebody scribing.' is taken up after a reformulation: 'who's writin' it.'. Note that, through a variety of strategies, members of the group manage their responses such that they do not have to take on the role of scribe. At line 5, Neil's 'Oh yeah:.' treats Barney's turn as news to him, and a proposal to be agreed with, rather than a request for action, and his subsequent nomination of Kay directs the role away from himself. M offers an account of why he cannot act as scribe: 'you can't read my writin'' (lines 6–8). By taking the opening turn and issuing the first pair part of an adjacency pair, Barney positions himself as someone requiring an answer or offer about who will 'scribe' rather than as someone who will take up the role. At line 8, Neil nominates Kay, his pointing gesture working in aggregate with the talk ('She wants to do it.') to accomplish the action, whilst also attributing agency to Kay for taking up the role. Her response at line 10, which overlaps with Mick's account, is to laugh rather than align with his suggestion. At line 11, Neil nominates Kay a second time, suggesting 'We:ll secretary an' female.', offering the category 'secretary' as a replacement for 'scribe', and juxtaposing 'female' with 'secretary'. Neil's second nomination accounts for the prior one, and its formulation displays his reasoning that coupling 'occupational' and 'gender' categories is commonsensically recognisable. A gloss might be, 'secretaries *in general* are female, you're female, so *you in particular* are our secretary'. Neil's turn achieves two things: it provides for a categorical identity for the person who will write for the group, and renders him (and the other group members) excluded from possible incumbency in that position.

Kay responds to Neil's second nomination by picking up her paper and pen, aligning herself with the role and carrying out its preliminary activities. However, she does not join in with his formulation of 'secretary' as 'female'. Instead, she produces a different characterological imputation for 'secretary': 'Yeah: I'm wearing glasses I must be the secretary' (line 16). This may demonstrate resistance to Neil's categorical references. Alternatively, it may offer further category-bound reasons for Kay to occupy the role. Following a prompt from Mick, 'Make a good start.' (line 27), she begins to write. The students return to the issue of her role on several occasions. At line 104, Kay asks 'am I wri:ting (then.)', and Neil confirms, 'Yes: go on.'. At lines 124–127, Mick and Neil further remind Kay of her role *as secretary* (rather than as 'student'), 'Are you getting all this down. =Come on.', 'gotta learn this short hand before you get into the- (0.4) the job market.' (see Stokoe, 2006, for further analysis of this extract).

What is clear from this sequence is not 'just' that gender categories crop up in interaction, and that we can point to instances of this happening, but that people *do things* with them. We can see how the

> participants' production of the world was itself informed by ... particular categorisation devices ... that the parties were oriented to that categorisation device in producing and understanding – moment-by-moment – the conduct that composed its progressive realisation.
>
> (Schegloff, 2007: 475)

However, I want to move on to discuss some potential objections to a category-based starting point for language and gender analysis – as well as some solutions and illustrations thereof.

Conversation analysis and categories: some methodological considerations

Readers familiar with conversation analysis (CA) will know that it is concerned with phenomena like sequence organisation and the shape, building blocks, prosodic features and action orientation of turns (see also Kitzinger, this volume). Categories, on the other hand, are a different, non-structural order of phenomenon, and are not obviously tied to, for example, a particular 'adjacency pair' (e.g., question-answer). Whereas the action of 'answer' normatively follows that of 'question', the lexical content of the turns that deliver these actions is less predictable. It is clear, then, that analysts interested in category-type topics such as 'gender' or 'ethnicity' cannot avoid studying them *as* categories (or 'person references', 'word selection', etc.), integrated into an analysis of the sequence-organisational structures of conversation. For this reason, I have argued for some time that Sacks's work on membership categories, and subsequent work on 'membership categorisation analysis' (MCA), is an obvious place for language and gender researchers to start (e.g., Stokoe, 1998; 2004).

Despite their shared origins in Sacks's (1992) lectures, CA and MCA have since developed along somewhat different paths. Schegloff (2007: 476) is critical of what he sees as MCA's engagement with 'promiscuous' analytic practices by importing and imposing the 'commonsense' knowledge needed 'for the argument-in-progress'. This kind of criticism has meant that, over the years, there has been little cross-fertilisation between Schegloffian CA, and MCA. It is interesting, then, that there has recently been something of a resurgence of interest in categories and person reference within CA (e.g., Enfield and Stivers, 2007; Raymond and Heritage, 2006; Kitzinger, 2005a). As Schegloff (2005: 450) writes, 'after a relatively quiet period during which attention has been focussed on other aspects of the organisation of interaction, efforts are underway to take up again issues of categorisation'. Schegloff's 'quiet period' refers to the work of conversation analysts preoccupied with turn and sequence organisation. Nevertheless, there has been plenty of ethnomethodological/CA work in that same period on 'categories', and 'categories in sequences' in general (e.g., Psathas, 1999; Antaki and Widdicombe, 1998; Hester and Eglin, 1997; Baker, 1984; Jayyusi, 1984; Watson, 1983), and on gender and sexuality in particular (Evaldsson, 2004; Stokoe, 2003; Eglin and Hester, 1999; Edwards, 1998; Nilan, 1994; Wowk, 1984).

Politics aside, the study of 'categories' remains a tricky issue. Because of the kind of phenomena they are, it is unlikely that we can predict *when* categories will crop up in interaction, and, as Pomerantz and Mandelbaum (2005) point out, it is also unlikely that when a category *is* used, it will be an instance of the same interactional phenomenon, or doing the same kind of action. Pomerantz and Mandelbaum therefore claim that 'because we cannot know in advance when a person will explicitly invoke a ... category, there is no way to plan data collection of them' (ibid.: 154). They propose two solutions to this. The first, demonstrated in their work on 'relationship categories', is to study members' *explicit uses of categories* found in existing data corpora. For example, Extract 4 comes from my own corpus of friends' talk, here chatting as they prepare for a night out:

Extract 4

```
001              (9.0)
002    S:   >I COUld've gone< spa::re when we was out that Saturday
003          though.=I could've gone spare. (.) when he,- (.) you
004          reme:mber when he jus' kinda like wa:lked pa:st.
005              (0.8)
006    S:   An' said hi: an:: jus' walked off.
007              (1.2)
008    C:   Y [eh.            ]
009    S:      [YOU KNOW] how say like you see people y[ou know]=
010    C:                                               [What on]=
011    S:   =[  but      ] aren't really friends with,
012    C:   =[Saturday? ]
013              (0.2)
014    S:   When we was in Extras.
015    C:   Ye:ah,
016    S:   An' y'know how sometimes y'see frie::nds,
017              (0.6)
018    C:   Oh:[:  ye::ah        ]
019    S:      [Like people  y']  not friends ↓with  [but you jus' go ]=
020    C:                                            [You jus' go you ]=
021    S:   =[up,       ]
022    C:   =[all right.]
023    S:   Yeh an' walk off.
024              (0.2)
025    S:   ↑HE did ↑↑THAT to me! I thought that is so fuckin'
026          ru:de,
027              (0.3)
028    C:   That is ru:de.
```

(#4 VH-1)

Sophie is recounting an incident in which she displays an understanding of the kinds of activities that are category-bound to 'friend'. She does this by contrasting the appropriate activities of 'friends' with the actions of one of her (unnamed) friends, as part of a complaint about him. Her complaint therefore turns on what 'friends' should and should not do when they meet each other. Her descriptions of this man's activities include that he 'jus' kinda like <u>wa:</u>lked pa:st' (line 4), and 'said <u>hi</u>: an:: jus' walked off.' (line 6). As Sacks (1992) shows, it is the fact that activities are category-bound that allows us to praise or complain about 'absent' activities. Sophie spells this out, by reasoning that while these kinds of activities may be appropriate for people that you 'aren't really <u>friends</u> with' (line 11), for this man to do it is 'fuckin <u>ru</u>:de,' (lines 25–26). Chloe ratifies this assessment with a second, 'That <u>is</u> ru:de.' Note that Chloe's second assessment is formulated as objective and independent from Sophie's 'subjective' one ('I thought …') – she is effectively as able as Sophie to assert what can be expected of a 'friend'. Thus the participants' complaint displays a shared understanding of the rights and obligations that are expectable of incumbents of the category 'friends' *in general*, and not just of this 'man' in particular (Benwell and Stokoe, 2006).

Pomerantz and Mandelbaum's second solution to the problem of researching 'categories' is to analyse conversations between 'incumbents of complementary pairs of relationship categories', showing how, for example, 'incumbents of the category of friend not only regularly greet each other and regularly update each other as to events in their lives; they also are accountable, and are called to task, for failing to perform these activities' (2005: 154). So, in the above sequence, Sophie and Chloe's display of shared knowledge and ratified assessments with regards to their complaint simultaneously functions to establish and maintain their own incumbency in the relational pair 'friend-friend' – *they are doing the things that 'friends' do.* However, this second solution is problematic for CA, in CA's own terms. While Pomerantz and Mandelbaum take care to point out that 'analysts should not assume that the conversational actions that incumbents of complementary relationship categories are necessarily associated with the relationship categories identified by the analyst', and that 'the burden is on the analyst to demonstrate an association between the activities, the relationship categories to which the participants *seem* oriented' (2005: 155, my emphasis), there is a danger of returning to explanations based in what the analyst 'knows' about a speaker's category memberships. For example, it is not clear how activities such as updating each other on life events is any more tied to 'friends' than to 'sisters', 'partners' or 'mothers'. And, of course, another complementary relationship category pair is 'male-female' – which takes us back to where we started!

In contrast to Pomerantz and Mandelbaum, I want to argue that it is possible to collect data in which the same categories routinely crop up. For example, in current work on neighbour complaints and disputes,[2] I have a large corpus of telephone calls to neighbour mediation centres and environmental health services, many of which include the category 'neighbour' in the caller's first substantive turn. The regular occurrence of a particular category allows for a systematic analysis of the work it is doing, as well as what happens in deviant cases. In the next section of the chapter, I demonstrate that and how the same *gender* categories crop up in the same interactional environment – a subset of the 'neighbour dispute' corpus comprising 150 police-suspect interrogations.

Doing denials with gender categories

Consider the following extract, in which a suspect (S) is being interviewed by police officers (P) following being arrested for beating up his male and female neighbours (who are partners). The suspect's account is that his neighbours have been taking photographs of him while he sits naked in his living room at night with the curtains open.

Extract 5

```
001  P1:  D'you remember kickin' 'e:r.=
002  S:   =No. Not 'er.
003            (0.8)
004  S:   I do the ma:n but not 'er: no.
005            (1.7)
006  P1:  .pt So you've not kicked her at all.
007            (0.9)
008  S:   °No.°
009            (2.2)
010  S:   Swung 'er about kept 'er off me that's all.
011            (2.4)
012  P1:  D'you remember 'er falling down to the gro:und.
013  S:   .hhhhhhhh
014            (0.3)
015  S:   ↑M:ye:ah. >See I-< I was pullin' 'er (0.2) ar- ar:
016       pullin' 'er arm to k- keep 'er awa:y from me like.=an'
017       I swung 'er a:rm like that.=Don't forget I'm still this
018       ra:ge an'- (0.4) an' uh she fell t- fell t- fell to the
019       la:wn.
020            (1.1)
021  S: → But the way's not to kick a ↑wo↓man as you might say.
022            (.)
023  S: → I wouldn't ↑do th:at. .shih
024            (0.8)
025  S:   Wouldn't be ri:ght.
026            (0.2)
027  S:   to: f'me to do ↓that.
028            ((papers rustling))
029  P2:  But   [you'd kick a bloke] in the 'ead three
030  S:         [(                  )]
031  P2:  ti:mes.
```

(#5 PN-61)

Earlier in this interview, S has admitted assaulting his male neighbour. This sequence begins after P1 has read out the female neighbour's statement, in which she alleges that S has kicked her to the ground. P1 asks S if he remembers 'kickin' 'e:r.' S's answer is built across two 'turn construction units', 'No. Not 'er', and another turn which follows a lack of uptake from P1 (line 4). S's answer therefore reiterates his earlier admission of kicking one neighbour, but not the other. At line 6, P1 formulates S's testimony 'So you've not kicked her at all.', which S treats as a redoing of the question. Again he denies the action of 'kicking' (line 8), but this time, after a lengthy gap develops, he admits to a much-downgraded action (with regards to its seriousness and criminal relevance) designed to halt the incident: 'Swung 'er about kept 'er off me that's all.'

P1 then asks if S remembers the woman 'falling down to the gro:und.' Note P1's use of the intransitive verb 'fall' at this point: S might well state that he saw his neighbour 'fall' (which does not imply agency on S's part), while not admitting to 'pushing' her to the ground. S answers '↑M:ye:ah.', then elaborates upon his earlier description at line 10, claiming to 'pull' the woman on her 'arm' to 'keep 'er awa:y from me like.' (line 16). S states that he 'swung 'er a:rm ... an' uh she fell t- fell t- fell to the la:wn.'. Note the details of this formulation: S also uses the intransitive verb 'fell', and reformulates P1's locative term 'ground' to 'lawn', which further works to downgrade the potential seriousness of S's actions, given that 'lawns' provide a relatively softer landing.

After a gap and no uptake from either police officer, S produces the target utterance, 'But the way's not to kick a ↑wo↓man as you might say. (.) I wouldn't ↑do th:at.' (lines 21–23). Note S's move from a general, scripted claim ('the way's ...', cf. Edwards, 1994) to a specific one ('I wouldn't...'), and the coupling of 'wouldn't' with a generalised formulation of the gender category 'a ↑wo↓man', rather than the particular woman he is accused of kicking. In addition, notice the way the turn is built: it starts with 'But the way's' and ends with 'as you might say'. These parts of the turn work to formulate the middle bit, 'not to kick a ↑wo↓man' as *common sense* and somewhat *idiomatic*, and, as such, reality constructing and maintaining with regards to gender relations. It is also a generalised *mundane moral* position (cf. Stokoe and Edwards, in press) which places the suspect in the 'category-of-men-who-don't-hit-women'. S then reiterates his denial: 'Wouldn't be ri:ght. (0.2) to: f'me to do ↓that.'

In police interviews, the suspect's main business is often *denying the charges* put to them. One methodical use of categories comes in environments where denials get done: the suspect categorises him/herself as *someone who does not harm a particular category of persons* – which, in the above extract, is 'women'. Based on the same police data corpus, Edwards has conducted a detailed analysis of the way the modal verb 'would' is used by suspects 'to claim a disposition to act in ways inconsistent with whatever offence they are accused of', its value being in the way that 'its semantics provide for a sense of back-dated predictability with regard to the actions in question' (2006b: 475). In other words, because the suspect *wouldn't* (in general) do the kind of action s/he is charged with, s/he *didn't* do it (this time). As we can see, one feature of suspects' 'would-based' denials is that they regularly co-occur with a categorical reference term.

Edwards (2006b) shows that a suspect's use of first person normative-dispositional 'would' ('I wouldn't ...') regularly follows the police officer's establishment of conflicting testimony regarding the offence for which the suspect has been arrested. This is the case above: the police officer is presenting, and the suspect denying, testimony relevant to an offence of 'causing bodily harm' (lines 1–12); the suspect then uses, in the context of a narrative account, a first person normative-dispositional *would*, plus a generalised categorial reference (lines 20–26). P2 invokes S's denial in his next question, 'But you'd kick a bloke in the 'ead three ti:mes' (lines 29–31), which S does not challenge. Note that P also uses a generalised gender category 'a bloke' here, that orients to 'a woman' as a member of a contrastive relational pair: both S and P are therefore oriented to the same membership categorisation device.

Extract 5 provides an initial example of the way suspects invoke gender categories as part of getting some business accomplished; here, doing a category-based denial. Such formats for doing denials featured regularly across the corpus of interviews (see Stokoe, 2006). Extracts 6 and 7 provide two further instances. In Extract 6, the suspect has been arrested for damaging his neighbours' fence and verbal abuse. In Extract 7, another suspect has been arrested for hitting her neighbour, which she denies, and so the police officer asks if 'somebody else' might have caused the injuries:

Extract 6

```
001  P:    You threaten 'er at all.
002             (0.4)
003  S:    No I didn't threaten 'er.
004             (0.8)
005  ?:    .hhhhh
006  S:  → I've got no reason to threaten 'e:r, I've never 'it a
007      → woman in my life.=and I never will 'it a woman in my life.
                                                      (#6 PN-63)
```

Extract 7

```
001  P:    D'you think [your husband hit her¿]
002  S:                [ N- my husband      ] would n:ever hit
003      → a woman,
004      →     (0.3)
005  S:    He would never EVer
                                                      (#7 PN-111b)
```

In Extract 6, the suspect is denying threatening his female neighbour. His denial is built as three items in a list, the first of which attends to the police-relevant issue of 'motive' 'I've got no reason to threaten 'e:r,' specifically addressing the woman in question. The second item, 'I've never 'it a woman in my life.', includes the general, anonymous category 'a woman' rather than the specific category of his neighbour. This works in the same way as the third item, which includes 'will', of which 'would' is a past tense form ('=and I never will 'it a woman in my life.'), categorising S as the kind of man who does not 'hit women' in general. These category-based denials are formulated in extreme terms, with the extreme case formulation 'never', which, as Pomerantz (1986) notes, can work to defend against or counter challenges.

In Extract 7, the category-based denial is occasioned by P's question about whether S's husband could have hit their neighbour. S denies that her husband hit their neighbour by claiming that he is the kind of man who 'would n:ever hit a woman,'. Following a gap in which there is no response from P, S reformulates her claim ('He would never EVer'), and again note the use of repeated and upgraded extreme case formulations that are combined with the category-based denial. Like Extract 5, S's denials are somewhat idiomatic. Indeed, the idiomatic quality of these category based denials is evidenced partly by the very juxtaposition of three different sequences in which the same kind of formulation is used.

Analysis of these short extracts has demonstrated, firstly, that the study of gender categories can be done in a robust way that ties them to particular actions (here, doing denials) done in particular kinds of sequential environments (here, following the presentation of counter-testimony). Second, the analysis reveals a members' method for doing denials; in this case, suspects' idiomatic use of self- and other-categorisations.

Concluding remarks: gendered 'reality analysis'

In this chapter, I have demonstrated a conversation analytic and ethnomethodological approach to the study of gender categories in interaction. I have shown how talk can be analysed in ways that reveal how *gender categories are routinely occasioned to accomplish some action*: narrative description, nominating someone for a task, doing denials. Through these analyses, we have seen how gender is realised – *what counts* as gender – in the interactional moments that comprise social life. We have seen how some categories are more situationally appropriate than others (e.g., 'girls/women', 'fellas/men'), that 'secretaries' are hearably 'female', and that being a man who hits women is morally sanctionable. Analyses of gender categories, then, should aim to explicate the *kinds of sequential environments* in which they crop up, and the *kinds of actions being done* in the turns in which they are embedded.

Having done this empirical work, I now want to consider the theoretical upshots of analysing 'gender' from an ethnomethodological (EM)/conversation analytic (CA) perspective, as it is difficult to engage in a study of 'gender' without an account of how it is to be theorised. I will focus particularly on the relationship between, and problematic conflation of, EM/CA and 'social constructionism'. Readers are likely to be familiar with the 'constructionist' view of gender as performance, enactment and so on, now something of a truism in contemporary gender studies, contrasting with the 'essentialist' perspective, which underpins 'gender difference' studies, criticisms of which are well-established (e.g., Crawford, 1995; Hare-Mustin and Maracek, 1990). However, there are some problems with the way constructionism-as-theory gets played out empirically, as well as some caricaturing of constructionism itself. I shall deal with each in turn.

First, as I have argued elsewhere, empirical translations of 'gender-as-construction' often end up making essentialist-sounding claims, particularly those that collect the talk of women or men, in interviews or natural settings, and then look at how *women* perform *femininities* and *men* perform *masculinities*. There is rarely a notion in such work of people *not* performing gender: if the data do not 'look like' recognisable femininity or masculinity, the 'finding' is that gender identity is not what we thought it was, or that it is variable, inconsistent, multiple or fragmentary (Edwards and Stokoe, 2004). Thus the performance of gender is explained or accounted for in a somewhat circular fashion, leaving what Velody and Williams (1998) call a 'realist residue'.

Second, there are problems with the way 'social constructionism' is (mis)understood by some language and gender researchers. Such misunderstandings are revealed in criticisms that, while constructionism is generally regarded as a 'good thing', it is also seen as 'dangerous' for ignoring 'facts [*sic*] about gender and language which have been repeatedly pointed out in the language and gender literature over the decades, and which, as socially responsible academics, we cannot and do not want to ignore' (Holmes and Meyerhoff, 2003: 9). For Holmes and Meyerhoff, a radically anti-essentialist position would result in the dissolution of the language and gender field, 'because gender would have become such an idiosyncratic quality that it would be non-existent as a category across individuals' (ibid.: 10). In everyday life, they argue, people treat gender as 'real', as social categories that matter, as a distinction that is 'crucial' and 'vital', and a stable essential distinction that, if threatened, is extremely disturbing (ibid.: 9–10).

However, these appeals to the 'actual' world of facts and reality are somewhat missing the point of constructionism. Holmes and Meyerhoff appear to want to accept two contradictory positions: that gender is socially constructed, but also that it is something that 'really' exists prior to its constitution in discourse. Here, social constructionism (vs. essentialism) is conflated with social/cultural (vs. biological) understandings of gender: it is treated as a construction *rather than* as biological, or as *only* a construction rather than real. The idea that 'construction' means that gender identities are 'only' constructions rather than real is itself a reiteration of essentialism (see Edwards, 1997, on the distinction between ontological and epistemic construction). There is no contrast between gender being 'constructed' and its being natural and prior to discourse. Its very existence as 'natural', 'essential' and prior to discourse is what gets constructed, in and through practices of all kinds (Stokoe, 2005). But this is not a social causation theory of gender itself. The issue for constructionists *and* ethnomethodologists is not whether gender is actually 'real' or 'true'; rather, it is the business of analysis to 'analyze the workings of those categories, not to merely use them as they are used in the world' (Jefferson, 2004: 118). Holmes and Meyerhoff's gloss on 'extreme' constructionism versus 'crucial', 'vital' and 'real' gender misunderstands the constructionist project, or at least does not attend sufficiently to constructionism as developed in arenas such as discursive psychology and the sociology of scientific knowledge (SSK) (see Edwards, 1997; Potter, 1996).

Both conversation analysis (CA) and ethnomethodology (EM) are often aligned with constructionism and thus anti-essentialism (e.g., Buttny's (1993) 'conversation analytic constructionism'). Lynch (1993: xiv–xv) argues that both EM and constructionism share a focus on the investigation of knowledge production. Both take an anti-foundationalist stance by 'seeking to describe the 'achievement' of social order and the 'construction' of social and scientific "facts"', and both 'explicitly renounce the use of transcendental standards of truth, rationality, and natural realism when seeking to describe and/or explain historical developments and contemporary practices' (ibid). Additionally, the SSK concept of methodological relativism parallels ethnomethodology's efforts to 'point to some of the ways in which the world is *rendered* objectively available and is *maintained* as such' (Heritage, 1984: 220). Both EM and SSK place reality temporarily in brackets, adopting the position of 'ethnomethodological indifference' (Garfinkel and Sacks, 1970: 63) in order to study how people maintain a sense of a commonly shared, objectively existing world.

However, despite these similarities, the relationship between CA/EM and constructionism is not straightforward. It is interesting, then, that feminist criticisms of CA often point to its perceived 'extreme' constructionist/relativist or anti-essentialist stance (e.g., Bucholtz, 2003a; Holmes and Meyerhoff, 2003). But it is not clear that CA practitioners regard themselves as 'constructionist'. Some ethnomethodologists stress that EM/CA 'takes no position on the continuum between realism and social constructionism (or any other dualisms either) and is, if anything, a-constructionist' (Wowk, 2004: 14). In particular, EM does not take up a particular ontological position with regards to the nature of 'reality'. Instead, it 'respecifies' (Button, 1991: 6) issues of what is real and authentic, including what is 'true' about identity, as matters for 'members' themselves to deal with. For EM, then, it is a 'basic mistake' to assume that we need to 'adopt a theoretical stance on 'reality' at all' (Francis, 1994: 105), partly because preoccupations about ontology inhibit close analysis of members' practices (Button and Sharrock, 2003). Indeed, EM is critical of some constructionist work for what it sees as subverting and ironising participants' sense of the integrity of their world (Watson, 1992). In everyday life, people generally treat 'gender' as a real thing that they can know about themselves and other people, and are not generally sent into a 'metaphysical spin' about ontological statuses (Francis, 1994). As we saw in the earlier analysis, speakers make reference to their own and others' gender as a routine matter within courses of action. When different speakers make the same kinds of reference, such as being a 'man-who-doesn't-hit-women', the categories take on a generalised, idiomatic and reality-constructing weight. And if people do question their own or someone else's membership of a gender category – that is, make it accountable – then this is something we can study. The focus then might be on members' orientations to identity *as* (un)stable, (in)consistent, (in)coherent and so on, and how they are produced as such in talk (Edwards and Stokoe, 2004; see also Speer and Parsons, 2006, on the gender reassignment clinic). In EM/CA, analysts work towards understanding *members' own 'reality-analysis'* (Hester and Francis, 1997) with regards to gender and how people constitute themselves as recognisably, take-for-grantedly, gendered, or hold each other accountable for normative membership in a category. I suggest that this way of understanding gender can usefully underpin our work on how it is relevant for everyday talk-in-interaction.

Notes

1 For a key to Jefferson's system of data transcription, see Kitzinger (this volume).

2 ESRC project *Identities in neighbour discourse: Community, conflict and exclusion* (RES-148-25-0010), co-holder Derek Edwards. The corpus includes approximately 250 calls to mediation centres, 170 calls to environmental health services, 120 police-suspect interrogations, 20 calls to anti-social behaviour services, and 20 hours of mediation data.

Part 4
Discursive Psychology

11

Discursive Psychology and the Study of Gender: A Contested Space

Nigel Edley and Margaret Wetherell

Introduction

In the social sciences many fields of enquiry with apparently clear and defined boundaries begin over time to fragment and subdivide. This is sometimes seen as a disruptive process, due to the 'narcissism of minor differences', yet it can also be viewed as a sign of health and growth. As people reflect on the original paradigm, exploring its strengths and weaknesses, new ideas and amalgams emerge and new conceptual frameworks begin to solidify around parts of original models. The aim of this chapter is to describe and review discursive psychological approaches to the study of gender, charting a process of division and creation of just this kind.

Early work on discourse and gender in social psychology took a broadly constructionist line – looking at gender as not 'always/already' in place, fixed as an essence, but as emergent from discourses which formulated and made available identity positions marked as masculine or feminine. This early work was also interested in the performance of gender in talk and texts, through interaction, as a local accomplishment.

Much of this work developed as a contrast to the traditional work on sex differences in psychology. In more recent times, however, discursive work in psychology has taken several different paths. Some practitioners have become much more focused on the fine-grain, following the prescriptions of conversation analysis, while others (including ourselves) have tried to build a path between post-structuralist discourse analysis and conversation analysis, extending the more integrative and synthetic starting points for discourse analysis in social psychology. The empirical consequences and the investigations of gender which result are nicely illustrated in the chapters of this volume with Kamada taking the integrative view and Stokoe and Kitzinger illustrating the conversation analytic path.

This chapter will review these developments and will argue for a discursive psychology of gender performances which continues to work across both the micro and the macro. We will recommend an analysis of what participants do in their talk which is informed by readings of the cultural and political contexts surrounding that talk and which is attentive also to the emergence of gendered subjectivities.

Psychology, gender and discourse

The 'turn to discourse' felt across the social sciences in the 1980s had a radical effect on psychological research on gender. It reinforced the burgeoning interest in the social and cultural foundations of gender identities and the impression that the study of fixed, biologically driven, sex differences could only provide a partial account. Evidence of historical and cultural variation in forms of masculinity and femininity showed that gender was relative, performative and negotiated. Crucially, the discursive turn opened up new ways for psychologists and other social scientists to conduct research on gender. For most of the twentieth century it would be fair to say academic psychologists studied a world of apparently silent individuals. Quantitative surveys measured (through paper and pencil) people's attitudes (understood as internal mental states) while psychological experiments focused on behaviour. The study of discourse expanded the concept of social action to include talk and texts of all kinds and it began to offer ways to work with people's words and communicative activities. It offered ways of moving past the increasingly sterile debates about what in sex/gender was biological and what was due to nurture and the environment.

Early work on discourse in psychology (Billig et al., 1988; Condor, 1988; Billig, 1987; Potter and Wetherell, 1987; Henriques, Hollway et al., 1984) established a number of principles bringing together themes from Austin and Searle's speech act theory, Foucauldian post-structuralism, ethnomethodology and Rom Harré's (1979) work on ethogenics among other sources. A core claim was that language was *constructive* or *constitutive*, rather than simply reflective (or referential). In other words, it was argued that language worked to *build* the world in addition to being a medium for talking *about* it. Potter and Wetherell (1987), for example, tried to show how various identities are 'worked up' from a stock of common resources, according to the demands of different interactional settings. What this meant for the analysis of gender was that, instead of seeing masculinity and femininity as something that both preceded and ushered from 'always/already' gendered subjects, it became understood as something that was produced and maintained in and through discourse (Wetherell, 1984). Echoing the ethnomethodological analyses of Garfinkel (1967), Kessler and McKenna (1978) and, later on, West and Zimmerman (1991), gender became understood as a social and discursive *accomplishment*; a performance rather than an essence – ideas which, famously, became extensively developed by Judith Butler (1990) as an elaborated and elegantly justified philosophy.

Throughout the 1990s a number of socio-psychological investigations appeared which applied broadly constructionist and discursive premises to look at gender in practice (e.g., Edley and Wetherell, 1999; Wetherell and Edley, 1999; Coyle and Morgan-Sykes, 1998; Gough, 1998; Edley and Wetherell, 1997; Willott and Griffin, 1997; Gill, 1993). One example, from our own research, looked at how, within a boys' independent school, inter-group relations were organised around and conducted through different constructions of masculinity (Edley and Wetherell, 1997). What we found here was, in effect, a clash of multiple masculinities. Of particular interest were the attempts by one group of young men to construct alternative identities to what was, in that context, a dominant ideal of macho masculinity. Our analysis charted the struggles inherent to such a project. As such, it offered an illustration of hegemony in action. A second study (Edley and Wetherell, 1999) explored the 'ideological dilemmas' (Billig et al., 1988) embodied within men's talk around fatherhood and domestic life. What this analysis showed was that, whilst the notion of the father-as-breadwinner was still a potent cultural commonplace, so too was the ideal of the fully involved, active or participant father. In other words, within the (then) contemporary ideological landscape, cultural common sense seemed to demand not only that the (post)modern father provided for his family, but also that he was physically there for them too. The young men we studied puzzled over this apparently impossible dilemma: either they went out to work and so failed as fathers or became stay-at-home dads and failed as men.

Common to most of these studies was an attempt to situate the local production of gender identities within a broader ideological or cultural context – for it was assumed that these two levels (the micro and the macro) were closely intertwined. As Kamada (Chapter 12, this volume) shows, for example, the creation of a positive new identity ('*daburu*') for Japanese multi-ethnic people only makes sense in the light of the already prevalent patterns of cultural denigration ('haafu'). This new discursive construct is a response to what was there before. Likewise, as we found, when the young men of the 1990s talked about their future as fathers, they were negotiating both older notions of masculinity and newer cultural versions. Negotiation of the new takes place in dialogue with already existing cultural contexts and social practices.

Discursive psychology and conversation analysis

The phrase 'discursive psychology' first made its appearance in a book of the same name by Derek Edwards and Jonathan Potter in 1992. This book set out to provide 'a thorough reworking of Psychology's subject matter' (Wooffitt, 2005: 113), or, as Potter and Hepburn (2007) put it, to 'look for psychology in a completely different place'. In contrast to traditional or mainstream psychology, which saw the mind and/or brain as the site of its main interest, Edwards and Potter focused their attention on a much more social domain:

> [r]ather than seeing discourse as a pathway to individuals' inner life, whether it be cognitive processes, motivation or some other mental stuff, we see psychological issues as constructed and deployed in discourse itself.
>
> (1992: 127)

Edwards and Potter didn't pick up on gender (the topic doesn't feature at all in the index), but their work acted as a catalyst, providing the impetus for a range of gender-specific studies, most notably in the writings of Susan Speer and Elizabeth Stokoe (Speer and Stokoe, forthcoming; Speer, 2005; Stokoe, 2005; Stokoe, 2004; Stokoe and Smithson, 2002; Speer, 2001; Stokoe and Smithson, 2001; Stokoe, 2000; see also Kitzinger, this volume). Unlike most work done during the 1990s, this body of research displayed a much closer alliance to the meta-theory and analytical foci of conversation analysis – indeed, to the point where, as Speer (2005) notes, the two disciplines have become quite hard to distinguish. As with conversation analysis, the contemporary discursive psychologist pays close attention to the action orientation (Atkinson and Heritage, 1984) and sequential organisation of talk. As with CA, they discourage 'ventur[ing] further than the limits of the text to explain *why* participants say what they do' (Speer, 2001: 107; emphasis in original). So, instead of going to the data to reveal the workings of patriarchy, hegemony or sexism, the post-millennial discursive psychologist is much more likely to restrict herself to the orientations, meanings and understandings of the participants themselves. In other words, gender is studied as a *participants' concern*; this work looks at how participants 'orient to' or make relevant matters of sex or gender (see Edwards, 1998, for an early example).

According to the main proponents of this new approach, there remains one significant point of difference between CA and DP – a point of distinction that centres upon the ideas of social constructionism (see Speer and Potter, 2002; Potter, 1996). As Speer (2005) points out, many conversation analysts reject the basic tenets of social constructionism, operating, instead, within a firmly realist paradigm. Discursive psychology, on the other hand, is said to:

> retain[s] a solid constructionist edge, treating discourse as the site in which the relevance and properties of what are traditionally taken to be mental phenomena are constituted and negotiated.
>
> (Wooffitt, 2005: 129)

It is important to take a moment to look at what is actually meant by *constructionism* here – especially in view of the fact that, in recent years, various commentators have claimed that it is not a unitary paradigm (see, for instance, Burkitt, 1999, 1998; Hacking, 1998; Danziger, 1997). In particular we are drawn to Edwards's (1997) distinction between what he calls the 'ontological' and 'epistemic' senses of construction.

Epistemic constructionism focuses analysis upon 'the constructive nature of *descriptions*, rather than of the entities that (according to descriptions) exist beyond them' (Edwards, 1997: 48; emphasis in original). Ontologic constructionism goes further and opens up a wider range of scholarly activities. Ontologic constructionists do not just analyse patterns in people's descriptions, but are interested in making claims about the patterning of the culturally constructed entities such as minds, worlds, selves, identities and sexualities which discourses bring into being. The new discursive psychology attempts to rigorously stick with epistemic construction while ontologic constructionism is more characteristic of cultural studies, cultural psychology, cultural anthropology and some work on social cognition. Ontological constructionists do not necessarily claim that their accounts of patterns in constructed social worlds are objective or true descriptions of the real nature of minds and worlds or, indeed, that these accounts are statements outside or immune from the constitutive nature of any discourse (including social scientists' discourse). But there is an attempt to apply scholarship to discuss the possible social consequences of the descriptions.

Edwards (1997) seeks to align discursive psychology much more with epistemic construction. The alternative, ontological, sense of social construction is cast out into the shady realms of cultural psychology. So, for example, when Speer (2005) subsequently writes of discursive psychology as embracing two senses of constructionism (within her book on gender talk), we find no trace of the ontological interpretation. The first sense, she says, considers the way that discourse 'is constructed from a range of conversational resources'. As regards the second:

> it studies the way that these resources are built and used in the course of performing specific social action – for example in asking questions, providing accounts, or managing blame and responsibility.
>
> (Speer, 2005: 91)

What this means is that, within these more recent discourse studies, there is no longer any sense of discourse as 'world building'; the whole notion of discourse 'constructing the object of which it speaks' (Foucault, 1972) is lost. Rather than retaining the post-structuralist elements of the original mix (found, for instance in Potter and Wetherell, 1987), discursive psychology now confines itself to talk about talk – or the analysis of 'talk-in-*interaction*' (see Coulter, 1999; Hibberd, 2005).

The implications of this strategy for the discipline of discursive psychology become clear when we focus on the topic of gender, for what ends up getting studied is, not how discourse produces subjects who think, act and feel in ways socially recognised as gendered, but the ways in which speakers use the vocabulary or discourse of gender (or 'gender talk') in the pursuit of everyday social actions (such as providing accounts, managing blame and so on and so forth). The point is that for us, as well as for a number of other critics (e.g., Coulter, 1999), such analyses appear as something of a 'side-show' to our principal concerns. It seems as if psychology has been abandoned rather than merely 're-specified' (Potter and Hepburn, 2007). As a consequence, what we are looking for is a broader understanding of constructionism, combining both its epistemic *and* ontologic senses. Indeed, it seems to us that any anti-essentialist understanding of gender both implies and *requires* an ontological 'take'; after all, from what other position can one investigate gender as a discursive accomplishment and not as some kind of mental or physiological substrate? A discursive psychology that embraces a post-structuralist as well as an ethnomethodological (or 'endogenous' – see Speer and Potter, 2002) sense of social construction is one that can not only appreciate gender as a discursive resource, but one that can also understand how discourse shapes people's sense of themselves (and others) as gendered beings. It is an approach that is capable, in other words, of showing how gender is brought into being – or realised as an efficacious social phenomenon – through a range of discursive practices.

Back to the future: towards an older discursive psychology of gender

At the heart of this chapter, then, is an argument about the constitution of discursive psychology in terms of how it approaches a topic like gender. As should now be clear, what we are advocating is an expanded version of discursive psychology; one that opens out from an exclusive focus on 'talk-in-interaction' so as to include a broader understanding of the *onto-formative* capacities of language. What we are arguing for is an approach that holds together a sense of how people both *do* and are *done by* gender talk; an approach that can illuminate how speakers construct (and use) gender categories and how they are constructed – as gendered beings – by those very categories. Commentators such as Wooffitt (2005) seem to feel that it is impossible to keep these two 'balls' in the air. In looking at the broader patterns of discourse, he says, the analyst is constantly drawn into underestimating or forgetting the interactional (i.e., 'local') context in and for which the talk was designed (ibid.: 173). Maybe this is a danger, but, even so, as far as we are concerned, it is better to attempt this juggling act rather than to drop one ball, under the (mis)apprehension of methodological rigour.

Having laid out these (largely) theoretical arguments, the time has come to try to substantiate our claims through the analysis of some empirical data. What we intend to do is present a piece of data that comes from our own research on men and masculinity. This data was first discussed in Wetherell (1998; see also Edley, 2001). Our aim is to reiterate the argument presented then and respond to a recent CA re-working of our analytic claims (Wooffitt, 2005). We hope to demonstrate that whilst the more conversation analytic-influenced style of discursive psychology provides some account of what is going on in the data, a fuller account can be found in a more synthetic approach which combines the micro-analyses of CA with a broader understanding of the rhetorical and ideological contexts that surround and lend substance to such conversational exchanges.

The data that we have chosen comes from fieldwork conducted amongst the sixth form of a UK-based single sex boys' school during the early 1990s (see Wetherell, 1994). Over the course of several months, interviews were held with three groups of white 17- to 18-year-old students – each lasting about one hour – with the aim of revealing the construction of masculine identities in a particular institutional site. The interviews covered various aspects of the young men's lives, including relations within the school, families and friends and their expectations for their future. The data that constitutes Extract 1 comes from one such interview and concerns the putative sexual activities of one of the participants. Just prior to the start of this extract, the interviewer (Edley) had interrupted the interview in order to put new batteries in the tape recorder and, during the hiatus, the young men had made several references to a weekend in which Aaron had supposedly 'struck it lucky' with a number of young women. Indeed, it was claimed that he had 'got off' with four in one night. With the machinery now restored to working order, line 1 sees Nigel asking for an account of those events.

Extract 1[1]

```
001  Nigel:   Okay yeah tell me about going with four people in one
002           night=
003  Phil:    [=All::right ((bangs table))       ]
004  Aaron:   [hhhhhhh hhhhhh hhhhhh h] hh no::=
005  Phil:    =Go on=
006  Paul:    On the record=
007  Phil:    =Was it was it this f .hh
008           (.)
009  Aaron:   I don't know I was a bit drunk=
010  Phil:    =I I'll tell he was drunk I'll tell you what I know
011           [because] I am never drunk
```

012	Nigel:	[Hm mm]
013	Phil:	Because I'm dead smug [erm:::]
014	Aaron:	[He's never] drunk it's true=
015	Phil:	=<u>Fri</u>day you went with Janesy on Friday?
016	Aaron:	I did yes:::
017	Phil:	Out <u>down</u> the pub I I <u>mi</u>ssed this completely a
018		<u>com</u>plete shock to me=
019	Aaron:	=.hhhh
020–066		((lines omitted - concerned with listing the names of the young women involved))
067	Aaron:	=We were very lucky that day
068	Phil:	We were erm and we were walking back and he says
069		oh I went with Janesy on Friday and I went yeah you
070		went with three birds last night you went with one on
071		Friday this was in his good month
072	Nigel:	Hm mm
073	Phil:	So that like took me aback somewhat (0.3) so that was
074		a good weekend for you
075		(.)
076	Nigel:	Is that <u>goo</u>d?
077	Phil:	Well in his books <u>yes</u> you know=
078	Aaron:	=hhhh.h [yeah]
079	Phil:	[The thing] is you got so much stick for it
080	Aaron:	Well yeah I could take the stick because it was
081		almost like (0.2) a good ego trip when everyone was
082		taking the stick oh you got off with her ah ha ha
083		yep I did so what's your problem? [Oh, er..errr]
084	Nigel:	[Hm mm]
085	Aaron:	[Errr]
086	Phil:	[None of them] were particularly pikey so you were
087		alright really
088	Aaron:	No (.) they weren't .hh none of them were like majorly
089		pikey .hh (.) one or two perhaps could have like
090		(.)
091	Phil:	I don't know I don't know I think I know this Cathy
092		bird I know Jenny I know Cathy thing I don't know who
093		the other one was and neither do you so can't tell=
094	Nigel:	=Yeah I mean I wasn't sort of saying is four in two
095		days good I mean it's <u>im</u>pressive [you know]
096	Aaron:	[hh [hhh] hh
097	Phil:	[hhhhh] hhhh
098	Nigel:	But I me::an like (.) it presumes that erm that's:: a
099		creditable thing (.) yeah? Is it?
100		(0.2)

101	Phil:	No because you're on the moral low ground
102	Aaron:	But I don't mind being on the moral [low ground]
103	Phil:	[Oh no you don't]
104		mind I I it didn't fuss me at all you know and I wasn't I
105		thought it was quite (.) it was quite impressive you
106		know you're sort of thinking that's shocking because it
107		never happens to me um:: .h hhh
108	Aaron:	Hhhh
109		(0.3)
110	Phil:	But he was (.) by some people in the group he was li
111		(.) they were just taking the piss it wasn't serious no-
112		one it didn't really <u>bo</u>ther anyone at [all]
113	Nigel:	[Hm mm]
114	Phil:	It was like Aaron was on the moral low ground because
115		he was like (.) gigolo Casanova whatever
116	Nigel:	Right (.) okay (0.2) what do you think Paul?
117		(0.3)
118	Paul:	Did you=
119	Phil:	=Are you ap [<u>pal</u>led?]
120	Paul:	[When you] .hh no just a sec (.)
121		[when you went out]
122	Nigel	[<u>a</u>re you appalled?]
123	Paul:	I jus I'll tell you in a minute when you went out
124	????:	hh[hhh]
125	Nigel:	[hhhh]
126	Paul:	When you went out on that Friday (.) evening you were
127		out on the pull yeah?=
128	Aaron:	=<u>No</u>
129	Paul:	This (.) you were not?=
130	Aaron:	=Just out [as a group]
131	Phil:	[Just out] as a group of friends
132	Paul:	On the Saturday you were out on the pull?
133	Phil:	No
134	Aaron:	.hh [not really]
135	Phil:	[He was] drunk=
136	Aaron:	=I <u>wasn't</u> drunk [unconscious] (.) I was <u>very</u> merry I
137	Phil:	[(inaudible)]
138	Aaron:	was like (.) all erm (.) all like social guards were down
139	Paul:	Yeah (0.2) and (0.3) whe::n (.) so and (0.4) when you
140		got off with the first one [did you]
141	Aaron:	[hhhhhhh hhh]
142	Phil:	Who was first? Can you remember?
143	Paul:	On the Friday
144	Aaron:	Er::::m on the Friday that that was Janesy

145	Paul:	Did you have any sort of like intonation (sic) of
146		carrying the relationship further?
147	Aaron:	No
148	Phil:	((inaudible undertone/one nighter))
149	Paul:	So so you basically went for as many pullings off as
150		you could get in a weekend?
151	Phil:	No
152	Aaron:	I didn't go for it it just
153		(.)
154	Paul:	It just happened?
155	Aaron:	Well yeah (.) it's not so much I thought <u>right</u> ((hits
156		the desk)) this weekend (.) keep your pecker up lad
157		you're away [it's] not like that it's just that I
158	Phil:	[hhh]
158		(.)
160	Paul:	With any of them [did you feel]
161	Aaron:	[I get lucky very (inaudible)]
162	Paul:	that there'd be like a follow on?
163	Phil:	He didn't know who <u>half</u> of them <u>were</u> do you .hh hh
164	Aaron:	Ah er I didn't (.) I mean it wasn't (.) I mean it wasn't
165		like a right gitty thing to do it was like the other
166		half knew as well that it wasn't gonna be
167		(0.4)
168	Phil:	Mm
169	Aaron:	Erm (0.2) no it's it's you're getting it all wrong it's
170		it's (0.2) it wasn't (0.4) errr Aaron come up with the
171		phrase you want to say (.) it wasn't alright this kid's
172		gonna get off with me then we're gonna go out oh no
173		we're not gonna go out what a git it was (0.2) I'm
174		gonna get off with this lad and that's alright
175	Phil:	Fancied a bit of rough you know
176	Aaron:	Fancied a bit of rough
177	Phil:	As and it was mutual I imagine

In the original analysis of this extract (Wetherell, 1998), it was suggested that what we have here is a populated ideological struggle between what Wendy Hollway (1984) described as three different discourses (or interpretative repertoires) of male sexuality: the 'male sex drive' discourse, the 'have and hold' discourse and the 'permissive' discourse. It was suggested that the different speakers are positioned – by themselves and by each other – within these various discourses. To begin with, the notion of promiscuity as an achievement is clearly evident in Phil's summary statement (lines 73 and 74), that it had been 'a good weekend' for Aaron. It is also implied insofar as Aaron's account of having been too drunk (to remember the details of the weekend in question) can be seen as a form of 'modesty device', whereby somebody else is compelled or invited to 'blow his trumpet' for him. The 'have and hold' discourse is most evident in Paul's contribution to the dialogue (particularly around lines 145–146 and 160–162, where he quizzes Aaron about whether or not he had any intentions of engaging the girls in question in longer term relationships), whilst the 'permissive' discourse figures mainly at the end (i.e., lines 164–177 – where Aaron and Phil jointly construct the encounters as entirely mutual or reciprocal). As feminist social psychologists we were interested in the fact that this group of middle-class white young men had reached a discursive settlement around a particular kind of permissive discourse. In response to Paul's invocation of 'have and hold' relational sexual morals, it was interesting that Aaron spent so much discursive energy establishing that the young women had wanted sex too and he had thus not acted in a 'right gitty' way. The data suggested that, for these young men, the subject positions associated with male sex drive discourse could constitute a troubled identity. More generally, the original analysis suggested that such patterns of 'trouble' (and examples of lack of trouble) were potentially very informative about the macro discursive environment and social change.

In his critical reinterpretation of this original analysis, Wooffitt (2005) argued that it is both unnecessary and unhelpful to look for the interplay of discourses or interpretative repertoires in data such as these. Part of his objection is that such practices direct attention away from the local business of talk-in-interaction. However, he also suggests that there is often no empirical evidence for the existence of these discourses; that they are, in effect, an analyst's fabrication. To illustrate his point, Wooffitt looks, in the extract above, at the notion of being 'out on the pull' (e.g., lines 126–127, and 132). He claims that the phrase doesn't belong to any particular discursive register (such as the 'have and hold' discourse) and neither, he insists, does it carry an inherent accusatory force. Rather, he says, the phrase is made to function as an accusation by virtue of its sequential location within what he describes as an 'inauspicious' environment or situation (whereby Paul – who uses the phrase – has been put on the defensive).

Perhaps the first thing to say, by way of a response, is that we don't disagree with a good deal of Wooffitt's analysis. In his close treatment of things like 'insertion sequences' and 'interjacent overlaps' he provides a persuasive account of how the talk unfolds. Neither do we disagree with his assertion that, whilst the phrase 'out on the pull' can carry an accusatory force, it can also be used in different ways (including, as Wooffitt notes, as a simple description of one's intentions for a night out). Like Hollway, we understand that promiscuity isn't inherently right or wrong/good or bad; it depends upon how it is framed. In this extract, it may well be that an upcoming accusation is signalled, as Wooffitt suggests, by the detailed organisation of Paul's talk at that very particular moment and the surrounding interactional inauspicious environment rather than, as we would suggest, by both the organisation of the talk and the available cultural meanings and connotations of 'being out on the pull'. Wooffitt, however, misses the point. What is so interesting in cultural and broader discursive terms (and for the study of gender) is that Aaron treats being 'on the pull' as a serious accusation which has to be countered, which is troubling and difficult for his identity. He need not have responded in this way – he need not have produced an elaborate defence. Unlike the conversation analyst, we think that, to explain why he did so and why the accusation did seem to be so troubling, we need to go beyond the patterns in this immediate interaction to reflect on broader culturally available discourses and changes in these over time.

What we are maintaining is that phrases like 'being out on the pull' often 'reference' or invoke sets of shared understandings (about, in this case, premeditation, agency and an overall sense of 'light-heartedness' – such that going 'out on the pull' is like some sort of sport or pastime), but also that these framings are themselves shared resources. People are familiar with the 'voice' or discourse of disapproval when it comes to promiscuity. The idea of sexual relations as the preserve of loving, monogamous relationships – rather than as the expression of some natural urge or the itch of lust – is clearly part of our own cultural (Christian) heritage. As Billig (1992, 1987) has ably demonstrated, it is not just the design of talk that relies on a certain cultural competence, the same is also true for the substance of conversation. In our view, taking such discourses or interpretative repertoires into account serves to enhance, rather than diminish, the quality of our analyses.

Let us take another example. Consider the interviewer's question on line 76. Clearly, 'Is that good?' stands as an utterance that works to problematise or unsettle the valorisation of male promiscuity evident in Phil's prior turn. However, what is interesting about the 17 lines that follow (77–93) is the way that this 'troubling' is resisted: the (de)merits of Aaron's actions do get discussed, but only in terms of the attractiveness of the young women involved ('pikey' here can be read as 'ugly'). In other words, the discussion remains firmly within the parameters of the same, celebratory, discourse. Then, in lines 94–99, Edley, as interviewer, has another go at formulating the question posed, initially, in line 76. But look at how this is done.

In the original analysis of this extract (Wetherell, 1998) this was described as 'a complex discursive act'. Indeed, it does seem complex. On the face of it, the interviewer *first* glosses Aaron's actions as 'impressive' but then goes on to question the 'credibility' of those same actions. So how are we to understand this bit of talk? The way that we believe it is best accounted for is in terms of *subject positions* found in different discourses or interpretative repertoires of male sexuality. What the interviewer is doing, in effect, is *skipping* between positions. The point is that 'four in two days' *is* impressive from within the register and logic of the male sex-drive discourse, just as it is reprehensible from without. Moreover, we would argue that this momentary identification with the male-sex drive discourse might help to explain the ripples of laughter that immediately ensue in lines 96 and 97. It is possible that Aaron and Phil are laughing at the irony of the interviewer's positioning, or maybe it marks the pleasure of a moment of 'male-bonding' (which sees the interviewer talking 'their language' – as opposed, perhaps, to the more 'responsible' or 'politically correct' line expected of someone in role as an adult social scientist). In the end, of course, it is difficult to say. Yet what does seem obvious, from the two analyses presented above, is that by drawing upon the concepts of subject position, interpretative repertoires and ideological dilemmas, discursive psychology is much better placed to provide us with a productive way of studying the construction of gender, both as talk-in-interaction and also as a lived or subjective reality.

Note

1 The transcript of this data has been slightly revised from how it appears in Wetherell (1998) – having returned once again to the original recordings.

Transcription notation

The form of transcription notation used above was modified from the system developed by Gail Jefferson (see Atkinson and Heritage, 1984).

One or more colons indicate **the extension of the previous sound**, e.g., Tha::t.

Laughter is marked by hh; the number of hh is a rough marker of duration of laughter.

.hh indicates **an audible intake of breath.**

A ? is used to mark **upward intonation characteristic of a question.**

Underlining indicates **stress placed on a word or part of a word.**

Extended square brackets mark **overlap between speakers.** The left bracket indicates the beginning of the overlap while the right bracket indicates the end, e.g.:

> hh[hhh]
> [hhhh]

Double parentheses indicate **transcriber's descriptions.**

Numbers in parentheses, e.g., (0.2), indicate **pauses** in tenths of a second while (.) indicates a **micropause.**

An equals sign = indicates **the absence of a discernable gap between the end of one speaker's utterance and the beginning of another speaker's utterance.**

12
Discursive 'Embodied' Identities of 'Half' Girls in Japan: A Multi-Perspectival Approach

Laurel D. Kamada

Introduction

This chapter illustrates a *multi-perspectival* discourse analytic approach, by examining how six Japanese-Caucasian adolescent girlfriends in Japan construct and, in particular, *combine* their multi-ethnic and gendered 'embodied' identities. Phillips and Jorgensen (2002) emphasise how multi-perspectivism fits well with the basic constructionist view of 'perspectivism' in bringing together several different theories and methods towards creating different forms of knowledge. While this study is mainly framed within Discursive Psychology (DP), it also incorporates analytic tools from Post-structuralist Discourse Analysis (PDA), particularly Feminist PDA (FPDA) (Baxter, 2003), drawing on the theoretical overlap between DP and FPDA (Baxter, 2003; Edwards and Potter, 1992; Wetherell, 1998).

Discursive psychology

As Edley and Wetherell (this volume) explicate, there are two main trajectories of discursive psychology: the detailed micro-analytic approach along the lines of conversation analysis which focuses on participants' displayed orientations, and the more integrative trajectory which combines elements of this micro-analysis along with a macro post-structuralist discourse analysis, which is informed by an examination of wider social and political contexts. In this chapter, I take the latter, integrative approach of discursive psychology in examining how discourses of ethnicity in Japan locally affect the ways in which Japanese-Caucasian adolescent girls construct their identities.

Rather than examining the 'attitude-system' of speakers, DP aims 'to see how the themes of ideology are instantiated in ordinary talk, and how speakers are part of, and are continuing, the ideological history of the discursive themes which they are using' (Billig, 2001: 218). Put simply, people draw on pre-existing vocabularies and resources – speech acts, such as apologies, requests, excuses, disclaimers, as well as silences – in order to describe their worlds. These 'realities' are not however mere descriptions, but *constructed versions* of events (Potter and Wetherell, 1987).

Edley writes that DP also aims 'to examine not only how identities are produced on and for particular occasions, but also how history or culture both impinge upon and are transformed by those performances' (2001: 190–1), and showed how 'lived' ideologies or the 'commonplaces' of culture can produce 'ideological dilemmas' that structure people's talk (ibid.: 203).

Feminist post-structuralist discourse analysis

In Baxter's (2002b, 2002c) Post-Structuralist Discourse Analysis (PDA) (later Feminist PDA (Baxter, 2003)), people are seen as *multiply* positioned, by themselves and others, within interconnected and competing discourses. Relatedly, PDA is concerned with the manner in which identities are displayed, enacted or performed with others in everyday talk as people draw on the various discourses available to them (see Baxter, this volume).

Feminist PDA incorporates 'an explicit feminist focus' (Baxter, 2002c: 840), where gender is seen as a site of struggle. It is 'a feminist approach to analysing the ways in which speakers negotiate their identities, relationships and positions in their world according to the ways in which they are located by competing yet interwoven discourses' (Baxter, 2003: 1). FPDA moves away from the 'second wave feminist perspective' which tended to see women and girls as *powerless victims* and instead views them 'as *potentially powerful* in terms of their multiple positioning within different discourses' of gender (ibid.: 41; my italics). Drawing on Baxter, I examine how multi-ethnic girls are 'simultaneously positioned as relatively *powerless* within a range of dominant discourses on [ethnicity and] gender, but [also] as relatively *powerful* within alternative and competing social discourses' (ibid.: 39; Baxter's italics; my inclusion of *ethnicity*). In particular, in this study I examine how multi-ethnic girls position themselves in terms of both their *ethnic* and *gendered* 'embodied' identities.

Multi-perspectivism

Wetherell (1998) has argued for an integrative, synthetic approach which combines micro-analytic features of discourse analysis with the post-structuralist analytic view of subject positioning constituted within discourses. In response to Schegloff's (1997) 'limited' perspective within Conversation Analysis, Wetherell called for a hybrid DP approach '[that] embodies many of the tensions between fine-grain analysis and more macro-social discourse work [and which] is defined inclusively rather than narrowly including both

Foucauldian and conversation analytic research on psychological issues' (2001: 189). The idea of a 'synthetic approach' to discourse analysis was also taken up by Baxter (2002b, 2002c), who proposed post-structuralist discourse analysis, not as a *better* methodological/theoretical framework than, for example, Schegloff's Conversation Analysis, but as a method that works 'supplementarily' with other methods. Baxter (2003) positively fosters this supplementarity within FPDA by promoting a 'plurality of versions' heard alongside one another.

DP and FPDA share many other commonalities, aside from the promotion of multi-perspectivism. Both grew out of a post-stucturalist social constructionist framework, where 'knowledge' and 'truth' are not seen as fixed, but contestable and negotiated. Both draw on the Foucauldian notion of how discourses inform the ways in which people position themselves in their day-to-day interactions with others and how they represent the world from particular perspectives. Although both DP and FPDA aim to resist determinism and 'grand narratives', they do allow for research that takes a particular political perspective (in the case of FPDA, alongside other perspectives) or can be used for feminist purposes. While DP doesn't champion only feminist concerns, it has been used for feminist purposes (see Edley and Wetherell, this volume; Hollway, 1984). Further, the concept of 'repertoires' characteristic of DP is similar to the notion of 'discourses' as used in FPDA: 'Both concepts invoke the idea of repositories of meaning; that is, distinctive ways of talking about objects and events in the world' (Edley, 2001: 202), any differential usage usually 'signal[ling] or signpost[ing] different conceptual and methodological positions within discourse analytical work' (ibid.). In this chapter, following Edley, I use the terms *discourse* and *repertoire* interchangeably.

'Embodied' ethnic identities of Japanese-white girls in Japan

This study shows how 'embodiment' is performed by looking at how both gender and ethnic discourses are drawn on in the construction of 'ethno-gendered' identity in Japan. Embodiment signifies how individuals make sense of themselves through the way they discursively position themselves and others based on their 'lived-body-selves' (Howson, 2005; Thapan, 1997). In gender studies, the notion of embodiment is used to show how identity is lived and performed at the physical site of the body (Bloustien, 2001; Thapan, 1997; Lovering, 1995). This is an identity over which one can exert agency. Budgeon (2003: 52) conceptualises the body, not as an object, but as an 'event' in an act of 'becoming' through continuous and multiple practices and interactions with others.

How this embodied identity is performed will be illustrated by examining a network of six adolescent multi-ethnic girlfriends of the same age, the participants of this study. These girls represent a relatively new, but growing, community of mixed ethnic children who were born and raised in Japan: each of the six has one Japanese parent and one foreign-raised, English-speaking Caucasian parent from the United Kingdom, the United States or Australia. Spread over a geographically broad community, they all attend different regular Japanese schools – as opposed to international or immersion schools – which socialise and enculture them in Japanese history, customs, mores, language and thought, together with their Japanese peers. They have known each other through their foreign parent's network of friends since pre-school and consider each other best friends.

The data consists of the girls' talk in six semi-structured (group) interviews and spontaneous conversations, audio-recorded over their early adolescence (ages 12–15). Throughout much of the data, I am the seventh participant. The data selected for this chapter comes mainly from our final meeting, called the 'Last Reunion', when five of the girls are 14 and one (Naomi) has turned 15. (See Appendix for transcription conventions and pseudonyms.)

Ethnic discourses/interpretive repertoires in Japan

While Sunderland (2004) proposes that after some analytic work, anyone can identify and name a discourse she also points out that reflexivity is important in documenting discourses and that, from a constructionist viewpoint, the naming of discourses is often a matter of *interpretation*. Baxter (2003: 138; and this volume) suggests four elements which can be used in discourse identification: words repeatedly used by the participant; commonly emerging themes; links apparent in the interactions between participants; and contradictions apparent in their interactions. With these points as a guide, and as a long-time resident of Japan, I have identified and named several dominant and alternative (competing) macro-level discourses or repertoires of gender and/or ethnicity in Japan (see Kamada, 2005a, 2005b, 2006), presented in the left-hand columns of Tables 12.1 and 12.2 below. Examples of how these discourses or repertoires are manifested as 'commonsense' expressions in present-day speech in Japan are listed in the right-hand columns.

A 'discourse of homogeneity' has been identified as an overarching, dominant discourse which has a broad effect on social, political and educational practices in Japan (e.g., Lie, 2001; Weiner, 1997). Underlying this discourse is a denial of the existence of ethnic diversity in Japan, and the promotion of a narrowly defined standard of *sameness* in terms of both *enacting Japaneseness* in a performative sense and *looking Japanese* in appearance. Related to this is a 'discourse of conformity', epitomised by the popular Japanese proverb, 'the nail that sticks up gets hammered down'. Ensuring group harmony and *using restraint* have always been highly valued social practices in Japanese society (LoCastro, 1990) and

Table 12.1   Dominant Japanese discourses/repertoires of ethnicity and examples
manifested in talk

Dominant discourses/repertoires of ethnicity in Japan	Dominant discourses/repertoires of ethnicity manifested in talk in Japan
'A discourse/repertoire of homogeneity' Denies ethnic diversity in Japan. 'Japaneseness' is equated with nationality, race, ethnicity, and language.	'Japan is a homogeneous/monolingual/ monocultural country/society.'
'A discourse/repertoire of conformity' Promotes the undesirability in Japan of standing out as different; people must work hard to perform or appear to be within Japanese norms, or can expect to be 'hammered down' into conformity.	'The nail that sticks up gets hammered down.' (Japanese proverb)
'A discourse/repertoire of gaijin otherness' Denies that people with non-Japanese features could be Japanese citizens or could understand Japanese customs, language or behaviour.	'Gaijin are not Japanese (citizens, race, ethnicity).' 'Gaijin speak English.' 'Gaijin cannot speak Japanese.' 'Gaijin cannot use chopsticks.' 'Gaijin cannot eat sushi.'
'A discourse/repertoire of multi-ethnic halfness' A deficit, subtractive discourse which constitutes multi-ethnicity as incomplete Japaneseness.	'She/he (Japanese-white person) is haafu (half)'

this discourse illustrates the notion of the disagreeableness of anyone standing out as different.

A dominant discourse of homogeneity denies that Japanese citizens with non-Japanese (or multi-) ethnicity exist in Japan, constituting people with non-Japanese features as foreigners and 'the other'. I have identified this as 'a discourse of *gaijin* (foreigner) otherness'. Intersecting with this discourse is, I propose, 'a discourse of multi-ethnic *halfness*'. The predominant word in common usage to refer to children of Japanese and white mixed-parentage multi-ethnic people is *haafu* (half). This constitutes multi-ethnic individuals on the basis of foreignness or of *incomplete* Japaneseness, in a subtractive manner within what has been called a 'discourse of deficit' (e.g., Sunderland, 2004).

In terms of alternative discourses of ethnicity, this deficit or 'subtractive' discourse of 'halfness' has, however, been contested and reconstituted in an 'additive' manner as 'doubleness' by the foreign-raised parents of multi-ethnic children within their communities in Japan, through their creation and use of an alternative word, *daburu* (from the English 'double'). This 'grass-roots'

Table 12.2 Alternative Japanese discourses/repertoires of ethnicity and examples manifested in talk

Alternative discourses/repertoires of ethnicity in Japan	Alternative discourses/repertoires of ethnicity manifested in talk in Japan
'A discourse/repertoire of diversity' Recognises and allows for the positive constitution of *difference* as enhancing and valuable.	'Japan is a multi-ethnic, multilingual, multicultural society'
'A discourse/repertoire of interculturalism' Promotes the value of intercultural 'savvy' as cultural capital – ability to: speak a foreign language; access global information; use the Internet in other languages; maintain connections, relatives or good friends overseas.	'People are different than they appear.'
'A discourse/repertoire of (*gaijin*) foreign/ethnic attractiveness' or 'a Western female beauty discourse' Positions white Westerners (and multi-ethnic Japanese-Caucasians) as more attractive than Japanese or Asians.	'Westerners have high noses (*hana ga takai*), prominent features or deep-set eyes (*hori ga fukai*).' 'Westerners have 'good body style': females: nice hips, breasts, legs; males: hunky chest, broad shoulders, tall.'
'A discourse/repertoire of multi-ethnic doubleness' A deconstruction of the deficit notion of 'halfness' in order for parents to offer their multi-ethnic children a more empowering discourse of ethnicity.	'She/he (Japanese/white person is *daburu* (double)).'

term emerged within this community as a new ideological discursive resource, through which these parents could offer their children a more empowering discourse. I call this 'a discourse of multi-ethnic doubleness'.

Another alternative discourse of ethnicity, which I call a 'discourse of diversity', competes with the dominant 'discourse of homogeneity' and allows for the *positive* constitution of difference. In addition, emerging from an earlier 'discourse of internationalisation' during the economic boom of the 1980s, linguistic traces have appeared in recent years of a third discourse which I have named a 'discourse of interculturalism', within which the mass media and advertising industries in Japan promote the value of intercultural skills such as foreign language proficiency, access to information and overseas connections.

A 'discourse of (*gaijin*) foreign/ethnic attractiveness' (or 'Western female beauty discourse') is a fourth alternative discourse of ethnicity. This was identified by Darling-Wolf (2003), although she did not refer to it specifically as a discourse. From a feminist perspective, she examined how 29 Japanese women in Japan negotiated and constructed attractiveness in the light of Westernised media representations. All her participants positioned white Westerners as more physically attractive than Japanese; for example, 'Westerners are more beautiful, they are tall, have high noses, big eyes, and a good sense of style', 'They have good [body] style, you know, compared to Japanese models, they have nice breasts, nice hips, longer legs' (Darling-Wolf, 2003: 165–6). Many of Darling-Wolf's Japanese participants constructed a hierarchy in which they placed 'whites' at the top, 'halves' in the middle and Japanese at the bottom. Below, I look at some data illustrating how the participants of this study also discursively draw on this discourse in the constitution of their identities.

Ethnically embodied 'ideal other'

During a group interview when the girls were 13 years old, I showed them a Japanese children's book on the human body. I pointed out the only three exceptions in the entire book of 128 pages (with illustrations and photos on every page) where *foreigners* had been used in place of *Japanese* people. I asked them to consider in one of these examples why, in order to showcase the human genitals, instead of using Japanese children, photos of naked (blonde-haired) white children were used. Several of the girls, drawing on a 'discourse of foreign attractiveness', observed that the 'style' of (White) foreigners was better than that of Japanese people. One girl said:

> G: **datte mune toka, dekaishi, nihonjin shoboi mon na**
> *after all their* (foreigners') *breasts and stuff are large, Japanese are plain*
> (poor-looking, lacking)

This multi-ethnic girl thus positioned herself (and the others present) as a member of an ethnically exotic and diverse group in contrast to Japanese people whom she positions as plain. Later, in the same 'Last Reunion' meeting, one of the girls, Hanna, asks everyone, 'what is special about being double?' Hanna chooses to use the alternative term 'double' instead of 'half', perhaps to signal a challenge to the deficit notion of 'halfness' and also to index in-group solidarity. Rina answers:

> R: **un, kanaa, kou, yappa, sugoi ekizochikkuna (laugh) kaodachi (?) ni narukara**
> **(laugh), uchi wa kekkou sukidashi, nanka**
> *um, what, because you would have an extremely exotic (laugh) facial shape*
> *(laugh), I really like that, somehow*

Rina draws on a 'discourse of ethnic attractiveness' in discursively creating for herself, and other multi-ethnic 'doubles', the positive 'embodied' capital of attractiveness based on their ethnicity.

During this meeting, I asked the girls to draw self-portraits of their own faces. While I was temporarily absent, a spontaneous (fortunately recorded) conversation ensues, when Hanna starts talking about the features of a girl not present, Jasmine. The other girls ask questions about Jasmine, first concerning her ethnicity: 'Is she Japanese?' Hanna answers, 'Chinese, but Japanese', leaving her ethnicity vague, while Rina describes her as, *'nihonjin-rashii kedo, bimyou'* ('she's kind of Japanese-like, but it's subtle'). As I show in Extract 1 below, Hanna positions Jasmine as more than *just* Japanese and as 'very cute', also drawing on a 'discourse of foreign/ethnic attractiveness'. The original talk was in Japanese, indicated in bold print below. Extract 1a provides the English translation.

Extract 1   Creating the ideal 'embodied' other

001   H: **Jazumintte hitona chou hada shirokute, hada meccha kirei yanenndena,**

002   **juuhassai nanyakedona, muccha na suppin yanon ni chou kirei yanenka hada ga,**

003   **dena, me ga na, konna Ajiajin yanoni meccha dekakutena,**

004   **me no shita, ko, (?) kou natteyan, are mitaiyan, meccha kawaii**

005   **dena, kuchibiru wa na usukutena, hana wa takainenka,**

006   **takai tteiuka meccha kireide totonottennen, chou kawaiide**

Extract 1a

001a   H: *that girl, Jasmine, has extremely white skin, her skin is really beautiful,*

002a   *and she is eighteen, her skin is really beautiful without using make-up, and*

003a   *her eyes, even though she's Asian, her eyes are really big, and*

004a   *and under her eyes, (?) it's like this, like that, totally cute*

005a   *and her lips are thin, her nose is high (prominent),*

006a   *not just high, but extremely pretty and well-featured, she's extremely cute*

Hanna appears enamored by Jasmine's attractiveness – her big eyes and white skin – and, in what might be a search for her own subjective ethnic embodied 'self', looks up to Jasmine (four years her elder) as an idealised role model. In her study of teenage girls, Bloustien (2001) examined how girls come to view their own bodies against a model of those they aspire to look like and be like. They negotiate a 'discourse of femininity', prevalent in the media and advertising, which constantly reinforces the idea of the 'idealised other'. Bloustien (2001) asserts that scrutinising and commenting on the physical features of others is a common, even universal, practice of adolescent girls. Hanna does this here in detail. Drawing on a 'discourse of *(gaijin)* foreign/ethnic attractiveness' ('Western female beauty discourse'), she points out Jasmine's exceptional *gaijin*-like alluring features (big eyes, thin lips, high nose, white skin), *in spite of* her Asian ethnicity, positioning Asians (in general) as less attractive and as outsiders. At the same time, Hanna creates for herself and the other girls the cultural capital of ethnic attractiveness as she self-identifies with having non-Japanese/non-Asian features of Western beauty.

In the following section I examine an excerpt where the girls work to deconstruct their own negative self-positioning.

Deconstructing disempowering ethnic embodiment

This section examines the second of three segments of an extract from the 'Last Reunion' meeting (see Kamada, 2006). In the first segment, the girls express their 'hatred' of being constituted as *half* when they were little. However, they agree that they are happy *now* to be *half*, using traces of a 'discourse of diversity', where difference is constituted as *good*. In the second segment (Extract 2, below), the girls talk about the difficulties they had during their elementary school years, when fewer empowering discourses of ethnicity were available to them. The extract starts after a statement from Anna who said that she hated a school trip photo in which only *her* face stood out as 'different':

Extract 2   I wanted to be Japanese

001	H:	mmm, issho, shougakkou gurai no toki wa meccha tsurakatta
002	L:	mmmm
003	G:	nanka, nihonjin ni naritai to omottetashi
004	G:	wakaru
005	G:	meccha omou
006	G:	minna (?) narou, narouto
007	G:	kaminoke kurokushitai to omoteittamon
008	L:	assonano?
009	G:	kaminoke dake ureshikatta, kao wa iyayatta (laugh)
010	N:	watashino kaminoke motto kurokatta karana
011	G:	itsumo (?)
012	L:	mmmm
013	R:	kinpatsu yatte shuugou shashin mitai (?) hitori dake na kin, kinpatsu ni kagayaiten na
014	G:	kakkoi
015	L:	ahountou? Naomi wa soiunakatta?
016	N:	ah, meccha iyayatta
017	L:	un
018	N:	nanka, meccha chicchai gakkou yakara, sugu naretakedo, sai-, nanka,
019		meccha, mukatsuku hito toka ga, sore o riyuunishite,
020		'anata haafu yakara' dounokouno haafu (?)

Extract 2a

001a H: *mmm, the same with me, it was really hard just during elementary school*

002a L: *yeah*

003a G: *I felt like I wanted to be Japanese and stuff*

004a G: *I know what you mean*

005a G: *I totally know (what you mean)*

006a G: *everyone becomes (?), tries to become*

007a G: *I felt like I wanted to darken my hair*

008a L: *oh really?*

009a G: *the only thing I was happy about was my hair, it was my face that I hated* (laugh)

010a N: *because my hair was darker then, than now*

011a G: *always (?)*

012a L: *uh-huh*

013a R: *I was blonde, in my school trip photo, I was the only one with blonde, sparkling blonde hair*

014a G: *that's cool*

015a L: *oh really? didn't that kind of thing happen to you Naomi?*

016a N: *ah, I totally hated it*

017a L: *uh-huh*

018a N: *somehow, because my school was extremely small, I got used to it soon but, somehow,*

019a   *there were totally disgusting people, using the reason,*

020a   *'because you're half', you're like this or that because you're half*

Within the dominant discourses of 'homogeneity' and 'conformity', the girls express feelings of powerlessness as a result of their physical salience. In the telling of their elementary school experiences, they co-construct the notion of Japanese conformity by positioning themselves as wanting to be something that they are not – dark haired and Japanese-looking: 'I felt like I wanted to be Japanese and stuff'; 'I felt like I wanted to darken my hair'; 'it was my face that I hated'. Repeatedly they resist and contest having been constituted in such a powerless manner, having then taken up these positions within dominant disempowering discourses. While drawing on a 'discourse of homogeneity' to express their feelings of shame based on their multi-ethnic features, they also work to deconstruct this discourse. In describing herself as conspicuous in her school photo with her 'blonde, sparkling blonde hair', Rina positions herself not only as 'different', but also as attractive, within a 'Western female beauty discourse'. This positioning is co-constructed by another girl: 'that's cool'. Now having other alternative discourses available to her, Naomi expresses a contesting voice: 'I totally hated it,' and takes the empowering role of positioning those who constituted her as 'totally disgusting people'. Naomi discursively positions herself as in control: 'I got used to it soon'. In her contestation she draws on a 'discourse of multi-ethnic halfness' by employing the word 'half' to index the voice of others who constitute her in a discriminatory manner solely on the basis of ethnicity.

The topic shifts in the third segment (not reproduced here) to the idea of being constituted as *gaijin* (foreigner). Up to this point, the girls had been co-constructing their disgust of being constituted as 'half' when they were younger, while reformulating the pejorative outsider aspect of 'halfness' into a positive, self-enhancing category. However, they do not take up the position of *gaijin* at all, not even in a reconstructed manner: 'it was like all over if they said "gaijin"'; 'that's totally disgusting'. They assert their agency to resist being positioned as *gaijin* and to contest being constituted within 'a discourse of *gaijin* otherness'.

Performing embodiment and 'fun femininity'

In this final section, I look at how these adolescent girls position themselves in relation to various discourses of gender and ethnicity through play. This, which I refer to as *fun femininity*, included the 'body work' (Bloustien, 2001) of teasing, touching and laughter that continued throughout the entire session of our final meeting. This 'Last Reunion' (named after the girls had been apart for four months, during which time Naomi and Hanna had attended school in Australia) takes place a few days after their return to Japan. From the very beginning of our session, sitting on the *tatami* mat floor around a low table, nearly every time Naomi takes the floor to speak, Rina, seated next to her, reaches out and pushes Naomi's breasts to accentuate them. The girls laugh at this, including Naomi who expresses little objection. Bloustien refers to this kind of touching 'play' as constituting 'different forms of exploration with the body, with space, with relationships' (2001: 109). Early on, however, Naomi responds with *'urusai'* ('you're annoying') to the laughter of all the girls. Then Rina asks:

R: **bura shiteiru, sore**
     are you wearing a bra, there

Naomi answers in the affirmative and then attempts to seriously address my questions. However, she is again immediately interrupted by Rina touching her:

R: **uchi ichiban chiisai**
     mine are the smallest

Here Rina positions herself as less femininely embodied than Naomi (and the other girls). Later in the session (Extract 3, below), *all* the girls focus on

Naomi's newly acquired cleavage, and begin to playfully tease her to see if her breasts are large enough for a pencil to stand up in her cleavage without dropping through to the floor. Speakers in the original extract used mostly Japanese (bold print). The original excerpt also included several 'code-switches' into English (regular print).

Extract 3 Holding a pencil in Naomi's cleavage

(R pushes N's breasts to accentuate them. All laugh, including N)

001 G: **hasameta**

(Gs try to stick a pencil into N's cleavage to see if it holds up without dropping through)

002 N: **mou hahaha** (laughter)
003 G: **misetterukara**
004 H: **nanbo hasameruka?**
005 G: **misetterukara**
[...]
014 G: **yattemite**
015 G: **yatte, yatte, yatte** (clapping hands in rhythm and chanting)
016 R: **Sara, (?) muriyone, wa uchi to onnajide muriyanen**
017 G: **muri**
018 L: I should take a picture right now.
019 N: no, no (laughs) no, no, no (laughs)
020 G: **zettai kyacchiyade (?)**
021 N: **saiaku** (laughing)
022 G: **yameteyo, to katte**
023 G: **yatteyo**
024 N: **iya**
025 L: can't find my camera
026 S: **henna puraido** (to Naomi)
027 S: **henna puraido** (to Naomi)
028 S: **henna puraido** (to Naomi)
[...]
034 N: **saiaku ya**
035 L: with Rina touching it
036 R: **Sa, Sara kochikara oo, oshite, tanima tsukutteageyou**
037 L: wait, **chottomatte**
038 R: **(?) OK sei no, Sara kochirakara oshite**
039 Gs: aaaahhhh (Girls yell as S and R simultaneously push N's breasts accentuating her cleavage)
040 G: **arie hentte**
041 L: **yokuitte**, OK, **chotto mouikkai** (takes a photo)
042   I'm not sure how

043	G:	mouikkai toka iushina
044	G:	pen hasame
045	N:	iya ha, ha (laughs)
046	G:	kore demo hasamareruyaro
047	L:	I'm not sure if that came out (about the photo)
048	G:	mouikkai
049	N:	iya, yamette
050	S:	nani sonna henna puraido
051	Gs:	(laugh)

Extract 3a

(R pushes N's breast to accentuate it. All laugh, including N)

001a G: *it holds it* (the pencil)

(Gs try to stick a pencil into N's cleavage to see if it holds up without dropping through)

002a N: *that's too much, ha ha ha* (laughter)
003a G: *because you're showing it*
004a H: *how many of them* (pencils) *will hold up* (in there)
005a G: *because you're showing it*
[...]
014a G: *let's try it*
015a G: *do it, do it, do it* (clapping hands in rhythm and chanting)
016a R: *Sara, you couldn't do it, right, you are the same as me, we can't do that*
017a G: *impossible*
018a L: I should take a picture of it right now.
019a N: no, no (laughs) no, no, no (laughs)
020a G: *you can definitely catch it* (on camera)
021a N: *this is the worst (laughing)*
022a G: *she said to stop it*
023a G: *do it*
024a N: *yuk*
025a L: can't find my camera
026a S: *you have a strange pride* (to Naomi)
027a S: *you have a strange pride* (to Naomi)
028a S: *you have a strange pride* (to Naomi)
[...]
034a N: *it's the worst*
035a L: with Rina touching it
036a R: *Sa, Sara, you pu- push from that side, let's give her a cleavage*
037a L: wait, *wait a minute*
038a R: *(?) OK, get ready, get set, Sara, push from that side*
039a Gs: aaaahhhh (Gs yell as S and R simultaneously push N's breasts accentuating her cleavage)

040a G: *that's strange*
041a L: (takes a photo) *that's good, OK, one more time*
042a I'm not sure how
043a G: *she said to do it one more time*
044a G: *stick a pen in there*
045a N: *yuk (laughs)*
046a G: *this could be stuck this in there too*
047a L: I'm not sure if that came out (about the photo)
048a G: *take another one*
049a N: *no, stop*
050a S: *why do you have such a pride (about it)*
051a Gs: (laugh)

Here the girls seem to be exploring and challenging the possibilities and limitations of their embodied identities (see Coates, 1999; Maybin, 2002). From a FPDA perspective, Extract 3 depicts the gendered performance of these adolescent girls as they co-construct the following two interconnected, but in some ways contradictory, themes:

(i) 'if you've got it, flaunt it'
(ii) 'if you flaunt it, you deserve what you get'

Both have been identified in similar terms elsewhere as discourses (Sunderland, 2004; Clark; 1998). 'If you've got it, flaunt it' could be seen as a trace of a 'discourse of liberation' (Sunderland, 2004), which implies the empowerment of girls and women through change or action. 'If you flaunt it, you deserve what you get' has also been previously referred to as a 'blame the victim' discourse (see Clark, 1998).

When Naomi tries to resist the 'fun', another girl states twice 'because you're showing it', positioning Naomi as deserving such teasing due to her purposeful flaunting within the second discourse. Some of the other girls discursively position themselves as bodily inferior in relation to a generalised 'ideal' of large breasts and to Naomi's body as an instantiation of that ideal. Rina, who is Naomi's closest friend, instigates much of the performance. As the girls playfully try the pencil trick, Rina says, 'Sara, you couldn't do it, right, you are the same as me, we can't do that'. Rina is implying that if she or Sara were to *try* to hold up a pencil between their 'smaller' breasts, it would drop to the ground, thus positioning them as less *femininely* embodied than Naomi.

I enter the play by producing my camera and preparing to take a photo. When Naomi begins to protest, Sara states, three times, 'you have a strange pride'. The Japanese word, *puraido*, despite deriving from the English *pride*, has the nuance of embarrassment or shame. Linguistic traces of 'if you've got it, flaunt it' can be seen in Sara's positioning of Naomi as 'strangely proud', implying that Naomi *should be* proud of her feminine embodiment, not ashamed. Sara positions Naomi as *strange* for not recognising, celebrating and freely flaunting her positive feminine 'asset'. Just as I prepare to take the photo, Rina tells Sara: 'push from that side, let's give her a cleavage'. As they do so, I take the photo.

I then suggest another photo, but Naomi refuses to pose for a second shot. In response, Sara asks for the fourth time, 'why do you have such a pride about it?', again suggesting that Naomi should be proud to flaunt what she's got, positioning her as 'strangely proud'. Sara here also implicitly positions herself as less femininely embodied than Naomi. Perhaps there is some tension here or 'serious play' (Bloustien, 2001), as some of the girls may have felt a sense of powerlessness in comparison to Naomi's greater 'embodied femininity'.

A discursive psychology lens might allow us to frame this co-constructed play as manifesting two juxtaposed gendered repertoires in the girls' talk:

Girls who flaunt themselves (physically attractive/sexy features), deserve foul play: ('because you're showing it [you're asking for this foul-play]')
and
Girls should be proud to flaunt their *good* (physically attractive/sexy) features: ('you have a strange pride [for not flaunting yourself more]')

If we see the production of these two contradictory repertoires as a co-construction, we can also identify an ideological dilemma in the talk of these multi-ethnic girls. In the data, it was not clear who used the first repertoire or if they were both expressed by the same person. Nevertheless, both seem to emerge from their talk. One 'commonsense' repertoire suggests that one should be proud of one's attractive physical attributes and show them off; the other, used by one of the girls to justify teasing Naomi, contradicts this, implying that if you are not careful to hide your attractiveness (or sexiness), you will be the object of foul play, for which *you* will be responsible ('blame the victim' discourse). Bloustien (2001) similarly examines what she refers to as the 'paradox' of adolescent girls working hard to be in the public gaze – to be attractive and to gain attention – while at the same time having to maintain 'vigilance' in not attracting the unsolicited gaze of sexual harassment or violence.

Of course, this gendered play or performance of *fun femininity* here takes place within a relatively *safe* atmosphere, characteristic of an in-group of (heterosexual) girls alone together. It can be seen as a celebration of the girls' femininity and their solidarity as 'femininely self-positioned' girls. While being the brunt of the joke, Naomi also celebrates this fun femininity, laughing throughout and resisting only slightly. This playfulness was not limited to these few selected excerpts, but continued at various points throughout the meeting. Bloustien refers to the 'joy of physicality' (2001: 107) among adolescent girls, noting that, compared with adult women, they are much more free, relaxed, silly and uncontrolled with their physicality, both in their individual body movements and contact with each other.

Underlying this play, these girls are performing their gendered identities while at the same time positively constituting their *ethnic* identities. Rina repeatedly makes mention of Naomi having returned from overseas with larger breasts (in relation to her own unchanged breasts), which she enviously constitutes as positive and valuable. This occurs against a backdrop of their earlier constructions which revealed traces of a 'discourse of foreign attractiveness' ('white-Western female beauty discourse') where the girls were seen as constituting their 'white' heritage as endowing them with bigger (and thus better) breasts, in comparison to Japanese who they had positioned as 'plain'.

Conclusion

This chapter has aimed to show how a multi-perspectival theoretical and methodological approach can positively contribute to our knowledge of how gender and ethnic identities are constructed. While there are many multi-perspectival combinations of DP with conversation analysis (Speer, 2005; see Benwell and Stokoe, 2006), work that combines and draws on the commonalities of the emerging disciplines of DP and FPDA is less common. Rather than using either approach on its own as an independent theoretical framework, I have drawn on overlapping theoretical notions and analytical tools found in both, aiming for a more integrated analysis of how identity can be discursively constructed. FPDA has helped to uncover linguistic traces of these girls' movement towards more empowering discourses of gender and ethnicity. DP has shed light on the discursive work involved in negotiating identities, and on how commonsense notions (interpretive repertoires) can appear as contradictory paradoxes (ideological dilemmas).

We can see here the effects of large-scale discourses, in which Western ideals of beauty impact on Eastern culture; but also evident is the 'bottom-up' generation or creation of new ideological/discursive resources, in the girls' reconstruction of the notion of 'halfness' into the more empowering one of 'doubleness'. Likewise, we have seen how the situated production of gender and ethnic identity on a micro-level was impacted by dominant and alternative discourses of ethnicity on a broader macro-level. These girls contest ethnic marginalisation within the limiting ethnic discourses of homogeneity, conformity, 'foreignness' and 'halfness', and position themselves within a wider array of alternative competing and more empowering ethnic discourses of diversity, interculturality and ethnic attractiveness.

As adolescent girls confronting issues of how they look, their ethnic embodiment is a foregrounded aspect of their identity. They celebrate their diversity and position themselves and each other within a privileging 'discourse of foreign/ethnic attractiveness', at the same time constituting 'Japanese' as 'ordinary' and as being without access to this 'special' cultural capital. In search of their own subjective ethnically embodied selves, these *daburu* girls negotiate notions of femininity and the 'idealised other', blending together their ethnic and gendered identities.

Acknowledgements

I would like to express my deepest gratitude to the six participants of this study who made this work possible in the first place. I would also like to sincerely thank Nigel Edley, Lia Litosseliti and Jane Sunderland for their generous and constructive comments on earlier drafts of this chapter. Any remaining errors or inaccuracies are entirely my own.

Transcription conventions

Convention	Explanation
(?)	undecipherable speech
?	rising intonation, question
(laugh)	laugh
,	(comma) continuing intonation (utterance not completed)
bold print	Japanese (actual speech) (Hepburn Romanisation System)
italic print	English translation of spoken Japanese
regular print	actual speech as spoken in English (not translation)
(explanation)	explanation or clarification in parenthesis
'quotation marks'	quoted speech or inferred voice of another person

The girls (pseudonyms):

R = Rina
N = Naomi
S = Sara
H = Hanna
A = Anna
M = Maya

Also:

L = Laurel (researcher)
G(s) = unidentified girl(s)

Part 5
Critical Discourse Analysis

13
Controversial Issues in Feminist Critical Discourse Analysis

Ruth Wodak

1 Introduction[1]

In recent years, we have experienced a huge amount of research in Gender Studies from many perspectives, including linguistic ones. The field of 'Gender and Language' is alive and well: new journals are popping up, new books, conferences, discussion forums and so forth.[2]

Thus, it is time to reflect: what are the most important agenda? Which are the (most) adequate methodologies and methods? What are their innovative aspects and which dimensions are now almost common knowledge? Most importantly, what are the relevant controversies and unsolved problems? Why do we need a 'Feminist Critical Discourse Analysis' (FCDA) as proposed by Michelle Lazar (2005), and how do FCDA and Critical Discourse Analysis (CDA) with all its various approaches differ? Let me briefly flag up each point in turn.

One issue of major importance for (F)CDA is the concern to isolate 'gender' as a variable or factor in investigating social phenomena. Clearly, every human being belongs to many groups and has multiple identities, some of which are sometimes backgrounded due to context, others foregrounded. The constellations change due to, *inter alia*, situational and socio-political contexts, functions of the interaction, intentions of the participants.

A feminist perspective would claim that many social problems are inherently gendered, thus not viewing 'gender' or 'sex' as isolated variables, but as dimensions informing theory and methodology in all research (see Donato et al., 2006: 19ff.). I return to Donato's specific proposals when presenting my short case study below in a discussion of what the specific feminist angle could be.

In this respect, Lazar rightly observes that CDA has been carried out mainly by white middle-class male researchers; while female and feminist researchers have been quoted, their research has not been adequately integrated (Lazar, 2005: 7ff.). This is right up to a point (Lazar is justified in claiming that this body of research remains relatively marginalised and that third world researchers are rarely invited as plenary speakers – neither non-Western male nor female colleagues); however, the huge amount of research noted above seems to contradict this opinion in some ways.

This leads us to a second important theoretical and methodological issue when undertaking CDA: how do we study the context of our texts, of the social problems we would like to tackle? Which context? This is, of course, not a new question.[3] However, attempts to operationalise the relevant aspects of co-texts and contexts are few and rarely successful.

In FCDA, we need to think even further: how and in which way does gender come into play when studying texts in contexts? How do we define and operationalise 'gendered discourses' or the influence of gender on communication? In my view, highly differentiated analysis of context and text is needed: often, each text is informed by multiple identities of speakers and receivers; the priority and relevance of gender in each specific context thus has to be carefully validated. Moreover, we need to consider Butler's (1990) claims that gender, as performed and constructed, also *(re)produces* context. Although I am opposed to generalising Butler's approach because performativity, in my view, is mostly applicable to women (and men) who are in powerful positions and thus able to define their roles, identities and practices much more easily than women from less privileged domains, everybody certainly influences and thus constitutes discourses and contexts through their activities (see Wagner and Wodak, 2006, for a discussion).

In relation to multiple identities, we also have to ask ourselves if 'gender' is always as relevant as often assumed in the literature. There are many situations where other identities *override* gender identities. An extreme historical example is the *Shoah* where the racist categorisation through the Nazis – that is, being perceived as Jewish, Roma, socialist, communist, homosexual and so on – determined deportation and extermination in concentration camps. Exclusion from all domains of life was primarily informed via a racist categorisation. Although the experiences of victims after deportation have varied along gender lines (see Kertesz, 2004; Klüger, 1973), ethnicity, religion, political affiliation, racialisation and sexual orientation were much more salient than gender. Other researchers have also challenged and interrogated the universality of the category 'woman', specifically from a feminist, ethnic, and lesbian perspective (see, e.g., Franklin, 1996).

This leads me to my fourth controversial issue: woman=/= woman=/=woman ....
Although many early feminists suggested that all women should, as 'sisters', behave in solidarity towards each other, this is clearly not the case (see Kotthoff and Wodak, 1997; Wodak, 1986, for a discussion). Such feelings and conflicts, which clearly affect our lives, professionally and privately, may be enacted differently amongst women, but enacted they are (Wagner and Wodak, 2006). Yet jealousy, envy and competition have been taboo for a long time as topics of feminist research. Female friendships have been studied extensively (Coates, 1997), but not patterns of conflict, except in the very young (Sheldon, 1997).

Conflicts among women also arise due to very different role models, ethical values, social class, as well as political affiliations. The debates about Angela Merkel or Maggie Thatcher becoming chancellor/prime minister of their respective countries illustrate such tensions well: many argued during the German elections 2005 that it would be important to 'have a woman in that position irrespective of their political beliefs', whereas others stated that the basic political party programmes were more relevant. I believe that such a dichotomist perspective which distinguishes between 'men' and 'women' belongs to the past (see, e.g., Mills, 2004, for a discussion).

In sum: if we take such problems into consideration, feminist critical linguists should be aware of the multiple contextual factors and their inter-dependency, multiple positionings and the multiple identities women and men perform and live. Moreover, linguists should work to integrate relevant interdisciplinary insights and multidisciplinary research – the wheel does not have to be reinvented![4] Analyses of texts (conversations, speeches, documents, media) should address all these.

I now discuss some of these 'open questions' in regard to theoretical and methodological aspects of gender and language study and in relationship to various traditions in Critical Linguistics and Critical Discourse Analysis. I also briefly present some proposals for 'Feminist Critical Discourse Analysis', elaborating Lazar's (2005) suggestions, and illustrate these with an empirical analysis of focus group discussions with migrant women, while adapting the discourse-historical CDA approach to issues of gender more specifically (Wodak, 2001a,b; Reisigl and Wodak, 2001).

2   Combining CDA and FCDA

> The marriage of feminism with CDA ... can produce a rich and powerful critique for action.
>
> (Lazar, 2005: 5)

> For feminist CDA, the focus is on how gender ideology and gendered relations of power are (re) produced, negotiated and contested in repre-sentations of social practices, in social relationships between people, and in people's social and personal identities in texts and talk.
>
> (Lazar, 2005: 11)

Starting with these two relevant principles, one problematic issue mentioned above immediately comes to mind – FCDA seems to focus on and define its focus mainly as *gender*; other identities seem to be ignored, other discursive and material practices too. The complex relationship(s) between the many important social factors and phenomena constituting our identities are rarely mentioned, even neglected. In opposition to much traditional research in CDA, such foregrounding of gender might make sense – however, many feminist researchers in CDA *have* been following these principles for a long time[5] (although Lazar's (2005) critique also relates to routine research practices and institutional practices of CDA, where Lazar does have a point). In my view, however, critical science and critical approaches need to *combine* many more perspectives; otherwise, we risk attracting accusations of reductionism. To avoid this, I suggest elaborating some of Lazar's proposals, thereby relating FCDA to CDA in more detail (see Wodak, 2004). (The list below, which relates primarily to CDA and specifically its Discourse-Historical Approach, is by no means comprehensive.)

1. The theoretical approach needs to be *interdisciplinary* because the problems to be investigated are too complex to be covered by only one traditional discipline. Donato and colleagues (2006) also stress this, specifically for migration studies. Interdisciplinarity, however, has always been at the core of CDA.
2. The theoretical and methodological frameworks are problem-oriented; thus social phenomena need to be investigated. Problems require specific adequate 'middle-range' theories as frameworks. Thus, when investigating voices of female migrants, we have to turn to research *outside* Communication Studies and Linguistics (see below).
3. These first two principles imply that the specific approach to a problem will necessarily be eclectic, abductive and retroductive, oscillating between theories, methodologies and data, and constructing an explicit approach adequate for the problem under investigation.
4. Multiple genres and public spaces should be included while studying a social phenomenon or problem, to allow for various perspectives (a form of triangulation). This implies taking intertextuality, interdiscursivity and recontextualisation into account as well as material practices. Moreover, inflationary terms such as 'discourse', 'identity' and 'context' need to be explicitly defined in relationship to a specific theoretical framework.
5. Such an approach needs to be context-dependent, contextualised and thus historically oriented. The notion of 'intertextuality' inherently implies taking synchronic and diachronic communicative events into account.
6. 'Critical' means constant self-reflection by the researcher, distance from the data, defining one's position and values as well as research interests explicitly, and being aware of multiple readings when analysing specific texts. Being critical means not taking social phenomena and processes for granted, opening up alternative options, and de-mystifying power relations, latent beliefs and ideologies while de-constructing texts and discourses systematically and precisely in a retroductable way. (This relates well to Lazar's definition of 'critical' (2005: 14ff.).)
7. Finally, practice and application should be aimed for. This principle is also endorsed both by CDA and FCDA (e.g., in proposing guidelines for non-discriminatory language behaviour).

Let us now summarise briefly more specific proposals which might be relevant to FCDA, taking some of the controversial issues mentioned above into account. This list is not to be viewed as an alternative to FCDA but as an attempt to specify its more general claims (Lazar, 2005: 4ff.) while including the traditional framework of CDA (specifically points 5 and 6):

1. Critical Research on gender should challenge simplistic dichotomies: the whole range of gendered identities in context needs to be considered.
2. Gender should be related to social class, ethnicity, profession, culture, religion and so forth, following the proposal to study multiple public spaces and genres related to a social problem. Gender is always present as a more (or less) salient factor, along with other factors; its specific relevance is context-dependent. Foregrounding gender in a specific investigation or piece of research needs to be justified (as in any research perspective).
3. Gender relations need to be studied over time and space. They change, due to sociopolitical developments. Thus, gender relations form part of larger and more complex social phenomena.
4. Gender can be viewed as an ideological construct. However, many material practices are also involved. Due to context, ideologies are often in stark contrast to material practices, which depend on complex decision-making. For example, gender equality and gender mainstreaming are part of most constitutions in Western democracies; daily practices, however, prove that often neither is the case (Wodak, 2003).
5. Critical studies of gender relations should aim at deconstructing the hegemony and symbolic violence of gender in sociopolitical contexts. Often gender is inherently linked to other identities and subject positions. This should be taken into account.

Of course, there are huge limitations in all programmatic statements. A combination of these two lists could be viewed as an 'ideal' research programme which can only ever be implemented partially. However, in sum, I believe that research on gender would benefit when asking some basic and constitutive questions by combining the two lists above, that is:

- being aware of the complex context – when does it make sense to foreground gender? Why?
- When analyzing gender issues and thus 'isolating' one of many variables, asking what this entails and what might accordingly be backgrounded or even neglected?
- When reducing complexity through focusing on gender, how restricted is the explanatory power of the analyst?
- Which contexts and variables are more salient in gender and language study than others?

As research always entails multiple selection procedures (of data, theories, methodologies), these questions should be borne in mind and the researcher should be aware of what each decision entails.

I now present aspects of a feminist, theoretical and methodological approach to CDA, addressing some of the above-mentioned issues. Illustrating the specific methodology, the data comes from focus groups of migrant women.

3   Migrant identities in context: combining the discourse-historical approach to CDA and FCDA

3.1   Defining the Problem

Extract 1

Well me for example I do feel like being in between (1.5) I feel as neither nor a foreigner (.) or or well I don't know (.) sometimes when I am between the Austrian girls (.) then I do feel like a foreigner (.) whereas I am not any I don't know I am not any pure foreigner I was only born here but my roots are in Turkey (0.5) and that is why I only know life as it is here (.) the life here and I do not know what it's like over there that is why when I go there I feel myself somehow different because because they are also well for example I do not know Turkish THAT well and so (0.5) and (0.5) well when I go there then they say' that I am born there' and so (.) and here when I come here then they say that I am I am well that I am Turkish (0.5) I am Turkish and so but (.) I am one but ((laughs)) I am not saying now that I am not but well I fell-I feel in between I don't know well I feel

(AT-F2)[6]

In this short text, this young Turkish woman who lives in Austria and has Austrian citizenship points to problems common nowadays in an articulate and moving way: where does she belong? Which identity/ies does she have?

Migrants experience the problem of 'not knowing where one belongs to' in an acute way. This problem is often more relevant for women because women are still explicitly treated differently and discriminated against in most host societies. This relates to employment, education and housing; discrimination has also become very visible in the 'headscarf' and 'veil' debates in France, Germany (Calavita, 2006; Silvey, 2006) and the United Kingdom where states seek to control women's bodies and where their bodies and religious beliefs are at the centre of the so-called 'equality' of cultures. Migration could thus be regarded as a gendered, religious and social-class issue (see below).

This young woman feels she does not belong anywhere anymore, neither to the country of her origin, nor to the host country. Wherever she moves, she does not (yet) belong, and she has not yet acquired a sense of identification; even if she or her family might already have citizenship in the host country. As repeatedly expressed in this short reflective quote, she just 'does not know'.

Such experiences of both female and male migrants must be seen in a broader European context, where migration has become frequently, and increasingly, stigmatised, both in public debates and in everyday encounters. In Europe in general, and in eight (Western, Central and Eastern) European countries in particular,[7] migration has had different meanings and been reacted to in various ways. Reactions depend on the country of origin (migrants from Germany or the United States are treated differently from those from Turkey), and on symbolic capital (how educated are they? which professions do they have?), language proficiency (how well do migrants speak the language of the host country?) and gender (Turkish women are treated differently from Turkish men; Nigerian women from Nigerian men, related to stereotypes and prejudices as well as values and norms of the respective women and their cultures of origin (Piper, 2006)). This necessarily non-finite list points to the complexity of the problem: gender is related to norms of upbringing, thus to culture, religion, social class, race, and to the beliefs, ideologies, membership categorisations and laws which prevail in the host country. In this illustrative case study, I focus on a few salient aspects of gendered migration: symbolic violence, recognition and everyday experiences of discrimination and exclusion.

Helena Flam and Brigitte Beauzamy (2006), in their research on symbolic violence (see Bourdieu, 1991 (1972), also Section 3.3.) against migrant women in the EU project mentioned above,[8] state that

> feminist research redefined symbolic violence to stand for denying the presence, skills or contributions of the 'other'. It called attention to real and symbolic status downgrading, showed how a male-dominated society denigrates women, renders their multi-facetted contributions virtually invisible, while turning down their demands for equal rights and social recognition (see also Krais, 1973).

Although some commonalities are observable (i.e., statistically, migration in Europe is on the rise, and it is emphasised throughout the EU that 'ageing Europe needs migration'), migrants are treated in various countries in highly ambivalent and discrete ways, according to official policies which usually aim at cultural, linguistic and other forceful 'assimilation' of migrants, rather than mutual 'integration'. Actions of the European Union seem to add to the ambivalence when approaching migration: while European 'richness in diversity' and the liberal stance on ethnic, linguistic, religious and cultural plurality of European societies is 'praised' on many occasions (e.g., in actions such as '2001 – EU Year of Languages' or in the recent 'Future of

Europe Debates' resulting in the widely debated 'EU Constitutional Treaty', cf. Krzyżanowski, 2005), the European Union's 'fortress Europe' excludes many migrants and denies their right to mobility and residence in European countries; it also makes 'combating (illegal) migration ... one of the top priorities of the European Union' (Busch and Krzyżanowski, 2007; Krzyżanowski and Wodak, 2007).

Thus, in the European context, where migration has been approached as a 'statistical' or 'demographic' need and a 'temporary anomaly' rather than a permanent and positive element of sociopolitical reality, the question of migrant identities and belonging becomes particularly important. However, too often, the gender dimension of migration is neglected (Tona, 2006; Mirdal and Ryynänen-Karjalainen, 2004).

When studying such a highly complex issue which relates to salient gender relationships, we thus need to contextualise our 'object under investigation' (following the principles spelt out above). The young Turkish woman who considers her 'belonging' or 'non-belonging' is one of many Muslim Turkish, Nigerian and Bosnian women which Michał Krzyżanowski, Fleur Ulsamer and I studied in focus group discussions in 2003/4 in various towns in Austria. Due to the fact that we had sampled a huge amount of everyday experiences from male and female migrants and had analysed many EU documents, national policy papers, media reports and political rhetoric, we were now in a position to draw more general conclusions which would extend the scope of this methodologically-oriented paper (see Jones and Krzyżanowski, 2007; Krzyżanowski and Wodak, 2007; Delanty, Jones and Wodak, 2008).

3.2 Brief theoretical considerations: sociopolitical analysis

The second important step in our context-dependent, critical analysis, which here serves illustrative aims, summarises some of the relevant theoretical literature and research which allow us to arrive at specific hypotheses and methodologies to operationalise our research questions (see Krzyżanowski and Wodak, 2006, and Donato et al., 2006[9] for extensive reviews of theories and methodologies related to migration, belonging and identification). This implies moving to interdisciplinarity (as proposed above) and integrating theoretical approaches from other, neighbouring disciplines.

The primary research questions could be formulated as follows: What makes gendered migrant identities so 'special'? Why is it still very difficult to analyse gender identities in the context of migration both theoretically and methodologically in an adequate way?

One possible solution to the problem of approaching migrant identities in general might consist of rethinking the way in which 'identity' is commonly conceptualised. Taking up Anne-Marie Fortier's approach to treat 'identity as threshold ... a location that by definition frames the passage from one space to another' (Fortier, 2000: 2) and to look at migrant identity 'as transition, always producing itself through the combined process of being and becoming' (ibid.) would explain why 'migrant identities' can never really be grasped – they are always undergoing change.[10]

Another way out of the dilemma consists in defining migrant identities as 'identity spaces in between' (Krzyżanowski, 2005) or as 'passages' (Probyn, 1996). These help to understand 'how transient, sometimes unclear relationships between self and other contribute to an individual's position *vis-à-vis* a collective identity' (Jones and Krzyżanowski, 2004: 5). To elaborate these assumptions, Krzyżanowski and Wodak (2007) have introduced a different perspective on the concept of *belonging*: we believe that the process of acquiring *feelings of belonging* 'captures ... the desire for some sort of attachment, be it to other people, places or modes of being' (Fortier, 2000: 2). This approach addresses some of the theoretical and methodological problems posed by research on (gendered) migrant identities.

Belonging allows us to focus on 'the ways in which individuals and groups are caught within wanting to belong, wanting to become' (Fortier, 2000: 2), while simultaneously emphasising 'narratives of identity as part of the longing to belong, as constituted by the desire for an identity, rather than surfacing from an already constituted identity' (ibid.). Thus, we emphasise the emotional perspective, feelings of desire and longing to belong which explain the ambivalence encountered in our first example above; moreover, the contradictions between structural membership categorisations through the host countries and subjective perceptions can be investigated.

As 'discourses of belonging' are sometimes strongly characterised by 'uncertainty stemming from the fact that he/she is not yet what he/she wants to become' (Rewers, 2000: 86), they also tend to highlight an urge to identify with 'the other', with 'them' and almost never with 'the same' or with 'us'. Hence, discourses of belonging are almost exclusively constructed on highlighting differences and juxtapositions. Gender comes into play at precisely this point: who do female migrants identify with? Who are their role models? How do they bridge the huge gap between different cultures of upbringing? How can a Western secular lifestyle be linked to a religious Islamic lifestyle in a Western society? Such complex questions require interdisciplinary theoretical and methodological approaches and need investigation in a detailed and differentiated way.

Following Jones and Krzyżanowski (2008), 'modes of belonging' (see Figure 13.1) are constructed in a gradual way, ranging from (a) most tentative *attachments*, through (b) various 'feelings' and other *modes of belonging*, to (c) forms of *membership* (official recognition of one's status, e.g. citizenship).

Once the construction of belonging enters the third stage, various forms of *membership* (e.g., residence or labour rights, citizenship, as well as many

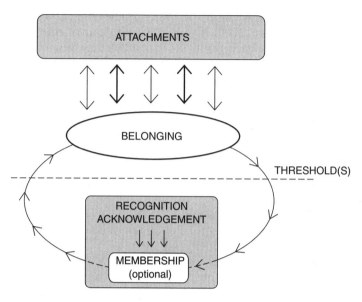

Figure 13.1   Schematic representation of processes associated with belonging
Source: Jones and Krzyżanowski, 2004: 9).

other forms of collective membership) are sought by a migrant. The importance of particular 'thresholds of membership' (see Bauböck, 1994) becomes apparent as numerous obstacles to becoming an accepted member of a particular real-life collective exist. *Recognition and acknowledgment* of one's rights and belonging are finally salient for the 'constructions' of one's belonging, as the latter cannot remain a question of choice, but must be recognised and respected by specific institutionalised sets of practices (e.g., citizenship). If membership in a particular (host) collective is recognised and granted, one's modes of belonging are further 'stabilised'. However, if recognition of one's status as a member is denied, a retreat to previous modes of 'belonging' may take place, thus reinforcing the feeling of remaining 'in-between' various collectives and not belonging to any of them (see Extract 1 above).

3.3   Macro-analysis: genre and topics

Having formulated the problem and some research questions, contextualised the problem and proposed a theoretical interdisciplinary framework, we start on the detailed analysis of our sample texts. In the first instance, here we are dealing with focus group discussions and with sequences taken out of context from a two-hour discussion which develops its own dynamic and conversational flow (see Benke, 2003; Wodak et al., 1999).

We thus encounter a hybrid genre consisting of some typical narrative sequences (Labov and Waletzky, 1967) as well as emotional utterances expressing ambivalent states – anger, sadness and so forth. Without being related to a specific experience or event, these enable us to generalise from many experiences or even use a 'meta-level evaluation' of such experiences. In past research on therapeutic discourse, I have labelled this genre *Problem Presentation* (Wodak, 1996, 1986a,b). There, it became very clear that women were able to present their emotional states much more explicitly than men; however, only working-class women and men were able to express their emotions directly – almost in the form of enacted scenes – whereas middle-class women told coherent stories.

In the case of migrant women, the 'problem presentations' seem to depend more on cultural norms and taboos surrounding the expression of emotions and specific topics as well as on social class. This means – returning to our controversial issues from Section 1 – that one necessarily needs to include other factors apart from gender in the analysis of migrants' experiences. The analysis of topics showed that most (male and female) migrants in our focus groups were concerned with thresholds of belonging – that is, how to arrive at citizenship, housing and jobs, on the one hand; on the other, with every-day experiences of discrimination due to insufficient language proficiency, unemployment and negative stereotypes (see also Bourdieu, 2004).[11]

Apart from categorising the contents of the data, the analysis of discourse topics allows the grasping of the range of themes surrounding the macro-topics developed while discussing the very general aspects of migrants' experiences, prompted by the moderator. When analysing the frequency of topics in detail related to modes of attachment (see Figure 13.1 above), it is striking that female migrants frequently report encountering different forms of discrimination than men (they are paid less for the same jobs, and find it more difficult to get employment other than cleaning or other badly paid, non-prestigious jobs) (see Essed, 1991). Thus, the experience of many non-migrant women is amplified through their migrant status. Moreover, most Muslim or non-White female migrants narrated experiences of being 'looked at' in derogatory and discriminatory ways. In the following, I present some typical qualitative examples related to this quantitative analysis.

Flam and Beauzamy (2008) investigated 'the gaze and the look' and other non-verbal behaviour towards female migrants in the narratives of the women in our groups. They emphasise:

that both our self-definition and our other-oriented dramaturgical acting are unthinkable without the constituting human gaze. But this gaze can turn into an instrument of superordination, superiority and contempt, of surveillance, control and discipline ... The gaze of the 'Other' simultaneously constitutes, judges and, in the very act of judgement, subordinates 'I' to the 'Other'. To reclaim the lost freedom 'I' must look back and thus acknowledge and seek to subordinate the 'Other' (see also Yar, 2002: 60–1).

I will now quote a few examples from Flam and Beauzamy's analysis of the recorded narratives to illustrate the topic of the symbolic power of the 'gaze' which is saliently directed at migrant women. Native glaring prevents migrants from feeling 'really at home', leaving them feeling 'uncomfortable', 'unwelcome', and 'afraid':

Extract 2

It can be hard to feel really at home in Britain ... people look at you like you sometimes (.) like you shouldn't be there and (1.0) like they don't want you there

(UK, Pakistan, F, 42)

Extract 3

... when you walk around the city people look at me (.) ... They do not want migrants to be seen ... Sometimes you are afraid to go out (↓)

(SW, Turkey, F)

Extract 4

... lots of young people were standing around us (-) and just looking at me (-) with my pitch-black HAIR (-) tanned skin (laughs) and dressed like ah a southerner (--) and then it got really uncomfortable (-) suddenly (-) so we left the fair pretty quickly (-) and drove back to the youth hostel (-) and I didn't dare go out on the street anymore (-) I couldn't wait (-) for the day (.) that we drove back two days later (--) it was not a great (--) great (.) great time

(D, Italy, M, 31)

In Sweden, Germany and in the United Kingdom, many migrants thus do not feel accepted. They strongly sense that they should be invisible or disappear. They feel threatened by 'the gaze'. In the case of the two women (Extracts 2 and 3), the headscarf plays an important role, signalling that they are Muslim. In Extract 4, black hair seems to suffice to mark difference.

Symbolic violence, according to Flam and Beauzamy (2008: 3, 29), is also evident in natives blaming migrants for some real or imagined general wrongs, such as run-down neighbourhoods, poor schools or high unemployment rates (see Bourdieu, 2004, for similar narratives from migrants in France). Reflecting current national discourses, many natives see migrants as 'too many parasites who either live off welfare or take the natives' work away from them'. These days they are often lumped together with illegal migrants and 'bogus' asylum seekers to constitute a category of 'immoral, foreign people' endangering one's nation and its welfare state (Wodak and van Dijk, 2000). All these discourses bestow visibility on migrants, but at a very high price. The gaze rests on both women and men; however, female migrants reported these experiences more often and also suffered more from being discriminated in this way because – as they often report – sexual humiliation might also be intended. Moreover, symbolic violence can also be 'patronising' when natives engage in a relationship with migrants on the condition that they accept the natives' superiority (Flam and Beauzamy, 2008). The patronising blend is displayed by Austrians, for example, when they teach migrants how to polish a car, or by Swedes when they show migrants how to celebrate Swedish Midsummer, as reported in other narratives in the focus groups. A female migrant from Mali has the strength to cry out 'Stop putting us down. It hurts' when reporting specific incidents in one of the French focus groups:

Extract 5

We are like you (.) look at the way you live (.) we live the same way (.) We had a misgiving in life which made us the way we are today (.) that's all (.) and it will work out (.) Stop putting us down (.) It hurts (.) It hurts somewhere, all this (.) You read French (.) so do I (.) you write it (.) so do it (.) You do something (.) I know how to do it as well you do (.)

(F, Mali, F, 39)

Flam and Beauzamy (2008) conclude that rather than developing several 'belongings', female migrants may end up with none – the new denied, the old lost. Thus, these – mostly Muslim and non-White – women turn into objects of unceasing harassment, symbolically and legally. Most of these women are also poor, have no adequate jobs (if any) and struggle to find good housing for themselves and their families. Social class, ethnicity, religion and gender interact in complex ways to perpetuate discrimination.

3.4 Micro-analysis

While Krzyżanowski and Wodak (2007) present an extensive and detailed discourse analysis of the narratives and problem presentations of migrants in focus group discussions, gender is not focused on. Here, I summarise just some relevant categories of analysis and illustrate these with brief examples, in terms of the discourse-historical approach to CDA discussed above, thus complementing the findings of Flam and Beauzamy (2008) through an explicit analysis of texts. The following categories are employed to analyze the narratives and problem presentations of 'belonging':

1. **Discursive strategies of self- and other-presentation.** I distinguish between: (a) reference and nomination; (b) predication; (c) perspectivation and involvement; and (d) intensification and mitigation (Reisigl and Wodak, 2001). This

analysis sheds light on how female migrants position actors/objects and which characteristics are attributed to these actors/objects.

2. **Argumentation/metaphors.** *Topoi* – 'content-related warrants or 'conclusion rules' that connect the argument or arguments with the conclusion' – are analysed to systematise argumentation patterns (Reisigl and Wodak, 2001: 75). Here, certain metaphors become particularly relevant (Koller, 2004b; Lakoff and Johnson, 1980).

3. **Grammatical categories – transitivity.** The analysis of verb categories portrays the 'emotionally-loaded' and ambivalent/sentimental constructions of attachments and 'belongings'.

In the following, I focus primarily on metaphors used in describing attachments. Extract 6 illustrates that *metaphors of attachments* ('home', 'sun') are highly emotional in their meaning, and are intensified by possessive pronouns ('my'):

Extract 6

Cuba is my home my family my sun. Everything is there I am here for love and because I wanted a better future but I do not belong here; everything in me says it I am not German ... and I would not like to become German either

(Leipzig-2, F1)

This emotionally laden discourse constructs a strong attachment to one's own group of origin. Attachment to the 'host' group is rejected by the statements 'I do not belong here' and 'I would not like to become German' which are connected through the reference 'here' (spatial deixis = Germany) in the first statement and 'becoming German' in the second. Such constructions show that attachments depict 'belonging' as dependent on one's place of living (geographical conditions). This example convincingly illustrates the dilemma for this female migrant of the difficulty in finding an object of identification, a role model.

The cultural norm of suffering for one's family (parents) is well developed in many parts of the analysed discourse, and strongly supports the *'topos of family'*:

Extract 7

I have my parents. My mother is over there, my father, my younger sisters, my brothers are over there. (...)We endure all this suffering in France to make our parents in Senegal happy.

(Paris, Senegalese, female, aged 33)

This *topos* is intensified by possessive pronouns ('me', 'our') implying that such an attachment may not only be individual (note the shifts in personal/possessive pronouns: 'I–my' to 'we–our'). Mental verbs referring to experience ('endure') intensify the emotional aspects experienced by this female migrant.

Referring to *family* occurs much more frequently with female migrants who would like to transfer their family networks and their family routines to the host country – these women define themselves through their family ties and not through other characteristics (such as professions). However, this is often not possible or is even forbidden. Such identifications point to traditional cultural norms, on the one hand; and to forms of exclusion, on the other, as they often do not have adequate employment.

Finally, I return to Extract 1 which illustrated the problem 'case study' for this chapter:

> Well me for example I do feel like being in between (1.5) I feel as neither nor a foreigner (.) or or well I don't know (.) sometimes when I am between the Austrian girls (.) then I do feel like a foreigner (.) whereas I am not any I don't know I am not any pure foreigner I was only born here but my roots are in Turkey (0.5) and that is why I only know life as it is here (.) the life here and I do not know what it's like over there that is why when I go there I feel myself somehow different because because they are also well for example I do not know Turkish THAT well and so (0.5) and (0.5) well when I go there then they say' that I am born there' and so (.) and here when I come here then they say that I am I am well that I am Turkish (0.5) I am Turkish and so but (.) I am one but ((laughs)) I am not saying now that I am not but well I fell-I feel in between I don't know well I feel

The *topos of multiple attachments* (identified through connectives as 'neither/ nor') is mitigated through particles ('well', 'but', 'somehow'). While mental verbs play a predominant role here ('feel', 'know'), the overriding strategy is further intensified by the *topos of illustration* ('for example ...'). Neither being attached to X nor Y is particularly constructed through deictic elements. While spatial deixis refers only to physical locations ('here' = Austria, 'there' = Turkey), the actual lack of any other groups is covered through the use of the impersonal and vague pronoun 'they' (both Austrians and Turkish: 'when I go there they say' and 'I come here they say'). Such contradictory argumentative constructions manifest the emotional state of ambivalence, of 'being in between'. She has left but not yet arrived. The ideal place for this young woman does not seem to exist.

4 Conclusions: which answers to which questions?

We can summarise the methodological steps of this analysis which follows CDA's Discourse-Historical Approach *and* FCDA as:

1. Historical and intertextual analysis
2. Socio-political analysis
   (these first two steps lead to distinct research questions and hypotheses)

3. Definition of methodology/ies to operationalise the research questions; data collection
4. Macro analysis: genre analysis, topical analysis (quantitative)
5. Micro discourse analysis (qualitative)
6. Interpretation/explanation; relating macro- and micro-levels to each other and detecting the complex relationships between the structural, broader context, gender, ethnicity, social class, religion, culture and so forth, and the subtle linguistic manifestations and discursive practices.

These six stages are linked to the proposals in the first section of this chapter.

I have tried to illustrate the many variables which are connected in complex ways when studying female migrant identities. (It was not possible to present details of the larger study on migrant discourses in other public spheres.) That such a complex issue requires interdisciplinary research should by now be obvious: sociological, political, anthropological and historical theories become important. Moreover, viewing migration in dichotomist terms seems obsolete. This is not a phenomenon where gender can be foregrounded; many other factors come into play.

Studying context does not stay an abstract *desideratum*. At least four levels of context were distinguished here:

- the broad sociopolitical context of migration in the EU since 2000
- the narrower context of specific migrant groups in eight EU member states
- the context of each focus group discussion (specific sub-topics, participants, dynamic of conversation)
- the context and co-text of each utterance of a female or male migrant (linguistic micro-analysis).

These levels are, of course, not clearly separated; they are linked to each other and overlap. Nevertheless, it makes sense to analyse them in chronological order and, at a second stage, relate them to each other as each singular utterance necessarily relates to all context levels (see also Wodak 2001a,b, 1996).

The critical discourse analysis of forms and meanings of belonging illustrates the complexity and multi-layered character of gendered migrant identities. The narratives and emotional, sometimes self-reflective problem presentations of female migrants analysed in this chapter highlight the constant uncertainty and ambivalence which women specifically encounter and are exposed to in their everyday lives in Europe. Everyday discrimination towards migrants tends to be stronger for Muslim and non-White women: they frequently experience particular (sexual) harassment as well as social exclusion and non-acceptance. All these features are reformulated in discourse to display how categorisation and differentiation of 'self' from the 'other' leave a mark on individual and collective identifications.

Gender, gender roles and gender stereotypes are clearly part of the social phenomenon of feeling 'in between'. However, gender has to be contextualised in relation to many other factors, without which this study would have neglected salient dimensions of migration in Europe.

Notes

1 I am very grateful to Anne-Marie Fortier, Veronika Koller and Jane Sunderland for their helpful comments on this chapter. I am, of course, solely responsible for the final version.

2 See Litosseliti (2006a); Sunderland (2006, 2004); Lazar (2005); Mills (2004); Essed, Kobayashi and Goldberg (2004); Holmes and Meyerhoff (2003); Litosseliti and Sunderland (2002); Kotthoff and Wodak (1997); Wodak (1997) for overviews and edited collections.

3 See debates in *Discourse and Society*, 1999; van Dijk (forthcoming); Blommaert (2005); Panagl and Wodak (2004); Wodak (1996).

4 See Barrett and McIntosh (1985); Bulkin, Pratt and Smith (1984); Maynard (1994); Franklin and Stacey (1986); Nicholson (1997).

5 See, for example, Wagner and Wodak (2006); Martin Rojo and Gomez Esteban (2005, 2003); Sunderland (2004); Wodak (2003); Koller, Chapter 14, and Kosetzi, Chapter 15 in this volume.

6 Key to Coding (all quoted examples): (a) country (AT = Austria, CY = Cyprus, FR = France, DE = Germany, IT = Italy, SE = Sweden, PL = Poland, UK = UK); (b) number of a focus group discussion in a particular country (FG 1, FG 2, FG 3, etc.); (c) participant's gender (F = female, M = male) and number (1, 2, 3, 4, 5, etc.).

Transcription symbols:

Symbol	Function
M1, M2, (or other)	Speakers
(.)	Short pause
(6.0), (8,0), (9,0), … 6.0 or 6,0?	Longer pause (six seconds, eight seconds, nine seconds, …)
(incomp. 6.0)	Incomprehensible elements of speech
[	Overlapping speech
Mhm. Eeeeeh	Paraverbal elements
((leans back)),((laughs))	Non-verbal behaviour
[Heimat]	Elements of original language (difficult to translate)
I would not say so	Normal speech
THIS	Accentuated/stressed element of speech
(↑)	Rising intonation (if significant)
(↓)	Falling intonation (if significant)

7 An EU-Fifth-Framework Research Project 'The European Dilemma: Institutional Patterns and Politics of Racial Discrimination', co-ordinated by Masoud Kamali (Uppsala University, Sweden, cf. www.multietn.uu.se), 2002–5, aimed at investigating sociopolitical developments and impacts as well as attitudes towards migration and mechanisms of social exclusion of migrants in eight European countries (Austria, Cyprus, France, Germany, Italy, Sweden, Poland, UK). At the University of Vienna, Michal Krzyżanowski, Fleur Ulsamer (research associates) and Ruth Wodak (PI) participated in the project as the Austrian partner institution. The data in this

chapter draw on 40 focus groups run and analysed during this project (Delanty, Jones and Wodak forthcoming). The summaries of the data, theoretical framework and parts of the analysis draw on Krzyżanowski and Wodak (2007).

8 Helena Flam was responsible for the German team, Brigitte Beauzamy for the French team.

9 Donato and colleagues (2006: 19–20) recommend three aspects to be integrated in feminist research on migration and gender: qualitative and quantitative methods; multidisciplinary teams; and alternative research practices (such as ethnography and questions tailored to suit both female and male migrants). These proposals are of course not new for CDA research.

10 Nobody's identities are stable or finite; however, migrants' identities are significantly different because of the sociopolitical and structural conditions as 'moments of exclusion'.

11 In the initial step of analysis, one needs to consider the topics put forward by the moderators of the focus groups. The first analysis systematised the sub-topics which relate to 'attachment, belonging and citizenship' without relating them to countries of origin, gender or social class in the first step (see Krzyżanowski and Wodak, 2006).

14
CEOs and 'Working Gals': The Textual Representation and Cognitive Conceptualisation of Businesswomen in Different Discourse Communities[1]

Veronika Koller

The case for cognitive critical discourse analysis

This chapter presents an integrated approach to gender and language study combining Critical Discourse Analysis with cognitive semantics, in particular metaphor. More specifically, it looks at the textual representation of women executives in two magazines to draw inferences about the way they are conceptualised at a cognitive level in and for different discourse communities. As shown throughout this volume, the study of discourse is amenable to being combined with other theoretical and methodological approaches, such as corpus linguistics (Part 2), conversation analysis (Part 3) and post-structuralism (Part 6). In this chapter, I discuss discourse in relation to cognition.

Although there is no direct link between discourse and cognition that allows writers' cognitive models to be read off texts, it still seems reasonable to assume a cognitive influence on both text production and text processing. One indicator is the relative stability of how utterances and texts are formulated, produced and received (Sanders, 2005: 63). While this consistency is partly due to discourse and genre conventions, production and understanding of (parts of) text also relies on relatively stable schematic and scriptural knowledge. This is especially relevant in synchronous spoken interaction that requires efficient cognitive processing to be possible at all (see Cicourel, 2006).

Not all cognitive states and models manifest themselves in interaction at all times, and those that do are abstract models rather than hard evidence. Discourse analysis alone cannot *prove* the existence of cognitive entities, but does allow for inferences about the models speakers utilise to structure texts, manage interactions and represent aspects of the world from a particular perspective. Gender models in discourse, gendered interaction and, more generally, gender as an ideological site, are some applications of an integrated study of language, mind and society. Discussing the results of text analysis not exclusively, but *also*, in cognitive terms, is an interpretative approach that provides a richer account of the reciprocal relation between discourse and cognition than theories that posit the primacy of one over the other. Such an interpretative framework stands in contrast to a positivist belief that what cannot be observed in linguistic behaviour cannot be studied in scientifically valid terms (Edwards, 2006b: 47).

The confrontational stance that opponents to cognitivist research sometimes adopt in discussion (and occasionally in writing, e.g., Coulter, 2005) gives rise to the suspicion that the debate might be about more than an academic disagreement on the (im)possibility of empirical observation and the consequent (in)validity of research. It sometimes appears as if work that attends to the cognitive aspects of discourse is regarded as a slippery slope that starts with legitimising individualism and ends with propounding essentialism and excusing social inequality. That is, the argument ultimately seems to be a political one. It seems more fruitful to, however, outline the position on cognition taken in this article and explain why I regard it as a useful complement to discourse studies.

To this end, in the next section I outline the relations between cognition and discourse and look especially at the role of metaphor here. My focus then turns to possible methods that can translate such an integrated research paradigm into empirical study. In the empirical part of this chapter I introduce the data and the way these were collected and analysed, and present the results of a contrastive text analysis. I close with a discussion of similarities and differences in how businesswomen are represented and conceptualised in two magazines and outline what this means for cognitive critical discourse analysis.

Research across boundaries

The recent surge in publications seeking to reconcile cognitive linguistics with critical approaches to language – variously referred to as 'cognitive text linguistics' (de Beaugrande, 2004), 'cognitive sociolinguistics' (Dirven and Kristiansen, forthcoming), 'cognitive pragmatics' (Nuyts, 2004) and 'socio-cognitive discourse studies' (van Dijk, 2006a) – should not obscure the fact that analysis of naturally-occurring language has addressed cognitive issues for some time. Few theories actually deny or ignore the existence of the mind. However, its *relation* to discourse has been discussed in very different, even diametrically opposed ways. For instance, as I show below, discursive psychology (in the Conversation Analysis rather than Foucauldian sense – see

Part 4) makes a strong anti-mentalist point: it 'inverts' the cognitive psychology belief that language is an expression of thought, rather seeing cognitive entities and processes as 'managed within discourse itself' (Edwards and Potter, 2005: 242–3). *Vice versa*, some researchers in CDA have utilised social cognition to complement the study of discourse (van Dijk, 2006a; Koller, 2005).

Discursive psychologists disagree with the cognitivist notion that language and its uses can be treated as a 'window on the mind', that is, that an individual's mental models are reflected in their discourse. Instead, cognitive entities such as beliefs, knowledge, intentions and mental states are seen not as phenomena underlying discourse, but as constructed by text and talk. Consequently, a discursive psychological analysis would look at how participants co-construct such entities by claiming and displaying them in linguistic interaction. Discursive psychology, as well as some strands within cognitive science itself, also takes issue with mainstream cognitive psychology in terms of methods (Potter and te Molder, 2005: 15–22), criticising it for relying on decontextualised laboratory settings – which are only sufficient if one believes that cognitive entities and operations are hard-wired in individuals – rather than on the authentic human interaction that needs to be studied if cognitive entities are seen as at least partly socially constructed. To remedy this, the CA branch of discursive psychology ascertains how orientation towards cognitive phenomena structures discourse, and how discourse constructs participants' understandings of aspects of the world. (In a Hallidayan reformulation, we could here identify the textual and ideational metafunctions of discourse, respectively.)

Discursive psychologists' focus on textually mediated interaction means that such 'activity is treated as primary, and reality and cognition are secondary' (Edwards and Potter, 2001: 15), because they are constructed by discourse. However, discursive psychology does not necessarily subscribe to discourse idealism in the tradition of Wittgenstein (1958), in which there would be no extra-discursive reality:

> Descriptions are constructive of their objects. That is not to say that talk brings things into the world, but rather, that descriptions are categorisations, distinctions, contrasts; there are always relevant alternatives available.
>
> (Edwards and Potter, 2005: 243)

Such a systemic view of discourse dovetails with the Hallidayan (1979) view of language as a system or repertoire drawn upon strategically in actual language use. The cognitive can equally be reintegrated into discourse analysis by using a systemic perspective that regards conceptual metaphors and other mental models as a pool of cognitive resources that speakers can draw on strategically for persuasive or argumentative purposes.

Discursive psychologists reserve their most fundamental criticism for the 'circularity' of cognitive discourse analysis: research that assumes discourse to be based on cognitive entities which in turn give rise to discourse is seen as 'circular' since one part of the model, cognition, is merely presupposed and the argument must return to what is observable, that is, discourse (Coulter, 2005).

Without wanting to split too many hairs, it still seems that what is called circular and hence invalid is actually *cyclical* or reciprocal: discourse activity is shaped (but not determined) by cognition, and cognition is shaped by discourse activity. However, in so far as discursive psychology does not rule out the existence of cognitive entities altogether, it maintains that 'instead of regarding cognition as determining action, we can view interaction as a source of cognition' (Drew, 2005: 181). Concerning script theory, for instance, discursive psychology would start with the observable, that is, the script as presented in talk and constructed there as a cognitive entity, rather than positing that mental scripts are formed in the mind via experience of the world and then expressed in talk (Potter and te Molder, 2005: 31–4). The question is whether one *has* to be assumed as primary at all. Such considerations sound suspiciously like chicken-and-egg problems and it might be more fruitful to assume a cyclical or reciprocal theoretical model in which each impacts on the other. Social cognition provides a valuable starting point from which to develop such a model.

For (critical) discourse analysis, or at least one branch of it, social cognition has been defined as 'the system of mental structures and operations that are acquired, used or changed in social contexts by social actors and shared by the members of social groups' (van Dijk, 2003: 89).[2] Such social contexts provide frames for textually mediated interaction by defining the social roles, identities and relations that impact on every interaction. Furthermore, participants hold models for particular contexts that control the production and comprehension of textual features (such as metaphor). Depending on their position and goal in the interaction, participants may seek to maintain or challenge the power structures that are inherent in interaction. One way is to influence social cognition. The models structured by social cognition are thus acquired and (re)produced in social, including discursive, interaction, and in addition help establish group cohesion by defining a group's membership, tasks/activities, goals, norms/values, position and resources (van Dijk, 1995b).

Work in socio-cognitive discourse analysis has looked at the factors impacting on discourse production (van Dijk, 2005), processing (O'Halloran, 2004) and comprehension (Wodak, 1987). The cognitive structure of ideology has also attracted interest (van Dijk, 2003), particularly in critical metaphor studies (Nerlich, 2005; Charteris-Black, 2004; Koller, 2004b; Musolff, 2004; Zinken, 2003).

Due to its dual nature as conceptual metaphor and metaphoric expression (Lakoff and Johnson, 1980), metaphor is positioned at the interface between cognition and discourse, providing an ideal entry point for research into relations between the two. Thus, the context models held by participants may conceptualise both the other participants as well as the topic of the text in metaphoric terms, which will be reflected in the metaphoric expressions found in the text under investigation. The complex nature of metaphor shows in the fact that it fulfils all three metafunctions posited for language (Halliday, 2004: 61). In addition to its textual function, metaphor helps conceptualise particular social (group) identities and organise relations within and between groups, by defining groups and being used strategically to reflect the models that recipients are assumed to share. As such, it fulfils an interpersonal metafunction. Thirdly, metaphor is ideational, in that it is used to construct reality from a particular viewpoint by conceptualising one thing in terms of another. As early as 1980, Lakoff and Johnson (1980: 156) observed that 'metaphors ... highlight and make coherent certain aspects of our experience ... metaphors may create realities for us, especially social realities'. In potentially performing all three metafunctions, metaphor can be deployed within a CDA tradition and its three-level embedded analytical framework (text; interaction between text producers, distributors and recipients; and the wider socio-economic and socio-cultural context; Fairclough, 1995a: 98). For example, the metaphoric conceptualisation of 'a company [as] an organic, living breathing thing' (*Fortune*, 2000, see below) not only serves to contrast other conceptualisations mentioned later, thus providing textual cohesion and coherence, but also ideationally constructs organisations in particular terms. Interpersonally, the metaphor communicates the speaker's values to the text recipient.

Critical discourse studies centre around social problems and social change, and the role that language – and, as I argue, cognition – play in the production, maintenance and/or subversion of social roles and relations. These will include complex, derived metaphors. The cognitive figures in so far as access to, and recombination of, complex metaphors and other models is limited by social and personal cognition. Thus, we can regard a person's values, stereotypes, memories and knowledge as parts of a system of options which are all potentially possible, although some are more motivated within a given interactional context. In a cyclical fashion, such selective and strategic usage of particular models to structure texts, define interpersonal, intra-group and inter-group relations, and construct reality will see particular models rise to prominence in discourse. Repeated exposure to preferred models under similar conditions would then have a cumulative effect in shaping cognitive models. Particular models could thus be reinforced or modified, or counter-models could emerge from alternative readings. Metaphor again takes a central role by dint of its dual nature (conceptual metaphor *and* metaphoric expression): while metaphor is primarily a cognitive resource, selective metaphor *use* can be seen as an ideologically vested discourse practice.

Certainly, text analysis based on this model does not show, prove or demonstrate the existence of mental models and other cognitive entities, although some conversation analytical studies strongly suggest that knowledge, plans, understanding and so on influence discourse production (e.g. Kitzinger, 2006a: 78–81; Drew, 2005; Heritage, 2005b). This is more difficult to claim of written communication, which is typically asynchronous and literally monologic.[3] Nevertheless, cognitive critical analysis of written texts allows a more comprehensive interpretation of the relations between discourse and cognition than approaches that regard one as primary. How then can cognitive critical discourse analysis be carried out on concrete texts?

Quantitative and qualitative paradigms

Given that conceptual metaphors and other mental models are to an extent constituted, reinforced and challenged intertextually, there is a strong case for harnessing empirical, especially quantitative, methods in cognitive critical discourse studies: if metaphoric models are dispersed within and between discourse communities, then we need to look at authentic data and could benefit from investigating large amounts of it. One tool for ascertaining how, say, metaphor is shared between members of a discourse community is the analysis of electronic text corpora. However, corpus analysis software is not intelligent, that is, it can search for strings of symbols but not identify the semantics of those strings, so mining corpora for metaphor in most cases involves searching for particular expressions. This not only risks missing other potentially important expressions (see Koller, 2006, for further discussion). Despite these obstacles, a number of corpus linguistic studies – with or without a critical angle – have tackled metaphor in discourse (Deignan, 2005; Stefanowitsch, 2005). Since the affordances and shortcomings of corpus linguistic methods for gender and language studies are discussed in Part 2, the focus here is on qualitative methods, which will reasonably supplement any first results gained through quantitative corpus analysis.

Looking at the textual function of metaphor, a qualitative analysis could look at how metaphoric expressions pattern into clusters and chains, lending coherence to a text. Further, metaphoric expressions can instantiate mental models such as beliefs, attitudes or stereotypes by being linked to linguistic parameters – mainly social actors and actions, modality, and attribution and evaluation (Fairclough, 2003; van Leeuwen, 1996) – that construct social roles and relations for discourse participants. Analysing metaphor in relation to other linguistic features provides cumulative evidence for models held by discourse participants. In verbs and verb phrases, for example, a FIGHTING metaphor[4] used to describe female executives could combine with a predominance of material process types and high-affinity epistemic modality to convey an image of forcefulness.

For any study addressing social roles and relations, it is potentially fruitful to look at how social actors are represented in terms of reference, including labels ascribed (van Leeuwen, 1996). Social actor categories are further fleshed out by the particular categories of actions ascribed to particular actors (Halliday, 2004: 170–5):[5]

- *material* processes impacting upon an object or another action
- *behavioural processes* representing an actor's behaviour that does not impact on an object
- *mental-affective processes* capturing what actors (are said to) think and feel
- *verbal-semiotic processes* describing an actor's communicative behaviour
- *relational processes* providing information about an actor's characteristics and attributes
- *existential processes* giving no information beyond the fact that the actor exists.

Lastly, the characterisation of social actors is achieved through attribution and evaluation, that is, the characteristics ascribed to them, which are often combined with the text producer's evaluation. Evaluation can be made explicit through attribution, for example, by calling an actor or her action 'impressive', 'despicable' and so on, or conveyed more subtly, through collocations and the connotations these have accumulated over time. For instance, 'to admit' collocates with entities and actions of negative value, and the sentence 'She admitted to being gay' therefore carries a very different evaluation from 'She stated that she was gay', or 'She came out as gay'.

Metaphor cuts across these parameters in that social actors as well as the actions and attributes ascribed to them can all be referred to in metaphoric form. For instance, a female executive's actions may be referred to in the phrases '[she] blew into [a company]', '[she has] a backbone of steel' and 'she is the lever in an urgently needed turnaround' (*Fortune*, 2000). In any given text, the different metaphoric expressions used can be derived from one or several metaphors. It is one aim of cognitive CDA to reconstruct the mental models as reflected in the text and afforded by the context (participants, topic, genre). Venturing beyond the level of individual texts, the researcher can also look at the scenario that characterises the genre or even discourse which a text constitutes, and is constituted by. A critical analysis will also look at whether the dominant metaphors contribute to or constitute an ideologically vested discourse, and discuss possible alternatives.

More parameters could be added – modality, intertextuality and interdiscursivity, narrative structure – all of which combine to reinforce, or indeed contradict, each other. Analysing texts for particular, clearly defined categories makes the study replicable, and since the categories are chosen with a view to how linguistic features help construct and possibly reinforce models of social actors, the analysis addresses both textual representation and cognitive conceptualisation.

Representing and conceptualising businesswomen for different audiences

In this empirical part of this chapter, I compare the representation of a particular social group, businesswomen, in two formats, business magazines and lesbian magazines. The context of each magazine gives rise to expectations on the part of the reader as to the structure and linguistic features used in the text. The observed similarities can be interpreted as a sign of interdiscursive alignment, with imported genres activating particular models that can modify expectations: the 'ranking' sub-genre (e.g., '500 largest companies') is imported from the business magazine format, which may be alien to most readers of lesbian magazines and hence requires careful introduction and adaptation. Its unexpected inclusion may further draw attention in a lesbian magazine, being inconsistent with readers' schema of such a magazine's appearance and contents. Differences on the other hand are best regarded as an effect of genre conventions, but also as indicating recipient design: the two texts are aimed at different audiences constituting different discourse communities, and the text producers will therefore not only use particular models of the topic under discussion, but also context models relevant for interacting with the respective target readership (van Dijk, 2006b: 170–3).

In terms of data, the study draws on the '50 Most Powerful Women in Business' list published in 2000 by US business magazine *Fortune*, and on the '10 Most Powerful Lesbians' list, published in 2004 by the US magazine *Curve*, explicitly following *Fortune*. These collections of portraits of female executives and entrepreneurs are analysed with a particular focus on actors and reference, process types, attribution and evaluation as well as the metaphoric expressions used to describe the women, to provide cumulative evidence of how they are conceptualised and represented. An extract from *Curve* is reproduced in the Appendix.

Businesswomen in the business magazine

In *Fortune* (extract not reproduced due to publisher's refusal), we can see that the two women in question, Debby Hopkins and Carly Fiorina, are mostly referred to by their last names and occasionally by their first and last names. In this respect, reference to them mirrors that of their male colleagues who feature in the article. This kind of reference is occasionally combined with the women's job titles.[6] More familiar forms of address, such as first names only, are relegated to quotes, and potentially problematic terms like *lady* and *girl* are mitigated by featuring only in indirect speech or formulaic phrases

('McGinn got the girl'). In this way, the writer adheres to a 'politically correct' code of conduct but can still add variation to the style of the article. One effect is that diminutive and much criticised references to professional women as *girls* come in through the backdoor.

As regards process types, material actions dominate, accounting for 44.44 per cent of all actions ascribed to the women. Several of the verbs involved in material processes, and some of those in relational processes, show the semantic feature [+FORCEFUL], for example, 'swept out the finance staff', 'manhandled the top brass' and 'was going full tilt'. Such actions furthermore tend to be grouped in tri-partite arguments to add rhetorical weight. This focus on outward activity that impacts on particular people and objects is corroborated by the relative scarcity of other process types, with behavioural processes accounting for 25 per cent, verbal ones for 11.11 per cent[7] and relational ones for a mere 8.52 per cent. Mental-affective processes are notably absent: readers' attention is drawn to the women's outward achievements while we learn nothing about their (reported) thoughts and feelings. Such a 'can-do attitude' and lack of contemplation is in many ways a characteristic of the culturally masculine corporate sector, extended here to its female members.

What relational processes there are point to the attributes ascribed to the women. Thus, they are represented and, we can infer, conceptualised as 'one of America's top ten CFOs', 'the lever in an urgently needed turnaround' and 'the woman on the verge'. Attribution here is indistinguishable from evaluation. The latter is defined by superlatives and intensifiers, most obviously so in the metaphoric self-description of lines 044–047 ADD, which is so exaggerated as to border on the ironic. Other attributions, such as 'her vibrant silk scarves and bold confidence', equally serve to not only describe but at the same time evaluate the actor. These adjectives can be seen as part of a coherent positive characterisation of someone who is also represented as engaging in forceful material actions. Furthermore, the combination of the stereotypical description of a woman in terms of fashion and clothing, and the non-traditional characterisation of her as courageous, mirror two different types of reference, namely 'politically correct', official terms, as well as more familiar and diminutive forms. Overall evaluation is positive, underscored by the narrative about how another actor's initially negative feelings toward one of the women turned into admiration, and by mentioning how she compensated for 'her poor pedigree'.

Many of these features are reflected in, and supported by, the use of metaphor in the text. Thus, the overall positive evaluation is reinforced by the primary spatial metaphor GOOD IS UP, as realised in the expressions 'rising stars' in the title, or 'top CFOs'. For more complex, derived metaphors, we find a cluster of conceptualisations all carrying the feature [+FORCEFUL], even [+AGGRESSIVE]. One such is the metaphor of NATURAL FORCE, instantiated in one woman's nickname 'Hurricane Debby', which is part of a chain of related expressions ('blew into Lucent', 'her force', and 'I kept blowing him off'). Linked to this is a metaphor of human force, paraphrasable as BUSINESS-WOMEN ARE MACHINES. This is expressed in referring to Debby Hopkins's 'backbone of steel' and as 'the lever in [a] turnaround', with a variation in 'financial reengineers' immediately afterwards. The metaphor is taken up again later, when Hopkins is seen 'going full tilt at Boeing'.[8] The concept of force is intensified by the WARRIOR metaphor, which finds an echo in the BOXER metaphor. As the most aggressive in the cluster of three, the WARRIOR metaphor is intensified but also mitigated, in that it is relegated to a self-description that could be read as ironic.

The metaphors that the writer uses to conceptualise businesswomen as warriors, boxers, machines or natural disasters are in stark contrast to that of BUSINESSWOMEN ARE CAREGIVERS, which is introduced by one of the women herself: by defining a company as 'an organic, living, breathing thing', the person who runs it by extension becomes a nurturer and caregiver. This metaphor is just as gendered as the WARRIOR metaphor: where one represents stereotypical femininity, the other captures a figure of hegemonic masculinity. In fact, the online edition of *Fortune* advertises the businesswomen ranking by drawing readers' attention to '50 women warriors': note how 'warriors' is qualified by the attribute 'women' to mark it as a special case. Interestingly, female executives are described, and describe themselves, disproportionately more often as warriors than do their male counterparts, in an exaggerated display and construction of non-traditional gender identity (Koller, 2004a). Gender-neutral metaphors are rare.

To sum up, the *Fortune* text features a double characterisation of business-women as professionals and 'girls', as feminine caregivers and masculine fighters. This apparent contradiction indicates the dilemmas brought about by shifting gender and professional roles (see Rojo-Martín and Gómez-Esteban, 2003; Wagner and Wodak, 2006) just as much as it helps to make the text stylistically varied and address different reader groups. Unifying features are positive evaluations of the women in both roles and a focus on forceful material actions, in line with the general ethos of the corporate sphere.

Businesswomen in the lesbian magazine

Although the *Curve* editorial that the extract chosen for analysis is taken from (see Appendix) makes explicit reference to *Fortune* as a model, the differences between how businesswomen are conceptualised and represented in the two magazines outweigh the similarities.

The women portrayed are similarly referred to by (first and) last names, or by job title. As in the business magazine, an alternative label is *girls*. While this was mitigated in the *Fortune* text, no such hedging exists in *Curve*, where reference is made not only to 'working girls' (line 005) but also to the even more informal 'gals' (line 015). Other labels relate, literally or metaphorically, to family and private life ('sisters in business' in line 012, 'lesbian mom' in line 030, and 'life partner' in lines 059–060). This feature is exclusive to *Curve*, where it contrasts with more public labels. Although the two means of reference can be juxtaposed (as in line 030), they do not merge: *lesbian* qualifies only private roles ('lesbian mom', not 'lesbian executive director') and sexual orientation is thus connected with the private sphere. This flies in the face of early feminist claims that the personal is political, and it is therefore questionable whether the label 'sisters' (line 012), which originated in the same context, is more than just a nod to lesbian feminist history. However, the two spheres do blend in the women's working lives in that most are seen working for LGBT commercial or human rights organisations. So while the personal and the political are kept apart linguistically, more than three decades of feminism and gay rights campaigning have indeed led to a specific professional sector.

Process types are also remarkably different. Fewer actions are ascribed to the women overall: while we find a normalised 54.69 such actions per 1000 words in *Fortune*, the *Curve* text pales in comparison, with only 32.04 actions. Furthermore, only three types of action – material, behavioural and relational – are realised, with percentages not showing the marked differences in *Fortune*: behavioural and relational processes both account for 35.71 per cent, material actions for only 28.57 per cent. These proportions make for an altogether more static representation of the women's actions, which is in sharp contrast to the represented dynamic, forceful activities that the women in *Fortune* were shown as engaged in.

A shared feature of the texts is the unabashedly positive evaluation of the women, which occasionally becomes celebratory. Intensifiers and superlatives are used most prominently (e.g. 'really big power lesbians' in line 006). Verb connotations are another evaluation device, as in 'who excel in their careers' (lines 012–13) or 'we anoint them' (line 017). Positive evaluation can also work indirectly, by linking the women with a company that is ascribed superlative attributes ('the country's largest funder' in line 028, 'one of the first major companies' in line 040). In contrast to the business magazine text, the *Curve* feature shows a conspicuous absence of interviews. This translates into a lack of verbal process types and intertextuality in general.

But perhaps the most striking feature of the *Curve* text is its use of only primary spatial metaphors: the familiar GOOD IS UP ('up-and-coming working women', lines 015–016), and POWERFUL IS BIG ('big power lesbians' in line 006, 'her decision was such a big one' in line 036). Interestingly, lesbian executives and their actions become more important, the more they are noticed by, and connected with, mainstream business – witness the dropping of names like 'Napster' (line 010), 'Harvard Business School' (line 038) and investment bank 'Charles Schwab' (line 040), which are only indirectly related to the women. The measure of success appears to be appraisal by mainstream society, reflected in modelling the magazine feature on that of a business magazine. However, one of the most defining characteristics of business magazines, the use of flamboyant metaphors, is conspicuously absent.

Despite these differences, the two texts still show enough similarities to allow us to speak of an interdiscursive alignment in which the *Curve* text is modelled on that in *Fortune*. The fact that *Curve* appropriates features of *Fortune* bears witness to the relative power and influence of business, and the media associated with it, over other sectors of society. Most obviously, it is the genre which is appropriated; while *Fortune* has published its ranking of businesswomen since 1998, the *Curve* text constitutes part of *Curve*'s first ever annual career feature in 2004.[9] (Figure 14.1).

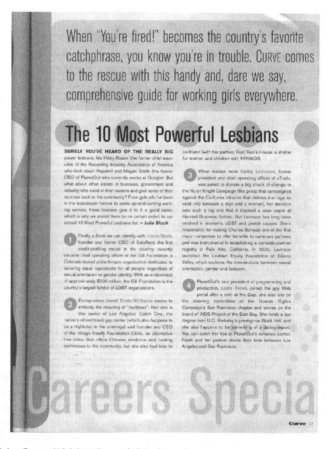

Figure 14.1 *Curve*, '10 Most Powerful Lesbians'

At the textual level, attribution and evaluation as well as some aspects of labelling and reference are similar. Both magazines further operate on the assumption that a professional career is desirable for, and relevant to, their readers.[10] However, the two texts are notably indebted to their respective genre conventions and the discourses informing them, and thus meet expectations brought about by the context of reading a particular type of magazine.

Curve profiles the businesswomen as ideal members of the lesbian community. The link is notable in the unmitigated familiar labels as well as the very criteria for being an ideal member: professionally success and, crucially, 'giv[ing] some of their success back to the community' (line 013). The image and evaluation of lesbian executives are the author's, who draws on assumed shared values of the community she writes for. It is this recurrent notion of a community that constitutes the most fundamental difference between the two texts and, by extension, the two discourse communities: although *Fortune* portrays the women as part of the wider business community, this link is nowhere made as explicit as the connections between lesbian executives and the wider lesbian community. Indeed, *Fortune*, in typical neo-liberal fashion, sees the women as high-achieving individuals, while *Curve* shows traces of feminist ideals in conceptualising and representing them as either collective actors or individuals supported by, and accountable to, their community.

Context models and recipient design

The differences discussed can partly be attributed to genre conventions, but partly reflect, and contribute to, different conceptualisations of women in the non-traditional role of executive and entrepreneur. The models at stake are two-fold: text producers operate with their own *and* their readers' perceived model of the social group in question. These models are activated by the context of text production and consumption and also shape the actual textual representation: context models 'subjectively "represent" relevant aspects of situations and society and directly interfere in the mental processes of discourse production' (van Dijk, 2006b: 163). They include assumptions about the communicative situation, the genre and topic, and the knowledge, values and beliefs assumed to be held by the audience. As such, they control the choice of linguistic features that are best suited to meet the communicative purpose.

As indicated, discourse analysis alone cannot prove the existence of these models. Indeed, claims about cognitive models underlying discourse, while making analysis more plausible, remain in the abstract hypothetical domain. Cognitive CDA, however, does provide circumstantial and cumulative evidence for their importance in discourse production and comprehension and helps to explain features of texts that might otherwise be overlooked. Going beyond the mere identification of metaphor in text, cognitive CDA regards metaphor as one form in which context-triggered models of topic and participants can be structured. Combining their textual realisation as metaphoric expression with an analysis of other parameters central to the text allows for tentative claims to be made about the nature of such models. The present analysis is one illustration of what an integrated approach to discourse and cognition has to offer: to give full credit to the rich and intricate relations between discourse, cognition and social life.

Acknowledgements

I am grateful for permission to reproduce 'The 10 Most Powerful Lesbians' (by Julia Bloch, *Curve*, November 2004, pp. 24–6).

Notes

1 I would like to thank Teun van Dijk and Ruth Wodak, as well as the editors, for their helpful comments on an earlier version of this chapter.
2 This definition is not universally shared; te Molder and Potter, for instance, claim that social cognition 'has largely focused on the explanation of social processes through the properties of individual cognition' (2005: 17) and contrast it with 'distributed cognition', which they say does account for how an individual's cognition is acquired through social interaction. Both theoretically and methodologically, early work in socio-cognitive psychology did indeed focus on the individual (see Koller, 2005, for a critique); the definition that van Dijk and other discourse analysts interested in cognition operate with can actually be seen as a subsequent development.
3 All discourse is of course dialogic in a metaphoric sense, in that it both assumes and anticipates an ideal reader, and intertextually engages with previous texts.
4 Following the conventions established in cognitive semantics, conceptual metaphors and semantic components will be indicated by small capitals.
5 The model of process types has an inherent flaw in that it was devised to categorise the functional properties of grammatical surface structures but uses semantic categories to do so. For instance, the verb phrase *to support someone/something* would have to be classified as an overt material process type since it involves an affected entity. At a 'covert', semantic level, however, it obviously addresses a mental state. Despite this drawback, process types remain a viable way of looking at the representation and conceptualisation of social actors.
6 Ironically, these job titles continue to feature the allegedly 'generic' masculine, e.g., 'Hewlett Packard Chairman' (*Fortune*, 2000).
7 Verbal processes are almost exclusively an effect of business magazine writers drawing quite heavily on interviews in their articles.
8 The latter instance may be partly triggered by the nature of Boeing as a manufacturer of aircrafts, weapons and defence systems; elsewhere, the writer mentions Hopkins's 'long runway' at that company.
9 The other national US lesbian magazine, *girlfriends*, published its first careers special in 1999.
10 This assumption is mitigated in *Curve*, in that the careers special includes a critical article on female poverty that problematises the notion of career as such.

Appendix

'The 10 Most Powerful Lesbians' (by Julia Bloch, *Curve*, November 2004, pp. 24–6.) Reproduced with permission.

001 When 'you're fired!' becomes the country's favorite catchphrase you know
002 you're in
003 trouble. Curve comes to the rescue with this handy and, dare we say,
004 comprehensive
005 guide for working girls everywhere.
006 Surely you've heard of the really big power lesbians, like Hilary Rosen (the
007 former
008 chief executive of the Recording Industry Association of America who took
009 down
010 Napster) and Megan Smith (the former CEO of PlanetOut who currently
011 works at
012 Google). But what about other sisters in business, government and industry who
013 excel in their careers and give some of their success back to the community?
014 From
015 gals who've been in the boardroom forever to some up-and-coming working
016 women,
017 these lesbians give 9 to 5 a good name, which is why we anoint them (in no
018 certain
019 order) to our 10 Most Powerful Lesbians list.
020 Finally, a Bush we can identify with: Linda Bush, founder and former CEO of
021 SafeRent, the first credit-profiling model in the country, recently became chief
022 operating officer at the Gill Foundation, a Colorado-based philanthropic
023 organisation
024 dedicated to securing equal opportunity for all people regardless of sexual
025 orientation
026 or gender identity. With an endowment of approximately $200 million, the
027 Gill
028 Foundation, is the country's largest funder of LGBT organisations.
029 ...
030 When lesbian mom Kathy Levinson, former president and chief operating
031 officer of
032 eTrade, was asked to donate a big chunk of change to the No on Knight
033 Campaign
034 (the group that campaigned against the California initiative that defines
035 marriage as
036 valid only between a man and a woman), her decision was such a big one
037 that it
038 inspired a case paper at Harvard Business School. But Levinson has long been
039 involved in women's, LGBT and Jewish causes: She's responsible for making
040 Charles Schwab one of the first major companies to offer benefits to same-sex
041 partners and was instrumental in establishing a domestic-partner registry
042 in Palo
043 Alto, California. In 2000, Levinson launched the Lesbian Equity Foundation of
044 Silicon Valley, which explores the intersections between sexual orientation,
045 gender
046 and Judaism.

047   ...
048   Speaking of power couples, Joan Garry, who worked at Showtime and helped
049   launch
050   MTV back in 1981, is now executive director of the gay and Lesbian Alliance
051   Against Defamation. GLAAD announced last summer that it would be
052   teaming up
053   with Logo, the new digital television network targeting queer viewers, to
054   broadcast
055   the 2005 GLAAD Media Awards, which celebrate fair and accurate representations
056   of the LGBT community in media and entertainment. One key consultant and
057   programmer over at Logo is none other than Eileen Opatut, former senior vice
058   president of programming and production at Food Network — and Garry's
059   life
060   partner. Talk about networking. (*continued*)

15
Harnessing a Critical Discourse Analysis of Gender in Television Fiction
Konstantia Kosetzi

1 Introduction

In this chapter, I discuss the contribution of CDA to the analysis of fictional television genres. CDA has been widely applied to non-fictional media (e.g., Chouliaraki, 2000; van Leeuwen, 1996; Fairclough, 1995b; van Dijk, 1995a), however, its application to fictional genres has been marginal. Here, I advocate that CDA *can* and *should* be applied to fiction more widely and propose an adaptation of Faircloughian CDA (mainly 2001a,b, 2003). I illustrate my methodological points with an example from *Σχεδόν Ποτέ* ('Almost Never', henceforth *ΣΠ*), a Greek fictional TV series[1].

ΣΠ is about four professionally successful, financially independent, and sexually liberated women, approaching 30 (Maria, Kalia, Vada and Stephania), who have 'set their minds on finding the right guy to fall in love with' (http://www.clproductions.gr/en/television/almost-never-1). Explicitly concerned with sex and with gender relations, *ΣΠ* is a clearly *gendered* site (cf. Sunderland and Litosseliti, 2002).

2 Key concepts: media, gender, fiction

2.1 Media

Media are seen as operating *within* the structures of societies (cf. Fairclough, 1995; Kastoras, 1990). There is a struggle over who/what is represented, how, and who/what is excluded, rendering the media ideological *in principle* (see e.g., Walsh, 2001; Chouliaraki, 2000; Fairclough, 1995b), where ideology is 'representations of aspects of the world which can be shown to contribute to *establishing, maintaining and changing social relations of power, domination and exploitation*' (Fairclough, 2003: 9, my emphasis). Not only do the media offer representations of the world, but there is also a *dialectical* relationship between media and society, that is, media *shape* and *are shaped* by it (see e.g., Litosseliti,

2006a; Fairclough, 1995b). I do not however take media to be ideological *a priori* (a common criticism of CDA, see, e.g., Blommaert, 2005; Verschueren, 2001). I did not originally see the series in this way, and only after I watched it did I realise that the issue was 'subtle sexism' (see below). Media are, I argue, 'central sites at which discursive negotiation over *gender* takes place' (van Zoonen, 1994: 41, emphasis in original). Arguably, '[*n*]*o* representations in the written and visual media are gender-neutral. They either confirm or challenge the status quo through the ways they construct or fail to construct images of femininity and masculinity' (Weedon, 1997: 101, my emphasis). And, of course, they may do both simultaneously.

2.2 Gender

Since the eighties, gender has been explicitly related to *discourse* (e.g., Wetherell, Stiven and Potter, 1987), marking a shift in language and gender research to what is said and how (e.g., Sunderland, 2004; Bucholtz, 2003a; Sunderland and Litosseliti, 2002; Cameron, 1998b). Discourse analysis has accordingly been seen as a flexible, incisive and valuable tool for the study of gender (Litosseliti, 2006a; Bucholtz, 2003a). Within discourse analysis, I find CDA particularly apt, as it is explicitly concerned with social issues and problems (e.g., Wodak, 2004; Fairclough, 2001b; van Dijk, 2001), gender being one. However, CDA has been critiqued in its application to gender research. Cameron (1998b), for instance, characterises CDA's founders as 'straight white men', who do not take on board feminists' work. However, there had been feminist work *within* CDA prior to 1998 (e.g., Wodak, 1997; Caldas-Coulthard, 1996; Talbot, 1995b; Lazar, 1993). More recently, Feminist Critical Discourse Analysis (FCDA) has also emerged (Lazar, 2005, and see Wodak (this volume)).

In a similar vein, Walsh (2001) criticises CDA approaches for marginalising gender, singling out Fairclough for 'privileg[ing] class above other determinants of power' (Walsh, 2001: 4), following CDA's Marxist origins. Nevertheless, Faircloughian CDA *has* been applied to gender (e.g., Kosetzi and Polyzou, forthcoming; Magalhães, 2005; Kosetzi, 2001; Talbot, 1998), and there are now more references to gender in Fairclough's own current work than previously (although the space devoted to gender is still relatively marginal[2]).

2.3 Fiction

Often associated with entertainment, fiction is sometimes not considered worth analysing (cf. Gledhill, 1997; Intintoli, 1984). However, fiction has been linked with producing and circulating values and cultural meanings (e.g., Gledhill, 1997; Weedon, 1997; Intintoli, 1984). Even though links between real-life social actors and practices and fictional representations may be difficult to establish, these have been argued for (e.g., van Leeuwen, 2005b; Machin and van Leeuwen, 2003; Stephens, 1992), representation being seen as a *recontextualisation* of social practices (e.g. Fairclough, 2003; Chouliaraki and Fairclough, 1999; van Leeuwen and Wodak, 1999; Bernstein, 1996,

1990)[3] (here of gender relations), and has also been linked to *ideology* (e.g. Sunderland, 2004; Stephens, 1992; Bakhtin, 1981). Bringing the *audience* as well into the 'equation', Intintoli (1984) and Stephens (1992) (working in the fields of soaps and children's fiction respectively) claim that for fiction to make sense to its audience, it must draw on some version of reality. As for production, the scriptwriter, in my case, is also socioculturally situated and her work bears the marks of socio-ideological-cultural influences (cf. Allen, 1985; Bakhtin, 1981).

In thus arguing for the validity of analysing TV fiction through CDA, I consider that any discourses (and associated themes within those) 'employed' in the series will be drawn from those currently circulating in the Greek context because of the need for the audience to recognise at least some of them (regardless of whether they then reproduce or challenge them), and because the scriptwriter recontextualises practices and discourses of the social contexts s/he belongs to. If the discourses in the series are not recognised, there will be no ratings,[4] meaning no profit, the *raison d'être* of commercial TV (cf. Papathanasopoulos, 2000; Valoukos, 1998). Given that Greek society is in flux (see below) regarding gender relations, these discourses are likely to be *competing*.

3   CDA and fiction

I turn now to the few cases of CDA being used to analyse fiction. Kress (1988) analyses a Mills and Boon novel and an advertisement for a drug. His overall point is that *all* texts can have the same ideological effects and thus there is the same need for analysis. Threadgold (1988) traces the same discourse of 'race and gender' in both fictional and non-fictional genres, identifying the same semantic and lexico-grammatical features. Neither Threadgold nor Kress make any distinction between fiction and non-fiction, but neither do they theorise any problems in this conflation.

Turning to fiction *per se*, analysing a horror and a romance novel, and two Mills and Boon romance novels, Talbot (1995a, 1997a) finds that whereas heroes are usually attributed transitive verbs, that is, active engagement with the world, heroines are attributed intransitive verbs, or are the subject of *mental* process verbs (as opposed to *material* process verbs, as is the case with men). However, like Threadgold and Kress, she does not consider special issues that might arise in analysing fiction.

In some contrast, Sunderland (2004), who employs a CDA of gender in award-winning US children's fiction identifying, *inter alia*, 'traditionally gendered' and feminist discourses, considers fiction's special characteristics, including the likely humour and irony (see below). Sunderland also discusses hegemonic and patriarchal discourses in fairytales and suggests that, because of the gendered discourses these draw on, 'they are not *just* imaginative books which provide pleasure for children' (2004: 145).

Paraphrasing this, I do not see TV fictional programmes as *just* providers of entertainment, but rather also as recontextualisations of discourses (and themes) circulating in the context from where these programmes emerge. Moving to *TV* fiction, Pollak and Wodak (2003) apply CDA to an episode of a popular TV detective series about an exhibition of the war-crimes committed by the German Wehrmacht during WWII. Wodak explains the rationale for CDA here, that is, as 'a good tool to analyse *text in context* ... we wanted to examine *critically* how the German media cope with the past and recontextualise it into a standard TV crime series'.[5] Recontextualisation underpins my argument, too, for the use of CDA in fictional TV (see Section 2), though using a rather dissimilar CDA *approach* (cf. Wodak's Discourse-Historical approach and Van Dijk's Socio-Cognitive approach; see Pollak and Wodak (2003)).

4 Issues in analysing fiction via CDA

As indicated above, there appears to be a lack of theorisation and complexification in the CDA of fictional data. One issue is what Sunderland (2004) refers to as *point of view*, in the sense that the narrator cannot be straightforwardly equated with the author (cf. Bakhtin, 1981: 314), and characters' words, practices and emotions cannot be seen as all having the author's approval. Accordingly, different characters may articulate 'progressive' and 'conservative' discourses (and/or themes) in order for the plot to progress. Characters can also draw on discourses ('conservative' and 'progressive') *critically*. However, this still supports the argument that, if a discourse is used, the expectation is that (part of) the audience will recognise it. Of course, there is always more than one reading of 'what is happening' in any fictional text: 'conservative' gendered discourses may be confirmed in one reading and challenged in another (cf. Kosetzi, 2007a; Unger and Sunderland, 2005).

Other elements in fiction which preclude a straightforward analysis are, as suggested, humour and *irony* (Sunderland, 2004). I incorporate such elements into my analytical framework (see below).

5 Theoretical framework

Of the main approaches to CDA (see Fairclough, 2003, 2001a,b, 1992a; van Dijk, 2003, 2001; Wodak, 2001b; Reisigl and Wodak, 2001; Chouliaraki and Fairclough, 1999; and Koller, this volume),[6] I use Fairclough (mainly 2003, 2001a,b), as this approach most explicitly links discursive change with social change[7] (see Section 1). Blommaert (2005: 6) considers Faircloughian CDA to be 'groundbreaking' in integrating social theory in the analysis of discourse and anchoring linguistic analysis in social contexts. Changes in society are thus linked with changes at the discursive level being *mediated* through *interdiscursivity* (see Section 6.2.4).

In this framework, *discourse* is used in two senses: 'as an abstract noun, meaning language and other types of semiosis as elements of social life'[8] and 'as a count noun, meaning particular ways of representing part of the world', that is, different discourses can represent the same 'part of the world' from different perspectives (Fairclough, 2003: 26). In this chapter, I focus on 'a social issue/problem' and use 'interactional analysis' (see Fairclough, 2001b: 229ff). However, in light of the special issues for CDA and fiction, and issues that emerged from my data (e.g., the narrator's role), my 'interactional analysis' includes considerations of social analysis, linguistic/semiotic analysis, including irony and visual analysis, the narrator's role and intertextuality.

6 Methodology of analysis

6.1 Fairclough's Stage 1: focus on a social issue/problem

The stimulus for this research came from an interest in whether the transitional phase that Greek society is going through in terms of gender relations (see Section 7.1) is represented in *ΣΠ*. After watching the series, I noticed that, whilst the heroines appear emancipated – they are financially independent, professionally successful and sexually liberated – they articulate traces of 'conservative' gendered discourses and themes. The issue/problem seemed to be *subtle* sexism (cf. Lazar, 2005; Wodak, 2005; Mills, 1998).

6.2 Fairclough's Stage 2c: interactional analysis

6.2.1 Social analysis

In this part of the analysis, I rely on others' sociological work in the Greek context and observations of the Greek media (see Section 7.1), delineating changes in Greek society in terms of gender relations regarding legislation, and women's strides in education, the workplace and interpersonal relations. Although these changes point to progress, the picture is far from idyllic.

6.2.2 Linguistic/Semiotic Analysis

Discourse identification is based on features of the text, which act 'on the one hand as *traces* of the productive process, and on the other hand as *cues* in the process of interpretation' (Fairclough, 1989: 24, emphasis in original). However, analysts' identification[9] of discourses has been criticised for lack of full 'evidential support' (Toolan, 1997: 33) and for selectivity and unsystematicity (Widdowson, 2004[10], 2000). I thus make transparent the linguistic traces and interdiscursive links/elements that led me to the identification of discourses (although because of interdiscursivity, the boundaries of discourses are not clear-cut, and discourse identification always complex; see Section 6.2.3). These traces are mainly *lexis*, *presupposition* and *denials/negatives*.

Regarding *lexis*, 'the emphasis is upon "key words"' (Fairclough, 1992a: 236) of significance – mainly, recurring items, although marginal instances of single lexical items (Fairclough, 2003) or phrases may be important, too. Lexis is important because 'the meanings of words and the wording of meanings are matters which are socially variable and socially contested, and facets of wider social and cultural processes' (Fairclough, 1992a: 185; see also Vološinov, 1973). Specifically, the meaning of a word or utterance in context can *maintain* unequal power relations as it legitimates, dissimulates, and/or reifies a state of affairs (e.g., Thompson, 1984), or *challenges* a state of affairs (e.g., West, Lazar and Kramarae, 1997). Thus, the choice of one specific lexical item over another is important, as well as the *presence* of the meaning (through the word), as opposed to its (potential) *absence*, in the first place.

Presuppositions are 'unstated premises of pieces of taken-for granted knowledge about the world' (Hall, 1982: 74), which in this way 'tend[] to pass unnoticed' (Talbot, 1995a: 63). Presuppositions can be seen as *ideological* 'when what they assume has the character of "common sense in the service of power"' (Fairclough, 1989: 154). Additionally, 'presupposed propositions are a way of incorporating the texts of others' (Fairclough, 1992a: 121): these may not be identifiable *per se*, but could include background knowledge or general opinion (Fairclough, 1992a, 1989).

Denials (or *negatives*) imply 'the assertion "elsewhere" of what is being denied' (Fairclough, 2003: 47). These are linked with *presuppositions* and *intertextuality*, as they 'incorporat[e] other texts only in order to contest and reject them' (Fairclough, 1992a: 121–2).

6.2.2.1   Irony

Irony, originating from the Greek *eironeia*, has been variously defined (e.g., Colebrook, 2004; Hutcheon, 1994). The working definition adopted here is simply 'two meanings in one utterance', drawing on Clift (1999), who in turn draws on Goffman's *footing* (1979) – see his distinction between (1) the animator of an utterance, the person who articulates it, (2) its author, the person who 'wrote' it, and (3) its principal, the person committed to its proposition. Clift argues that, in irony, there is a 'footing shift', from 'committed participant to detached observer' (1999: 532). This shift of footing achieves two meanings, or, to use Goffman's (1974) terminology, *framing*: there is one meaning inside the other, one framing the other. In this sense, when there is footing shift, 'the ironist frames what is said, thus becoming principal of an outside – framing – meaning' (Clift, 1999: 533).

What is of utmost importance here is irony's *function*. Irony can be seen as a tool to *reinforce* the status quo (e.g., see Litosseliti, 2006a; Benwell, 2004, 2002; Jackson, Stevenson and Brooks, 2001; but also Gauntlett, 2002). However, irony has also been seen as inherently subversive: a 'self-critical, self-knowing, self-reflexive mode' (Hutcheon, 1994: 30), having the power to *challenge* dominant discourses. Speer's study of sexism and leisure showed participants 'exploit[ing] sexist arguments in an ironic fashion to expose and challenge sexist assumptions' (Speer, 2002: 247). Similarly, in an analysis of an extract from a television documentary on the 1998 Gay Games in Amsterdam presented by an 'out' gay man, Richard Fairbrass, commenting on a football match between a gay and a straight team, mocks the heterosexual stereotype of football playing, thus 'highlight[ing] the social construction of sexuality and the mechanisms through which heterosexuality comes to be seen as normative' (Speer and Potter, 2002: 173). Irony worked similarly in El Refaie's (2005) study of Austrian newspapers: a small number of articles ironically highlighted the absurdity of prejudice and racism, common in other articles, thus challenging their naturalness. In my data, irony similarly seems to *challenge* 'conservative' discourses and themes (Kosetzi, 2007b).

6.2.2.2 Visual analysis
ΣΠ requires visual analysis for a number of reasons. As language, image and sound coexist, television is characterised by multi-modality (e.g., Norris, 2004; Kress and van Leeuwen, 2001, 1996). In his latest versions of CDA (2003, 2001a,b), Fairclough includes the notion of *semiosis* when defining discourse, and semiotic analysis in the analysis of discourse, which would include visual analysis (see also Litosseliti, 2006a; Lazar, 2000). Further, like words, images do not only represent reality or social interaction, but also *produce* meanings and are therefore ideological (see, e.g., Walsh, 2001; Kress and van Leeuwen, 1996; Stephens, 1992). Visual choices *per se* are important, since they entail other choices not being made, with ideologies being behind and within these choices, in that producers are interested in specific meanings being represented. (Nevertheless, viewers can make their own meanings (but see below).)

I focus on instances of shots classified by *camera angle*. These are important since different camera angles for people can represent them in particular (possibly oppositional) relations which reflect and arguably produce unequal power relations. The convention established in cinema and TV is that if one looks down on something/somebody, one has symbolic power, whereas that something/somebody is rendered 'small', insignificant' and 'subordinate'. Arguably, it is the other way round when one looks up at something/someone, while there is symbolic equality if the camera is at eye-level (cf. Jewitt and Oyama, 2001; Kress and van Leeuwen, 1996; Katz, 1994; and see Section 7.2).

Reflecting on the process of analysing visuals, I align myself with the claims that

- visuals are culture-bound (e.g., Kress and van Leeuwen, 1996)
- meanings are not inherent in images (e.g., Jewitt and Oyama, 2001; Iedema, 2001)
- there are many possible but not unlimited meanings (e.g., Jewitt and Oyama, 2001)
- analysts come up with their own readings (e.g., Iedema, 2001).

However, I also concur with the view that viewers are *positioned* by camera angles to 'read' visuals in specific ways, that is, to see (power) relations in ways suggested by those angles (see, e.g., Jewitt and Oyama, 2001; Kress and van Leeuwen, 1996), even though they may *reject* this positioning.

6.2.3 The narrator's role

In *ΣΠ*, as well as dialogue, there is *narration*, in the form of voice-overs (VO). Maria is both narrator and main character (cf. Rimmon-Kenan, 2002; Bal, 1997) – a friend of the other main characters. She 'knows' their pasts, and part of her role is to convey these to the audience. As narrator, Maria comments on what they say/do and, indeed, on herself in ways that (may) dialogically challenge a discourse/theme, often through *ironic* comment (see above).

6.2.4 Interdiscursive analysis

Interdiscursivity, a type of intertextuality, a major focus of Bakhtin's work (1986, 1981), with Kristeva (1986) coining the term, refers to how a given text is constituted by (a number of) genres, discourses and styles (e.g., Fairclough, 1992a: 85). My focus here is the amalgam of *gendered* discourses (and themes within those). An interdiscursive *analysis* involves 'identifying which discourses are drawn upon, and how they are articulated together' (Fairclough, 2003: 128). Any stretch of language can be seen as interdiscursively containing traces of more than one discourse (e.g., Kress, 1988: 134), in part because many discourses are closely related with no clear-cut boundaries (e.g., Sunderland, 2004; Wodak, 2001b, 1997). This brings the inevitable difficulty of distinguishing between similar discourses and of classifying them as complementary, subordinate or overarching (see, e.g., Sunderland, 2000b on 'discoursal *hierarchies'*, and Litosseliti, 2006a on relations between discourses in general).

Interdiscursivity is especially important in Faircloughian CDA because of its link with social change: in periods of intense social-cultural change, Fairclough (e.g., 1992b) argues, there is a particular linguistic and intertextual heterogeneity of texts (see also Lazar, 2005, 2000; Fairclough, 2003, 1995a,b; Martín Rojo and Gómez Esteban, 2003; Walsh, 2001). Often, this 'intertextual heterogeneity' includes the co-existence of *competing/contradictory* discourses.[11] This co-existence may be *'conservative'* or *'progressive'* (see Sunderland, 2007), some researchers supporting that competing discourses *maintain traditional ideology* (e.g., see Lazar, 2005, 2000; Martín Rojo and Gómez Esteban, 2003; Wetherell, Stiven and Potter, 1987), others seeing contradiction more positively. For Hollway, for example, 'every practice to some extent articulates ... contradictions and therefore is a site of potential change as much as it is a site of reproduction' (1984: 260), and Fairclough (2001b) sees contradictions in networks of practices as progressive. I would argue similarly: since discourses are specific to locations and times (e.g., Wodak, 2001a, 1995), these are arguably hospitable for such discourses (cf. Blommaert,

2005). If change is in a 'progressive' direction, then (at least some of) the discourses and/or themes articulated will also be progressive. Even if one argues that feminist ideas are included in a given text *just* because of their diffusion in a specific context, and not because things have indeed changed, the mere fact that feminist ideas *are* included is telling. (Of course, to what ends these feminist ideas are employed, such as stimuli for consumption (e.g., see Talbot, 2000; Mills, 1998), is another issue.)

7 Sample analysis

7.1 Social analysis

Regarding *legislation*, the Constitution of 1975 stipulates that Greek men and women have equal rights and obligations and are equal before the law (cf. General Secretariat for Equality (henceforth GSE), 2004). The 2001 Revision of the Constitution includes a new article according to which *positive* measures, which were legislated not to constitute gender discrimination (GSE, 2001), must be taken to promote equality between women and men (GSE, 2004; Teperoglou and Psara, 2001).

Currently in Greece there is also a National Action Programme for Gender Equality (2001–6) aiming at the efficient use of human resources, irrespective of gender, and the elimination of any discrimination against women. The conceptual tool is 'gender mainstreaming', that is:

> the reorganisation, improvement, development, and the evaluation of the process of implementing policy in order to integrate the perspective of gender equality in all policies in all levels and stages by the agencies that are involved in implementing policies.
>
> (Kethi, 2006)

Broadly, the goals of this Programme are to develop strategies promoting women's position in the economy, lifelong learning, the workplace and decision-making, to improve knowledge of legislation, and to promote equality in everyday life including changing stereotypes about gender roles (Tzavella, 2004).

As regards *education*, women's participation in higher education increased between 1994 and 1999 (GSE, 1999: 21); in 2001, 59 per cent of university students were women, as well as 50 per cent of students on Masters courses, while the percentage of women students in the 'hard' sciences rose (Fotopoulou, undated). However, the percentage of illiterate women (mainly in rural areas and in older age groups) remains higher than that of men (GSE, 1999).

In *employment*, during 1991–2000, *inter alia*, the percentage of working women increased and women's unemployment rates decreased (Athanasiadou, Petropoulou and Mimikou, 2001; GSE, 1999).

However, despite these changes and the improvement of working women's qualifications, women's unemployment is twice that of men (Athanasiadou, Petropoulou and Mimikou, 2001): Greece (with Spain) has the lowest percentage of women's participation in the labour force in the EU (Simeonidou, 2005a). Additionally, the proportion of women in high-ranking professional positions is still low (Kaitanidi, 2005; Athanasiadou, Petropoulou and Mimikou, 2001), and there is a gender pay gap (Karamesini and Ioakeimoglou, 2003).

In relation to *media*, both research and Greek newspaper articles have centred round the issues of women *not* occupying senior positions in the hierarchies of media institutions (cf. Kafiri, 2002; Diamantakou, 1994). Regarding women's *representation* in fictional TV genres, in the past women were represented as naïve, ignorant, and having many problems (usually in comedies), and as housewives/mothers and victims (in dramatic series) (Diamantakou, 1994; Parlas, 1992; Sarris, 1992). Additionally, women were represented as 'complementing' men, the latter always being represented in a more positive light (Diamantakou, 1994; Sarris, 1992; Doulkeri, 1990). These studies did not take into account the irony and/or exaggeration characteristic of fiction. What was noted, though, is that these representations did not go hand in hand with actual social change (e.g., an increase in independent, working women; Diamantakou, 1994; Sarris, 1992). Doulkeri also identified a lack of 'feminist' series, that is, 'related to women's emancipation, and their claims in the workplace, family and society in general' (1990: 43, my translation). However, programmes with feminist *elements* are identified, including women's sexual liberation (Doulkeri, 1990).

More recently, after the Fourth World Conference on Women in Beijing, the Greece National Report acknowledged progress regarding both women's promotion to senior positions of media institutions and gender representation (GSE, 1999). However, it also pointed to continuing stereotypical representations (GSE, 1999: 93).

Currently, what is frequently heard in the media is that gender roles in personal relationships have changed, that is, that nowadays the woman is the 'hunter'.[12] This identified change does not, however, seem evident in other areas of women's and men's interpersonal lives. For instance, despite the fact that men are no longer the (only) breadwinners, according to a 1999 survey, men's participation in household chores and children's upbringing is still limited (women spend twice as much time on these tasks as men), even though in theory men are in favour of sharing these activities (Simeonidou, 2005a,b). In a recent *European* study, Greek fathers rank second lowest (to Portuguese) as regards time spent with their children (Aggelopoulos, 2005). Substantial gender equality in Greece thus appears to have a long way to go.

7.2   Linguistic/semiotic and interdiscursive analyses

I now illustrate how the Faircloughian CDA framework can be further operationalised through an example. Analysing the original (Greek), I follow

Fairclough (1992b: 196) who contends that 'discourse analysis papers should reproduce and analyse textual samples in the original language, despite the added difficulty for readers' (see also Stubbs, 1997). However, the data is translated for non-speakers of Greek.

A HOTEL BEDROOM DOOR, EXTREME CLOSE UP (ECU) OF A 'DO NOT DISTURB' SIGN, IMPLYING THAT PEOPLE ARE HAVING SEX.	MAPIA (V.O.) TALKING ABOUT KALIA[13]
ECU of half of Kalia's naked body, lying on a bed, a tattoo on her hip, looking up at Panos who is getting dressed, walking away from bed	[MARIA (V.O.) SHE IS THE ONE WHO WANTS TO GET MARRIED MORE THAN ALL OF US AND IS NOT ASHAMED OF SAYING SO... NOW, WHY DID SHE CHOOSE PANOS, WHO IS MARRIED, OUT OF ALL POSSIBLE MEN? MAYBE, BECAUSE HE IS EVIDENTLY NOT AFRAID OF
Panos turns round, looks down at Kalia	COMMITMENT, AS SHE SAYS.]

Drawing on a theme I name 'Marriage: women's natural goal/happiness', based on lexical traces of *presuppositions* and *denials* in my data, Maria construes Kalia as wanting to marry – like the rest of the heroines, evident in the *presupposition* behind the *comparison* [more than all of us]. Their only concern is admitting it. (The notion of marriage as 'natural' for women was also noted by Litosseliti (2006a) in her discussion of ads.)

The man who Kalia wants to marry, Panos, is, however, already married. There are several issues here. First, Panos is evidently not afraid of commitment (see below on the ironic aspect of Maria's claim). The *presupposition* behind the *negative* is that other men *are* thus afraid, a linguistic trace of a 'Men are afraid of commitment' theme, according to which men are afraid to commit themselves in a (marital) relationship (cf. Kosetzi and Polyzou, forthcoming; Jackson, Stevenson and Brooks, 2001). Panos is thus 'the exception that proves the rule'. Women are therefore construed as wanting marriage, and men as afraid of it. These two themes, *interdiscursively* linked, are indeed themes of a 'Gender Differences' discourse (cf. Kosetzi and Polyzou, forthcoming; Sunderland, 2004; Hollway, 1989, 1984).

However, even though he is 'not afraid of commitment', the married Panos cannot marry Kalia, giving the lie to his being an 'exception'. Later, Maria's *tone* of *voice* and comment *per se* as narrator are *ironic*: Maria distances herself from what she 'reports' to the viewers. As she says, these are Kalia's words and not her own. Maria is the 'animator' here and not the 'author' or 'principal' of the words, in Goffman's terminology (1979), marking a *footing shift* and *framing* a mockery of the situation (see Section 6.2.2.1).

Having an affair with a married man and waiting for *him* to file for divorce positions Kalia as powerless. This is also conveyed visually: Kalia looks up at Panos and he down upon her. As suggested, the person who is looked up at – the man in this case – can be read as being in a position of power (see Section 6.2.2.2).[14] One way viewers are thus positioned to read this scene is to see the woman as, if not inferior, being in a weak position, *or* to see the man as seeing her as inferior and powerless.

8 Conclusion

In this chapter I have argued that CDA can and should be employed to analyse (TV) fiction in order for the politics of fiction to be recognized and analysed appropriately. To this end, I have adapted Fairclough's model (2003, 2001a,b) by adding the analytic categories of irony, the role of the narrator and visual analysis, to account for the requirements of fictional texts in analysis.

CDA sees a *dialectical* relationship between discourse and the extra-discursive (e.g., Chouliaraki and Fairclough, 1999); it rejects 'discourse idealism', that is, 'seeing the social as nothing but discourse' (see ibid.: 28). To address this, like others, I advocate supplementary *ethnographic* research (e.g., Fairclough, 2003; Wodak, 2001a; Chouliaraki and Fairclough, 1999), which is indeed sometimes conducted within CDA itself (e.g., see Muntigl, Weiss and Wodak, 2000; Chouliaraki, 1998). Here, ethnographic *production* research could have been of use, addressing the producers' and scriptwriter's point of view, as well as the ways in which such media texts are *consumed* and drawn on by women in everyday life.

Acknowledgements

I am grateful to Ruth Wodak, Jane Sunderland, Veronica Koller and Alexandra Polyzou for their useful comments on earlier drafts of this chapter. Responsibility for the final text lies entirely with me.

Notes

1 This chapter is part of a broader research project undertaken for my PhD thesis, where both the series *and* the audience (female focus groups) were analysed in order to address the overarching question: 'How are the changes in gender relations taking place in (urban) Greek society represented in this TV series? And how are these representations consumed by young Greek women viewers?'

2 But see Wodak (this volume), who argues that gender should be studied in relation to other factors, such as class, race, religion, with gender foregrounded in the *research questions*.

3 Aligning myself with such a position does not mean that I equate fiction and reality, or examine whether the series is 'realistic'. Instead, my argument concerns the discourses (and associated themes) in fictional texts and the contexts from where these texts emerge (see below).

4 Of course, this process is not so straightforward; other factors come into play regarding the popularity of a programme (plot, time slot, actors, directors), the study of which are beyond the scope of this chapter.

5 Ruth Wodak, personal communication (23.11.2004, my emphasis).

6 For a more detailed overview of approaches within CDA, see, e.g., Wodak, 2004.

7 Other studies make reference to social change (e.g., Kovács and Wodak, 2003; Wodak and van Dijk, 2000); however, a theorisation of the link between discourse and social change does not occupy a central place in those.

8 The notion of *discourse* is distinguished from *text*: 'A text is a product rather than a process – a product of the process of text production. ... *discourse* ... refer[s] to the whole process of social interaction of which a text is just a part' (Fairclough, 1989: 24). Texts include forms of semiosis other than the written and oral (e.g., Fairclough, 2003).

9 As well as analysts, the audience/readers identify discourses (and themes within those), too (see Meinhoff and Smith, 2000; Sunderland, 2004). As Sunderland (2004: 164) contends, '[t]he extent to which readers do co-construct gendered discourses is an avenue for further research'.

10 For a reply, see Wodak, 2006.

11 Interdiscursivity can also signal 'ideological dilemmas' (see Billig et al., 1988), attempts to accommodate multiple audiences or stylistic reasons.

12 In, e.g., *Stoma me Stoma*, a prime time show, 9.1.2004; *Apokleistika*, an afternoon gossip TV programme, 1.6.2004; *Auto pou Theloun oi Gunaikes*, an early evening, live, competition-like TV programme, 24.12.2004, 27.12.2004, 30.12.2004; broadsheet newspapers (Kaitanidi, 2004); gossip magazines, e.g. *Shock*, 9.2.2006; informal personal observations.

13 Kalia is having a relationship with Panos, who is married. She has just received a phone-call from him about meeting for half an hour at a hotel. After having sex, Kalia starts complaining about him not spending much time with her and asks when he is getting divorced. He assures her that he will.

14 Later, when she addresses him and complains about him wanting to leave early, she raises herself up, while still lying on the bed, and he continues to look down at her. However, as the discussion progresses and she asks him to take action regarding his wife, she stands and they are at the same eye level, which may be read as a mark of equality.

Part 6

Feminist Post-Structuralist Discourse Analysis

16
Feminist Post-Structuralist Discourse Analysis – A New Theoretical and Methodological Approach?

Judith Baxter

Introduction

In recent years, a number of gender and language researchers have begun to explore and experiment with the use of a *new* theoretical and methodological approach to gender and language study: that of Feminist Post-Structuralist Discourse Analysis (FPDA). While there is a growing international interest in the FPDA approach, it is still relatively unknown in the wider community of discourse analysts. There is little published work as yet which directly draws on FPDA, but much fascinating work in the pipeline. At the moment, it is just a small fish in the big sea of discourse analysis; its future is far from certain and it may well be swallowed up whole by larger varieties, or choose to swim with the tide of Critical Discourse Analysis, which to some extent it resembles.

This chapter serves three very important functions within this collection. First, it aims to make the existence of FPDA better known to both gender and language researchers and to the wider community of discourse analysts, by outlining FPDA's own theoretical and methodological approaches. This involves locating and positioning FPDA in relation, yet in contradistinction to, the fields of discourse analysis to which it is most often compared: Critical Discourse Analysis (CDA) and, to a lesser extent, Conversation Analysis (CA). Under this first aim, the chapter actively serves to *evolve* the thinking presented in my book, *Positioning Gender in Discourse* (2003), which sought to define the FPDA approach.

Secondly, the chapter serves a vital *symbolic* function. It aims to contest the authority of the more established theoretical and methodological approaches represented in this collection, which currently dominate the field of discourse analysis. This is a vital function of the post-structuralist approach to theory and methodology. Lesser known methodologies like FPDA offer a *resistant* value in challenging fashionable or entrenched approaches, which tend to transform themselves into 'grand narratives ... grounding truth and meaning in the presumption of a universal subject and a predetermined goal of emancipation' (Elliott, 1996: 19). In Foucault's terms, any paradigm of knowledge, as it becomes more established, inevitably systematises itself into a 'regime of truth' (1980: 109–33). However benign the approach, the 'will to truth' is also 'a will to power'. FPDA considers that an established field like gender and language study will only thrive and develop if it is receptive to new ways of thinking, divergent methods of study, and approaches that question and contest received wisdoms or established methods.

Thirdly, the chapter aims to introduce some new, experimental and ground-breaking FPDA work, including that by Harold Castañeda-Peña and Laurel Kamada (this volume). I indicate the different ways in which a number of scholars are imaginatively developing the possibilities of an FPDA approach to their specific gender and language projects.

1   FPDA: the theoretical approach

So, what has FPDA to offer gender and language study in relation to its better known partners of CDA and CA? This is a question I explore at some length elsewhere (Baxter, 2002a; 2003), and it is not my intention to recycle my arguments here. However, since then, I have been challenged at different conferences to justify FPDA as a distinct theoretical and methodological approach in its own right. Doesn't FPDA sound very much like Feminist *Critical* Discourse Analysis in both name and sentiment? Am I not, perhaps, on an empire-building mission to attach my name to a new theoretical approach?

Perhaps the most important response is that FPDA has no interest in competing with other approaches for prospective punters. One of the key values of FPDA is that it offers itself as a 'supplementary' approach, simultaneously complementing and undermining other methods. There is much value to be gained from a *multi-perspectival* approach that combines different methodological tools in a functional way as befits the task in hand. Phillips and Jorgensen (2002) emphasise how multiple viewpoints fit well with the basic constructionist view of 'perspectivism' in bringing together several different theories and methods to create divergent forms of knowledge. Such textual interplay between competing terms, methods and sets of ideas allows for more multiple, open-ended readings, and distinguishes the post-structuralist approach from more modernist versions of discourse analysis. Castañeda-Peña (Chapter 17) makes FPDA his central approach for analysing the speech of pre-schoolers in Colombia, but also draws upon CA to micro-analyse sequences of conversational turns, as well as applying a CDA critique. Kamada (Chapter 12) combines FPDA with discursive psychology and non-discourse analytic principles, that is, Bourdieu's (1977) theories of cultural and symbolic capital, to analyse the construction of ethnic identities among six Japanese-Caucasian girlfriends. Of all the leading approaches to discourse analysis in the field, FPDA has most in common with CDA. Yet, FPDA and CDA have quite different theoretical and epistemological orientations. While they share commonalities in theory and methodology, the two approaches arguably have *contrasting* outlooks on the world and seek divergent outcomes. I shall therefore expand on the background to this in order to clarify views I have expressed elsewhere (2002a, 2003). At the 2005 BAAL/CUP Seminar (see Chapter 1), I defined FPDA as:

> an approach to analysing intertextualised discourses in spoken interaction and other types of text. It draws upon the post-structuralist principles of complexity, plurality, ambiguity, connection, recognition, diversity, textual playfulness, functionality and transformation.
>
> The *feminist* perspective on post-structuralist discourse analysis considers *gender differentiation* to be a dominant discourse among competing discourses when analysing all types of text. FPDA regards gender differentiation as one of the most pervasive discourses across many cultures in terms of its systematic power to discriminate between human beings according to their gender and sexuality.
>
> (Baxter, 2005)

This definition of FPDA developed from the ideas of the formalist Bakhtin (1981) and the poststructuralists, Derrida (1987) and Foucault (1980), in relation to power, knowledge and discourses. It has also been inspired by the feminist work of Walkerdine (1998), and Weedon (1997), among others. In my empirical research, I have deployed FPDA in relation to classroom spoken interactions, and, more recently, to management meetings and the construction of gendered leadership in the boardroom. I refer briefly to both studies by way of illustration below.

Theoretically, FPDA has definite connections and parallels with current versions of *feminist* CDA (Lazar, 2005a; Caldas-Coulthard, 2003; Wodak, this volume). Here, I recognise that CDA is in no way a monolithic construct, but rather a multidisciplinary perspective drawing upon diverse approaches. As far as it is possible to generalise, both FPDA and feminist versions of CDA share a key principle: *the discursive construction of subjectivity*. Accordingly, such approaches would probably agree on the following principles (which are also associated with performativity theory (Butler, 1990)):

- *Discourse as social practice* (rather than, or additional to, 'language above the sentence' or as 'language in use' (Cameron, 2001)).

- *The performative (rather than essentialist or possessive) nature of speakers' identities*; gender is something people enact or do, not something they are or characterise.
- *The diversity and multiplicity of speakers' identities*: thus, gender is just one of many cultural variables constructing speakers' identities (e.g., regional background, ethnicity, class, age), though it is still viewed as potentially highly significant.
- *The construction of meaning within localised or context-specific settings or communities of practice* such as classrooms, board meetings, TV talk shows.
- *An interest in deconstruction*: working out how binary power relations (e.g., males/females, public/private, objective/subjective) constitute identities, subject positions and interactions within discourses and texts, and challenging such binaries.
- *Inter-discursivity*: recognising ways in which one discourse is always inscribed and inflected with traces of other discourses, or how one text is interwoven with another.
- *The need for continuous self-reflexivity*: being continuously explicit and questioning about the values and assumptions made by discourse analysis.

If this is the case, wherein lies the difference? CDA follows a tradition from post-Marxism through cultural materialism to critical linguistics, critical theory, literary theory, and other branches such as genre studies and discursive psychology. Common to this tradition is an explicit emphasis upon emancipatory social theory on behalf of dominated and oppressed groups (Fairclough and Wodak, 1997). Early versions of CDA were broadly cultural materialist in outlook (e.g., Fairclough, 1995). More recent CDA, however, as defined by scholars such as Caldas-Coulthard, 1996, and Wodak, this volume), have defined it in more social constructionist or even post-structuralist terms. For example, Wodak (2001a: 9) cites the Duisburg School of CDA as 'massively influenced by Michel Foucault's theories' in terms of its view that discourses are historically founded, socially constitutive and always interwoven.

Nevertheless, FPDA has its theoretical roots firmly in postmodernism rather than post-Marxism, and its quest is epistemological rather than ideological. This has three key implications which in *my* view makes FPDA fundamentally different from CDA:

- *FPDA does not have an emancipatory agenda, but a 'transformative quest'.*

This is not just juggling with words. While CDA has an avowedly ideological agenda committed to focusing on social problems and working on behalf of the oppressed (e.g., Wodak, 2001a), FPDA cannot support any agenda that, in Foucault's terms (1980: 109), may become 'a will to truth' and therefore 'a will to power'. In other words, FPDA cannot support a political or indeed, a theoretical mission which might one day become its own 'grand narrative'.

On the other hand, according to post-structuralist principles (Foucault, 1984: 46), FPDA can support small-scale, bottom-up, localised social transformations that are vital in its larger quest to challenge dominant discourses (like gender differentiation) that inevitably become grand narratives. In line with Bakhtin's (1981) ideas on heteroglossia, FPDA means giving space to marginalised or silenced voices (such as certain girls who say little in classroom settings, or those women whose voices are overlooked or silenced in management settings). So as a methodological approach, FPDA is thus best suited to small-scale, ethnographic case studies in which subjects have some degree of agency to change their conditions.

• *FPDA believes in complexity rather than polarisation of subjects of study.*

Because CDA has an emancipatory agenda, it has tended on occasions to polarise subjects of study into two categories – the *more* powerful: those (people, groups, systems) who wield power over others, and the *less* powerful, or those who suffer its abuse. This dichotomised attitude is illustrated in van Dijk's answer to the question, 'What is CDA?':

> CDA research combines what perhaps somewhat pompously used to be called 'solidarity with the oppressed' with an attitude of opposition and dissent against those who abuse text and talk in order to establish, confirm or legitimate their abuse of power ... that is, CDA is biased – and proud of it.
>
> (2001: 96)

CDA's critique is often therefore a binary one in that it is directed *against* those institutional discourses that tend to serve hegemonic interests, and it is working *for* the various social groups whose interests are peripheralised by such dominant discourses. In terms of gender and language studies, CDA is concerned to target and deconstruct patriarchal or masculinist discourses on behalf of 'oppressed' social groups such as women or homosexuals (e.g., Lazar, 2005a).

FPDA, on the other hand, challenges ways in which modernist thinking tends to structure thoughts in oppositional pairs, placing one term over the other. Centring the marginal and marginalising the central, as CDA purports to do – 'a perspective that is consistent with the best interests of dominated groups' (van Dijk, 2001: 96) – itself creates another hierarchy that requires overturning. (There are, of course, notable exceptions to this binary pattern in CDA research. Wagner and Wodak's (2006) study of powerful women, for example, points to the complexity and ambiguity of female leadership identities.) Equally, FPDA is concerned *not* to polarise males as villains and females as victims in any oppositional sense, nor even to presume that women as a category are necessarily powerless, disadvantaged or oppressed by 'the other'. Rather, it argues that female subject positions are complex, shifting and multiply located. It suggests that the ceaseless interaction of competing discourses means that speakers will continuously fluctuate between subject positions on a matrix of powerfulness and powerlessness. This shift can happen across a range of *different* speech events, within a single speech context, or literally *within* a few moments of interaction. It can even happen *simultaneously*; for example, being powerful or powerless in different ways at the same moment in time. So at this micro-level, FPDA can help analysts to pinpoint an exact moment in discourse when a speaker shifts between states of relative powerfulness and powerlessness. The approach also helps to explain the complex pattern of discoursal relations that produce such sudden and dramatic shifts of power.

- *FPDA is anti-materialist in tendency.*

CDA assumes discourse to work *dialectically* (Fairclough and Wodak, 1997) in so far as the discursive event is shaped by, and thereby continuously reconstructs, 'real' or 'material' events, situations or structures. FPDA, on the other hand, adopts an *anti*-materialist stance in its view that social realities are always discursively produced. In other words – and this is the contentious bit – speakers do not exist outside discourse. From the moment we are born, we enter a social world that is infused by competing discourses. We make sense of our existence through such discourses – pre-existing knowledge systems which constantly mediate our thoughts and experiences. In Foucault's (1972: 49) terms, discourses operate as 'practices that systematically form the object of which they speak'. This means that a stretch of speech or talk is continuously reconstructed or reproduced *through* discourses, never outside it. So CDA's distinction between text and context (Fairclough, 1995a) is collapsed by FPDA in favour of the concept of inter-discursivity, where one discourse is always negotiated, challenged, evolved and adjusted through the lens of other discourses.

Does this mean that for post-structuralist discourse analysts, material reality does not exist? This was debated at the BAAL/CUP Seminar after the FPDA papers were presented, and it is worth answering more formally here. My own view – not necessarily shared by all feminist post-structuralists – is that *of course* material reality exists. If a woman experiences physical pain at childbirth, this pain is a material state. But the experience of enduring pain in childbirth is felt or understood principally through cultural and social discourses about childbirth pain, which classify and categorise these experiences. The often-intense physical feelings produced by childbirth are inseparable from the cultural forms of expression by which women process that pain – as inevitable, beneficial, containable, or whatever. This may be further mediated, or complicated, by the mixed messages – or contradictory discourses – that different cultures produce about the experience of female pain. This in itself is bound up with issues of power relations, which offer women competing subject positions about how to make sense of pain – some relatively powerful, many far less so. For FPDA, this is not, as CDA would have it, a dialectical process (Fairclough and Wodak, 1997). The personal experience of pain is culturally embedded and constituted in competing and often contradictory ways. So, for example, counter-discourses on childbirth pain such as those promoted by The National Childbirth Trust in Britain have reconstructed the experience not as a medical condition which needs to be controlled, classified and treated by expert obstetricians, but as a joyous, 'natural' occasion, over which pregnant women should be allowed maximum choice, control and involvement. This once resistant discourse has increasingly become more mainstream and therefore approved, within medical practices in Britain. Whether women now experience childbirth pain differently, even reconstituting it as a joyous or celebratory set of sensations, is almost impossible to 'prove' using conventional research methods, but personal testaments suggest it may be so (Talbot, 1998).

What the anti-materialist approach means for FPDA at least is that research practices are themselves always highly discoursal and textualised. FPDA thus draws attention to the constructedness of its own conceptual framework and 'foundational rhetoric' in relation to its subject of study. In line with feminist ethnography (Middleton, 1993), FPDA takes the principle of self-reflexivity one step further than CDA might do, by likening the textualising process of research to a *literary form*. In other words, the business of text-making will constitute the analyst as literally an *author* with a certain control over his or her work. But this 'control' is tempered by hegemonic constraints: the number of subject positions made available to authors/ researchers by the conventions of academic research and publishing practices is limited.

To bring this down to earth, I may *want* to conduct my FPDA research in the spirit of Derrida's (1987) textual playfulness and Barthes's (1977) 'writerly' practices, but the dominant version of academic reality says that I must produce some closure to my arguments to satisfy the demands of peer review research practice. The least I can do, as a self-reflexive researcher, is to make the *constructedness* of this whole process more transparent and explicit.

So far, this chapter has focused on clarifying the theoretical principles of FPDA in order to demonstrate its distinctive approach to gender and language study; and on indicating the symbolic value of this lesser known theoretical approach as a force for resistance. In order to complete these aims, I now turn to what is distinctive about FPDA's methodology by considering two features by way of example: sources of data, and textual analysis. Again, my discussion here aims to evolve and move forward my original case on FPDA methodology (Baxter, 2003).

2 FPDA: the methodological approach

2.1 The use of data

FPDA has developed an approach to data that differs significantly from mainstream approaches to discourse analysis. First, while established approaches such as CA and CDA generally offer a unitary perspective of the data by single or multiple authors, FPDA aims to provide *multiple* voices and accounts in accordance with Bakhtin's (1981) principle of 'polyphony'. This effectively means providing space in a discourse analysis for the coexistence of distinctively different voices and accounts, such as those of the research participants, other researchers on the project, and possibly even people who review and comment on the research. If these different voices and accounts can be juxtaposed with a minimum of the usual interweaving authorial comments, they can then make their own comments by *supplementing* each other.

The polyphonic approach to data dovetails with a second methodological feature: competing voices and accounts according to Bakhtin's (1981) principle of 'heteroglossia'. This aims to include *minority* voices alongside more official and openly recognised accounts in order to make space for voices that would otherwise be silenced. This might literally be the representation of people who never speak. In my classroom study (Baxter, 2003), I foregrounded the voices of certain 15-year-old girls who rarely spoke in class, and were damningly considered 'good listeners'. In my management study (Baxter, 2003), I highlighted the voice of a female personal assistant whose institutional position determined that she should never speak at meetings. My purpose was to enable her to express her views alongside those of her six male and one female bosses, because she was clearly an essential presence within the management team. 'Heteroglossia' is thus a post-structuralist principle for both data collection and presentation that produces a particular range, richness and plurality of meanings.

2.2 Textual analysis

A key aspect of FPDA, like CDA, is the identification and naming of significant discourses within spoken and written texts. Conversation analysts (e.g., Widdicombe, 1995) have rightly asked other (critical) discourse analysts for their 'warrant' for naming specific discourses in their studies, suggesting that at times CDA seems to generate random discourses to suit their ideological purposes. This is commented on by Sunderland (2004), who has drawn up a list of discourses which have been named and identified by Critical Discourse analysts, amongst others. But the fact that discourses are thus identified does not mean that they *exist*, except in the written text of the analyst who coined their names.

CA, in contrast, bases its own warrants on its claim that any larger patterns it detects in micro-analyses of 'talk-in-interaction', such as evidence of gendered behaviour, can always (and only) be located, turn by turn, within specific speech exchanges. This is not an approach that Critical Discourse analysts have traditionally deployed – there has been a tendency on their side to see a discourse as simply 'out there' waiting to be 'bird-spotted' through a combination of socially informed intuition, critical judgement and supporting textual analysis. That discourse is then often taken 'on trust' and applied as a research category to the critique of other texts. Such a discourse may well be widely recognised by communities of analysts, but CA would question whether it has been identified and named through the application of rigorous and retrievable research methods. In its defence, CDA would posit the importance of analysts' insights as members of society, who self-reflexively acknowledge the constructedness of their categorisations of discourse (Billig, 2000).

FPDA suggests that both a *synchronic* and a *diachronic approach* to this methodological issue might be the answer to the question of what counts as a discourse. Its *diachronic* or ethnographic perspective analyses the language of a particular social group over a longish period of time. This allows for recording overall patterns and developments in the discursive relationships of a given social group. In my management study (Baxter, 2003; 2006b), I observed and recorded the spoken interactions of a group of managers over several months, charting the ways in which working relationships evolved and changed. It was only over this period of time that it became obvious to me (and the other research participants) that there existed organised patterns of speech and behaviour that were discursively shaped by particular versions of reality. In the end, the choice of a name to be attached to these identified 'discourses' is clearly subjective and interpretive, but such a bank of ethnographic evidence, shared by a given community of practice, supports their presumed existence.

The second, synchronic aspect is a detailed, micro-analysis of stretches of text associated with a particular speech event, and is very much in line with CA. My own approach (Baxter, 2003) borrows from the semiotic and literary stylistic methods of Barthes (1977), Eco (1990) and others. Parallel methods are increasingly being explored by Critical Discourse analysts interested in written and multi-modal communication (e.g., see Koller, this volume). The FPDA approach to micro-analysis works on two levels: *denotative* and *connotative* (Barthes, 1977). On the first level, the denotative aims to describe the verbal and non-verbal interactions of a social group in close, but basically non-evaluative detail. Here, the methods of CA provide useful tools in giving a relatively uncontroversial *description* of events. On the second level, the 'connotative' analysis aims to *interpret* the data according to the ways in which speakers are constantly jockeying for positions of power according to competing and intertextualised discourses. (Here, I have adapted the original semiotic meanings of denotation/connotation for the purposes of analysing speech data.) In my management study (Baxter, 2003), I plotted in two 'discourse maps' interrelationships between four key discourses which seemed to be shaping the experiences of this management team. The first map, *discourse combination*, showed how institutional discourses can work together to shape the team's sense of reality in mutually productive ways. The second map, *discourse tension*, showed how the same discourses can also compete with each other, creating a site of struggle within the team.

This plotting of discourses is not just an academic exercise; it can have a functional and practical outcome in the world – always of key importance to the FPDA quest. The discourse maps were used by the management team to confront some of the difficulties in their professional relationships, and encouraged individuals, both male and female, to negotiate some of their gender-stereotyped assumptions. Ultimately, the discourse maps allowed for an important transformation to happen in the business practices of this group: these managers gained a clearer understanding of both their shared aspirations and competing interests, enabling them to resolve conflicts and work together more harmoniously as a team.

3   FPDA work in the pipeline

I suggested at the start of this chapter that, while there is a growing international interest in FPDA, especially in recent scholarship, it is still a relatively unknown approach in the wider community of discourse analysts. Since the publication of my book in 2003, a number of doctoral and post-doctoral students around the world have begun to explore FPDA in their own projects. Little of this work is as yet published. I shall now therefore introduce the work of the five speakers who attended the BAAL/CUP seminar in 2005, of whom Harold Castañeda-Peña, is represented in this section, and Laurel Kamada[1] in the Discursive Psychology section, drawing upon their own words and descriptions of their work (denoted by quote marks). In different ways, each scholar has subjected the FPDA approach to test, and has adapted and extended its methodology to suit their own purposes.

Laurel Kamada aims to 'embellish' existing notions of FPDA by incorporating the factor of *ethnic* subjectivity into the 'mix' of competing discourses she examines. She includes ethnicity alongside gender in her exploration of how multi-ethnic, Japanese-Caucasian girls are simultaneously positioned as relatively powerful and powerless within a range of dominant discourses. Kamada reports how she is able to produce analyses of the conversations among the six girls by combining both longer term, 'diachronic' and moment-specific, 'synchronic' methods. Her focus is 'embodiment': how individual girls make sense of themselves through the way they discursively position themselves and others based on their 'lived-body-selves' – not only how they speak together, but how they enact the 'body work' of friendship: teasing, touching and laughter. Kamada demonstrates how the girls work to construct their identities within and across competing discourses of ethnicity, arguing that 'FPDA has been shown to have an application wider than just gender studies and can well answer the theoretical and methodological needs in a broad range of social science, linguistics and discursive fields of research.'

Surin Kaur (2005) draws primarily upon Performativity theory in her work on the performances of gendered identities in online discussion boards. Her hypothesis is that gender is a series of repetitious acts, bodily and discursive, that are imposed upon people by normative discursive definitions of gender and sexuality. However, she argues that Performativity theory on its own is not able to show us what is actually happening because of the levels of abstraction at which it works. Her supplementary use of FPDA allows for the detailed *textual* examination of the discourses that continuously compete with each other in the performance of gender – enactments of gender that allow members of online discussion boards to take up multiple and sometimes conflicting subject positions. Kaur notes that one of the key points of 'intersection' between Performativity theory and FPDA is a specifically functional one. The combination of these frameworks provides an 'ensemble of tools' necessary to analyse the ways in which gender is performed in cyberspace. FPDA in particular provides the methodology for a detailed linguistic analysis of the ways in which members of virtual communities negotiate ambiguous and complex positions for themselves, which would be far less possible to sustain in the 'material' world. FPDA provides the tools to analyse these 'virtual' relationships that are ephemeral, constantly shifting, and subject to dispersal.

Harold Castañeda-Peña analyses the social construction of gender identities through a case study of Colombian pre-schoolers learning English as a foreign language. Castañeda-Peña carried out ethnographic, qualitative research into the classroom speech and behaviour of his research participants, which gave him time to build up a dossier of evidence on the existence of particular classroom discourses. He finds that FPDA offers a very specific, focused micro-analytical tool to locate the ways in which a number of gendered discourses operate intertextually to situate the pre-schoolers' voices within the classroom interaction. He notes how the pre-schoolers, both male and female, are never uniformly powerful or powerless, but constantly shift between different subject positions in relation to the different discourses, sometimes between one conversational turn and the next. He suggests that FPDA 'seems to open a new self-reflexive theoretical framework to the study of the interface of gender, EFL learning and early childhood education', in his view a highly under-researched area. Castañeda-Peña's development of a sequential, turn-by-turn denotative analysis, building on CA methods, also advances the approach used in my own work (2003, 2002a), by focusing on how conversations can be co-constructed between participants.

Tamara Warhol (2005) is developing methods of FPDA to investigate how students at an American, non-denominational, divinity school learn 'exegesis': the interpretation (in this case) of biblical texts – suggesting that FPDA can be equally applicable to written as well as spoken texts. Drawing on Bakhtin (1981), Warhol argues that all utterances are dialogical in nature; they cannot be read or heard in isolation. Instead, they respond to utterances that precede them and anticipate utterances that will respond to them. Meaning is not found in one text alone, but amidst a dialogue of interacting voices. Any original text, such as a version of the Bible, will be re-inflected by new voices. Through a close, micro-analysis of spoken transcripts, Warhol shows that in one seminar, the exegesis of Galatians 1:11–24 by a group of students and their teacher, presents multiple voices: the characters *within* the biblical text; the voices of theological scholars *outside* the text; and the voices of the seminar participants themselves. Warhol adds her own voice to this mix, and suggests that readers of her papers will add their supplementary voices to the exegesis process. Thus, 'an infinite number of voices echo through the interpretation of the biblical text'. Warhol therefore uses FPDA to challenge the modernist quest of much current theological teaching that seeks closure by deriving a single, correct meaning from a text, presumed to be that of the author. Warhol advances the approach by showing how FPDA can be used to analyse multi-voiced, heteroglossic, *written* texts such as the Bible, and, more importantly to analyse how students make sense of these competing accounts in their seminar discussions.

Finally, Gabrielle Budach (2005), currently completing an ethnographic study of three literacy centres in Ontario, Canada, is interested in the connections between language, gender and speech community. Such literacy centres are part of a francophone network designed to improve the literacy skills and political confidence of monolingual, French speakers in Canada: they thus represent an important site for the construction and contestation of social meanings, including debates on what counts as legitimate language capital and who counts as francophone. On one hand, the centres are represented by their management as a space organised and primarily run in the interests of francophone women; on the other, both learners and outsiders perceive the centres as unnecessarily excluding of men, and French/English bilingual speakers in general. While drawing on a number of theoretical paradigms, Budach finds FPDA valuable in its role as an 'additional' methodology, offering an 'alternative' set of strategies to CA and CDA (cf. Baxter, 2003: 44). Furthermore, she uses a number of 'biographic interviews' of managers, teachers and learners to display the plurality of voices and perspectives on this issue. While Budach does not use discourse analysis as such, she does juxtapose extracts from her interview extracts to illustrate the competing and discordant accounts of her subjects. The principle of post-structuralism, in Budach's words, is that 'there are no fixed meanings once and for all, but contestations and redefinitions revealed by different readings within different contexts'. Her contrastive analysis of various case studies points to heterogeneity and tension inside the literacy centres arising from different life experiences and attitudes to language – despite the managerial representation of the institution as 'a homogeneous gendered space'.

3 Conclusion

It has been my intention in this chapter to make FPDA, and its manifestations in current scholarship, a little better known to the wider community of gender and language researchers and discourse analysts. Does FPDA offer a new theoretical and methodological approach to gender and language study? I propose that it does so in the following five ways:

- FPDA draws attention to the provisional, constructed nature of all research and to its status as a textualising and fictionalising practice.
- It is concerned to widen the range of possible meanings by challenging the notion of the single authorial account: it should offer space for competing voices and diverse accounts of experience and resist a single line of argument or closure.
- FPDA explores the differences within and between girls/women including their experiences of the complexities and ambiguities of power. In refusing to constitute gender in binary terms, FPDA offers a potentially empowering and celebratory vision.
- It aims to support transformative feminist processes provided these are specific, localised, action-driven, functional and temporary.
- FPDA offers a 'supplementary' approach to the 'grand narratives' expounded by the established schools of discourse analysis represented in this volume: CDA and CA (as well as Interactional Sociolinguistics). This means that it can be effective as a supplementary methodology, offering an *alternative* set of strategies alongside any of the more well-known approaches.

FPDA may just be a small fish in a big sea, but, vulnerable as this makes it, this is also its position of strength. As a theoretical and methodological approach, FPDA has a mandate to contest grand narratives; it is not concerned to found a new school of discourse analysis. At the moment I consider FPDA as a vital antidote to the increasing institutional power of both CA and CDA. As Billig (2000) has said, CDA must be prepared to open up possibilities for new forms of discourse analysis that 'expose the self-interest and political economy of the sign, "critical" '. I consider that FPDA does exactly that.

Note

1 Laurel Kamada adopts a multi-perspectival approach to her work, which draws upon discursive psychology, CDA and FPDA.

17
Interwoven and Competing Gendered Discourses in a Pre-School EFL Lesson

Harold Andrés Castañeda-Peña

Introduction

In this chapter I set out a Feminist Post-Structuralist Discourse Analysis (FPDA) approach to study classroom interactions in a pre-school English as a Foreign Language (EFL) lesson. After analysing an EFL lesson, I show how FPDA has contributed to my own research and highlight a possible development of FPDA studies in relation to gender and EFL learning in pre-primary education.

The methodological decisions for my study have been informed by a post-structuralist understanding of gender, power and discourse. Gender, within such a stream of thought, is fluid, unstable and unfixed. Consequently, I tend to interpret gender relationally: not as a binary opposition or differentiation, but as multiplicity. It is important to note, as Paechter (2003: 541) does (also in an educational context), that the recognition of belonging to a group of males or females 'is related to the development of performances of masculinity and femininity'. Therefore, there is not one particular performance of masculinity, but performances of masculinities; not one single performance of femininity, but performances of femininities. These performances constitute and reconstitute subjects in discourse, establishing permanently changing and asymmetrical (rather than fixed and symmetrical) relationships. This understanding of gender thus renders it transitory within multiple discourses.

Discourse(s), as Carabine (2001: 274) argues, is (are) related to 'historically variable ways of speaking, writing and talking about, as well as practices around, an issue'. In this sense my research examines the social construction of gender as and through discursive practices, in relation to which pre-schoolers (here) might or might not directly cite gender. Certainly, pre-schoolers *perform* gender on a daily basis.

The pre-school EFL lesson I analyse below in this exploratory study is potentially 'telling' because these children are being taught, through myriad resources and activities, the English personal pronouns '*He*', '*She*' and '*I*'. Thus, the curricular topic orients the children towards particular constructions and performances of gender by this focus on what are in effect traces (Talbot, 1998) of a gendered discourse: the importance of the binary. My warrant (Swann, 2002) for identifying gender in this classroom context is threefold: the EFL class topic, the 'performative gender work' (Cameron, 1997b) elaborated by the pre-schoolers via their use *in situ* of these pronouns, and what has been called 'talk around a gendered text' (Sunderland et al., 2002).

Feminist post-structuralist discourse analysis (FPDA)

From both a theoretical and methodological perspective, I find FPDA particularly useful for describing and interpreting gendered interactions in the EFL pre-school classroom. Baxter (2002c: 10) conceives of FPDA 'both as a theoretical framework and as a research tool'. As a theoretical framework, FPDA 'specialises in identifying the range of discourses at play within varying social contexts in order to ascertain the interwoven yet competing ways in which such discourses structure speakers' experiences of power relations' (Baxter, 2003: 46).

FPDA uses two levels of analysis. The first is descriptive and microanalytical ('denotative'). The second is an interpretative ('connotative') commentary based on the evidence gathered from the first level (Baxter, 2002b, 2002c, 2003, and previous chapter).

While there is a considerable body of work to date on gender and second/ foreign language education (see Sunderland, 2000) – and Baxter herself considers a first language classroom (a Year 10 English lesson at a UK co-educational secondary school) – the construction of masculinities and femininities in the context of *pre-schoolers* learning a (foreign) language has, however, been neglected. Only Hruska (2004) to my knowledge has examined gender and English language learning in pre-primary settings. In order to address this situation, it is the pre-school setting, and the verbal and non-verbal construction and performance of masculinities and femininities here, that constitute the focus of this study.

The study

I now present a single case from my own study,[1] occurring in a specific (synchronic) moment – a lesson videoed in June 2005 – taken from a diachronic qualitative study conducted 2004–6. The findings were drawn from a *Transición*[2] EFL lesson at the Goldmedal Kindergarten (not its real name) in Zipaquirá, an urban town in Colombia. A female teacher (T), five male students (Nando = N, aged 5; Pablo = P, Andy = A, Oscar = O and Juan = J, all aged 6) and one female student (Carolina = C, aged 6) are the research participants. Another female teacher (T2) is also present. All speak Spanish as their first language. The lesson was videoed (by a male camera operator). The resultant transcript includes the spoken interactions and gestures, proxemics and other modes structuring the lesson (see Norris, 2004): these include the teacher's physical commands and students' responses, a text played back on a tape recorder (TR), a folding book and texts written on the board.

The lesson

For the purposes of this chapter, the transcript[3] has been edited (see the denotative analysis after the transcript for a description of the omitted turns). The *full* transcript contains 348 turns (where a turn is bounded by the initiation and ending of completely delivered propositional content, or by an interruption used to gain the floor or overlap concurrent with someone else's utterances). I call the lesson **The 'HE', 'SHE', 'I' Lesson**. This name is derived from the pronouns written by the teacher on the board. The transcribed extracts take up less than 5 minutes.

The 'HE', 'SHE', 'I' lesson

This lesson starts with two listening exercises – the first about professions, the second about English sounds. Students are expected to repeat after they listen to the tape in both exercises. Then the teacher plays back a short story which is illustrated in a folding book.
[Introductory sentence omitted.]

122	TR:	Who is she? I asked my mom! She's a bus driver
123	S:	[a bus driver]
124	T:	Okay, who is she?
125	C:	Whooo iiis sheee?
126	A:	Who/
127	T:	[She is]
128	C:	She is (1)=
129	A:	[a bus driver]
130	T:	Bus driver
131	C:	Bus driver
132	T → Ss:	I can't hear
133	Ss:	Bus driver

{18 turns omitted}

152	T:	**¿Por qué helper? Por que está ayudando a la mamá** [Why a helper? Because he is helping mom] Okay now ((*T returns to her desk*))
153	C:	**Yo también ayudo a mi mami a recoger los regueros** [I also help my mum to tidy up]
154	N:	**Yo también** [Me too]

{43 turns omitted}
198 T: **¿Qué es I? Yo**
             [What is 'I'? I]
199 Ss: **[Yo]**
             [I]
200 T: I
201 Ss: {inaudible}
202 A → T: **¿Entonces donde está la I es un hombre y una mujer?**
             [So, wherever you see the capital I, does it refer to both
             a man and a woman?]
             {A refers to what he sees written in the board 'He', 'She', 'I'}
203 T → A: **No porque es yo yo okay entonces=**
             [No, because it is 'I' 'I' Okay so=]
204 N: **[un hombre y una mujer puede ser yo]**
             [both a man and a woman could be 'I']
{029 turns omitted}
234 T → Ss: Okay!
             She!
             ¿Y quién es 'She'? {sic}
             [And who is 'She'?]
235 Ss: *((All male classmates point to Carolina. Carolina smiles and
             puts her hands together on her chest, her gaze is directed
             towards the desk))*
236 T → Ss: Aha! Exactly!
{058 turns omitted}
295 T → Ss: Okay! To the floor
296 S: Floor
             ((All Ss sit on the floor))
297 T: I am standing up
298 S: Standing up
             ((All Ss stand up))
299 T: I am running
300 Ss: *((All Ss run {vigorously}))*
301 T: I am dancing
302 N: Jumping
             {SS seem to be confused about the action they have to
             perform}
             ((Ss do not perform an action at all))
303 T: daaan dancing
304 Ss: *((All Ss start dancing alone where they are standing up))*
305 T: **[Cojan parejos]**
             [Pick male-dancing partners]
306 T: Dance
307 Ss: *((Carolina is smiling and seems to freeze for a while))*

> *((Oscar dances with T))*
> {Pablo and Andy are out of sight}
> *((Andy jumps into Carolina to get her as his dance partner, separating her from the closest boys (Pablo and Juan) who seem to be about to hug her))*
> *((T leaves Oscar, who is embraced by Nando. Oscar doesn't reject Nando))*
> *((Pablo and Juan look at the others and do not get dance partners))*

{3 turns omitted}

311 T: and she is sitting down
312 S: Sitting down Sitting down
             ((All Ss start looking for chairs to sit down))
313 T: [she she she]
314 Ss: *((Some male students remain standing up))*
             She
315 T: [She
316 J → P: Shee no heee
             ((The male Ss who sat down stand up))

{30 turns omitted}

347 T: **¡Yo creo que les quedó claro!**
             [I think they understood]

Denotative analysis

The transcript above is my own reconstruction of the videotaped data. Below, I use FPDA to analyse the 'HE', 'SHE', 'I' lesson, basing my description on the whole lesson extract. Turns are indicated in brackets.

'She is a bus driver'

Participants work on two listening exercises (turns 1–121) for the most part. The first involves the repetition of texts on an audiotape about professions. The texts are isolated words (*officer, nurse*), pronouns (*she*) and sentences (*She is a bus driver*). The second listening exercise is of the sounds /pē/, /kū/ and /ah/, in a chant. This exercise unfolds similarly to the first. Then the teacher links a text from the audiotape to a folding-book page containing a story entitled 'The shopping trip'. In the four-page story a boy and his mum see various people.

Each page is represented in the audiotape by an interactive model: '*Who is she? I asked my mom! She's a bus driver*' (turn 122). The contents of the pages include the representation of a male police officer (omitted) and a female bus driver (turns 122–33). The teacher introduces the question '*who is she?*' (turn 124). This is replicated by Carolina (turn 125), followed by Andy (turn 126) who is interrupted by the teacher (turn 127) apparently with a two-fold purpose: to exemplify the type of complete answer she wants from the students and to provide the beginning of the answer. This is repeated once again by Carolina (turn 128) and overlapped by Andy (turn 129). Then the teacher illustrates the second part of the answer (turn 130) and Carolina completes the construction of her own answer (turn 131). At that moment the teacher produces a whole-class question (turn 132) and obtains a choral reply containing the second part of the answer (turn 133).

'Me too'

From this point, the lesson is structured with more texts from the audiotape and the folding book. The content of these texts include a male shopkeeper (omitted) and a male 'helper' at the store (omitted). The teacher emphasises in Spanish her explanation of the word 'helper' (turn 152); she again uses the marker *'Okay'* and without pausing introduces *'now'* to initiate a new activity. Carolina launches a follow-up comment in Spanish (turn 153), acknowledged by Nando (turn 154).

'Both a man and a woman could be "I"'

Afterwards, the teacher writes the pronouns on the board and asks questions (omitted) about their meaning (turns 198–200). The teacher also points to all the male students, to Carolina, and to herself, relating the subjects 'on the spot' to the pronouns. Students repeat when nominated by the teacher and start pointing to their classmates. Andy, referring to the written word 'I' on the board, initiates a direct question in Spanish (turn 202). The teacher answers back, finalises with the marker *'Okay'* and initiates a new question with *'[So]'* (turn 203), all in Spanish. Nando formulates an overlap (turn 204) containing his appreciation of the signifier 'I'.

'He' and 'She' / 'Miss' and 'Mr'

At this point, the teacher conducts a series of 'Point to someone' exercises (omitted). Students randomly point to their classmates (turns 234–237). The initiation exchange is marked by the teacher's use of *'Okay'* followed by the pronoun *'She'*. The teacher also utters in Spanish *'[And who is "She"?]'*, wanting the male students to point to Carolina, which they do (turn 235). Finally the teacher introduces an acceptance and evaluative act (turn 236).

'Pick male-dancing partners'

The lesson continues with a 'Do as I say' exercise. The teacher asks the students to lie down on the floor (turn 295) in order that they can work with actions such as 'standing up' (turns 297–298), 'running' (turns 299–300) and 'dancing' (turns 301–307) using either 'He' or 'She'. In the last turns, the teacher reiterates her instruction (turn 303) that had been misunderstood by the pre-schoolers (probably because in turn 302 Nando utters a different interpretation). The students start dancing alone where they had been standing (turn 304). The teacher interweaves a request in Spanish (turn 305) and adds the command *'Dance'* (turn 306) and dances with Oscar (turn 307).

'Sheee no heee'

Other practice turns are set up (omitted). The teacher then uses a new model (turn 311). As she sees that the male pre-schoolers are looking for chairs to sit down and some actually sit when they are not supposed to (according to the logic of her linguistic model), she overlaps *'she she she'* (turns 313–315). Some students also utter *'she'* (turn 314). Then Juan addresses Pablo with a clarification in which there is rising intonation as the vowel sounds are elongated (turn 316). The boys comprehend this clarification and the ones who sat down immediately stand up. The teacher initiates a new series of 'point to someone' exercises (omitted) and ends the class (turn 347).

The 'HE', 'SHE', 'I' lesson thus portrays a teacher and her pre-schoolers structuring exchanges in which verbal and non-verbal answers are provided to specific linguistic models framed within definite activity types: listening and drilling exercises, 'Do as I say' and 'Point to someone' activities, reading texts from a folding book and from the board. Additionally, the interactions are structured by the simultaneous use of English and Spanish by both teacher and students.

Connotative (FPDA) analysis

From a post-structuralist point of view, the 'HE', 'SHE', 'I' lesson is the outcome, manifestation and indeed recontextualisation of interwoven and competing gendered discourses which render the research participants at times powerful and at other times less so, through specific subject positions which I will comment on below.

'She is a bus driver'

It is self-evident that the texts in the materials used in the 'HE', 'SHE', 'I' lesson are linguistically gendered. However, in their non-gender-stereotypical representations, they arguably also draw on a 'Gender equality discourse' (Sunderland, 2004), which includes the idea that women do, can or should perform the same professional activities as men (*She is a bus driver, She is a police officer*). The same iconic image is portrayed in the 'shopping trip' story: *'Who is she? I asked my mom! She's a bus driver'*. In this moment, the female bus driver, representing a trace of the 'Gender equality discourse', competes with a more mainstream 'Gender differences discourse' (ibid.). For example, the police officer is represented by a more traditional male character in the story. Both 'The shopping trip' and the audiotape bring into the 'HE', 'SHE', 'I' lesson intertextual traces of gendered discourses that then reappeared during listening and drilling exercises (e.g., *He's a police officer* vs. *She's a police officer*).

Of course, the female teacher directly acknowledged neither the 'Gender equality discourse' nor the 'Gender differences discourse'. From an FPDA perspective, the teacher arguably did not notice the gendered traces in the teaching materials and neither had she noticed the ways in which such content could subject-position her students. An FPDA approach might argue that the 'Gender equality discourse' was short-lived in this lesson precisely *because* this discourse was not acknowledged; even when it was intertextually related to the 'Gender differences discourse' within the teacher's own instructional decisions (e.g., the teacher could have highlighted that a woman was the bus driver, and that the police officer was a man but *could* have also been a woman (as the students heard before in the listening exercise)). From an FPDA standpoint, it could be said that in this highly situated context, noticing gendered discourses could be vital because, in Colombia, *inter alia*, women are not frequently seen performing the role of bus driver.[4] This could contribute to position women in less stereotypical roles in girls' and boys' early socialisation processes in the EFL classroom.

Obviously, as Teutsch-Dwyer argues about masculinities – and, I would add, femininities – gendered discourses 'may vary not only within one individual, one group of individuals, but also across cultures' (2001: 176). From an FPDA point of view, the cases of Carolina and Nando could be telling here, as I illustrate below.

'Me too'

It is precisely the moment when Carolina comments '*[I also help my mum to tidy up]*' and Nando adds '*[Me too]*' that the 'Gender differences discourse' fades in support of the 'Gender equality discourse'. Within an FPDA approach, it could be said that both Carolina and Nando seem to align power relationships and/or positions for males and females in the context of housework because both can take up the role of 'helper'. Adapting Sunderland and colleagues' (2002) model of 'talk around a text', it could be said that Carolina's and (especially) Nando's talk around this gendered text simultaneously endorse non-traditional *and* traditional representations of gender. In this highly situated site, these pre-schoolers come across texts that at times go beyond the traditional representation of gender roles, and seem to critically extend that content to their personal experiences. Nando's voice can be seen as 'equalising' traditionally gendered roles, as a response to Carolina. It could also be said though that both Carolina and Nando might be competing for a subject position in which being a 'helper' is significant and even powerful. Speaking from a post-structuralist standpoint, Walkerdine (1998: 66) found in a nursery school that, for the boys, 'the domestic is a site for opposition and resistance to the power of women'. Carolina takes up an arguably powerful position precisely in a 'site of boys' resistance', but soon that position is shared with Nando for whom the domestic seems *not* to be a site of struggle. Both pre-schoolers appear to construct in this moment their own positive masculinities and femininities as mum's 'helpers'.

'Both a man and a woman could be "I"'

These pre-schoolers' comments around the written texts on the board also raise the issue of language representation and how both Spanish and English denote and connote a binary gendered content at the pronoun level. (As we know, a number of languages have a gender-differentiated pronoun system.) When Andy asks *'[So, wherever you see the capital I, does it refer to both a man and a woman?]'*, he seems to be exploring how this pronoun in the foreign language is a discourse marker of identity for either women or men, drawing on his own knowledge of his first language. He appears to be considering the possibility that the 'I' could be used for self-construction (Sunderland, 2004) and in that sense might constitute a shared position for him (as well as both men and women). Although the teacher seems to avoid addressing Andy's hypothesis, saying *'[No, because it is "I" "I"]'*, Nando comments on this gendered topic, in spite of the teacher's reply to Andy correctly maintaining that *'[both a man and a woman could be "I"]'*.

More research is needed to understand how gendered meanings might be acquired or learned in the EFL classroom and socially enacted to position subjects. Specifically, it is relevant to understand how in the EFL pre-school context, through the new language, a pre-schooler 'negotiates a sense of self...and gains access to – or is denied access to – powerful social networks that give [her/him] the opportunity to speak' and consequently to construct and perform her/his identities as a gendered being and as a language learner (see Norton, 2000: 5). I would like to highlight how Andy's and Nando's comments around gender take place after traces of two gendered discourses ('Gender equality' and 'Gender difference') have emerged and appear to have been silenced (ignored) – twice – by the instructional design and/or pedagogical discourse of the teacher. And it is precisely Nando – the youngest boy – who has formerly drawn on the 'Gender equality discourse', who verifies Andy's linguistic hypothesis by making a logical inference about how the language operates at the pronoun level.

'He' and 'She' / 'Miss' and 'Mr'

Another case of identity construction in the target language occurs a few turns later. A close look at the data shows that Carolina constantly asserts her 'right to speak' in the class by echoing the teacher. If the teacher utters half a request, Carolina echoes it. Carolina has been keen to demonstrate her understanding of the lesson content and has positioned herself in several turns as the articulate knower, becoming (as Walkerdine (1998: 66) established in a nursery school context) 'the sub-teacher'. Carolina is fully permitted to do so by the teacher, in a form of the 'Teacher Approval discourse': 'the extent to which a teacher appear[s] to favour or privilege one student as a speaker over another' (Baxter, 2002a: 10). However, things change for Carolina during the 'point to someone' exercise when the teacher asks the pre-schoolers to point to a classmate according to her choice of 'He' or 'She'. At the pronoun level Carolina is thus constructed as the only signified of 'She' and the five male pre-schoolers as five possible 'He's'. When the option is 'He', the boys randomly point to each other and so does Carolina. When the option is 'She', all the boys point to Carolina, who smiles and puts her hands together on her chest; her gaze directed towards the desk. This singling out might be uncomfortable for Carolina in two ways. Firstly, from being a 'sub-teacher', in a powerful position, she is positioned as an arguably less powerful subject (object?) of a 'gender binary' discourse through the boys' construction of 'She'. Secondly, as a learner, Carolina keeps echoing the teacher, providing the physical responses and mimicking as requested by the teacher. However, at this precise moment her gaze is directed towards her desk, her hands are on her chest and she, as a learner, is not able to provide a physical response. It is only later, towards the end of the lesson (not transcribed), when Carolina bounces back and announces that along with her female teacher that the other *Miss* (Teacher 2) is also in the classroom, so that both female teachers correspond to 'She' and *Mr* (the cameraman) is another 'He'.

'Pick male-dancing partners'

The male pre-schoolers also find themselves performing gender work within the intertextual combination of diverse gendered discourses in the lesson. The parameters of what has been called a 'Bounded masculinity/Unbounded femininity' discourse (Sunderland, 2004) are culturally shaped: transgression of normative practices of gender are understood differently according to specific contexts. For example, while in some cultures males dancing in pairs or men choreographing other men is acceptable, in other cultures dancing is constructed as a gendered practice traditionally performed by male-female pairs. Both femininities and masculinities could thus be bounded or unbounded. In the 'HE', 'SHE', 'I' lesson, the female teacher organises a 'Do as I say' exercise using 'I' with an action in progress. When she says *'I am dancing'*, the immediate physical response is that all students start dancing alone where they are standing. Her solicit *'[Pick male-dancing partners]'* indirectly gives Carolina the power to choose her own partner. However, it is the boys who seem to choose their partners. Although there is a covert dispute over Carolina between Andy, Pablo and Juan, only Andy accomplishes his goal. Pablo and Juan do not embrace each other and end up with no dancing partner, perhaps feeling awkward with the alternative. The three boys can be seen as doing gender work within the 'Bounded masculinity discourse' in which (proper) boys construct themselves as not dancing with other boys. On the other hand, Nando embraces Oscar and Oscar goes along with being held as his dance partner. This appears to be a transgression of this same discourse and could be interpreted as a form of 'Unbounded masculinity' in which Nando overtly and happily constructs himself as a boy for whom it is fine to dance with another boy in the context of a class exercise.

'Sheee no heee'

The 'Bounded masculinity discourse' thus appears as a significant discourse in this lesson and can be seen in an intertextual relation to the 'Boy-as-OK/ Girl-as-not-OK discourse' (Sunderland, 1995, 2004). It could be OK for a boy to sometimes dance with a boy, but not always 'not OK' for a boy to identify himself as a girl when learning EFL. In Sunderland's iconic example of young adolescents learning German as a foreign language, it is observed that the word *girl* could be used to ridicule a boy (hence 'Girl-as-not-OK'). In contrast, in that lesson, a couple of girls volunteered enthusiastically to read a German dialogue with *'We're boys/We're boys, miss'* with no one laughing at their words ('Boy-as-OK'). In the 'HE', 'SHE', 'I' lesson, some boys sit (*'She's sitting down'*) when only Carolina was expected to do so. The teacher introduces immediate feedback repeating *'She, she, she'*, perhaps in the hope that the boys would realise that she did not say *'He'*. But it is Juan who emphasises *'Sheee no heee'*, directing his gaze towards Pablo. This has two, (simultaneously) plausible interpretations. First, that Pablo did not understand the instruction and should correct his mistake. Second, that Juan is censuring Pablo for taking up the role of a girl, which is not admissible even for the purposes of the exercise, because this puts a male in an 'inferior' position where 'she' is constructed as part of a binary set occupying an asymmetrical place. Juan seems not to be repeating/echoing the teacher's solicit; he rather elongates his pronunciation of the vowels to make his point clearer.

All in all, the 'HE', 'SHE', 'I' lesson is the result of multiple, emerging, interwoven and competing gendered discourses which can be traced intertextually within the interactions that construct the whole episode. In a less-than five minute extract from the complete lesson, traces of the 'Gender equality', 'Gender differences', 'Teacher approval', 'Bounded masculinity and unbounded femininity', 'Unbounded masculinity' and 'Boy-as-OK/Girl-as-not-OK' discourses were identified (see Sunderland, 2004). The teacher and the pre-schoolers draw on those discourses to position each other interactively in dominant and at times less dominant positions. Carolina positions herself as a 'sub-teacher' and is positioned as an object of the boys' constructions of 'She'. Less noticeably, Carolina positions her male classmates as the object of her solitary construction of 'He'. Carolina and Nando seem to share an egalitarian subject position when it comes to performing the role of mum's 'helper'. Andy and Nando make inferences about the representation of gendered discourses in their attempt to understand the possibilities for constructing 'I' in the foreign language. Nando constantly appears to present and position himself overtly within a 'Gender equality discourse'. He also positions himself and performs within an 'unbounded masculinity discourse' involving Andy, who seems to be in a less powerful position compared to the gendered performances of Juan, Pablo and Oscar, who seem oriented more to a 'bounded masculinity discourse'. Positioning himself outside this last discourse might or might not lead a male pre-schooler to be 'reprimanded' by his male classmates. It looks however as if Juan is telling Pablo off for taking up the role of 'She'. Finally and very significantly, the teacher does not appear to notice the salient discourses of 'Gender equality' and 'Gender differences' offered by the class materials and her own instructional design. From an FPDA viewpoint this could be a missed opportunity for transformative action in which, for instance, gendered content in the EFL classroom may be used to produce discourses that position and construct women and men as equals, occupationally at least.

An implication of this episode for language education may be that a *number* of transformative actions may be needed locally. Teachers may need to be made more aware of the salient gendered discourses offered by teaching materials, and of how these discourses position students within the structure of the lesson. More importantly, EFL teachers might pay attention to the comments pre-schoolers make around gendered texts used in the classroom. They might also examine more closely the instructional activities used during EFL lessons which might prompt pre-schoolers to negotiate subject positions through gendered discourses that, in Goodwin's words, 'do not treat peers as co-equals' (2002: 723). In my current research I have found, for example, that shifting versions of femininity may marginalise or support the discoursal construction of girl-teachers. Although this identity construction carries a burden for girls – because of boys' and other girls' resistance – it still seems to be a position of girl empowerment in the EFL classroom. In the 'HE', 'SHE', 'I' lesson, different versions of femininities (e.g., the teacher girl) and masculinities (bounded and unbounded) emerge, compete, shift and disappear through interwoven and diverse gendered discourses.

The special role of language education in the construction and performance of myriad masculinities and femininities in EFL pre-school settings needs more research. Within an FPDA approach, it is necessary to examine systematically how shifting masculinities and femininities relate to EFL clasroom processes, and how, across different EFL pre-school contexts (all-boys, all-girls, mixed), those shifting positions relate to the construction of gender identity and to the performance of gender work in interaction with gendered texts and discourses brought in by the teacher and the educational institution.

What is FPDA's contribution to this book?

FPDA as a theoretical framework could be said to facilitate the understanding of both gender and discourse as *multiplicity* within a post-structuralist feminist focus. In the 'HE', 'SHE', 'I' lesson, sometimes pre-schoolers are silenced, on other occasions they struggle for the 'right to speak', and they constantly live between and within shifting versions of masculinities and femininities. FPDA enables us to pin down in an interaction exactly where salient gendered discourses emerge: here, for example, evolving gendered discourses of equity and differentiation were put into action by the teacher and by the pre-schoolers' comments around gendered texts. More importantly, FPDA pinpoints how gendered discourses operate (and intertextually compete), situating interlocutors, or participants' voices, in different subject positions. Thus subject-positioning is the result of power distribution being used to structure not only the interaction but also the interlocutors' own experiences of such power: here, Carolina was at times powerful as a 'sub-teacher' and at other times arguably less powerful as the 'object' of the male pre-schoolers' construction of 'She'.

One distinctive and significant feature of FPDA is its welcoming of 'working partnerships' and 'supplementarity' between different theoretical and methodological perspectives: the analysis presented at the denotative level includes the representation of turn-taking as adjacency pairs, and a sequential analysis (with a number of omissions) achieves a detailed CA-like description of how the 'HE', 'SHE', 'I' lesson was co-constructed co-operatively by the research participants.

Finally, FPDA focuses on small-scale transformations: for those EFL pre-school teachers and foreign language teachers reading this study, FPDA suggests a more heightened awareness of the gendered discourses competing in their lessons and consequent transformative actions.

Notes

1 This research study has been partially sponsored by the European Union Programme of High Level Scholarships for Latin America, Alβan Programme, scholarship No. (E04D031582CO).
2 The Goldmedal Kindergarten, a private school, offers a three-year EFL programme. The official names for each corresponding year are *Pre-Jardín*, *Jardín* and *Transición*.
3 {} indicate transcriber's notes. [] indicate overlap. [] after bold text enclose transcriber's translations. *(( ))* indicate descriptions of proxemics and gestures.
4 1.5 per cent of women out of 4000 men are employed by the most important transport system in Bogotá as bus drivers.

Part 7
Queer Theory

18

The Contributions of Queer Theory to Gender and Language Research

Helen Sauntson

This chapter explores some of the contributions made by queer theory, and the related sub-discipline of queer linguistics, to the study of gender and language. At times, the study of sexuality and language has been treated as separate and distinct from the study of gender and language, and there are good reasons for maintaining this distinction in terms of both theory and methodology (see, e.g., Cameron and Kulick, 2003; Kulick, 2000). However, other work, particularly in sociology and social theory as well as linguistics, has noted rather a special relationship between gender and sexuality, arguing and illustrating how the two are inextricably linked (Butler, 2004; 1997; 1990; Halberstam, 1998; Munt, 1998; Livia and Hall, 1997). Bucholtz and Hall (2004) and other researchers included in Livia and Hall's (1997) collection have utilised relevant aspects of queer and feminist theory to further the study of both language and gender and language and sexuality. Drawing on such work, key questions asked in this chapter are 'what has the study of gender and language got to do with the study of sexuality and language?' and, given that the study of sexuality and language is often rooted in fundamental elements of queer theory, 'why does gender and language need queer theory?' In order to address these questions, this chapter starts by outlining some key developments in the history of queer theory and then considers how elements of queer theory have influenced the study of language, gender and sexuality. I then introduce Bucholtz and Hall's (2004) 'tactics of intersubjectivity' analytical framework as an example of how linguistic methodologies are starting to emerge from queer theory in conjunction with feminist theories and applied linguistic frameworks. I present examples from Bucholtz and Hall's explanation of the framework and my own work on lesbian and gay coming out narratives.

Some key developments in queer theories[1]

The term 'queer' became popularised in the 1990s but its meanings remain quite diverse. It can be used simply as shorthand for 'lesbian and gay' and has historically been used in certain contexts as a term of abuse directed towards those who identify as non-heterosexual. Intellectually, it refers to that which is not aligned with any particular identity and resists categorisation.

Until recently, queer theories (it is perhaps more appropriate to refer to them in the plural as there is no singular 'queer theory'), have sat at the margins of linguistics with their main applications occurring within social theory and literature (e.g., Hall, 2003; Sedgwick, 1990). A possible reason for this is that queer theories do not espouse any particular methodology applicable to the study of language. An oft-cited criticism of queer theory is that its uses and applications are limited both within and outside the academy, given its largely theoretical nature. Linguistics, by its very nature, demands a certain methodological and analytical rigour which queer theories, by *their* nature, do not offer.

However, certain publications have considered how selective aspects of queer theory may be used alongside other approaches and methodologies to further our understanding of gender and language. Livia and Hall's (1997) *Queerly Phrased* was the first to consider the role that queer theory might play in the study of language, gender and sexuality. Chapters in *Queerly Phrased* consider the complex historical relationship between queer and feminist theories and work towards finding complementary ways in which the two can fruitfully be used in the linguistic study of gender and sexuality. Such work has subsequently been developed by Morrish and Sauntson (2007), Bucholtz and Hall (2004) and Campbell-Kibler and colleagues (2002), as I will show.

Social, political and academic influences

Queer theory has been influenced by the work of Butler (2004; 1997; 1991; 1990), Fuss (1991), Sedgwick (1990), Foucault (1978; 1976) and Althusser (1971). Although purportedly not restricted to the domain of sexuality and gender, a key line of development of queer theories can be traced back to the homophile,[2] feminist, and lesbian and gay liberation movements of the 1950s, 1960s and 1970s. Jagose (1996) describes how homophile movements were generally characterised by being conservative and integrationist, whilst gay liberation movements were seen as more radical with their agenda of challenging and overturning existing social relations and institutions. Although queer theory shares some characteristics with gay liberation, it also partly arose out of a critique that gay liberation still espoused a commitment to some kind of 'natural' sexual identity, one which could only be understood in terms of power and oppression.

Feminism, particularly lesbian feminism, has been influential in revealing how oppressions surrounding sexuality are intricately tied to oppressions surrounding gender. Rich (1993), for example, explores how practices which function to naturalise heterosexuality and pathologise lesbianism simultaneously function to privilege (heterosexual) masculinity. She describes heterosexuality as 'a political institution which disempowers women' (ibid.: 227) and proposes challenging and denaturalising heterosexuality by arguing that it is more 'natural' for women to align themselves with other women (epitomised by lesbianism but also realised as other heterosocial relationships between women) and for men with other men. Wittig (1993) also proposes that the categories of gender (i.e., 'women' and 'men') are political categories which are complicit in the maintenance of heterosexuality. But, unlike Rich, Wittig places lesbianism outside the categories of gender by arguing that 'the refusal to become (or to remain) heterosexual always meant to refuse to become a man or a woman' (ibid.: 105). Thus, to refuse heterosexuality is the most direct way to refuse male economic, ideological and political power. However, both authors share a commitment to challenging and destabilising what Rich terms 'compulsory heterosexuality' and it is this aspect of lesbian feminism which has informed queer theory. Butler (1990), for example, develops this notion in her claims that heterosexuality is naturalised by the performative repetition of normative gender identities.

Queer theories differentiate themselves from gay liberationist and (lesbian) feminist models by resisting their commitment to notions of a coherent lesbian or gay subject and community. Jagose (1996) notes that the non-specificity of 'queer' protects it from criticisms made of the exclusionary and essentialising tendencies of referring to identity categories such as 'lesbian' and 'gay'.

Performativity, gender, sexuality and language

Butler's (1991; 1990) theories of performativity and appropriations of language styles are crucial to understanding queer perspectives and have recently been applied to gender and sexuality work (e.g., Morrish and Sauntson, 2007; Livia and Hall, 1997). Butler's claims about identity, of which gender is an integral component, have been influential both in queer theories and approaches to the study of language, gender and sexuality (including, in this volume, Baxter and Leap). For Butler, identity is not fixed or inherent in the individual or society, but is rather fluid, shifting with different contexts of interaction. In Butler's notion of performativity, identities do not pre-exist, but rather are brought into being by a series of 'citational' acts – including linguistic acts – which are understood to produce those identities. In this performativist paradigm, Butler argues that 'gender is a kind of imitation for which there is no original' (1991: 6) and posits that gender is something we 'do', not what we 'are'. Butler's work, if not cited directly, is echoed in several chapters in this collection. Within a performativist paradigm, different contexts of interaction will produce subtly different gendered identities – a further tenet of approaches in this book (e.g., FPDA, CDA).

Also as exemplified in many of the chapters here, under the influence of Butlerian queer theory, recent work in gender and language continues to problematise the binary divide of genders, sexes and sexualities. Issues surrounding how men and women might resist expectations about their gendered linguistic performances, questions about agency and volition, and explorations of the relationship between gender and sexuality all owe a great deal to Butler's theoretical work. In linguistics, Livia and Hall (1997) were the first scholars to use the term 'queer' to refer generally to non-normative performances of resistance. Chapters in their volume consider linguistic applications of performativity in gay, lesbian, bisexual and trans-gendered contexts. What is revealing about this and subsequent sexuality and language work (Morrish and Sauntson, 2007; Sauntson and Kyratzis, 2007; Bucholtz and Hall, 2004; Campbell-Kibler, Podesva et al., 2002) is that it becomes evident that in making performative statements about sexuality, we inevitably make performative statements about gender, and vice versa. Thus, despite the claims of some queer theorists that gender and sexuality follow separate lines of enquiry, once we begin to examine real-life language practices, gender and sexuality interact to such an extent that it becomes impossible to completely separate them in linguistic analysis. This issue is addressed below.

'Knots that must be undone'

Butler suggests that the categories of gender and sexuality have been 'causally entangled in knots that must be undone' (1998: 225–6) and readings of queer theory often reveal apparently contradictory positions regarding gender and sexuality. On the one hand, gender and sexuality cannot be separated, on the other, it is sometimes necessary to separate them in academic enquiry. This point is supported in other work within queer theory (e.g., Sedgwick, 1990) and linguistics (e.g., Cameron and Kulick, 2003) and is an ongoing debate which has yet to (but may never) be resolved. A point noted by Butler (1998), Sedgwick (1990) and Rubin (1984) is a peculiarity of the relationship between gender and sexuality, as opposed to gender and any other social variable. Rubin (1984) has claimed that, although sexuality and gender studies have historically constituted different avenues of enquiry, they frequently overlap and influence each other, lending them a unique relationship. In a development of Rubin's position, Sedgwick argues that although there is potential to create some 'analytic distance' between gender and sexuality, they are inextricable in that one can only be expressed in terms of the other. Quite simply, without the concept of gender, there could be no concept of homo/heterosexuality, and vice versa. Sedgwick notes that other dimensions of sexual choice (e.g., age) have no definitional connection with gender. Sexuality tends to be discursively constructed using culturally recognisable sex and gender categories as its key terms of reference. On a basic level, one can identify and construct oneself as a lesbian by expressing sexual desire for and/or identification with other women, where 'women' is socially understood as a gender category or as a biological sex category. One does not say, for example, that one is 'white' or 'working class' because one desires or identifies with women. Gender is not an integral resource in the enactment of other forms of social identity in the way that it is in the enactment of sexual identity. Work by Coates (2007, 2003), Morrish and Sauntson (2007), Kiesling (2002), Cameron (1997b), Leap (1996) and others has shown that the semiotic resources associated with gender categories are deployed as a means of constructing sexual identities in and through discourse. Such work suggests that there is a clear relationship between gender and sexuality, that the two are not experienced separately, and cannot be separated for the purpose of analysis.

Of course, it is important to be wary of over-simplifying the relationship between gender and sexuality and of uncritically conflating the two terms. We should take heed of Cameron and Kulick's useful summation that 'Sexuality and gender may be interdependent, but they are not reducible to one another' (2003: 53). However, it seems clear that the study of gender and language would undoubtedly benefit from investigating the 'knots that must be undone' in terms of gender and sexuality. Linguistic-based work which explicitly examines sexuality alongside gender has suggested that sexuality is produced in relation to particular material conditions and relations of power and has revealed some of the ways in which people deploy the semiotic resources culturally associated with gender to perform sexual identity in discourse (e.g., Morrish and Sauntson, 2007; and chapters in Livia and Hall, 1997). Moreover, people frequently draw on ideologies of gender essentialism to understand and construct sexual identities for themselves and others. For example, Morrish and Sauntson's (2007) analysis of coming out narratives reveals that evaluative references to gender are commonly deployed in such texts as a means of enabling the narrators to organise and understand sexual identities (see below). Both queer theory and queer linguistics are, therefore, careful to point out that what Spivak terms 'strategic essentialism' (Spivak, cited in Landry and MacLean, 1996: 204–5) is sometimes a useful organising concept for social actors in their processes of identity construction.

Hierarchies of constraint

These issues relate to Butler's more recent work in which she is careful to highlight notions of constraint rather than claiming gender can be simply performed at will (a common misreading of Butler's work). Whilst retaining a commitment to queer notions of performativity, Butler defines sexuality as 'an improvisational possibility within a field of constraints' (2004: 15) and argues that both gender and sexuality are mobilised and incited by social constraints as well as extinguished by them. Thus, genders and sexualities are 'hierarchised' under constraint, and this constraint often comes from essentialist ideologies of gender and sexuality. The result of this hierarchisation is that idealised or hegemonic masculinities and femininities stereotypically associated with heterosexuality are ranked higher than the marginalised genders typically associated with homosexuality. Drawing on the work of Connell (1995) and Kiesling (2002) as well as Butler, Coates (2007, 2003) notes that heterosexuality is an integral identifying component of the most powerful genders – 'hegemonic' masculinity and femininity – in society. Without heterosexuality, the most powerful genders lose their hegemonic status. Thus, hegemonic gender and heterosexuality are mutually perpetuating – gender hierarchies serve to maintain the ideological power of heterosexuality and vice versa. Moreover, powerful ideological mechanisms for linking gender to biological sex are crucial for maintaining hierarchies of gender. When performances of gender are enacted in the social world, that very performance becomes subject to interactional practices which place the performance within a gender hierarchy that is constantly under construction. In other words, gender performances are interactively constructed as normal/normative or deviant/marginal. Some past gender and language work has uncritically attributed discursive performances of 'femininity' to women and of 'masculinity' to men, thus perpetuating this ideology. This rather reductionist approach (which Nicholson, 1994, has termed the 'coat-rack' approach) harks back to the essentialist arguments that 'discourse' approaches to gender and language purport to resist.

An important aspect of the relationship between gender and sexuality is that hierarchies of gender are produced by heterosexuality and challenged by homosexuality and certain forms of 'non-normative' heterosexual practice. Halberstam's work on female masculinity (1998), for example, is important for revealing how masculinity, as a gender category, is not just the domain of men, but can also be performed by women, sometimes more effectively. Furthermore, she claims, it is often women who 'police' the boundaries and properties of what constitute acceptable forms of masculinity in society.

Working with criticisms of queer theory

Queer theories are not without their criticisms; indeed, one job of any gender and language scholar is to adopt a critical and self-reflexive stance in relation to the theoretical approach being applied. One key criticism of queer theory is its loss of specificity, rendering it 'apolitical'. Another is that the term 'queer' still carries negative connotations for many lesbians and gays who would, therefore, wish to resist the term, even in an academic context. A further concern is that many self-identified 'queers' have oppressed gender non-conformists within their own communities (e.g., Livia, 2002, has noted the oppression of butch-identified women within lesbian communities) and there is a danger of re-rendering invisible already oppressed groups which have previously fought for visibility (e.g., women, lesbians, non-white people, transgendered people). Some have claimed that it would, therefore, be more helpful to consider queer theories alongside feminism (Bucholtz and Hall, 2004; Livia and Hall, 1997). Queer theories have also been criticised for being white-, male-, and middle-class oriented and restricted to those in a university environment, for being elitist and inaccessible and for ignoring the economic and material conditions surrounding gender and sexuality (Hennessy, 2000; Ebert, 1996). Hall (2003) argues that a more productive way forward is for queer theorists and political activists to listen to each other and to those working in the area of gender and language.

Despite these theoretical and methodological concerns, I would argue that if queer theory is utilised selectively, in conjunction with feminist lines of enquiry, it can provide an effective contribution to developing understandings of relationships between gender, sexuality and language. Leap (this volume) provides an illustration of such an application. Jagose (1996) offers an understanding of queer theory not as standing in opposition to any approach or movement which requires an amount of identity politics (e.g., feminism) to achieve its purpose, but as a theory which may be utilised to enhance our understanding of 'identity' in the contexts under scrutiny:

> Instead of theorising queer in terms of its opposition to identity politics, it is more accurate to represent it as ceaselessly interrogating both the preconditions of identity and its effects.
>
> (Jagose, 1996: 131–2)

Applications of queer theory to gender and language research

Queer theories, then, take 'normality' as their object of investigation and Butler's notion of performativity has been important in enabling us to question socially sanctioned notions of normality in relation to gender and sexuality. Important contributions of queer theorists such as Butler, Sedgwick and Fuss have been to question the naturalisation of heterosexuality in both academic study and outside academia. Gender and language research has too often been guilty of colluding in the privileging of heterosexuality over other forms of sexuality (see McElhinny, 2003, for a more detailed account) and queer theory may help address such issues. Gender and language-related research which focuses upon social actors who do not identify as heterosexual has often occurred at the margins of the field (e.g., as token chapters in edited collections and occasional journal article), whilst work which takes language and homosexuality as its primary focus (e.g., Morrish and Sauntson, 2007; Livia and Hall, 1997; Leap, 1997, 1995; Moonwomon, 1995) has incorporated fuller discussions of heterosexuality and gender. Research which adopts the latter focus is beginning to reveal how a dual focus on gender and sexuality within linguistics can enhance our understanding of both.

Like feminist post-structuralist discourse analysis discussed by Baxter (this volume), queer theories try to resist producing their own totalising discourses. As Hall explains:

> [As] the concept 'queer' emphasises the disruptive, the fractured, the tactical and contingent, then certainly any implication that queer theorisation is itself a simple monolith would be hypocritical.
>
> (2003: 5)

And, as Butler points out, 'normalising the queer' would indeed signal its end. Historically and intellectually, then, it may at first be quite difficult to see how queer theories, with their emphasis on non-specificity and the erasure of identity, may be reconciled with feminist theories, with their more overtly political agenda focused around recognisable, if constantly shifting, identities. Indeed, much current work in the field of gender and sexuality across a range of disciplines has sought to resolve this conundrum – how is it possible to retain a commitment to a political and emancipatory agenda whilst, at the same time, resisting notions of 'identity' as something which is fixed, stable and inevitable? Livia and Hall (1997), Bucholtz and Hall (2004), and Morrish and Sauntson (2007), have all dealt with such issues, attempting applications of the work of Butler and other queer theorists to the field of gender, sexuality and language. Some of this methodological work, most notably Bucholtz and Hall's work, will now be discussed.

Tactics of intersubjectivity

A potential problem with utilising queer theories within language study is that they have no clearly definable methodology. 'Queer' resists methodological classification and organisation in the same way that it resists definition and categorisation. Queer theories, despite their theoretical consistencies with approaches such as FPDA, do not have a rigorous methodology, therefore their potential application to systematic analyses of language and gender may initially seem questionable. However, a practical solution may be found in the work of Bucholtz and Hall (2004). Their 'tactics of intersubjectivity' model has been conceived with gender and sexual identities in mind and, drawing on a combination of selective aspects of queer and feminist theories, offers a new and revealing framework for the analysis of the relationship between identity and language. The model provides an effective means of incorporating elements of queer theory into enquiry which wants to retain a commitment to some notion of 'identity', however fluid that notion may be. For researchers to completely disinvest from notions of identity would call into question other valuable approaches in gender and language (FPDA and CDA are, in some ways, dependent on notions of recognisable gender identities). 'Tactics of intersubjectivity' shares characteristics with approaches such as sociolinguistics (perhaps most closely aligned with a communities of practice sociolinguistic framework[3]), FPDA and CDA in that it has been developed in the recognition that identities emerge in context, that they may be temporary and multiple, and that they are negotiated with other social actors and in relation to structures of power (Bucholtz, 2003b). Like queer theory, the tactics of the intersubjectivity framework treats 'identity' not as an empirical category, but as a product of processes of identification. This is, in many ways, similar to a sociolinguistic 'communities of practice' approach whereby identities are discursively produced in localised contexts of interaction. But tactics of intersubjectivity *develop* this notion by offering an explicit methodological framework for considering how gender and sexual identities are produced in and through situated discourse.

'Tactics of intersubjectivity' are 'analytic tools to call attention to salient aspects of the discourse situation' (Bucholtz and Hall, 2004: 493). They identify three pairs of 'tactics' through which identity is intersubjectively constructed in local contexts of language use – *adequation* and *distinction; authentication* and *denaturalisation; authorisation* and *illegitimation*. Bucholtz and Hall prefer the term 'intersubjectivity' to 'identity' because they define the process of identification as a bivalent one in which the subject is both the author of social processes as well as the subject of them. Therefore, identification is not the property of individuals, but inherently relational. For example, as Caron (2005) notes, one can only be gay (heterosexual, bisexual) with other people. This relationality is addressed in the first pair of tactics, *adequation* and *distinction*, which refer to social sameness and difference so that, in the process of identity formation, the subject may attempt to suppress those social practices which are not consistent with the desired identity (distinction), and to highlight those practices which are (adequation). These processes are illustrated in the following examples which are all taken from an electronic corpus of coming out narratives.[4] The first example illustrates the tactic of *adequation*:

> Highschool was a great time for me because I met other girls who were just like me.

In this example, it is through the discovery of social sameness ('other girls who were just like me') that the narrator's sense of normality and acceptability comes to be defined. The next two examples illustrate the opposing tactic of *distinction* in which the narrators intersubjectively construct themselves as different from, rather than the same as, other social actors in the same context:

> I'm the boring old cliché of feeling different from my friends ... was the typical-tomboy with older brother when I was really young

> I was harassed for being feminine, who did not fit the masculine mold, not liking to participate in sports, and having the best grades in my class.

Here, the narrators' feelings of 'difference' are interpreted retrospectively as indicators of their emerging homosexuality. They both produce social differentiation by disaligning themselves from other social actors with whom they feel they are expected to align themselves.

The second pair of tactics of intersubjectivity are *authentication* and the corresponding *denaturalisation*. Bucholtz and Hall propose that 'authentication concerns the construction of a true or veridical identity, denaturalisation foregrounds untruth, pretence, and imposture in identity positioning.' (2004: 498). Authentication and denaturalisation do not simply equate to static and essentialised notions of 'real' and 'false' identities but, instead, highlight those linguistic practices by which identities come to be verified or authenticated. Examples of *authentication* from the corpus are:

> Then I discovered the new hit show from Showtime, Queer as Folk. I don't know what it was about that show, but it made me proud to be gay ... I think that show had the biggest influence on my coming out ....

> At that time I had been making a lot of online friends and discovering that I wasn't weird or screwed up after all but a lot of others out there just like me.

In both of these examples, the narrators' gay identities are verified, contextualised and authenticated through their initiation into aspects of gay culture (in the first example, media, and, in the second, gay cultural space on the Internet). The narrator in the second example reflects that, once his identity had been authenticated, he no longer felt 'weird or screwed up'. It is worth noting that this example simultaneously refers to a process of adequation whereby the narrator appeals to the social sameness of 'others out there just like me'. The next example illustrates the tactic of *denaturalisation*:

> I made new friends at my school in a few months, though I remained in the closet, pretending to be heterosexual.

Here, the narrator engages in a process of pretence to construct a sexual identity which they do not see as being authentic. The sexual identity of the narrator is thus interactionally constructed as incredible in the particular school context to which he is referring. This stands in contrast to the examples of authentication in which the narrators' identities are verified through a process of engagement with recognisably gay cultural space, or what may be termed a gay community of practice.

Bucholtz and Hall's final tactics of intersubjectivity pair is *authorisation* and *illegitimation*. *Authorisation* denotes a state whereby a subject is afforded some degree of institutional recognition, and *illegitimation* one of structural marginalisation. They state that, 'authorisation is the use of power to legitimate certain social identities as culturally intelligible, while illegitimation is the revoking or withholding of such validation from particular identities' (Bucholtz and Hall, 2004: 503). Queer theory responds to the most prevalent forms of sexual authorisation in society – heteronormativity and homophobia. Morrish (in Morrish and Sauntson, 2007) provides an illustration of authorisation and illegitimation in her discussion of teachers' strategies for revealing and concealing homosexual identity in the classroom. Morrish (ibid.) observes that whilst it is acceptable for references to heterosexuality to form part of the content of a lesson, it feels threatening for a gay teacher to reference homosexuality in similar ways. She cites the use of references to heterosexual nuclear family interactions in linguistics textbooks, noting the following examples from Grundy's (1995) book on pragmatics:

Not long ago my wife and I went out for lunch with two other couples.

(1995: 5)

if I say it late at night it may count as a way of excusing myself and getting off to bed before my wife.

(1995: 10)

What strikes Morrish is Grundy's taken-for-granted entitlement to reveal these obviously heterosexual familial and marital contexts – even to publish them in an academic textbook. The British higher education context clearly allows subjects to engage in this kind of institutional authorisation of heterosexuality whilst any alternative sexual identity is rendered illegitimate. For a lesbian or gay teacher to use similar examples to Grundy might at the very least cause some discomfort in the classroom, and, in the previous climate of Section 28 in Britain, might have invited accusations of 'promoting' homosexuality. Thus, heterosexual relationships and identities are institutionally authorised whilst non-heterosexual identities are rendered invisible, unintelligible and illegitimate. In the coming out stories corpus, the narrators often construct their sexual identities through processes of illegitimation and draw explicit attention to this in contexts such as the school.

I was taught, in school, that being gay was wrong.

[My mother] left me with the advice not to broadcast my identity to my school because it is really conservative and I wont be accepted too well.

These examples illustrate the narrators engaging with a process of illegitimation whereby homosexual identities are marginalised and denied institutional recognition. The tactics of intersubjectivity framework thus enables an application of queer theory's principle aim of uncovering the ways in which heterosexuality is naturalised and how other forms of sexual identity are 'queered'. The framework does this without dispensing with notions of identity, but recognises that identity construction is intersubjective, contextual and never complete. Bucholtz and Hall stress that these pairs of intersubjective tactics are not always distinct and often work together in an ongoing process of identity construction. The tactics are not inherent in speakers or in social practices or ideologies, but they do function as helpful analytical tools for drawing attention to salient aspects of any discourse situation in processes of identity construction. Thus, the framework makes use of both the non-specificity of queer theories, and the political necessity of retaining some kind of commitment to notions of 'identity' in feminist enquiry, in complementary ways.

In a field of study whose current focus is predominantly on discursive constructions of gender, using a range of theoretical and methodological approaches such as those covered in this volume, this use of queer theory to interrogate underlying preconditions of gender identity, and how these may be enacted and formulated in discourse has the potential to be extremely useful.

Notes

1   For overviews of theoretical and methodological developments in the study of sexuality and language, see Cameron and Kulick (2003) and Bucholtz and Hall (2004).

2   The homophile movement was an international movement active during the 1950s and 1960s whose main agenda was to work towards political reform surrounding sexuality and, in particular, to increase tolerance of homosexuality. Strategies included setting up educational programmes to counter homophobia and lobbying political parties and governments. Homophile organisations were often criticised for masculine-bias or largely ignoring the needs of lesbians.

3   See Part 1, the Sociolinguistics and Ethnography section of this volume.

4   All coming out narrative examples are taken from: http://www.comingoutstories. com. Further discussion of this data can be found in Sauntson (2007) and Morrish and Sauntson (2007). I am grateful to David Ralphs for giving permission to use data from this website.

19
Queering Gay Men's English

William L. Leap

What do queer theories have to offer researchers of gender and language? As Sauntson explains in the preceding chapter, the utility of the queer position seems limited, given that queer theories do not always use gender identity as the entry point for their discussion. In contrast, in language and gender research, the identity of the (speaking) subject is often named from the outset, a goal of the inquiry being to explore the language use of that subject in various domains.

Identity-centred linguistic inquiry was the approach to language and gender research taken in *Word's Out: Gay Men's English* (Leap, 1996, hereafter WO). The first section of this chapter uses key arguments from queer theory to disclose weaknesses in WO's identity-based discussion of gay English text-making. The remainder of the chapter considers what a description of 'gay men's English' might entail, if the 'identity' of the speaking subject were *not* named at the outset of inquiry while WO's other interests in language and gendered practices 'at the site' were maintained. Taken together, this chapter addresses key concerns that queer theory brings to the study of gender and language, including:

1. Gender is not a static construction but is always in formation.
2. Linguistic practices provide sites for those formations; they do not simply index a gendered presence that enters the social moment already constructed.
3. Gendered identity builds on understandings of normality and difference that are reflected in sexual, racial, ethnic and/or class-related identities.
4. Meanings of gender are expressed through linguistic practice, but these expressions are not limited to any single feature of linguistic practice.

Word's Out was not a 'queer text'

For years, studies of gay men's English were largely confined to discussions of gay-related vocabulary. Descriptions of gay men's language use in social settings were concerned with social practices – dynamics of public sex, social organisation of gay commercial venues, gay folklore, the rhetoric of homophobia. Linguistic data provided evidence for these larger concerns, but were not the focus of discussion in their own right.

My intent in writing WO was to demonstrate that gay men's English was not limited to erotic vocabulary, 'camp' expressions and other features of the so-called 'lavender lexicon' – the impression presented in much academic and popular literature at that time. In contrast, I used a close reading of gay men's conversations, oral narratives and written sources to argue that gay men's English should be described in terms of the linguistic practices – for example, turn-taking, style-shifting, lexical choices, narrative organisation, integration of affect – that enable gay men's communication, as gay men, within the linguistic moment. Frequently, the 'gay content' associated with gay English texts is not explicitly marked, but emerges through speaker/listener co-construction as the text-making unfolds. Similarly, while gay men's English is often found in contexts dominated by other forms of gay visibility, it is also evidenced in settings where explicit statements of sexually transgressive themes are actively discouraged, and where gay presence itself is a form of risk-taking. Speakers and listeners adjusting their linguistic practices accordingly, and how those adjustments are negotiated, were also addressed in WO.

In short, WO describes gay men's English as a type of linguistic work associated with a particular category of speaking subject. WO never argued that the linguistic practices associated with the speaking subject were 'inherently' gay or unique to gay text-making; examples show how different forms of language use gained this attribute through association with gay-identified speakers and messages at the site. And, as noted, gay-related messages themselves are often products of the linguistic moment, and not necessarily encoded directly in the text. Here, as Kulick (2000) and others correctly observe, the argument in WO took on a certain circularity: the 'source' of the 'gayness' of gay men's English is the gay identity claimed by one or more of the speaking subjects, yet linguistic practices are one of the primary means through which speakers construct and proclaim gay identity in public and private settings.

Admittedly, WO did not address this circularity. Having already named the identity of the speaking subject at the outset of the analysis, the chapters described how the named speaking subjects used English in conversation and other social action in the given setting. So if the logic was circular, the research task was unquestionably linear in its analytical direction. Invoking what Spivak (1993) has termed the 'risk' of 'strategic essentialism', WO made some claims about gay men's language use, illustrated those claims with examples of conversation and narrative, and opened this argument to critical discussion.

Naming the subject (i.e., as 'gay men') imposed limitations on WO's argument, however. For example, when I organised material for the book, discussions of the English language use of African-American, Hispanic or other same-sex identified men of colour that are available today were just beginning to appear in print. WO's examples drew heavily on research and personal experiences that were almost exclusively nested within urban US settings and within domains of whiteness, and that placed considerable restriction on the understandings of male sexual sameness that informed WO's discussion of gay men's English.

From a queer theoretical perspective, this focus was highly objectionable. Queer theory stresses that gender is closely tied to assumptions of normativity that assign value to all forms of subject position within the social setting. In fact, particular claims to gender have become so closely connected with claims to race and class that '[i]n the US today, the dominant image of the typical gay man is a white man who is financially better off than most everyone else', while the primary themes in the nation's 'gay rights agenda' – same-sex marriage, equal access to military service – remain detached from 'supposedly non-gay issues such as homelessness, unemployment, welfare, universal health care, union organising, affirmative action and abortion rights' (Berube, 2001: 234, 235). WO could have used gay men's English as an entry point for exploring the workings of normativity. But to do this, the discussion would need to examine language use outside the domains of gay experience and outside the domains of whiteness; WO did not do this. And even though the volume's focus on whiteness is acknowledged in the introductory chapter (1996: xviii–xvix), how whiteness (and white privilege) may help shape gay men's gendered stances, linguistic practices, and the expressions of these stances and practices 'at the site' are not addressed.

Nor did WO consider the extent to which assumptions about masculinity influenced gay men's linguistic practices, even though some of the elements of gay men's text-making resemble features of an English language-based linguistic masculinity (Coates, 2003; Cameron, 1997b). The presence of these features strengthens gay English connections to broader patterns of normativity in US society, and WO acknowledged the possibility of such a connection (1996: xi). Yet, despite the whiteness of the speaking subject being acknowledged, the implications of this alliance remained unexamined in the book's examples.

Queering gay men's English: an example from Cape Town, South Africa

But what would a discussion of 'gay men's English' look like, if the identifiers particular to the speaking subject were *not* named at the outset of the inquiry – if the analysis treated identity formation as a product of the speaker's linguistic practices rather than the foundation on which they are based? Such an inquiry builds on queer theory's assertion (point 1, above) that gender is a point of reference constantly in formation, that is, 'an ongoing discursive practice…open to intervention and resignification' (Butler, 1990: 33). This 'ongoing discursive practice' unfolds within particular moments of social interaction, and a queer-centred exploration of gay men's English would focus attention on the social interaction and the moment where it unfolds, tracing claims to gendered (and other) identity as they unfold within that setting. Bucholtz and Hall (2004) proposed a framework for such inquiry in their discussions of 'tactics of intersubjectivity' (see Sauntson, preceding chapter). Rather than looking at language use in formal terms, their framework focuses on forms of conversational practice as embedded within different categories of social interaction, each of which helps speakers establish claims to a subject position at the site, as gendered persons and in other ways.

In the following paragraphs, I consider the intersubjective formation of gendered identity in the context of story-telling – specifically, as part of the telling of a life-story narrative.[1] I use *life-story narrative* to refer to what Linde (1993: 20) terms 'oral units of social interaction', whose details are culled from a larger, more inclusive inventory of interrelated 'stories and associated discourse units' that are:

> told by an individual during the course of his/her lifetime [and] have as their primary evaluation a point about the speaker, not a general point about how the world is.

> (ibid.: 20–1)

The speaker-centred, highly reflective focus of these narratives makes them an especially useful resource in language and gender research. Moreover, life stories are accessible to researchers; people are often willing to tell stories about themselves, even when they may be reluctant to talk about other issues facing them in daily life. Heavily gendered moments figure prominently in life-story narratives: for gay men, such moments include 'coming out' experiences, the discovery of key sites in the urban terrain, 'how I met my boyfriend,' as well as descriptions of face-to-face encounters with homophobia. Life stories then provide entry points to further discussion.

Life stories are also of interest to speakers themselves, who often use the telling of a story (whether in an interview or a context of everyday life) as an occasion for working through conflicting assumptions of identity and proposing claims to subject positioning which can then be evaluated, and accepted or rejected, by other participants in the story-telling. The enduring popularity of life stories rests, in part, with the way that speakers can vary their subject position in the story line without disrupting the overall coherence of the narrative.

'Bob's story' is an example of a life-story narrative, where the speaker's sexuality and other components of his subject position are very much in formation and where the details of that formation are key elements in the linguistic work of the story-telling. In this story, Bob, an 18-year-old Black African man, describes his first visit to a gay club in the City Centre of Cape Town,

South Africa, and situates that visit within competing meanings of masculinity, homosexuality and racial status in the final moments of apartheid. The interview took place in May 1996; the interviewer, Mfume, was a 21-year-old Black African woman. Bob and Mfume were good friends and students at the University of Cape Town at this time; Mfume was enrolled in a seminar I was teaching at UCT. She conducted this interview as part of a class project, and, with Bob's consent, agreed to have the text reproduced here. The incident at the City Centre gay club took place in July 1995. At that time, Cape Town's City Centre, which had been a white-only terrain under apartheid, had been officially desegregated, and people of Colour now had access to the City Centre's public spaces and commercial terrains, gay clubs included. Even so, white mistrust of Coloured and Black intention and other legacies of apartheid tradition were still in evidence, as Bob's story indicates. The personal experiences that his story describes are infused with social themes, only one of which has to do with male-centred, same-sex desire.

Background: life stories as queer texts

Life-story narratives are 'queer texts' in the sense of the four points introduced in the opening section of this chapter. They are created in specific moments of social interaction. Their construction enunciates speakers' claims to gendered and other forms of social identity, yet the process of construction does not require that those claims already be formed. Instead, telling these stories becomes a context for (ex)pressing those claims, especially when events in those stories are framed in relation to broader expectations of power and authority. Understandably, Plummer has argued, 'we live in a world of sexual stories' and we reveal 'who we are through accounts of our identity struggles' (1995: 5).

But life stories are not self-contained statements, by any means. These stories have often been told before, and telling them again brings that history into the narrative moment. They are constantly revised and updated as a consequence of retelling, and in response to new events and new discoveries about older and familiar experiences. In other words, while life stories may appear scripted, in some sense, they are also texts in formation, and understanding how these stories are constructed is as important to life-story analysis as is understanding the basics of the story line.

Accordingly, rather than emphasising the life story's formal detail, more recent interests examine the internal form of the text as part of the speaker's engagement with memory, value and voice, within the historical and social moment, and beyond (James, 2000; Portelli, 1993; Kleinman, 1988). Under this framework, life stories cease to be sites of coherence, and become statements of assumption, contradiction and omission, features that provide opportunities for the active engagement of the audience in the development of the narrative.

Bob's story

Speaker: Bob; Interviewer: Mfume

[Mfume: *When did you come out?*]
I haven't really come out. The question should be when did I get into the scene. I've known about myself ever since I was in Standard 7. I'd gone through some literature about it, but I've never had the guts to practice it. Until I almost committed suicide. I had to stop fighting with myself. Then I came back to varsity. I used to stay in [a men's residence hall at UCT]. They had this poster about this place [names the club]. Then I decided to go there, but they didn't allow me to come in. I didn't know anything about clubbing at that stage. I was just a nerd. Clubs sounded far and weird. [Mfume: Why far?]

Because of where I lived I had a funny perception about what went on there. I thought people would just grab you and do things to you.

[Mfume: *So after you went there and they didn't let you in?*]
I went to Foreplay.[2] It's not really a life you know, it's a game. There are some funny rules you have to play by. I met a stranger at a porno shop. I was very much into cruising then. I wouldn't like to go further into that. He gave me this list, a brochure, a list of all these clubs and bars, and after that I tried Foreplay.

[Mfume: *Why didn't they let you in at (names club)?*]
They said members only. I actually went early, before they opened for the night. I stood at the door and they had the chairs on the tables and I think they were getting ready to open. I stood there and the manager came running, looked at me strangely like I was some kind of thief. Maybe not a thief but somebody who had invaded some kind of territory. But then I heard about ABIGALE.[3] I decided then, I don't know, through some literature, oh! it was through the UCT Diary so I decided to find out about these people.

Bob's story: useful fictions of incompleteness

At first reading, and without paying attention to contextual details, Bob's story is very much about competing expectations of masculinity, and his efforts to locate himself within that contested terrain of those expectations. Importantly, and contrary to older claims about life-story construction, his efforts are not presented in terms of a strict chronology, nor is the context of these experiences fully described. In fact, Bob's story-telling assumes that listeners will recognise the defining themes in recent South African cultural and political history, particularly the ways that apartheid rule used meanings of *place* to draw distinctions between, for example, male and female bodies, Black, Coloured and white bodies, authoritative and powerless bodies, and to assign value to locations that have ties to white, masculine authority. So Bob does not clarify the apartheid-related meanings of phrases like *township, City Centre, where I lived* (see below), *thief, invad[er] of some kind of territory,* and Mfume did not ask Bob to explain these. Both being Black South Africans, township residents by birth, and residents of the Cape Town area during the indicated time period, such clarification was not necessary. In effect, Bob's story-telling did not produce a static, self-contained narrative, but a text in formation, whose details were deeply dependent on his interaction with Mfume during the story-telling, on the particulars of historical moment within which the story-telling was taking place, and on his lingering memories of apartheid rule.

It is doubtful that Bob would tell this story in similar terms to another audience, or at a later point in his life. Alterations would not, however, mean that earlier versions of the story were defective. If, as queer theory claims, gender (and other formations related to normativity) are always *in* formation, then stories like Bob's where formations of gender are described will *themselves* be contingent, never emerging in final form. In this sense, life-story narratives resemble what Laclau (1996: 53) terms an *empty signifier*. That is, they contain inconsistent references, gaps in information, and other shortcomings; yet their value as statements of personal meaning encourages speakers and listeners to proceed as if the narratives contained no such 'flaws'. The fiction of completeness that surrounds these narratives resembles 'the appearance of substance, of a natural sort of being' that Butler (1990: 33, and see note 1) associates with gender and this may be one reason why speakers use life-story narratives to answer questions about their gender (and other) identity when such questions are raised by others (or themselves).

Escaping township homosexuality

One of the topics where Mfume did ask questions concerned township homosexuality. This is an area with which she may have been familiar, but one on which she wanted to hear Bob's point of view. And contrary to the image of the naïve and uninformed subject that he presented in the opening segment of his story, Bob's responses to Mfume's questions revealed that he knew a lot about the township 'scene' and that what he 'knew about himself' while living at home was shaped by this information as well as by the literature that he read.

Bob never identifies himself as a Black South African in this text, however. In one sense, he did not need to do so: the fact was already foregrounded in the assumptions of emplacement and embodiment that surrounded Bob's and Mfume's presence in the narrative moment. By treating 'Blackness' as the unmarked racial reference, Bob's discussion becomes dominated by references to whiteness. That message is underscored by references to locations where forms of normativity may be contested, but never entirely undermined. These locations include: the secondary school classroom, the university, the college residence hall – and the gay dance club. His discomfort with these sites marks him as different, and marks his story as a narrative about difference, even if the specifics of difference have yet to be named.

Bob began to engage the tensions of normativity and difference once he discussed his unfamiliarity with the club scene: *Clubs sounded far and weird*, he noted, and when Mfume asked *Why far?*, Bob responded: *Because of where I lived.* *Where I live(d)* is a South African township English phrasing that dates from the apartheid period, when 'persons of colour' were officially assigned to a single residence, whose location was then indicated on the speaker's identity documents; any deviation from this violated the state's efforts to enforce racial segregation and made the individual subject to legal action. Because township residents often had to leave home to seek employment or for other reasons, township English speakers distinguished *where I live*, the official address, from *where I stay*, the residence the speaker occupies for a shorter period of time. Thus, by using *where I lived* to frame his answer to Mfume's question, Bob makes clear his sense of the *weird*ness of city centre gay clubs, and his *funny perception about what went on there* was based on his understandings of male homosexuality as practiced in his home township. In effect, without employing explicit references to do so, Bob's remarks are 'queering' the City Centre's gay terrain: that is, he is using township perspectives as a benchmark against which City Centre-related assumptions of white gay masculinity can then be exposed.

During a later part of the discussion, Bob turned his queer gaze onto the assumptions structuring township-based homosexuality. He explained to Mfume that township homosexuality is dominated by *people who are into cross-dressing … drag queens.* He continued:

Bob: … They wear make-up and stuff … They're trying to be women. I really hate that, you know. People think that if you are gay then it means you are trying to be a woman … To white people they just think of you as a guy attracted to other guys. In black communities they'll go so far as determining your taste. In the townships they're very cliquey. They associate you with a group …. They are very forward there. They just start fiddling with you. They grab you by force. At [city centre clubs] they're very snobbish, so they have restraint. And in townships they're very nosy so they've got to know even what you do in bed.

Mfume: So privacy's important to you?

Bob: Yes, and there's not much of it in the townships. At least if I go to [city centre clubs] no one knows me.

Mfume: Did you know a lot of gay people in [home township]

Bob: No. I couldn't even think of practicing it. Maybe it was one of the reasons I wanted to be out of [home township], so I could start practicing this thing.

Mfume then asked more pointedly why Bob couldn't *practice this thing* in his home township:

Bob: My family of course. My brother would have killed me. Literally. And my mother would have disowned me.

Mfume: Did your mother ever make comments that made you believe that?

Bob: Ja, lots of things like: 'If someone ever did that, I wouldn't even let them into my house.'

Mfume: And your brother?

Bob: When I came home in first term, he asked me if I had a girlfriend. I said 'No,' and he said; 'Why? You're a man. I just hope you're not queer because those white universities have all these facilities for people to practice homosexuality. It's easy there. No one gives a damn in white universities.'

As these remarks suggest, one of Bob's reasons for leaving his home township and *coming to varsity,* was to find an alternative to the assumptions regarding Black (heterosexual) masculinity that are widely maintained within the township 'scene'. Another reason was to escape the surveillance of family and close friends whose distaste for homosexuality (and especially its ties to whiteness) resembles anti-gay discourses widely articulated throughout sub-Saharan Africa (Epprecht, 2004; Aarmo, 1999; Murray, 1998).

Indeed, while leaving his home township allowed Bob to get away from township-defined homosexuality and the ever-watchful supervision of his family, it also meant that he was moving out of a historically Black-proclaimed terrain and into an area that had been heavily inscribed for whiteness. The sites where Bob hoped to find homosexual opportunities that were more to his liking were historically white locations; and, in this sense, what Bob's brother reportedly said about *white universities having facilities for people to practice homosexuality* was quite accurate. And for a time, as Bob discovered, *no one gives a damn in white universities* or in any other white locations, especially if the would-be subject is a person of colour. What he would learn about the city centre scene, and about the assumptions regarding white-defined masculinity that are widely maintained there, he would have to learn for himself.

Not exactly a coming out story

In some ways, then, what Bob's story describes is akin to the coming out experience that figures prominently in gay men's life stories in North

Atlantic settings (Leap, 1996; Liang, 1997). These stories also resemble the heroic narratives described by Campbell (1949). In this framework, coming out unfolds as a journey that takes the subject into unfamiliar, mysterious terrain. There the subject is confronted by a series of demanding challenges related to sexual (and related) identity, some of which the subject transcends, others of which present temporary setbacks. Usually, the subject engages with the challenges alone, and this increases their difficulty. But the subject perseveres, and is ultimately able to make a public affirmation of sexual orientation. This may restore relations with family or friends, or further widen the distance between them. Either way, the story ends with the triumphant ending of the subject's journey – self-acceptance, articulation, visibility – even if the subject has now come to the threshold of a new journey, and equally unfamiliar terrain.

Similarly, Bob first presents himself as uninformed and inexperienced about aspects of homosexual life, and explains the failure of his first visit to a gay club in terms of his own naiveté: *I didn't know anything about clubbing at this stage. I was just a nerd. Clubs sounded far and weird.* Even so, being refused entrance to the city centre gay club did not render him powerless. Bob went on to make contact with (presumably gay) men at other locations in the city centre, and eventually found his way to a bookstore that was a popular meeting place for same-sex identified white men and men of colour. He learned, in the process, that *there [were] some funny rules that you have to play by,* and people like *the stranger at the porno shop* helped him master these. Still, Bob remains the primary actor, the source of initiative, the subject of a largely self-managed socialisation. Thus, just as he moved from the gay clubs to the porno shop and other City Centre locations, then he moved on to Foreplay. And then he *heard about ABIGALE ... and decided to find out about those people,* which broadened his contacts with the Cape Town area gay resources, and added a political dimension to his 'coming out' experience.

In other ways, however, this example does not fit so easily into the North Atlantic based 'coming out' story framework. For one thing, his relationship with Mfume excepted, the disclosure of sexual orientation to family and friends, always a key event in North Atlantic narratives, is not attested here. We don't know whether Bob has ever told his family, and, given his remarks, it seems unlikely that he would ever do so.

Moreover, while this is a narrative about Bob's experience, as a sexual subject, it also addresses issues of normativity that are much broader than Bob's own life story and more complex than a disclosure of personal sexual preference. Township homosexuality, with its assumption that all sexuality is framed in terms of 'men' or 'women,' and its emphasis on cross-dressing and other obligations of taste, contrasts with City Centre gay sexuality, defined in terms of *guy[s] attracted to other guys,* and framed within a commercial geography rather than networks of kinship and friendship ties. The racialised messages embedded within this contrast connect these competing forms of sexual sameness to the workings of apartheid technology and the regulation of South African society that this technology enabled.

Thus, from a township perspective, homosexuality emerges in Bob's text as either a Black construction, and therefore local and familiar, or as something that is white, alien, and linked to oppressive rule. These assumptions of normativity did not vanish as apartheid rule transitioned to democratic government. Access to City Centre gay geography made the 'alien terrain' accessible, but did not erase its associations with whiteness. Thus Bob's first visit to the City Centre gay terrain found him labelled *a thief...somebody who had invaded some kind of territory*. And this forces him to find City Centre territory where he is not judged out of place. The cruising locations, where white men and men of colour could meet and negotiate private liaisons, were much more accepting in that regard; this is where he learned the *funny rules you have to play by*.

Ironically, Bob's dislike of township homosexuality had to do with the township's treatment of the homosexual person as if he were a commodity – something that may be acquired, exchanged, used and discarded without regard for the person's well-being:

> In black communities they'll go so far as determining your taste...They are very forward there. They just start fiddling with you. They grab you by force.

The City Centre gay venues provided a space of escape from township experience, yet they also imposed a different type of commodification. Here, while the object of desire is still a 'pawn' in the game of public sex, the object is now defined in racialised as well as sexualised terms. And here, even though Bob *wouldn't like to go further into that*, the object can claim a position of agency, both by *becoming very much into cruising* and ultimately by seeking out ABIGALE and anchoring his homosexuality in terms of an anti-apartheid-related politics. Neither actions were open to him within the township setting, and both of them become attempts to undermine the authority of the township/City Centre and Black/White binaries.

Certainly, 'coming out' themes are deeply embedded in this work; but to summarise the whole of Bob's experiences with this label would divert attention from the dynamics of social and political settings in favour of context-free psychological themes. If queer theories intend to 'investigate...the underlying preconditions of gender identity, and how they are enacted and formulated in discourse', as Sauntson (this volume) explains, attention to social and political setting cannot be ignored.

Is Bob's story a gay English text?

Given how much can be learned about Bob's story if we add a queer theory perspective and refuse to 'name the subject' in advance of the analysis, it seems worthwhile to ask whether anything is gained here by labelling Bob's story as a gay English text. Indeed, Bob's story is not a narrative about 'gay experience' as such. The discussion of 'identity' is heavily inflected with issues of racial and class tension, not confined solely to a male-oriented same-sex attraction, and the understanding of homosexuality on which the discussion is based is not constrained by North Atlantic, and increasingly transnational, constructions of sexual privilege. And Bob does not refer to himself as a 'gay man' or as any other sexual category. In this sense, referring to Bob's story as a 'gay English text' is misleading. It mistakenly implies that a single, fixed identity anchors the issues addressed in this narrative, and that the linguistic practices that enable text-making are oriented in terms of a similar, singular focus.[4]

A text where gay English is refused?

At the same time, Bob's story is, in part, a narrative about 'gayness'. The narrative displays his repeated attempts to engage with meanings of 'gay identity' that circulate within the contexts of the City Centre, and with the comparable sexual meanings confronting him in the township settings. When access to one component of township or City Centre terrain was denied, Bob turned to other locations and the meanings of sexual subjectivity which were possible in those settings. The intersubjectively constructed language of the narrative – including Mfume's sequencing of the narrative through her questions, and both participants' repeated reliance on implicit meanings at key points to mark key moments in the narrative – captures this ongoing engagement. None proved to be satisfactory, however, and, hearing about ABIGALE, Bob shifted focus, away from township and the City Centre, towards a more politicised, Black/Coloured affirming, sexualised terrain. Bob's remarks do not indicate whether this multi-layered, politicised subject position will also become a foundation for further exploration, rather than a fixed identity; given the overall direction of the narrative, such an outcome would not be surprising.

In this sense, Bob's story could be called a 'gay English text' provided we make clear that in this instance, gay English usage shows how gay identity was engaged and then rejected, that is, this is a 'gay English text' where gay English itself is ultimately refused. This is a very different meaning of 'gay English text' from that found in North Atlantic settings, where linguistic practices encode gay experience more directly and more consistently throughout the text.

A text whose language affirms gender as a flexible accumulation?

If there is a dominant or centralising theme in Bob's story, I suggest that it rests in Bob's struggle to claim a particular position of masculinity and to fashion a text where linguistic practices capture these gendered claims.

Multiple meanings of 'masculinity' are attested in these texts, including his family's assumptions about hetero-manliness, township-centred expectations of M-to-F (male-to-female) cross-dressing and transgender performance, urban attraction of gay opportunity and gay privilege, and Black political masculinity; tensions between Blackness and whiteness and other forms of opportunity and privilege lend further texture to these meanings.

To say that Bob's story is merely about gender is limiting, however. Here, gender as relevant to this text is not singular, fixed and stable, but has been fashioned along lines that resemble the processes of flexible accumulation that characterise commodity production (Harvey, 1989), citizenship (Ong, 1999) and other dominant themes in late modernity. I have suggested (Leap, 2003, and elsewhere) that the differences in linguistic practices associated with gendered text-making in various late modern settings can be read productively in terms of these accumulation processes. Perhaps it is time to consider 'gay men's English' as a particular expression of those processes, even if at times the processes and their outcomes are not so flexibly expressed.

Conclusions: how queer theory can be helpful for studies of language and gender

Queer theory may appear to be a mode of inquiry that is detached from real-world experience. But the discussion in this chapter suggests that this appearance may be misleading, at least in so far as language and gender studies are concerned. Queer theory's interests in the decentring of subject position and in the non-specificity of theory provide helpful constraints for researchers interested in understanding how meanings of gender become constructed, negotiated and contested through forms of linguistic practices. Besides asking *who* is speaking, and *how* they invoke language to express gendered meanings, queer theory insists that the inquiry disclose connections between gender and other forms of social location that are being addressed within the social moment. This requires a close reading of text, and careful consideration of speaker biography and speaker intention, but it also requires social and historical perspectives that extend far beyond the textual boundary.

Other approaches to discourse analysis argue in favour of attention to contextualisation and archive in studies of text (Blommaert, 2005). Missing in Blommaert, and in other treatments of discourse analysis, is an insistence that gender be a foregrounded category in the discussion. Queer theory may not always foreground discussions of gender, but it does not allow gender to be pushed into the sidelines so that a-historical, highly generic political process can move into centre stage. By keeping the subject out of the discussion, initially, and by inviting researchers to trace how speakers bring the subject into the text – or, in the sense of Bob's story, how speakers may refuse to do so – queer theory enriches the understandings of language and gender that other modes of critical inquiry currently provide.

Notes

1 Story-telling and conversation are similar in certain ways. Story-telling involves exchange between the narrator and other participants in the event, as shown in Mfume's questions to Bob and Bob's shaping his narrative in response to them. Importantly, in oral narrative, one speaker (the narrator) is the dominant voice in the turn-taking and that status is usually not contested. In other genres of everyday conversation, such assertions of privilege would probably be contested.

2 A Cape Town City Centre adult bookstore.

3 Lesbian/gay activist organisation, specifically for persons of colour.

4 Orthodox queer theorists would likely respond here that no such text, whether South African or North American in basis, would be oriented in terms of such fixed identity. I suggest that such orientation *guides* some men's stories of, e.g., their attempts to negotiate a pathway through 'a desert of nothing' and toward an oasis of gay identity (Leap, 1996: 125–39). The foregrounding of sexuality over other aspects of speaker subject position may well be a marker of privilege, but it is still a narrative style attested in the North Atlantic terrain.

References

Aarmo, M. 1999. How homosexuality became 'un-African': The case of Zimbabwe. In Blackwood, E. and Wieringa, S. (eds) *Same-Sex Relations and Female Desires: Transgender Practices across Cultures*. New York: Columbia University Press. 255–80

Aggelopoulos, G. 2005. Greeks are the worst fathers: They rank second lowest in Europe regarding the time they devote to their children. *Ta Nea* 17.6.2005: 51

Ahmad, F. 2003. Still in progress? Methodological dilemmas, tensions and contradictions in theorising South Asian Muslim Women. In Puward, N. and Raghuram, P. (eds) *South Asian Women in the Diaspora*. Oxford: Berg. 43–66

Allen, R. 1985. *Speaking of Soap Operas*. Chapel Hill: University of North Carolina Press

Althusser, L. 1971. *Lenin and Philosophy and Other Essays*. London: New Left Books

Antaki, C. and Widdicombe, S. (eds) 1998. *Identities in Talk*. London: Sage

Archer, L. 2002. 'It's easier that you're a girl and that you're Asian': Interactions of 'race' and gender between researchers and participants. *Feminist Review* 71: 108–32

Aries, E. 1996. *Men and Women in Interaction: Reconsidering the Difference*. New York: Oxford University Press

Arnold, N. 1990. A bit too close to Homer: Gender and writing in the junior school. In *National Writing Project: What are Writers Made of? Issues of Gender and Writing*. Walton-on-Thames: Nelson

Athanasiadou, C., Petropoulou, S. and Mimikou, G. 2001. The conditions of women's employment in Greece: 1980–2000. http://www.kethi.gr/greek/meletes/index.htm (Accessed 21.11.2005)

Atkinson, J. and Heritage, J. (eds) 1984. *Structures of Social Action: Studies in Conversation Analysis*. Cambridge: Cambridge University Press

Baker, C. 1984. The search for adultness: Membership work in adolescent-adult talk. *Human Studies* 7: 301–23

Baker, P. 2006. *Using Corpora for Discourse Analysis*. London: Continuum

Baker, P. 2005. *Public Discourses of Gay Men*. London: Routledge

Bakhtin, M. 1986. *Speech Genres and Other Late Essays*. Austin: University of Texas Press

Bakhtin, M. 1981. *The Dialogic Imagination: Four Essays*. Austin: University of Texas Press

Bal, M. 1997. *Narratology: Introduction to the Theory of Narrative* (2nd edn). Toronto: University of Toronto Press

Bargiela-Chiappini, F. and Harris, S. 1997. *Managing Language: The Discourse of Corporate Meetings*. Amsterdam: Benjamins

Barrett, M. and McIntosh, M. 1985. Ethnocentrism and socialist feminism. *Feminist Review* 17: 3–19

Barrett, R. 1999. Indexing polyphonous identity in the speech of African American drag queens. In Bucholtz, M., Laing, A. and Sutton, L. (eds) *Reinventing Identities: The Gendered Self in Discourse*. New York: Oxford University Press. 313–31

Barthes, R. 1977. *Image-Music-Text*. New York: Hill & Yang

Bateson, G. 1987/1972. A theory of play and fantasy. In Bateson, G. (ed.) *Steps to an Ecology of Mind: Collected Essays in Anthropology, Psychiatry, Evolution and Epistemology*. London: Jason Aronson. 177–93

Bauböck, R. 1994. *Transnational Citizenship: Membership and Rights in International Migration*. Aldershot: Edward Elgar

Bauman, G. 1997. Dominant and demotic discourses of culture: Their relevance to multi-ethnic alliances. In Werbner, P. and Moodod, T. (eds) *Debating Cultural Hybridity: Multi-cultural Identities and the Politics of Anti-Racism*. London: Zed Books. 209–25

Baxter, J. (ed.) 2006a. *Speaking Out: The Female Voice in Public Contexts*. Basingstoke: Palgrave Macmillan

Baxter, J. 2006b. Putting gender in its place: A case study on constructing speaker identities in a management meetings. In Barrett, M. and Davidson, M. (eds) *Gender and Communication at Work*. Aldershot: Ashgate. 154–65

Baxter, J. (2005) Feminist poststructuralist discourse analysis. Paper delivered at BAAL/CUP Seminar: *Theoretical and Methodological Approaches to Gender and Language Study*, 18–19 November 2005, The University of Birmingham, UK

Baxter, J. 2003. *Positioning Gender in Discourse: A Feminist Methodology*. Basingstoke: Palgrave Macmillan

Baxter, J. 2002a. Jokers in the pack: Why boys are more adept than girls at speaking in public. *Language and Education* 16 (2): 81–96

Baxter, J. 2002b. Competing discourses in the classroom: A poststructuralist analysis of pupils' speech in public contexts. *Discourse and Society* 19 (6): 827–42

Baxter, J. 2002c. A juggling act: A feminist post-structuralist analysis of girls' and boys' talk in the secondary classroom. *Gender and Education* 14 (1): 5–19

Beach. W. 2000. Inviting collaborations in stories about a woman. *Language in Society* 29: 379–407

Beattie, G. 1981. Interruption in conversational interaction and its relation to sex and status of interactants. *Linguistics* 19: 15–35

Belt, V. 2002. Capitalising on femininity: Gender and the utilisation of social skills in telephone call centres. In Holtgrewe, U., Kerst, C. and Shire, K. (eds) *Re-Organising Service Work: Call Centres in Germany and Britain*. Aldershot: Ashgate. 123–45

Benke, G. 2003. We are facing a new order in Europe: Neutrality versus Nato. In Kovacs, A. and Wodak, R. (eds) *Nato, Neutrality and National Identity: The case of Austria and Hungary*. Vienna: Böhlau. 281–310

Benwell, B. 2004. Ironic discourse: Evasive masculinity in men's lifestyle magazines. *Men and Masculinities* 7 (1): 3–21

Benwell, B. 2002. Is there anything 'new' about lads? : The textual and visual construction of masculinity in men's magazines. In Litosseliti, L. and Sunderland, J. (eds) 149–74

Benwell, B. and Stokoe, E. 2006. *Discourse and Identity*. Edinburgh: Edinburgh University Press

Bergvall, V., Bing, J. and Freed, A. 1996. *Rethinking Language and Gender Research*. London: Longman

Bernstein, B. 1996. *Pedagogy, Symbolic Control and Identity: Theory, Research, Critique*. London: Taylor & Francis

Bernstein, B. 1990. *The Structuring of Pedagogic Discourse: Class, Codes and Control* Volume 4. London: Routledge

Berube, A. 2001. How gay says white and what kind of white it says. In Rasmussen, B., Klineberg, E., Mexica, I. and Wray, M. (eds) *The Making and Unmaking of Whiteness*. Durham, SC: Duke University Press. 234–65

Besnier, N. 2003. Crossing genders, mixing languages: The linguistic construction of transgenderism in Tonga. In Holmes, J. and Meyerhoff, M. (eds) 279–301

Biber, D., Conrad, S. and Reppen, R. 1998. *Corpus Linguistics: Investigating Language Structure and Use.* Cambridge: Cambridge University Press

Biber, D., Johansson, S., Leech, G., Conrad, S. and Finegan, E. 1999. *Longman Grammar of Spoken and Written English.* London: Longman

Billig, M. 2001. Discursive, rhetorical and ideological messages. In Wetherell, M., Taylor, S. and Yates, S. (eds) *Discourse Theory and Practice: A Reader.* London: Sage. 210–21

Billig, M. 2000. Towards a critique of the critical. *Discourse and Society* **11** (3): 291–2

Billig, M. 1999. Whose terms? Whose ordinariness? Rhetoric and ideology in conversation analysis. *Discourse and Society* **10** (4): 543–58

Billig, M. 1992. *Talking of the Royal Family.* London: Routledge

Billig, M. 1987. *Arguing and Thinking: A Rhetorical Approach to Social Psychology.* Cambridge: Cambridge University Press

Billig, M., Condor, S., Edwards, D., Gane, M., Middleton, D. and Radley, A. 1988. *Ideological Dilemmas: A Social Psychology of Everyday Thinking.* London: Sage

Bing, J. and Bergvall, V. 1996. The question of questions: Beyond binary thinking. In Bergvall, V., Bing, J. and Freed, A. (eds) 1–30

Blommaert, J. 2005. *Discourse: A Critical Introduction.* Cambridge: Cambridge University Press

Blommaert, J., Collins, J., Heller, M., Rampton, B., Slembrouck, S. and Verschueren, J. 2003. Introduction (special issue): Ethnography, discourse and hegemony. *Pragmatics* **13** (1): 1–10

Bloustien, G. 2001. Far from sugar and spice: Teenage girls, embodiment and representation. In Baron, B. and Kotthoff, H. (eds) *Gender in Interaction: Perspectives on Femininity and Masculinity in Ethnography and Discourse.* Amsterdam: John Benjamins. 99–136

Blyth, C. Recktenwald, S. and Wang, J. 1990. I'm like 'Say what?!' A new quotative in American oral narrative. *American Speech* **65** (3): 215–27.

Bourdieu, P. 2004. *The Weight of the World.* London: Polity Press

Bourdieu, P. 1998. *Practical Reason: On the Theory of Action.* Cambridge: Polity Press

Bourdieu, P. 1993. *The Field of Cultural Production.* Cambridge: Polity Press

Bourdieu, P. 1991. *Language and Symbolic Power.* Cambridge: Polity Press

Bourdieu, P. 1990. The scholastic point of view. *Cultural Anthropology* **5** (4): 380–91

Bourdieu, P. 1977. *Outline of a Theory of Practice.* Cambridge: Cambridge University Press

Brah, A. 1996. *Cartographies of Diaspora.* London: Routledge

Buchanan, D. 1992. An uneasy alliance: Combining quantitative and qualitative research methods. *Health Education Quarterly* **19**: 117–35

Bucholtz, M. 2003a. Theories of discourse as theories of gender: Discourse analysis in language and gender studies. In Holmes, J. and Meyerhoff, M. (eds) 43–68

Bucholtz, M. 2003b. Sociolinguistic nostalgia and the authentication of identity. *Journal of Sociolinguistics* **7**: 398–416

Bucholtz, M. 1999a. 'Why be normal?': Language and identity practices in a community of nerd girls. *Language and Society* **28**: 203–23

Bucholtz, M. 1999b. Bad examples: Transgression and progress in language and gender studies. In Bucholtz, M., Liang, A. and Sutton, L. (eds) *Reinventing Identities: The Gendered Self in Discourse.* New York: Oxford University Press. 3–24

Bucholtz, M. and Hall, K. 2004. Theorizing identity in language and sexuality research. *Language in Society* **33**: 469–515

Budach, G. 2005. Language, gender and community in French Ontario: Exploring a feminist poststructuralist perspective. Paper delivered at *BAAL/CUP Seminar:*

Theoretical and Methodological Approaches to Gender and Language Study. University of Birmingham, UK

Budgeon, S. 2003. Identity as an embodied event. *Body and Society* 9 (1): 35–55

Bulkin, E., Pratt, M. B., and Smith, B. (1984) *Yours in Struggle: Three Feminist Perspectives on Anti-Semitism and Racism.* New York: Long Haul Press

Burkitt, I. 1999. Between the Light and the Dark: Power and the material contexts of social relations. In Nightingale, D. and Cromby, J. (eds) *Social Constructionist Psychology: A Critical Analysis of Theory and Practice.* Buckingham: Open University Press. 121–31

Burkitt, I. 1998. Relations, communication and power. In Velody, I. and Williams, R. (eds) 69–82

Busch, B. and Krzyżnowski, M. 2007. Outside/inside the EU: Enlargement, migration policies and the search for Europe's identity. In Anderson, J. and Armstrong, W. (eds) *Geopolitics of the European Union Enlargement.* London: Routledge.

Butler, J. 2004. *Undoing Gender.* New York: Routledge

Butler, J. 1999. *Gender Trouble: Feminism and the Subversion of Identity* (2nd edn). New York: Routledge

Butler, J. 1998. Afterword. In Munt, S. (ed.) 225–30

Butler, J. 1997. *Excitable Speech.* New York: Routledge

Butler, J. 1991. Imitation and gender subordination. In Fuss, D. (ed.) 13–31

Butler, J. 1990. *Gender Trouble: Feminism and the Subversion of Identity.* New York: Routledge

Buttny, R. 1993. *Social Accountability in Communication.* London: Sage

Buttny, R. and Williams, P. 2000. Demanding respect: The uses of reported speech in discursive constructions of interracial contact. *Discourse and Society* 11: 109–33

Button, G. (ed.) 1991. *Ethnomethodology and the Human Sciences.* Cambridge: Cambridge University Press

Button, G. and Sharrock, W. 2003. A disagreement over agreement and consensus in constructionist sociology. In Lynch, M. and Sharrock, W. (eds) *Harold Garfinkel.* London: Sage

Calavita, K. 2006. Gender, migration, and law: Crossing borders and bridging disciplines. *International Migration Review* 40 (1): 104–32

Caldas-Coulthard, C. 2003. Cross-cultural representation of 'otherness' in media discourse. In Weiss, G. and Wodak, R. (eds) 272–96

Caldas-Coulthard, C. 1996. Women who pay for sex and enjoy it: Transgression versus morality in women's magazines. In Caldas-Coulthard, C. and Coulthard, M. (eds) *Texts and Practices: Readings in Critical Discourse Analysis.* London: Routledge. 250–70

Cameron, D. 2006. Theorising the female voice in public contexts. In Baxter, J. (ed.) 3–20

Cameron, D. (2005a). Language, gender and sexuality: Current issues and new directions. *Applied Linguistics* 26 (4): 482–502

Cameron, D. (2005b). Relativity and its discontents: Language, gender and pragmatics. *Intercultural Pragmatics* 2 (3): 321–34

Cameron, D. 2003. Gender and language ideologies. In Holmes, J. and Meyerhoff, M. (eds) 447–67

Cameron, D. 2001. *Working with Spoken Discourse.* London: Sage

Cameron, D. 2000a. *Good to Talk: Living and Working in a Communication Culture.* London: Sage

Cameron, D. 2000b. Styling the worker: Gender and the commodification of language in the globalized service economy. *Journal of Sociolinguistics* 4 (3): 323–47

Cameron, D. 1998a. 'Is there any ketchup, Vera?': Gender, power and pragmatics. *Discourse and Society* 9 (4): 437–55

Cameron, D. 1998b. Gender, language and discourse: A review essay. *Signs: Journal of Women in Culture and Society* 23 (4): 945–73

Cameron, D. 1997a. Theoretical debates in feminist linguistics: Questions of sex and gender. In Wodak, R. (ed.) 21–35

Cameron, D. 1997b. Performing gender identity: Young men's talk and the construction of heterosexual masculinity. In Johnson, S. and Meinhof, U. (eds) *Language and Masculinity*. Oxford: Blackwell. 47–64

Cameron, D. 1996. The language-gender interface: Challenging co-optation. In Bergvall, V., Bing, J. and Freed, A. (eds) 31–53

Cameron, D. 1995a. Rethinking language and gender studies: Some issues for the 1990s. In Mills, S. (ed) *Language and Gender: Interdisciplinary Perspectives*. London: Longman. 31–44

Cameron, D. 1995b. *The Feminist Critique of Language. A Reader*. London: Routledge

Cameron, D. 1992. *Feminism and Linguistic Theory* (2nd edn). Basingstoke: Macmillan

Cameron, D. 1990. Demythologising sociolinguistics: Why language does not reflect society. In Joseph, J. and Taylor, T. (eds) *Ideologies of Language*. London: Routledge. 79–96

Cameron, D. and Kulick, D. 2003. *Language and Sexuality*. Cambridge: Cambridge University Press

Cameron, D., McAlinden, F. and O'Leary, K. 1988. Lakoff in context: The social and linguistic functions of tag questions. In Coates, J. and Cameron, D. (eds) *Women in Their Speech Communities*. London: Longman. 74–93

Cameron, D., Frazer, E., Harvey, P., Rampton, M. and Richardson, K. (eds) 1992. *Researching Language: Issues of Power and Method*. London: Routledge

Campbell, J. 1949. *The Hero With a Thousand Faces*. Princeton: Princeton University Press

Campbell-Kibler, K., Podesva, R., Roberts, S. and Wong, A. (eds) 2002. *Language and Sexuality: Contesting Meaning in Theory and Practice*. Stanford, CA: CSLI

Candlin, S. 2003. Issues arising when the professional workplace is the site of applied linguistic research. *Applied Linguistics* 24 (3): 386–94

Carabine, J. 2001. Unmarried motherhood 1830–1990: A genealogical analysis. In Wetherell, M. et al. (eds) *Discourse as Data: A guide for Analysis*. London: Sage. 267–310

Caron, D. 2005. Shame on me! or The naked truth about me and Marlene Dietrich. Paper delivered at *Lavender Languages and Linguistics XII*. American University, Washington, DC

Carranza, I. 1999. Winning the battle in private discourse: Rhetorical-logical operations in storytelling. *Discourse and Society* 10 (4): 509–41

Charteris-Black, J. 2004. *Corpus Approaches to Critical Metaphor Analysis*. Basingstoke: Palgrave Macmillan

Chesebro, J. (ed.) 1980. *GaySpeak: Gay Male and Lesbian Communication*. New York: Pilgrim Press

Cheshire, J. 1982. *Variation in an English Dialect: A Sociolinguistic Study*. Cambridge: Cambridge University Press

Chouliaraki, L. 2000. Political discourse in the news: Democratizing responsibility or aestheticizing politics? *Discourse and Society* 11 (3): 293–314

Chouliaraki, L. 1998. Regulation in 'progressivist' pedagogic discourse: Individualized teacher-pupil talk. *Discourse and Society* 9 (1): 5–32

Chouliaraki, L. and Fairclough, N. 1999. *Discourse in Late Modernity: Rethinking Critical Discourse Analysis.* Edinburgh: Edinburgh University Press

Christie, C. 2002. Politeness and the linguistic construction of gender in parliament: An analysis of transgressions and apology behaviour. http://www.shu.ac.uk/wpw/ politeness/christie.htm (Accessed 28.2.2006)

Cicourel, A. 2006. The interaction of discourse, cognition and culture. *Discourse Studies* 8 (1): 25–9

Cicourel, A. 1964. *Method and Measurement in Sociology.* New York: Free Press

Clark, K. 1998. The linguistics of blame: Representations of blame in *The Sun's* reporting of crimes of sexual violence. In Cameron, D. (ed.) *The Feminist Critique of Language* (2nd edn). London: Routledge. 183–97

Clift, R. 1999. Irony in conversation. *Language in Society* 28: 523–53

Coates, J. 2007. 'Everyone was convinced that we were closet fags': The role of heterosexuality in the construction of hegemonic masculinity. In Sauntson, H. and Kyratzis, S. (eds) 41–67

Coates, J. 2004. *Women, Men and Language: A Sociolinguistic Account of Gender Differences in Language* (3rd edn). London: Longman

Coates, J. 2003. *Men Talk: Stories in the Making of Masculinities.* Oxford: Blackwell

Coates, J. 1999. Changing femininities: The talk of teenage girls. In Bucholtz, M., Liang, A. and Sutton, L. (eds) *Reinventing Identities: The Gendered Self in Discourse.* Oxford: Oxford University Press. 123–43

Coates, J. 1997. Competing discourses of femininity. In Kotthoff, H. and Wodak, R. (eds) 285–314

Coates, J. 1996. *Women Talk: Conversation between Women Friends.* Oxford: Blackwell

Coates, J. 1995. Language, gender and career. In Mills, S. (ed.) *Language and Gender: Interdisciplinary Perspectives.* London: Longman. 13–30

Coates, J. 1993. *Women, Men and Language.* New York: Longman

Coates, J. 1989. Gossip revisited: An analysis of all-female discourse. In Coates, J. and Cameron, D. (eds) *Women in Their Speech Communities.* London: Longman. 94–122

Colebrook, C. 2004. *Irony.* London: Routledge

Condor, S. 1988. 'Race stereotypes' and racist discourse. *Text* 8: 69–91

Connell, R. 1995. *Masculinities.* Cambridge: Polity Press

Corbett, G. 1991. *Gender.* Cambridge: Cambridge University Press

Coulter, J. 2005. Language without mind. In te Molder, H. and Potter, J. (eds) 79–92

Coulter, J. 1999. Discourse and mind. *Human Studies* 22: 163–81

Coyle, A. and Morgan-Sykes, C. 1998. Troubled men and threatening women: The construction of 'crisis' in male mental health. *Feminism and Psychology* 8 (3): 263–84

Crawford, M. 1995. *Talking Difference: On Gender and Language.* London: Sage

Crystal, D. 1992. *An Encyclopedic Dictionary of Language and Languages.* London: Penguin Books

Danziger, K. 1997. The varieties of social construction. *Theory and Psychology* 7 (3): 399–416

D'Arcy, A. 2004. Contextualising St. John's English within the Canadian quotative system. *Journal of English Linguistics* 32 (4): 323–45

Darling-Wolf, F. 2003. Media, class, and western influence in Japanese women's conceptions of attractiveness. *Feminist Media Studies* 3 (2): 153–72

Davies, B. 1995. *Feminist Post-structuralism and Classroom Practice.* Melbourne: Deakin University Press de Beaugrande, R. 2004. Language, discourse, and cognition: Retrospects and prospects. In Virtanen, T. (ed.) *Approaches to Cognition through Text and Discourse*. Berlin: de Gruyter. 17–31

Deery, S., Iverson, R. and Walsh, J. 2004. The effect of customer service encounters on job satisfaction and emotional exhaustion. In Deery, S. and Kinnie, N. (eds) *Call Centres and Human Resource Management*. Basingstoke: Palgrave Macmillan. 201–22

De Francisco, V. 1997. Gender, power and practice: Or, putting your money (and your research) where your mouth is. In Wodak, R. (ed.) 37–56

De Francisco, V. 1991. The sounds of silence: How men silence women in marital relations. *Discourse and Society* 2: 413–24

Deignan, A. 2005. *Metaphor and Corpus Linguistics*. Amsterdam: Benjamins

Delanty, G., Jones, P. and Wodak, R. (eds) 2008. *Voices of Migrants*. Liverpool: Liverpool University Press

del-Teso-Craviotto, M. 2006. Words that matter: Lexical choice and gender ideologies in women's magazines. *Journal of Pragmatics* 38 (11): 2003–21

Derrida, J. 1987. *A Derrida Reader: Between the Blinds*. Harvester Wheatsheaf

Derrida, 1981.

Derrida, J. 1976. *Of Grammatology*. London: John Hopkins University Press

Diamantakou, P. 1994. Women's characters: How modern women are presented in the world of our television. *Kathimerini* 27/3/1994: 24

Dirven, R. and Kristiansen, G. (eds) Forthcoming. *Cognitive Sociolinguistics*. Berlin: de Gruyter

Donato, K., Gabaccia, D., Holdaway, J., Manalansan, M. and Pessar, P. 2006. A glass half full? Gender in migration studies. *International Migration Review* 40 (1): 3–26

Doulkeri, T. 1986. *The Greek Woman's Participation in Family and Labour*. Athens: Sakkoula

Drew, P. 2005. Is confusion a state of mind? In te Molder, H. and Potter, J. (eds) 161–83

Duranti, A. 1997. *Linguistic Anthropology*. Cambridge: Cambridge University Press

Dynes, W. 1985. *Homolexis: A Historical and Cultural Lexicon of Homosexuality*. New York: Gay Academic Union

Eakins, B. and Eakins, G. 1978. *Sex Differences in Human Communication*. Boston, MA: Houghton Mifflin.

Ebert, T. 1996. *Ludic Feminism and After*. Ann Arbor: University of Michigan Press

Eckert, P. 2000. *Linguistic Variation as Social Practice: The Linguistic Construction of Identity in Belten High*. Oxford: Blackwell

Eckert, P. 1998. Gender and sociolinguistic variation. In Coates, J. (ed.) *Language and Gender: A Reader*. Oxford: Blackwell. 64–75

Eckert, P. 1989. *Jocks and Burnouts: Social Categories and Identity in the High School*. New York: Teachers College Press

Eckert, P. and McConnell-Ginet, S. 2003. *Language and Gender*. Cambridge: Cambridge University Press

Eckert, P. and McConnell-Ginet, S. 1995. Constructing meaning, constructing selves: Snapshots of language, gender and class from Belten High. In Hall, K. and Bucholtz, M. (eds) *Gender Articulated: Language and the Socially Constructed Self*. London: Routledge. 469–507

Eckert, P. and McConnell-Ginet, S. 1992. Think practically and look locally: Language and gender as community-based practice. *Annual Review of Anthropology* 21: 461–90

Eco, U. 1990. *The Limits of Interpretation.* Bloomington: Indiana University Press
Edley, N. 2001. Analysing masculinity: Interpretative repertoires, ideological dilemmas and subject positions. In Wetherell, M. et al. (eds) 189–228
Edley, N. and Wetherell, M. 1999. Imagined futures: Young men's talk about fatherhood and domestic life. *British Journal of Social Psychology* **38** (2): 181–94
Edley, N. and Wetherell, M. 1997. Jockeying for position: The construction of masculine identities. *Discourse and Society* **8** (2): 203–17
Edwards, D. 2006a. Facts, norms and dispositions: Practical uses of the modal *would* in police interrogations. *Discourse Studies* **8** (4): 475–501
Edwards, D. 2006b. Discourse, cognition and social practices: The rich surface of language and social interaction. *Discourse Studies* **8** (1): 41–9
Edwards, D. 2005. *Conversation and Cognition.* Cambridge: Cambridge University Press
Edwards, D. 1998. The relevant thing about her: Social identity categories in use. In Antaki, C. and Widdicombe, S. (eds) 15–33
Edwards, D. 1997. *Discourse and Cognition.* London: Sage
Edwards, D. (1994). Script formulations: A study of event descriptions in conversation. *Journal of Language and Social Psychology* **13** (3): 211–47
Edwards, D. and Potter, J. 2005. Discursive psychology, mental states and descriptions. In te Molder, H. and Potter, J. (eds) 241–59
Edwards, D. and Potter, J. 2001. Discursive psychology. In McHoul, A. and Rapley, M. (eds) *How To Analyse Talk in Institutional Settings: A Casebook of Methods.* London: Continuum. 12–24
Edwards, D. and Potter, J. 1992. *Discursive Psychology.* London: Sage
Edwards, D. and Stokoe, E. 2004. Discursive psychology, focus group interviews, and participants' categories. *British Journal of Developmental Psychology* **22**: 499–507
Eglin, P. and Hester, S. 1999. 'You're all a bunch of feminists': Categorization and the politics of terror in the Montreal Massacre. *Human Studies* **22**: 253–72
Ehrlich, S. 2003. Coercing gender: Language in sexual assault adjudication processes. In Holmes, J. and Meyerhoff, M. (eds) 645–70
Elliott, A. 1996. *Subject to Ourselves.* Oxford: Polity Press
El Refaie, E. 2005. Our purebred ethnic compatriots: Irony in newspaper journalism. *Journal of Pragmatics* **37**: 781–97
El-Salanti, N., Wiegman, I-M. and Sørensen, O. 2004. Call Centre i Danmark 2004: Ledelse, Samarbejde og Teknologi. http://www.casa-analyse.dk/files/pdf/Call_centre_i_Danmark_2004~.pdf (Accessed 27.10.2006)
Enfield, N. and Stivers, T. (eds) 2007. *Person Reference in Interaction: Linguistic, Cultural and Social Perspectives.* Cambridge: Cambridge University Press
Epprecht, Mark. 2004. *Hungochani: The History of a Dissident Sexuality in Southern Africa.* Montreal: McGill-Queen's University Press
Essed, P. 1991. *Understanding Everyday Racism.* Newbury Park: Sage
Essed, P., Kobayashi A. and Goldberg, D. (eds) 2004. *A Companion to Gender Studies.* London: Blackwell
Evaldsson, A.-C. 2004. Shifting moral stances: Morality and gender in same-sex and cross-sex game interaction. *Research on Language and Social Interaction* **37** (3): 331–63
Fairclough, N. 2003. *Analysing Discourse: Textual Analysis for Social Research.* London: Longman
Fairclough, N. 2001a. Critical discourse analysis as a method in social scientific research. In Wodak, R. and Meyer, M. (eds) *Methods of Critical Discourse Analysis.* London: Sage. 121–38
Fairclough, N. 2001b. The discourse of new Labour: Critical discourse analysis. In Wetherell, M. et al. (eds) 229–66

Fairclough, N. 1995a. *Critical Discourse Analysis*. London: Longman

Fairclough, N. 1995b. *Media Discourse*. London: Arnold

Fairclough, N. 1992a. *Discourse and Social Change*. Cambridge: Polity Press

Fairclough, N. 1992b. Discourse and text: Linguistic and intertextual analysis within discourse analysis. *Discourse and Society* 3: 193–219

Fairclough, N. 1989. *Language and Power*. London: Longman

Fairclough, N. and Wodak, R. 1997. Critical discourse analysis. In van Dijk, T. (ed.) *Introduction to Discourse Analysis*. London: Sage. 258–84

Finch, J. 1984. 'It's great to have someone to talk to': The ethics and politics of interviewing women. In Bell C. and Roberts H. (eds) *Social Researching: Policies, Problems and Practice*. London: Routledge & Kegan Paul. 70–87

Fishman, P. (1983) Interaction: the work women do. In Thorne, B. et al. (eds) *Language, Gender and Society*. Rowley, MA: Newbury House

Fishman, P. 1978. Interaction: The work women do. *Social Problems* 25: 397–406

Flam, H. and Beauzamy, B. (2008). Symbolic Violence. In Delanty, G., Jones P. and Wodak, R. (eds), *Migrant Voices: Discourses of Belonging and Exclusion*. Liverpool: University of Liverpool Press (in press)

Fortier, A.-M. 2000. *Migrant Belongings*. Oxford: Berg

Fortune. 2000. Available at: http://money.cnn.com/magazines/fortune/fortunearchive/2000/10/16/289643/index.htm (accessed 09/05/08).

Fotopoulou, E. n.d. The Profile of the Contemporary Greek Woman. *Ine*: 40–2

Foucault, M. 1984. What is enlightenment? In Rabinow, P. (ed.) *The Foucault Reader*. London: Penguin. 32–50

Foucault, M. 1980. *Power/Knowledge*. Brighton: Harvester Press

Foucault, M. 1978. *The History of Sexuality* (Volume 1). Trans. Robert Hurley. London: Penguin

Foucault, M. 1972. *The Archaeology of Knowledge*. London: Tavistock

Francis, D. 1994. The golden dreams of the social constructionist. *Journal of Anthropological Research* 50 (2): 1–22

Franklin, S. (ed.) 1996. *The Sociology of Gender*. London: Routledge

Franklin, S. and Stacey, J. (eds) 1986. *Lesbian Perspectives in Feminism*. London: Routledge

Freed, A. 2004. Sex or gender: Still a conundrum in language and gender research. Paper delivered at *Third Biennial Conference of the International Gender and Language Association*. Cornell University

Freed, A. 2003. Epilogue: Reflections on language and gender research. In Holmes, J. and Meyerhoff, M. (eds) 699–721

Freed, A. and Greenwood, A. 1996. Women, men and type of talk: What makes the difference? *Language in Society* 25: 1–26

Fuss, D. (ed.) 1991. *Inside/Out: Lesbian Theories, Gay Theories*. New York: Routledge

Gal, S. 1991. Between speech and silence: The problematics of research on language and gender. In di Leonardo, M. (ed.) *Gender at the Crossroads of Knowledge: Feminist Anthropology in the Postmodern Era*. Berkeley, CA: University of California Press. 175–203

Gal, S. 1979. *Language Shift: Social Determinants of Linguistic Change in Bilingual Austria*. New York: Academic Press

Gal, S. 1978. Peasant men can't get wives: Language change and sex roles in a bilingual community. *Language in Society* 7: 1–17

Garfinkel, H. 1967. *Studies in Ethnomethodology*. New Jersey: Prentice-Hall

Garfinkel, H., and Sacks, H. 1970. On formal structures of practical actions. In McKinney, J. and Tiryakian, E. (eds) *Theoretical Sociology: Perspectives and Developments*. New York: Appleton-Century-Crofts. 337–66

Gauntlett, D. 2002. *Media, Gender and Identity: An Introduction.* London: Routledge

General Secretariat for Equality 2004. *Equality between Women and Men* (1983–2003). Athens: Ministry of Interior Public, Administration and Decentralisation

General Secretariat for Equality 2001. *National Action Programme for Equality* (2001–2006). Athens: Ministry of Interior Public, Administration and Decentralisation

Gill, R. 1995. Relativism, reflexivity, and politics: Interrogating discourse analysis from a feminist perspective. In Wilkinson, S. and Kitzinger, C. (eds) 165–86

Gill, R. 1993. Justifying injustice: Broadcasters' accounts of inequality in radio. In Burman, E. and Parker, I. (eds) *Discourse Analytic Research: Readings and Repertoires of Texts in Action.* London: Routledge. 75–93

Gledhill, C. 1997. Genre and gender: The case of soap opera. In Hall, S. (ed.) *Representation: Cultural Representations and Signifying Practices.* London: Sage. 337–86

Goffman, E. 1979. Footing. *Semiotica* 25: 1–29

Goffman, E. 1974. *Frame Analysis.* New York: Harper & Row

Goodwin, M. 2002. Building power asymmetries in girls' interaction. *Discourse and Society* 13 (6): 715–30

Goodwin, M. 1990. *He-Said-She-Said: Talk as Social Organization Among Black Children.* Bloomington, IA: Indiana University Press

Gough, B. 1998. Men and the discursive reproduction of sexism: Repertoires of difference and equality. *Feminism and Psychology* 8 (1): 25–49

Gough, B. and Edwards, G. 1998. The beer talking: Four lads, a carry out and the reproduction of masculinities. *Sociological Review* 46 (3): 409–35

Grabe, W. and Stoller, F. 1997. Reading and vocabulary development in a second language: A case study. In Coady, J. and Huckin, T. (eds) *Second Language Vocabulary Acquisition.* Cambridge: Cambridge University Press. 98–122

Graddol, D. and Swann, J. 1989. *Gender Voices.* Oxford: Blackwell

Granger, S. (ed.) 1996. *Learner English on Computer.* London: Longman

Green, J. and Bloome, D. 1997. Ethnography and ethnographers of and in education: A situated perspective. In Flood, J., Heath, S. and Lapp, D. (eds) *A Handbook of Research on Teaching Literacy through the Communicative and Visual Arts.* New York: Macmillan. 181–202

Greenwood, A. 1996. Floor management and power strategies in adolescent conversation. In Bergvall, V., Bing, J. and Freed, A. (eds) 77–97

Grundy, P. 1995. *Doing Pragmatics.* London: Edward Arnold

Gumperz, J. 1982. *Discourse Strategies.* Cambridge: Cambridge University Press

Haas, M. 1944. Men's and women's speech in Koasati. *Language* 20: 142–9

Hacking, I. 1998. On being more literal about construction. In Velody, I. and Williams, R. (eds) 49–68

Hacking, I. 1990. *The Taming of Chance.* Cambridge: Cambridge University Press

Halberstam, J. 1998. *Female Masculinity.* Durham, NC: Duke University Press

Hall, D. 2003. *Queer Theories.* Basingstoke: Palgrave Macmillan

Hall, K. 1995. Lip service on the fantasy lines. In Hall, K. and Bucholtz, M. (eds) *Gender Articulated: Language and the Socially Constructed Self.* London: Routledge. 183–216

Hall, K. and O'Donovan, V. 1996. Shifting gender positions among Hindi-speaking Hijras. In Bergvall, V., Bing, J. and Freed, A. (eds) 228–66

Hall, S. 1982. The rediscovery of ideology: Return of the oppressed in media studies. In Gurevitch, M., Bennett, M., Curran, J. and Woollacott, J. (eds) *Culture, Society and the Media.* London: Methuen. 56–89

Halliday, M.A.K. 2004. *An Introduction to Functional Grammar* (3rd edn). London: Arnold

Halliday, M.A.K. 1979. *Language as Social Semiotic: The Social Interpretation of Language and Meaning*. London: Arnold

Hamilton, H. 1998. Reported speech and survivor identity in on-line bone marrow transplantation narratives. *Journal of Sociolinguistics* 2 (1): 53–67

Hammersley, M. 2006. Ethnography: Problems and prospects. *Ethnography and Education* 1 (1): 3–14

Hammersley, M. 2003. Conversation analysis and discourse analysis: Methods or paradigms? *Discourse and Society* 14 (6): 751–81

Hammersley, M. and Atkinson, P. 1995 *Ethnography: Principles in Practice* (2nd edn). London: Routledge

Hare-Mustin, R. and Maracek, J. (eds) 1990. *Making a Difference: Psychology and the Construction of Gender*. New Haven: Yale University Press

Harré, R. 1979. *Social Being: A Theory for Social Psychology*. Oxford: Blackwell

Harvey, D. 1989. *The Political-Economic Transformation of Late Twentieth Century Capitalism: The Condition of Post-Modernity*. Oxford: Blackwell

Hellinger, M. and Bußman, H. (eds) 2001. *Gender across Languages: The Linguistic Representation of Women and Men* (Volumes 1–3). Amsterdam: John Benjamins

Hennessy, R. 2000. *Profit and Pleasure*. New York: Routledge

Henriques, J., Hollway, W., Urwin, C., Venn, C. and Walkerdine, V. 1984. *Changing the Subject: Psychology, Social Regulation and Subjectivity*. London: Methuen

Heritage, J. 2005a. Conversation analysis and institutional talk. In Fitch, K. and Sanders, R. (eds) *Handbook of Language and Social Interaction*. Mahwah, NJ: Lawrence Erlbaum

Heritage, J. 2005b. Cognition in discourse. In te Molder, H. and Potter, J. (eds) 184–202

Heritage, J. 1984. *Garfinkel and Ethnomethodology*. Cambridge: Polity Press

Heritage, J. and Raymond, G. 2005. The terms of agreement: Indexing epistemic authority and subordination in assessment sequences. *Social Psychology Quarterly* 68: 15–38

Hesse-Biber, S., Gilmartin, C. and Lyndenberg, R. 1999. *Feminist Approaches to Theory and Methodology*. Oxford: Oxford University Press

Hester, S. and Eglin, P. (eds) 1997. *Culture in Action: Studies in Membership Categorization Analysis*. Boston, MA: International Institute for Ethnomethodology and University Press of America

Hester, S. and Francis, D. 1997. Reality analysis in a classroom storytelling. *British Journal of Sociology* 48 (1): 95–112

Hibberd, F. 2005. *Unfolding Social Constructionism*. New York: Springer

Hoey, M. 2005. *Lexical Priming*. London: Routledge

Holden, C. 1993. Giving girls a chance: Patterns of talk in cooperative groupwork. *Gender and Education* 5 (2): 179–89

Hollway, W. 1989. *Subjectivity and Method in Psychology: Gender, Meaning and Science*. London: Sage

Hollway, W. 1984. Gender differences and the production of subjectivity. In Henriques, J. et al. (eds) 227–63

Holman, D. and Wood, S. 2002. Human resource management in call centres. http://esrccoi.group.shef.ac.uk/pdf/hrm_in_callcentres.pdf (Accessed 28.2.2006)

Holmes, J. 2006. *Gendered Talk at Work*. Oxford: Blackwell

Holmes, J. 2003a. Women's talk at the top. *Boardroom: Journal of the Institute of Directors* 1: 1–2

Holmes, J. 2003b. How top women talk. *Paanui: Ministry of Women's Affairs* 6–7

Holmes, J. 1997a. Story-telling in New Zealand: Women's and men's talk. In Wodak, R. (ed.) 263–93

Holmes, J. 1997b. Women, language and identity. *Journal of Sociolinguistics* **1** (2): 195–223

Holmes, J. 1996. Women's role in language change: A place for quantification. In Warner, N., Ahlers, J., Bilmes, L., Oliver, M., Wertheim, S. and Chen, M. (eds) *Gender and Belief Systems: Proceedings of the Fourth Berkeley Women and Language Conference.* Berkeley, CA: Berkeley Women and Language Group. 313–30

Holmes, J. 1995. *Women, Men and Politeness.* London: Longman

Holmes, J. 1984. Hedging your bets and sitting on the fence: Some evidence for hedges as support structures. *Te Reo* **27**: 47–62

Holmes, J. and Major, G. 2003. Nurses communicating on the ward: The human face of hospitals. *Nursing New Zealand* **8** (11): 14–16

Holmes, J. and Meyerhoff, M. 2003. *Handbook of Language and Gender.* Oxford: Blackwell

Holmes, J. and Meyerhoff, M. 1999. The community of practice: Theories and methodologies in language and gender research. *Language in Society* **28** (2): 173–84

Holmes, J. and Sigley, R. 2002. Looking at girls in corpora of English. *Journal of English Linguistics* **30**: 138–57

Holmes, J. and Stubbe, M. 2003a. 'Feminine' workplaces: Stereotype and reality. In Holmes, J. and Meyerhoff, M. (eds) 573–99

Holmes, J. and Stubbe, M. 2003b. *Power and Politeness in the Workplace: A Sociolinguistic Analysis of Talk at Work.* Harlow: Pearson

Holstein, J. and Gubrium, J. 1997. Active interviewing. In Silverman, D. (ed.) *Qualitative Research: Theory, Method and Practice.* London: Sage. 113–29

Howson, A. 2005. *Embodying Gender.* London: Sage

Hruska, B. 2004. Constructing gender in an English dominant kindergarten: Implications for second language learners. *TESOL Quarterly* **38** (3): 459–85

Hutcheon, L. 1994. *Irony's Edge: The Theory and Politics of Irony.* London: Routledge

Hymes, D. 1996. *Ethnography, Linguistics and Narrative Inequality.* London: Taylor & Francis

Hymes, D. 1974. *Foundations in Sociolinguistics: An Ethnographic Approach.* London: Tavistock

Iedema, R. 2001. Analysing film and television: A social semiotic account of hospital: An unhealthy business. In van Leeuwen, T. and Jewitt, C. (eds) *Handbook of Visual Analysis.* London: Sage. 183–204

Intintoli, M. 1984. *Taking Soaps Seriously: The World of Guiding Light.* New York: Praeger

Jackson, P., Stevenson, N. and Brooks, K. 2001. *Making Sense of Men's Magazines.* Cambridge: Polity Press

Jagose, A. 1996. *Queer Theory: An Introduction.* New York: New York University Press

James, D. 2000. *Dona Maria's Story: Life, History, Memory and Political Identity.* Durham, NC: Duke University Press

James, D. and Clarke, S. 1993. Women, men, and interruptions: A critical review. In Tannen, D. (ed.) *Gender and Conversational Interaction.* Oxford: Oxford University Press. 231–80

James, D. and Drakich, J. 1993. Understanding gender differences in amount of talk: A critical review of research. In Tannen, D. (ed.) *Gender and Conversational Interaction.* Oxford: Oxford University Press. 281–312

Jayyusi, L. 1984. *Categorization and the Moral Order.* London: Routledge

Jefferson, G. 2005. Glossary of transcript symbols with an introduction. In Lerner, G. (ed.) *Conversation Analysis: Studies from the First Generation*. Amsterdam: John Benjamins. 13–31

Jefferson, G. 2004. A note on laughter in 'male-female' interaction. *Discourse Studies* 6: 117–33

Jefferson, G. 1986. Notes on 'latency' in overlap onset. *Human Studies* 9: 153–83

Jefferson, G. 1980. On 'trouble-premonitory' response to inquiry. *Sociological Inquiry* 50 (3–4): 153–85

Jesperson, O. 1922. *Language: Its Nature, Development and Origin*. London: Allen & Unwin

Jewitt, C. and Oyama, R. 2001. Visual meaning: A social semiotic approach. In van Leeuwen, T. and Jewitt, C. (eds) *Handbook of Visual Analysis*. London: Sage. 134–56

Jiménez Catalán, R. 2003. Sex differences in L2 vocabulary learning strategies. *International Journal of Applied Linguistics* 13 (1): 54–78

Jiménez Catalán, R. 1997. Análisis de los intereses sociales y personales de alumnos navarros de secundaria. In Jiménez Catalán, R. (ed.) *Los Temas Transversales en la Clase de Inglés*. Pamplona: Gobierno de Navarra, Departamento de Educación y Cultura. 7–27

Jiménez Catalán, R. M. and Ojeda Alba, J. 2007. La carta como instrumento de identificación personal e interacción comunicativa en L2: Análisis del vocabulario de los saludos y despedidas. In Martínez, Ramírez (coord) *La lengua escrita*. SEDLL/ Universidad de La Rioja, CD

Johnson, S. and Meinhof, U. (eds) 1997. *Language and Masculinity*. Oxford: Blackwell

Johnstone, B. 1993. Community and contest: Midwestern men and women creating their storyworlds in conversational storytelling. In Tannen, D. (ed.) *Gender and Conversational Interaction*. New York: Oxford University Press. 62–80

Johnstone, B. 1990. *Stories, Community and Place: Narratives from Middle America*. Bloomington: Indiana University Press

Jones, A. 1993. Becoming a girl: Poststructuralist suggestions for educational research. *Gender and Education* 5 (2): 157–66

Jones, P. and Krzyżanowski, M. 2008. Belonging. In Wodak, R. et al. (eds) *Voices of Immigrants in Europe. Research Report within the EU-FP5 Research Project 'The European Dilemma: Institutional Patterns and Politics of Racial Discrimination'*. Unpublished. http://www.ling.lancs.ac.uk/staff/wodak/papers/RacisminAustriaFinalReport2006. pdf (Accessed 26.7.2007)

Kafiri, K. 2002. Gender and mass media: Overview study. http://www.kethi.gr/greek/ meletes/index.htm (Accessed 5.11.2005)

Kahneman, D. and Tversky, A. 1973. On the psychology of prediction. *Psychological Review* 80: 237–51

Kaitanidi, M. 2005. 'Mrs Manager': A minority. *Ta Nea* 19.2.2005: 18

Kaitanidi, M. 2004. Single white female. *Ta Nea* 6.3.2004: 35

Kamada, L. 2006. Multiethnic identities of 'haafu/daburu' girls in Japan. *JALT 2005 Conference Proceedings*. Tokyo: Japan Association for Language Teaching

Kamada, L. 2005a. Celebration of multi-ethnic cultural capital among adolescent girls in Japan: A post-structuralist discourse analysis of Japanese-Caucasian identity. *Japan Journal of Multilingualism and Multiculturalism* 11: 19–41

Kamada, L. 2005b. Interpretive repertoires and ideological dilemmas of gender: Japanese-Caucasian girls in Japan. *Aomori Akenohoshi Tanki Daigaku Research Reports* 31: 31–43

Karamesini, M. and Ioakimoglou, I. 2003. The determinants of the pay gap between men and women. http://www.kethi.gr/greek/meletes/index.htm (Accessed 21.11.2005)

Kastoras, S. 1990. *Audiovisual Mass Media*. Athens: Papazisis

Katz, E. 1994. *The Film Encyclopedia* (2nd edn). New York: HarperCollins

Kaur, S. 2005. The performance of gender in online discussion boards. Paper delivered at *BAAL/CUP Seminar: Theoretical and MethodologicalApproaches to Gender and Language Study*. University of Birmingham, UK

Keenan, E. 1974. Norm-makers, norm-breakers: Uses of speech by men and women in a Malagasay Community. In Bauman, R. and Sherzer, J. (eds) *Explorations in the Ethnography of Speaking*. Cambridge: Cambridge University Press. 125–43

Kelly, J. 1991. A study of gender differential linguistic interaction in the adult classroom. *Gender and Education* 3 (2): 137–43

Kendall, S. and Tannen, D. 1997. Gender and language in the workplace. In Wodak, R. (ed.) 81–105

Kertesz, I. 2004. *Fatelessness*. London: Vintage Books

Kessler, S. and McKenna, W. 1978. *Gender: An Ethnomethodological Approach*. New York: John Wiley

Kethi (Research Centre for Gender Equality) *Gender Mainstreaming*. http://www.kethi. gr/english/entaxi/index.htm (Accessed 1.1.2006)

Kiesling, S. 2002. Playing the straight man: Displaying and maintaining male heterosexuality in discourse. In Cambell-Kibler, K. et al. (eds) 249–66

Kilgariff, A. and Tugwell, D. 2001. WASP-Bench: An MT lexicographers' workstation supporting state-of-the-art lexical disambiguation. *Proceedings of MT Summit VII*. Santiago de Compostela. 187–90

Kitzinger, C. 2007. Is 'woman' always relevantly gendered? *Gender and Language* 1 (1): 39–49

Kitzinger, C. 2006a. After post-cognitivism. *Discourse Studies* 8 (1): 67–83

Kitzinger, C. 2006b. Talking sex and gender. In Drew, P., Raymond, G. and Wrinberg, D. (eds) *Talk in Interaction in Social Research Methods*. London: Sage. 155–70

Kitzinger, C. 2005a. Speaking as a heterosexual: (How) does sexuality matter for talk-in-interaction. *Research on Language and Social Interaction* 38 (3): 221–65

Kitzinger, C. 2005b. Heteronormativity in action: Reproducing normative heterosexuality in 'after hours' calls to the doctor. *Social Problems* 52 (4): 477–98

Kitzinger, C. 2000. Doing feminist conversation analysis. *Feminism and Psychology* 10: 163–93

Kleinman, A. 1998. *The Illness Narratives: Suffering, Healing and the Human Condition*. New York City: Basic Books

Klüger, R. 1973. *The Last Escape*. New York: Doubleday

Koller, V. 2006. Of critical importance: Using corpora to study metaphor in business media discourse. In Stefanowitsch, A. and Griess, S. (eds) *Corpus-Based Approaches to Metaphor and Metonymy*. Berlin: de Gruyter. 229–57

Koller, V. 2005. Critical discourse analysis and social cognition: Evidence from business media discourse. *Discourse and Society* 16 (2): 199–224

Koller, V. 2004a. Businesswomen and war metaphors: 'Possessive, jealous and pugnacious'? *Journal of Sociolinguistics* 8 (1): 3–22

Koller, V. 2004b. *Metaphor and Gender in Business Media Discourse: A Critical Cognitive Study*. Basingstoke: Palgrave Macmillan

Kollock, P., Blumstein, P. and Schwartz, P. 1985. Sex and power in interaction: Conversational privileges and duties. *American Sociological Review* 85: 34–46

Kosetzi, K. 2007a. *Representations of Women in Terms of Gender Roles and Sexual Practices in Σχεδόν Ποτέ (ΣΠ) ('Almost Never'): The Text and the Audience.* Unpublished PhD, Lancaster University, Lancaster

Kosetzi, K. 2007b. 'Challenging (?) Conservative discourses: The case of Σχεδόν Ποτέ *(ΣΠ)* ('Almost Never'). In S. Santaemilia, P. Bou, S. Marduenda and G. Zaragoza (eds), *International Perspectives on Gender and Language.* Valencia: University of Valencia, 706–25

Kosetzi, K. 2001. *The Construction of Fatherhood in Greek Parenting Magazines.* Unpublished MA dissertation. Lancaster University, Lancaster

Kosetzi, K. and Polyzou, A. forthcoming. 'The perfect man, the proper man': Representations of masculinities in *Nitro*, a Greek men's lifestyle magazine. Paper delivered at *14th Symposium on Critical Discourse Analysis.* University of Athens, Athens

Kotthof, H. and Wodak, R. (eds) 1997. *Communicating Gender in Context.* Amsterdam: John Benjamins

Kovács, A. and Wodak, R. 2003. Preface. In Kovács, A. and Wodak, R. (eds) *NATO, Neutrality and National Identity: The Case of Austria and Hungary.* Wien: Bóhlau Verlag. 347–405

Krais B. 1993. Gender and symbolic violence: Female oppression in the light of Pierre Bourdieu's theory of social practice. In Calhoun, C., LiPuma, E. and Postone, M. (eds) *Bourdieu: Critical Perspective.* Cambridge: Polity Press. 156–77

Kress, G. 1988. Textual matters: The social effectiveness of style. In Birch, D. and O'Toole M. (eds) *Functions of Style.* London: Pinter. 126–41

Kress, G. and van Leeuwen, T. 2001. *Multimodal Discourse: The Modes and Media of Contemporary Communication.* London: Arnold

Kress, G. and van Leeuwen, T. 1996. *Reading Images: The Grammar of Visual Design.* London: Routledge

Kristeva, J. 1986. Word, dialogue and novel. In Moi, T. (ed.) *The Kristeva Reader.* Oxford: Blackwell. 34–61

Kroløkke, C. and Sørensen, A. 2006. *Gender Communication: Theories and Analyses.* London: Sage

Krzyżanowski, M. 2005. European identity wanted! On discursive dimensions of the European convention. In Wodak, R. and Chilton, P. (eds) 137–64

Krzyżanowski, M. and Wodak, R. 2007. Multiple identities, migration and belonging: Voices of migrants. In Caldas-Coulthard, C. and Iedema, R. (eds) *Identity Troubles.* Basingstoke: Palgrave Macmillan

Kulick, D. 2000. Gay and lesbian language. *Annual Review of Anthropology* 29: 243–85

Kulick, D. 1999. Transgender and language: A review of the literature and suggestions for the future. *GLQ* 5: 605–22

Kulick, D. 1998. *Travesti: Sex, Gender and Culture among Brazilian Transgendered Prostitutes.* Chicago: University of Chicago Press

Kvale, S. 1996. *Interviews: An Introduction to Qualitative Research Interviewing.* London: Sage

Labov, W. 1990. The intersection of sex and class in the course of linguistic change. *Language Variation and Change* 2 (2): 205–51

Labov, W. 1966. *The Social Stratification of English in New York City.* Washington, DC: Center for Applied Linguistics

Labov, W. 1963. The social motivation of a sound change. *Word* 19: 273–309

Labov, W. and Waletzky, J. 1967. Narrative analysis: Oral versions of personal experience. In Helm, J. (ed.) *Essays on the Verbal and Visual Art.* Seattle: University of Washington Press. 12–44

Laclau, E. 1995. *Emancipation(s)*. London: Verso

Lakoff, G. and Johnson, M. 1980. *Metaphors We Live By*. Chicago: University of Chicago Press

Lakoff, R. 2003. Language, gender and politics: Putting 'women' and 'power' in the same sentence. In Holmes, J. and Meyerhoff, M. (eds) 161–78

Lakoff, R. 1975. *Language and Woman's Place*. New York: Harper & Row

Land, V. and Kitzinger, C. 2005. Speaking as a lesbian: Correcting the heterosexual presumption. *Research on Language and Social Interaction* 38 (4): 371–416

Landry, D. and MacLean, G. (eds) 1996. *The Spivak Reader*. London. Routledge

Larson, C. 1997. Re-presenting the subject: Problems in personal narrative inquiry. *Qualitative Studies in Education* 10 (4): 455–70

Laufer, B. 1997. The lexical plight in second language reading. In Coady, J. and Huckin, T. (eds) *Second Language Vocabulary Acquisition*. Cambridge: Cambridge University Press. 20–34

Lave, J. and Wenger, E. 1991. *Situated Learning: Legitimate Peripheral Participation*. Cambridge: Cambridge University Press

Lazar, M. 2005. *Feminist Critical Discourse Analysis: Gender, Power and Ideology in Discourse*. Basingstoke: Palgrave Macmillan

Lazar, M. 2002. Consuming personal relationships: The achievement of feminine self-identity through other-centredness. In Litosseliti, L. and Sunderland, J. (eds) 111–28

Lazar, M. 2000. Gender, discourse and semiotics: The politics of parenthood representations. *Discourse and Society* 11(3): 373–400.

Lazar, M. 1993. Equalizing gender relations: A case of double-talk. *Discourse and Society* 4 (4): 443–65

Leap, W. forthcoming

Leap, W. 2007. 'Where do I have to stay for the night and what do I have to do?'Apartheid geography, township sexuality, and the discursive public sphere. Unpublished.

Leap, W. 2003. Language and gendered modernity. In Holmes, J. and Meyerhoff, M. (eds) 401–22

Leap, W. 1996. *Word's Out: Gay Men's English*. Minneapolis: University of Minnesota Press

Leap, W. (ed.) 1995. *Beyond The Lavender Lexicon: Authenticity, Imagination, and Appropriation in Lesbian and Gay Languages*. Luxembourg: Gordon & Breach

Leap, W. and Boellstorff, T. (eds) 2003. *Speaking in Queer Tongues: Globalization and Gay Language*. Urbana: University of Illinois Press

Leet-Pellegrini, H. 1980. Conversational dominance as a function of gender and expertise. In Giles, H., Robinson, W. and Smith, P. (eds) *Language: Social Psychological Perspectives*. Oxford: Pergamon. 97–104

Leidner, R. 1993. *Fast Food Fast Talk: Service Work and the Routinisation of Everyday Life*. Berkeley: University of California Press

Lerner, G. 2000 Turn-sharing: The choral co-production of talk in interaction. http://www.soc.ucsb.edu/faculty/lerner/pub/Turn_Sharing.pdf (Accessed 27.7.2007)

Lerner, G. 1996 On the 'semi-permeable' character of grammatical units in conversation: Conditional entry into the turn-space of another speaker. In Ochs, E., Schegloff, E. and Thompson, S. (eds) *Interaction and Grammar*. Cambridge: Cambridge University Press. 238–76

Lerner, G. 1991. On the syntax of sentences-in-progress. *Language in Society* 20: 441–58

Levey, S. 2003. Reported dialogue and pragmatic particles in the narratives of preadolescents. *World Englishes* 22 (3): 305–21

Liang, A. 1997. The creation of coherence in coming-out stories. In Livia, A. and Hall, K. (eds) 287–309

Lie, J. 2001. *Multiethnic Japan*. Cambridge: Harvard University Press

Linde, C. 1993. *Life Stories: The Creation of Coherence*. New York: Oxford University Press

Litosseliti, L. 2006a. *Gender and Language: Theory and Practice*. London: Arnold

Litosseliti, L. 2006b. Constructing gender in public arguments: The female voice as emotional voice. In Baxter, J. (ed.) 40–58

Litosseliti, L. and Sunderland, J. (eds) 2002. *Gender Identity and Discourse Analysis*. Amsterdam: Benjamins

Livia, A. 2002. The future of queer linguistics. In Campbell-Kibler, K. et al. (eds) 87–97

Livia, A. and Hall, K. (eds) 1997. *Queerly Phrased: Language, Gender, And Sexuality*. Oxford: Oxford University Press

Löbner, S. 2002. *Understanding Semantics*. London: Arnold

LoCastro, V. 1990. *Intercultural Pragmatics: A Japanese-American Case Study*. Unpiblished PhD. University of Lancaster, UK

Louw, B. 1993. Irony in the text or insincerity in the writer? The diagnostic potential of semantic prosodies. In Baker, M., Francis, G. and Tognini-Bonelli, E. (eds) *Text and Technology*. Amsterdam: John Benjamins. 157–76

Lovering, K. 1995. The bleeding body: Adolescents' talk about menstruation. In Wilkinson, S. and Kitzinger, C. (eds) *Feminism and Discourse: Psychological Perspectives*. London: Sage. 10–31

Lynch, M. 1993. *Scientific Practice and Ordinary Action: Ethnomethodology and Social Studies of Science*. Cambridge: Cambridge University Press

Machin, D. and van Leeuwen, T. 2003. Global schemas and local discourses in *Cosmopolitan*: *Journal of Sociolinguistics* 7 (4): 493–512

Magalhães, I. 2005. Interdiscursivity, gender identity and the politics of literacy in Brazil. In Lazar, M. (ed.) 181–204

Maltz, D. and Borker, R. 1982. A cultural approach to male-female miscommunication. In Gumperz, J. (ed.) *Language and Social Identity*. Cambridge: Cambridge University Press. 196–216

Martín-Rojo, L. and Gómez Esteban, C. 2005. The gender of power: The female style in labour organization. In Lazar, M. (ed.) 61–89

Martín-Rojo, L. and Gómez Esteban, C. 2003. Discourse at work: When women take on the role of manager. In Weiss, G. and Wodak, R. (eds) 241–71

Mason, J. 2002. *Qualitative Researching* (2nd edn). London: Sage

Maybin, J. 2006. *Children's Voices: Talk, Knowledge and Identity*. Basingstoke: Palgrave Macmillan

Maybin, J. 2002. 'What's the hottest part of the Sun? Page 3!': Children's exploration of adolescent gender identities through informal talk. In Litosseliti, L. and Sunderland, J. (eds) 257–73

Maynard, M. 1994. 'Race', gender, and the concept of difference in feminist thought. In Afshar, H. and Maynard, M. (eds) *The Dynamics of 'Race' and Gender: Some Feminist Interventions*. London: Taylor & Francis. 9–25

McElhinny, B. 2003. Theorizing gender in sociolinguistics and anthropology. In Holmes, J. and Meyerhoff, M. (eds) 21–42

McElhinny, B. 1998. 'I don't smile much anymore': Affect, gender and the discourse of Pittsburgh police officers. In Coates, J. (ed.) *Language and Gender: A Reader*. Oxford: Blackwell. 309–27

McElhinny, B. 1995. Challenging hegemonic masculinities: Female and male police officers handling domestic violence. In Hall, K. and Bucholtz, M. (eds) *Gender Articulated: Language and the Socially Constructed Self*. London: Routledge. 217–43

McEnery, T. and Wilson, A. 1996. *Corpus Linguistics*. Edinburgh: Edinburgh University Press

McIlvenny, P. (ed.) 2002. *Talking Gender and Sexuality*. Amsterdam: John Benjamins

Meara, P. 1996. The dimensions of lexical competence. In Brown, G., Mamkjaer, K. and Williams, J. (eds) *Performance and Competence in Second Language Acquisition*. Cambridge: Cambridge University Press. 35–53

Meinhoff, U. and Smith, J. 2000. The media and their audience: Intertextuality as paradigm. In Meinhoff, U. and Smith, J. (eds) *Intertextuality and the Media: From Genre to Everyday Life*. Manchester: Manchester University Press. 1–17

Middleton, S. 1993. *Educating Feminists: Life Histories and Pedagogy*. London: Teachers College Press

Miller, G. 1997. Building bridges: The possibility of analytic dialogue between ethnography, conversation analysis and Foucault. In Silverman, D. (ed.) *Qualitative Research: Theory, Method and Practice*. London: Sage. 24–44

Miller, J. and Glassner, B. 1997. The 'inside' and the 'outside': Finding realities in interviews. In Silverman, D. (ed.) *Qualitative Research: Theory, Method and Practice*. London: Sage. 99–112

Mills, S. 2004. *Discourse: The New Critical Idiom* (2nd edn). London: Routledge

Mills, S. 1998. Post-feminist text analysis. *Language and Literature* 7 (3): 235–53

Mills, S. 1997. *Discourse: The New Critical Idiom*. London: Routledge

Milroy, L. 1987. *Language and Social Networks* (2nd edn). Oxford: Basil Blackwell

Milroy, L. 1980. *Language and Social Networks*. Oxford: Basil Blackwell

Mirdal, G. and Ryynänen-Karjalainen, L. 2004. *Forward Look on Research in Migration and Transcultural Identities*. Strasbourg: European Science Foundation

Mirza, M. 2006. Religiosity and the politics of identity. Paper delivered at *Multicultural Britain: From Anti-Racism to Identity Politics to...? Centre of Research for Nationalism, Ethnicity and Multi-culturalism conference*. Roehampton University, UK

Montgomery, M. 1986. *An Introduction to Language and Society*. London: Routledge

Moonwomon, B. 1995. Lesbian discourse, lesbian knowledge. In Leap, W. (ed.) 45–64

Morrish, E. and Sauntson, H. 2007. *New Perspectives on Language and Sexual Identity*. Basingstoke: Palgrave Macmillan

Morrison, A., White, R. and van Velsor, E. 1987. *Breaking the Glass Ceiling: Can Women Reach the Top of America's Largest Corporations?* Reading, MA: Addison-Wesley

Mullany, L. (2007) Gendered Discourse in the Professional Workplace. Basingstoke: Palgrave Macmillan

Mullany, L. and Litosseliti, L. 2006. Gender and language in the workplace. In Litosseliti, L. Gender and Language: Theory and Practice. London: Arnold. 123–48

Muncie, J. 2002. Process writing and vocabulary development: Comparing lexical frequency profiles across drafts. System 30: 225–35

Munt, S. (ed.) 1998. *Butch/femme: Inside Lesbian Gender*. London: Cassell

Muntigl, P., Weiss, G. and Wodak, R. (eds) 2000. *European Union Discourses on Un/Employment: An Interdisciplinary Approach to Employment Policy-Making and Organizational Change*. Amsterdam: John Benjamins

Murray, S. 1998. Sexual politics in contemporary Southern Africa. In Murray, S. and Roscoe, W. (eds) *Boy-Wives and Female Husbands: Studies in African Homosexualities*. New York: St. Martins' Press. 243–53

Murray, S. 1988. The sound of simultaneous speech, the meaning of interruption *Journal of Pragmatics* 12: 115–16

Murray, S. 1985. Toward a model of members' methods for recognising interruptions. *Language in Society* **14**: 31–40

Musolff, A. 2004. *Metaphor and Political Discourse: Analogical Reasoning about Europe.* Basingstoke: Palgrave Macmillan

Mynatt, C., Doherty, M. and Tweney, D. 1977. Confirmation bias in a simulated research environment: An experimental study of scientific inference. *Quarterly Journal of Experimental Psychology* **29**: 85–95

Nagar, I. 2005. Language, gender and identity: The case of Kotis. Paper delivered at *BAAL/CUP Seminar: Theoretical and Methodological Approaches to Gender and Language Study.* University of Birmingham, UK

Nerlich, B. 2005. 'A river runs through it': How the discourse metaphor crossing the rubicon structured the debate about human embryonic stem cells in Germany and (not) the UK. *Metaphorik de* **8**: 71–104

Nichols, P. 1983. Linguistic options and choices for Black women in the rural South. In Thorne, B., Kramarae, C. and Henley, N. (eds) *Language and Sex: Difference and Dominance.* Rowley, MA: Newbury House

Nicholson, L. (ed.) 1997. *The Second Wave: A Reader in Feminist Theory.* London: Routledge

Nicholson, L. 1994. Interpreting gender. *Signs* **20** (1): 79–105

Nilan, P. 1994. Gender as positioned identity maintenance in everyday discourse. *Social Semiotics* **4** (1–2): 139–63

Norman, K. (ed.) 1992. *Thinking Voices: The Work of the National Oracy Project.* London: Hodder & Stoughton

Norris, S. 2004. *Analyzing Multimodal Interaction: A Methodological Framework.* London: Routledge

Norton, B. 2000. *Identity and Language Learning: Gender, Ethnicity and Educational Change.* London: Longman

Nuyts, J. 2004. The cognitive-pragmatic approach. *Intercultural Pragmatics* **1** (1): 135–49

O'Barr, W. and Atkins, B. 1998. 'Women's language' or 'powerless language'? In McConnell-Ginet, S., Borker, R. and Furman, N. (eds) *Women and Language in Literature and Society.* New York: Praeger. 93–110

Ochs, E. 1992. Indexing gender. In Duranti, A. and Goodwin, C. (eds) *Rethinking Context: Language as an Interactive Phenomenon.* Cambridge: Cambridge University Press. 335–58

O'Halloran, K. 2004. *Critical Discourse Analysis and Language Cognition.* Edinburgh: Edinburgh University Press

Okamoto, D., Rashotte, L. and Smith-Lovin, L. 2002. Measuring interruption: Syntactic and contextual methods of coding conversation. *Social Psychology Quarterly* **65**: 38–55

Ong, A. 1999. *Flexible Citizenship: The Cultural Logics of Transnationality.* Durham, NC: Duke University Press

Orr, S. 2006. Women's work, women's talk? An investigation of gender and language practices in a Glasgow call centre. Paper delivered at *16th Sociolinguistic Symposium.* Limerick University, Eire

Ostermann, A. 2003. Communities of practice at work: Gender, facework and the power of habitus at an all-female police station and a feminist crisis intervention center in brazil. *Discourse and Society* **14** (4): 473–505

Paechter, C. 2003. Learning masculinities and femininities: Power/knowledge and legitimate peripheral participation. *Women's Studies International Forum* **26** (6): 541–52

Panagl, O. and Wodak, R. (eds) 2004. *Text und Kontext*. Würzburg: Königshausen and Neumann

Parlas, K. 1992. The contemporary woman in television. *Kathimerini* 5/1/1992: 10–11

Papathanasopoulos, S. 2000. *Television and its Audience*. Athens: Kastaniotis

Pauwels, A. 1998. *Women Changing Language*. New York: Longman

Pels, D. 2002. Everyday essentialism: Social inertia and the Munchhausen effect. *Theory, Culture and Society* **19** (5/6): 69–89

Philips, L. and Jorgensen, M. 2002. *Discourse Analysis: As Theory and Method*. London: Sage

Philips, S. 2003. The power of gender ideologies in discourse. In Holmes, J. and Meyerhoff, M. (eds) 252–76

Pichler, P. Forthcoming. *Talking Young Femininities*. Basingstoke: Palgrave Macmillan

Pichler, P. 2007. Talking traditions of marriage: Negotiating young British Bangladeshi femininities. *Women's Studies International Forum* **30** (3): 201–6

Pichler, P. 2006a. 'This sex thing is such a big issue now': Sex talk and identities in three groups of adolescent girls. In Sauntson, H. and Kyratzis, S. (eds) 68–95

Pichler, P. 2006b. Multifunctional teasing as a resource for identity construction. *Journal of Sociolinguistics* **10** (2): 226–50

Piper, N. 2006. Gendering the politics of migration. *International Migration Review* **40** (1): 133–64

Plummer, Ken. 1995. *Telling Sexual Stories*. London. Routledge

Pollak, A. and Wodak, R. 2003. The scene of crime: The Wehrmacht exhibition. In Heer, H., Manoschek, W., Pollak, A. and Wodak, R. (eds) *How History is Made: On the Construction of Memories of Wehrmacht and the Second World War*. Wien: Czernin Verlag. 225- 245. Reprinted 2007 in English translation as *The Discursive Construction of History*. Basingstoke: Palgrave Macmillan

Pomerantz, A. 1986. Extreme case formulations: A way of legitimizing claims. *Human Studies* 9: 219–30

Pomerantz, A. and Mandelbaum, J. 2005. Conversation analytic approaches to the relevance and uses of relationship categories in interaction. In Fitch, K. and Sanders, R. (eds) *Handbook of Language and Social Interaction*. Mahwah, NJ: Lawrence Erlbaum Associates. 149–74

Portelli, A. 1993. *The Death of Luigi Trastulli and Other Stories: Form and Meaning in Oral History*. Albany: SUNY Press

Potter, J. 1996. *Representing Reality: Discourse, Rhetoric and Social Construction*. London: Sage

Potter, J. and Hepburn, A. 2007. Discursive psychology: Mind and reality in practice. In Weatherall, A., Watson, B. and Gallois, C. (eds) *Language, Discourse and Social Psychology*. Basingstoke: Palgrave Macmillan

Potter, J. and te Molder, H. 2005. Talking cognition: Mapping and making the terrain. In te Molder, H. and Potter, J. (eds) 1–54

Potter, J. and Wetherell, M. 1987. *Discourse and Social Psychology: Beyond Attitudes and Behaviour*. London: Sage

Probyn, E. 1996. *Outside Belongings*. London: Routledge

Psathas, G. 1999. Studying the organization in action: Membership categorization and interaction. *Human Studies* 22: 139–62

Psathas, G. (ed.) 1995. *Conversation Analysis: The Study of Talk-in Interaction*. London: Sage

Puwar, N. 2003. Melodramatic postures and constructions. In Puwar, N. and Raghuram, P. (eds) *South Asian Women in the Diaspora*. Oxford: Berg. 43–66

Rampton, B., Tusting, K., Maybin, J., Barwell, R., Creese, A. and Lytra, V. 2004. UK linguistic ethnography: A discussion paper. http://www.lancs.ac.uk/fss/organisations/lingethn/ (Accessed 15/06/05)

Raymond, G. and Heritage, J. 2006. The epistemics of social relations: Owning grandchildren. *Language in Society* **35** (5): 677–705

Rayson, P., Leech, G. and Hodges, M. 1997. Social differentiation in the use of English vocabulary: Some analyses of the conversational component of the British National Corpus. *International Journal of Corpus Linguistics* **2** (1): 133–52

Read, K. 1980. *Other Voices: The Style of a Male Homosexual Tavern*. San Francisco: Chandler & Sharp

Reisigl, M. and Wodak, R. 2001. *Discourse and Discrimination: Rhetorics of Racism and Anti-Semitism*. London: Routledge

Rewers, E. 2000. *Language and Space: The Poststructuralist Turn in the Philosophy of Culture*. Frankfurt: Lang

Rich, A. 1993. Compulsory heterosexuality and lesbian existence. In Abelove, H., Barale, M. and Halperin, D. (eds) *The Lesbian and Gay Studies Reader*. London: Routledge. 227–54

Richards, J. and Schmidt, R. 2002. *Longman Dictionary of Language Teaching and Applied Linguistics*. London: Longman

Rimmon-Kenan, S. 2002. *Narrative Fiction: Contemporary Poetics* (2nd edn). Routledge: London

Roberts, C., Cooke, M., Baynham, M. and Simpson, J. 2005. Ethnographic-style bilingual interviews: Practical concerns and implications. Paper delivered at *UK Linguistic Ethnography Forum*. University of Bristol, UK

Roberts, C. and Sarangi, S. 2003. Uptake of discourse research in professional settings: Reporting from medical consultancy. *Applied Linguistics* **24** (3): 338–59

Rogers, B. 1972. *The Queens' Vernacular: A Gay Lexicon*. San Francisco: Straight Arow Books

Romaine, S. 2001. A corpus-based view of gender in British and American English. In Hellinger, M. and Burmann, H. (eds) *Gender Across Language* (Volume 1). Amsterdam: John Benjamins. 153–75.

Romaine, S. 1984. The status of sociological models and categories in explaining linguistic variation. *Linguistische Berichte* **90**: 25–38

Romaine, S. and Lange, D. 1991. The use of 'like' as a marker of reported speech and thought: A case of grammaticalization in progress. *American Speech* **66** (3): 227–79

Rubin, G. 1984. Thinking sex: Notes for a radical theory of the politics of sexuality. In Vance, C. (ed.) *Pleasure and Danger: Exploring Female Sexuality*. New York: Routledge. 267–319

Sacks, H. 1992. *Harvey Sacks: Lectures on Conversation*. Oxford: Blackwell

Sacks, H. 1984. Notes on methodology. In Atkinson, J. and Heritage, J. (eds) *Structures of Social Action: Studies in Conversation Analysis*. Cambridge: Cambridge University Press. 21–7

Sacks, H. 1972. On the analyzability of stories by children. In Gumperz, J. and Hymes, D. (eds) *Directions in Sociolinguistics: The Ethnography of Communication*. New York: Holt, Rinehart & Winston. 329–45

Sacks, H. and Schegloff, E. 1979. Two preferences in the organization of reference to persons in conversation and their interaction. In Psathas, G. (ed.) *Everyday Language: Studies in Ethnomethodology*. New York: Irvington. 15–21

Sacks, H., Schegloff, E. and Jefferson, G. 1974. A simplest systematics of turn-taking for conversation. *Language* **50** (4): 696–735

Sanders, R. 2005. Validating 'observations' in discourse studies: A methodological reason for attention to cognition. In te Molder, H. and Potter, J. (eds) 57–78

Sarangi, S. and Candlin, C. 2003. Trading between reflexivity and relevance: New challenges for applied linguistics. *Applied Linguistics* **24** (3): 271–85

Sarangi, S. and Roberts, C. 1999. The dynamics of interactional and institutional orders in work-related settings. In Sarangi, S. and Roberts, C. (eds) *Talk, Work and Institutional Order: Discourse in Medical, Mediation and Management Settings*. New York and Berlin: Mouton de Gruyter. 1–57

Sarris, N. 1992. *Greek Society and Television 1 and 2: Series of Essays for the Public*. Athens: Gordios

Sauntson, H. (2007) Education, culture and the construction of sexual identity: An appraisal analysis of lesbian coming out narratives. In Sauntson, H. and Kyratzis, S. (eds) 140–64

Sauntson, H. and Kyratzis, S. (eds) 2007. *Language, Desires and Sexualities: Cross-Cultural Perspectives*. Basingstoke: Palgrave Macmillan

Saville-Troike, M. 2003. *The Ethnography of Communication: An Introduction* (3rd edn). Oxford: Blackwell

Schegloff, E. 2007. A tutorial on membership categorization. *Journal of Pragmatics* **39**: 462–82

Schegloff, E. A. 2006. *A Primer in Conversation Analysis II: Sequence Organisation*. Cambridge: Cambridge University Press

Schegloff, E. 2005. On complainability. *Social Problems* **52** (4): 449–76

Schegloff, E. 2001 Accounts of conduct in interaction: Interruption, overlap and turn-taking. In Turner, J. (ed.) *Handbook of Sociological Theory*. London: Kluwer Academic

Schegloff, E. 2000 Overlapping talk and the organisation of turn taking for conversation. *Language in Society* **29**: 1–63

Schegloff, E. 1999. 'Schegloff's texts' as 'Billig's data': A critical reply. *Discourse and Society* **10** (4): 558–72

Schegloff, E. 1998. Reply to Wetherell. *Discourse and Society* **9** (3): 413–16

Schegloff, E. 1997. Whose text? Whose context? *Discourse and Society* **8** (2): 165–87

Schegloff, E. 1996a. Some practices for referring to persons in talk in interaction. In Fox, B. (ed.) *Studies in Anaphora*. Amsterdam: John Benjamins. 437–85

Schegloff, E. 1996b. Confirming allusions: Toward an empirical account of action. *American Journal of Sociology* **104**: 161–216

Schegloff, E. 1992. In another context. In Duranti, A. and Goodwin, C. (eds) *Rethinking Context*. Cambridge: Cambridge University Press. 191–227

Schegloff, E. 1991. Reflections on talk and social structure. In Boden, D. and Zimmerman, D. (eds) *Talk and Social Structure*. Berkeley, CA: University of California Press. 44–70

Schegloff, E.A. 1987. Between macro and micro: Contexts and other connections. In Alexander, J., Giesen, B., Much, R. and Smelser, N. (eds) in *The Micro-Macro Link*. Berkeley: University of California Press. 207–34

Schegloff, E., Jefferson, G. and Sacks, H. 1977. The preference for self-correction in the organization of repair in conversation. *Language* **53**: 361–82

Schiffrin, D. 1996. Narrative as self-portrait: Sociolinguistic constructions of identity. *Language in Society* **25** (2): 167–203

Schmid, H.-J. and Fauth, J. 2003. Women's and men's style: Fact or fiction? New grammatical evidence. Paper delivered at *Corpus Linguistics Conference*. Lancaster University, UK

Scott, M. 1996. Comparing corpora and identifying key words, collocations, and frequency distributions through the *WordSmith Tools* suite of computer programs. In Ghadessy, M. and Roseberry, R. (eds) *Small Corpus Studies and ELT: Theory and Practice*. Amsterdam: John Benjamins

Sealey, A. 2005. Linguistic ethnography: An applied linguistic perspective. Paper delivered at *British Association of Applied Linguistics Conference*. University of Bristol, UK

Sedgwick, E. 1990. *The Epistemology of the Closet*. Berkeley, CA: University of California Press

Segall, K. 2005. *Social Voices: Characterising the Use of Reported Dialogue in Conversation*. Unpublished PhD. Roehampton University, UK

Shain, F. 2003. *The Schooling and Identity of Asian Girls*. Stoke on Trent: Trentham Books

Sheldon, A. 1997. Talking power: Girls, gender enculturation and discourse. In Wodak, R. (ed.) 225–44

Sidnell, J. (2003) Constructing and managing male exclusivity in talk-in-interaction. In Holmes, J. and Meyerhoff, M. (eds.) *The Handbook of Language and Gender*. Oxford: Blackwell

Sigley, R. and Holmes, J. 2002. Girl-watching in corpora of English. *Journal of English Linguistics* 30 (2): 138–57

Silverman, D. 2001. *Interpreting Qualitative Data: Methods for Analysing Talk, Text and Interaction* (2nd edn). London: Sage

Silvey, R. 2006. Geographies of gender and migration: Spatializing social difference. *International Migration Review* 40 (1): 64–81

Simeonidou, C. 2005a. The distribution in the workplace and the household: Results of the Panhellenic survey of 1999. Paper presented at *Gender is Changing: Research, Theory and Politics of the Gendered Reality in the 21st Century* conference. Athens

Simeonidou, C. 2005b. Formation and breaking-up of the family in Greece. In Ziomas. D., Kappi, C., Papailiou, O., Papapetrou. G. and Fagadaki, E. (eds) *The Social Portrait of Greece 2003–4*. Athens: National Centre for Social Research, Institute of Social Policy. 17–36

Sinclair, J. 1991. *Corpus, Concordance, Collocation*. Oxford: Oxford University Press

Smith, D. 1981. *The Experienced World as Problematic: A Feminist Method. Sorokin Lecture No. 12*. Saskatoon: University of Saskatchewan

Smith, Z. 2000. *White Teeth*. London: Penguin

Speer, S. 2005. *Gender Talk: Feminism, Discourse and Conversation Analysis*. London: Routledge

Speer, S. 2002. Sexist Talk: Gender categories, participants' orientations and irony. *Journal of Sociolinguistics* 6 (3): 347–77

Speer, S. 2001. Reconsidering the concept of hegemonic masculinity: Discursive psychology, conversation analysis and participants' orientations. *Feminism and Psychology* 11 (1): 107–35

Speer, S. 2000. Sexist talk: Gender categories, participants' orientations and irony. *Journal of Sociolinguistics* 6 (3): 347–77

Speer, S. 1999. Feminism and conversation analysis: An oxymoron? *Feminism and Psychology* 9 (4): 471–8

Speer, S. and Parsons, C. 2006. Gatekeeping gender: Some features of the use of hypothetical questions in the psychiatric assessment of transsexual patients. *Discourse and Society* 17 (6): 785–812

Speer, S. and Potter, J. 2002. From performatives to practices: Judith Butler, discursive psychology, and the management of heterosexist talk. In McIlvenny, P. (ed.) 79–109

Speer, S. and Stokoe, E. Forthcoming. *Conversation and Gender*. Cambridge: Cambridge University Press

Spender, D. 1990. *Man Made Language* (2nd edn). London: Pandora

Spender, D. 1980. *Man Made Language*. London: Pandora

Spivak, G. 1993. *'In a Word: Interview.' In Outside in the Teaching Machine*. New York: Routledge. 1–24

Spivak, G. 1985. Subaltern studies: Deconstructing historiography. In Landry, D. and MacLean, G. (eds) 203–36

Spradley, J. 1979. *The Ethnographic Interview*. Belmont, CA (USA): Wadsworth

Stefanowitsch, A. 2005. The function of metaphor: Developing a corpus-based perspective. *International Journal of Corpus Linguistics* **10** (2): 161–98

Stenström, A., Andersen, G. and Hasund, I. 2002. *Trends in Teenage Talk: Corpus Compilation, Analysis, and Findings*. Amsterdam: John Benjamins

Stephens, J. 1992. *Language and Ideology in Children's Fiction*. London: Longman

Stewart, K. 1992. *A Space at the Side of the Road*. Austin: University of Texas Press

Stivers, T. 2005. Modified repeats: One method for asserting primary rights from second position. *Research on Language and Social interaction* **38**: 131–58

Stokoe, E. in press. 'Girl – woman – sorry!': On the repair and non-repair of consecutive gender categories. In Speer, S. A. and Stokoe, E. (eds), *Conversation and Gender*. Cambridge: Cambridge University Press

Stokoe, E. 2006. On ethnomethodology, feminism, and the analysis of categorial reference to gender in talk-in-interaction. *Sociological Review* **54** (3): 467–94

Stokoe, E. 2005. Analysing gender and language. *Journal of Sociolinguistics* **9** (1): 118–33

Stokoe, E. 2004. Gender and discourse, gender and categorization: Current developments in language and gender research. *Qualitative Research in Psychology* **1** (2): 107–29

Stokoe, E. 2003. Mothers, single women and sluts: Gender, morality and membership categorization in neighbour disputes. *Feminism and Psychology* **13** (3): 317–44

Stokoe, E. 2000. Toward a conversation analytic approach to gender and discourse. *Feminism and Psychology* **10** (4): 552–63

Stokoe, E. 1998. Talking about gender: The conversational construction of gender categories in academic discourse. *Discourse and Society* **9** (2): 217–40

Stokoe, E. 1997. An evaluation of two studies of gender and language in educational settings. *Gender and Education* **9** (2): 233–44

Stokoe, E. 1995. Gender differences in undergraduates' talk: Contrasting analyses and what they offer. *Feminism and Psychology* **5** (1): 99–104

Stokoe, E. and Edwards, D. In press. Mundane morality and gender in familial neighbour disputes. In Cromdal, J. and Tholander, M. (eds) *Children, Morality and Interaction*. London: Equinox

Stokoe, E. and Smithson, J. 2002. Gender and sexuality in talk-in-interaction: Considering conversation analytic perspectives. In McIlvenny, P. (ed.) 79–109

Stokoe, E. and Smithson, J. 2001. Making gender relevant: Conversation analysis and gender categories in interaction. *Discourse and Society* **12** (2): 217–44

Stokoe, E. and Weatherall, A. 2002. Gender, language, conversation analysis and feminism. *Discourse and Society* **13** (6): 703–13

Stubbs, M. 2001. *Words and Phrases: Corpus Studies of Lexical Semantics*. London: Blackwell

Stubbs, M. 1997. Whorf's children: Critical comments on critical discourse analysis (CDA). In Ryan, A. and Wray, A. (eds) *Evolving Models of Language: Papers from the Annual Meeting of the British Association for Applied Linguistics*. Clevedon: Multilingual Matters. 100–16

Stubbs, M. 1996. *Text and Corpus Analysis*. London: Blackwell

Sunderland, J. 2007. Contradictions in gendered discourses: Feminist readings of sexist jokes? *Gender and Language* **1** (2)

Sunderland, J. 2006. *Language and Gender: An Advanced Resource Book*. Abingdon: Routledge

Sunderland, J. 2004. *Gendered Discourses*. Basingstoke: Palgrave Macmillan

Sunderland, J. 2000a. Issues of language and gender in second and foreign language education. *Language Teaching* **33** (4): 203–23

Sunderland, J. 2000b. Baby entertainer, bumbling assistant and line manager: Discourses of fatherhood in parentcraft texts. *Discourse and Society* **11** (2): 249–74

Sunderland, J. 1995. 'We're boys, miss!': Finding gendered identities and looking for gendering of identities in the foreign language classroom. In Mills, S. (ed.) *Language and Gender: Interdisciplinary Perspectives*. London: Longman. 160–78

Sunderland, J. and Litosseliti, L. (eds) 2002. *Gender Identity and Discourse Analysis*. Amsterdam: Benjamins

Sunderland, J., Cowley, M., Rahim, F., Leontzakuo, C. and Shattuck, J. 2002. From representation towards discursive practices: Gender in the foreign language textbook revisited. In Litosseliti, L. and Sunderland, J. (eds) 223–55

Swann, J. (2003) Schooled language: Language and gender in educational settings. In Holmes, J. and Meyerhoff, M. (eds.) *The Handbook of Language and Gender*. Oxford: Blackwell.

Swann, J. 2002. Yes, but is it gender? In Litosseliti, L. and Sunderland, J. (eds) 43–67

Swann, J. 1992. *Girls, Boys and Language*. London: Blackwell

Swann, J. et al., 2004. *A Dictionary of Sociolinguistics*. Edinburgh : Edinburgh University Press.

Tagliamonte, S. and D'Arcy, A. 2004. He's like, she's like: The quotative system in Canadian youth. *Journal of Sociolinguistics* **8** (4): 493–514

Tagliamonte, S. and Hudson, R. 1999. *Be like* et al. beyond America: The quotative system in British and Canadian Youth. *Journal of Sociolinguistics* **3** (2): 147–72

Tainio, L. 2003. 'When shall we go for a ride?' A case of the sexual harassment of a young girl. *Discourse and Society* **14** (2): 173–90

Talbot, M. 2003. Gender stereotypes: Reproduction and challenge. In Holmes, J. and Meyerhoff, M. (eds) 468–86

Talbot, M. 2000. 'It's good to talk?' The undermining of feminism in a British Telecom advertisement. *Journal of Sociolinguistics* **4** (1): 108–19

Talbot, M. 1998. *Language and Gender: An Introduction*. Cambridge: Polity Press

Talbot, M. 1997a. 'An explosion deep inside her': Women's desire in popular romance fiction. In Harvey, K. and Shalom, C. (eds) *Language and Desire: Encoding Sex, Romance and Intimacy*. London: Routledge. 106–22

Talbot, M. 1997b. 'Randy fish boss branded a stinker': Coherence and the construction of masculinities in a British tabloid newspaper. In Johnson, S. and Meinhof, U. (eds) 173–87

Talbot, M. 1995a. *Fictions at Work*. London: Longman

Talbot, M. 1995b. A synthetic sisterhood: False friends in a teenage magazine. In Hall, K. and Bucholtz, M. (eds) *Gender Articulated: Language and the Socially Constructed Self*. New York: Routledge. 143–65

Tannen, D. 1994. *Gender and Discourse*. Oxford: Oxford University Press

Tannen, D. 1993. The relativity of linguistic strategies: Rethinking power and solidarity in gender and dominance. In Tannen, D. (ed.) *Gender and Conversational Interaction*. Oxford: Oxford University Press. 165–88

Tannen, D. 1991. *You Just Don't Understand: Women and Men in Conversation*. London: Virago Press

Tannen, D. (1990). *You Just Don't Understand!* London: Virago

Tannen, D. 1989. *Talking Voices: Repetition, Dialogue and Imagery in Conversational Discourse*. Cambridge: Cambridge University Press

Tashakkori, A. and Teddie, C. 1998. *Mixed Methodology: Combining Qualitative and Quantitative Approaches*. London: Sage

Taylor, P. and Bain, P. 1999. 'An assembly line in the head': Work and employee relations in the call centre. *Industrial Relations Journal* **30** (2): 101–17

Taylor, P., Mulvey, G., Hyman, J. and Bain, P. 2002. Work organization, control and the experience of work in call centres. *Work, Employment and Society* **16** (1): 133–50

te Molder, H. and Potter, J. (eds) 2005. *Conversation and Cognition*. Cambridge: Cambridge University Press

Teperoglou, E. and Psara, M. 2001. *Women and Politics: Overview Study*. http://www.kethi.gr/greek/meletes/index.htm (Accessed 5.11.2005)

Teutsch-Dwyer, M. 2001. (Re)constructing masculinity in a new linguistic reality. In Pavlenko, A. et al. (eds) *Multilingualism, Second Language Learning, and Gender*. Berlin: de Gruyter. 175–98

Thapan, M. (ed.) 1997. *Embodiment: Essays on Gender and Identity*. Delhi: Oxford University Press

Thompson, J. 1984. *Studies in the Theory of Ideology*. Cambridge: Polity Press

Threadgold, T. 1988. Stories of race and gender: An unbounded discourse. In Birch, D. and O'Toole, M. (eds) *Functions of Style*. London: Pinter. 169–204

Tona, C. 2006. But what is interesting is the story of why and how migration happened: Ronit Lentin and Hassan Bousetta in conversation with Carla De Tona. *Forum Qualitative Social Research* **7** (3) http://www.qualitative-research.net/fqs/ (Accessed 26.7.2006)

Toolan, M. 1997. What is critical discourse analysis and why are people saying such terrible things about it? *Language and Literature* **6** (2): 83–103

Tracy, K. 1998. Analysing context: Framing the discussion. *Research in Language and Social Interaction* **31** (1): 1–28

Trudgill, P. 1972. Sex, covert prestige and linguistic change in the urban British English of Norwich. *Language in Society* **1**: 179–95

Tzavella, P. 2004. *General Secretariat for Equality: Role and Fields of Exercising Politics*. Athens: Panteion University of Social and Political Sciences

Unger, J. W. and Sunderland, J. 2005. Gendered discourses in a contemporary animated film: Subversion and confirmation of gender stereotypes in *Shrek*. *CLSL Working Paper 124*. http://www.ling.lancs.ac.uk/groups/clsl/wpapers.htm

Valoukos, S. 1998. *Greek Television: Television Series Guide 1967–1998*. Athens: Egokeros

Van Dijk, T. Forthcoming. *Context*. Cambridge: Cambridge University Press

van Dijk, T. (ed.) 2006a. *Discourse Studies* **8** (1)

van Dijk, T. 2006b. Discourse, context and cognition. *Discourse Studies* **8** (1): 159–77

van Dijk, T. 2005. Contextual knowledge management in discourse production: A CDA perspective. In Wodak, R. and Chilton, P. A. (eds) *A New Agenda in (Critical) Discourse Analysis*. Amsterdam: Benjamins. 71–100

van Dijk, T. 2003. The discourse-knowledge interface. In Weiss, G. and Wodak, R. (eds) 85–109 van Dijk, T. 2001. Multidisciplinary CDA: A plea for diversity. In Wodak, R. and Meyer, M. (eds) *Methods of Critical Discourse Analysis*. London: Sage. 95–120

van Dijk, T. 1995a. Power and the news media. In Paletz, D. (ed.) *Political Communication and Action*. Cresskill, NJ: Hampton Press. 9–36

van Dijk, T. 1995b. Discourse analysis as ideology analysis. In Schäffner, C. and Wenden, A. (eds) *Language and Peace*. Aldershot: Dartmouth. 17–33

van Leeuwen, T. 2005a. Three models of interdisciplinarity. In Wodak, R. and Chilton, P. (eds) *A New Agenda in (Critical) Discourse Analysis: Theory, Methodology and Interdisciplinarity*. Amsterdam: John Benjamins. 3–18

van Leeuwen, T. 2005b. *Introducing Social Semiotics*. London: Routledge

van Leeuwen, T. 1996. The representation of social actors. In Caldas-Coulthard, C. and Coulthard, M. (eds) *Texts and Practices: Readings in Critical Discourse Analysis*. London: Routledge. 32–71

van Leeuwen, T. and Wodak, R. 1999. Legitimising immigration control: A discourse-historical analysis. *Discourse Studies* 1 (1): 83–118

van Zoonen, L. 1994. *Feminist Media Studies*. London: Sage

Varga, O. 2005. 'Sex' and 'gender': A corpus analysis of British and American English. Paper delivered at *BAAL/CUP Seminar: Theoretical and Methodological Approaches to Gender and Lanaguge Study*. University of Birmingham, UK

Velody, I. and Williams, R. (eds) (1998) *The Politics of Constructionism*. London: Sage

Verschueren, J. 2001. Predicaments of criticism. *Critique of Anthropology* 21 (1): 59–81

Vološinov, V. 1973. *Marxism and the Philosophy of Language*. Trans. Matejka, L. and Titunik, I. New York: Seminar Press

Vygotsky, L. 1978. *Mind in Society: The Development of Higher Psychological Processes*. London: Harvard University Press

Wagner, I. and Wodak, R. 2006. Performing success: Identifying strategies of self-presentation in women's biographical narratives. *Discourse and Society* 17 (3): 385–411

Walkerdine, V. 1998. *Counting Girls Out: Girls and Mathematics*. London: Routledge Falmer

Walkerdine, V. 1990. *Schoolgirl Fictions*. London: Verso

Walsh, C. 2001. *Gender and Discourse: Language and Power in Politics, the Church and Organisations*. London: Longman

Warhol, T. 2005. Feminist poststructuralist discourse analysis and biblical authority. Paper delivered at *BAAL/CUP Seminar: Theoretical and Methodological Approaches to Gender and Language Study*. University of Birmingham, UK

Warren, C. 1974. *Identity and Community in the Gay World*. New York: John Wiley

Watson, D. 1983. The presentation of victim and motive in discourse: The case of police interrogations and interviews. *Victimology: An International Journal* 8 (1–2): 31–52

Watson, G. 1992. When Orietta visits, reflexivity is not a trouble. Paper presented at *Discourse Analysis and Reflexivity Group*. Brunel University, UK

Watson, J. 1977. *Between Two Cultures: Migrants and Minorities in Britain*. Oxford: Blackwell

Weatherall, A. 2002. *Gender, Language and Discourse*. London: Routledge

Weatherall, A. 2000. Gender relevance in talk-in-interaction and discourse. *Discourse and Society* 11 (2): 290–2

Weedon, C. 1997. *Feminist Practice and Poststructuralist Theory* (2nd edn). Oxford: Blackwell

Weiner, M. (ed.) 1997. *Japan's Minorities: The Illusion of Homogeneity*. London: Routledge

Weiss, G. and Wodak, R. 2003. *Critical Discourse Analysis: Theory and Inter-Disciplinarity*. Basingstoke: Palgrave Macmillan

West, C. 1979. Against our will: Male interruptions of females in cross-sex conversations. In Orasanu, J., Slater, M. and Adler, L. (eds) *Language, Sex and Gender: Annals of the New York Academy of Sciences 327*. New York: New York Academy of Sciences. 81–97

West, C. and Zimmerman, D. 1991. Doing gender. In Lorber, J. and Farrell, S. (eds) *The Social Construction of Gender*. Newbury Park: Sage. 13–37

West, C. and Zimmerman, D. 1987. Doing gender. *Gender and Society* 1 (2): 125–51

West, C. and Zimmerman, D. 1983. Small insults: A study of interruptions in cross-sex conversations between unacquainted persons. In Thorne, B., Kramarae, C. and Henley, N. (eds) *Language, Gender and Society*. Rowley, MA: Newbury House. 103–17

West, C., Lazar, M. and Kramarae, C. 1997. Gender in discourse. In van Dijk, T. (ed.) *Introduction to Discourse Analysis*. London: Sage. 119–43

Wetherell, M. 2001 Themes in discourse research: The case of Diana. In Wetherell, M., Taylor, S., and Yates, S. (eds) *Discourse Theory and Practice: A Reader*. London: Sage. 14–28

Wetherell, M. 1998. Positioning and interpretative repertoires: Conversation analysis and post-structuralism in dialogue. *Discourse and Society* 9 (3): 387–412

Wetherell, M. 1994. Men and masculinity: A socio-psychological analysis of discourse and gender identity. *End of Award Grant Report: ESRC grant No. R000233129*.

Wetherell, M. 1984. Writing gender. In Potter, J., Stringer, P. and Wetherell, M. (eds) *Social Texts and Context: Literature and Social Psychology*. London: Routledge. 9–29

Wetherell, M. and Edley, N. 1999. Negotiating hegemonic masculinity: Imaginary positions and psycho-discursive practices. *Feminism & Psychology* 9 (3): 335–56

Wetherell, M., Stiven, H. and Potter, J. 1987. Unequal egalitarianism: A preliminary study of discourses concerning gender and employment opportunities. *British Journal of Social Psychology* 26: 59–71

Widdicombe, S. (1995) Identity, politics and talk: A case for the mundane and everyday. In Wilkinson, S. and Kitzinger, C. (eds) *Feminism and Discourse: Psychological Perspectives*. London: Sage.

Widdowson, H. 2004. *Text, Context, Pretext: Critical Issues in Discourse Analysis*. Oxford: Blackwell

Widdowson, H. 2000. Critical practices: On representation and the interpretation of text. In Sarangi, S. and Coulthard, M. (eds) *Discourse and Social Life*. London: Longman. 155–69

Widdowson, H. 1995. Discourse analysis: A critical view. *Language and Literature* 4 (3): 157–72

Wilkinson, S. and Kitzinger, C. 1995. *Feminism and Discourse: Psychological Perspectives*. London: Sage

Willott, S. and Griffin, C. 1997. 'Wham bam, am I a man?' Unemployed men talk about masculinities. *Feminism and Psychology* 7 (1): 107–28

Wittgenstein, L. 1958. *Philosophical Investigations*. Trans. Anscombe, G. Oxford: Blackwell

Wittig, M. 1993. One is not born a woman. In In Abelove, H., Barale, M. and Halperin, D. (eds) *The Lesbian and Gay Studies Reader*. London: Routledge. 103–9

Wodak, R. 2006. Review article: Dilemmas of discourse (analysis). *Language in Society* 35: 595–611

Wodak, R. 2005. Gender mainstreaming and the European Union: Interdisciplinarity, gender studies and CDA. In Lazar, M. (ed.) 90–113

Wodak, R. 2004. Critical discourse analysis. In Seale, C., Gobo, G., Gubrium, J. and Silverman, D. (eds) *Qualitative Research Practice*. London: Sage. 197–215

Wodak, R. 2003. Multiple identities: The roles of female parliamentarians in the EU parliament. In Holmes, J. and Meyerhoff, M. (eds) 671–98

Wodak, R. 2001a. What CDA is about: A summary of its history, important concepts and its developments. In Wodak, R. and Meyer, M. (eds) 1–13

Wodak, R. 2001b. The discourse-historical approach. In Wodak, R. and Meyer, M. (eds) 63–94

Wodak, R. (ed.) 1997. *Gender and Discourse*. London: Sage

Wodak, R. 1996. *Disorders in Discourse*. London: Longman

Wodak, R. 1995. Critical linguistics and critical discourse analysis. In Verschueren, J., Östman, J. and Blommaert, J. (eds) *Handbook of Pragmatics*. Amsterdam: John Benjamins. 204–10

Wodak, R. 1987. 'And where is the Lebanon?' A socio-psycholinguistic investigation of comprehension and intelligibility of news. *Text* 7 (4): 377–410

Wodak, R. 1986a. *Language Behavior in Therapy Groups*. Los Angeles: University of California Press

Wodak, R. 1986b. *The Language of Love and Guilt*. Amsterdam: Benjamins

Wodak and Kovács, 2004.

Wodak, R. and Meyer, M. (eds) 2001. *Methods of Critical Discourse Analysis*. London: Sage

Wodak, R. and van Dijk, T. (eds) 2000. *Racism at the Top: Parliamentary Discourses on Ethnic Issues in Six European States*. Klagenfurt: Drava

Wodak, R., de Cillia, R., Reisigl, M. and Liebhart, K. 1999. *The Discursive Construction of National Identity*. Edinburgh: EdinburghUniversity Press

Wooffitt, R. 2005. *Conversation Analysis and Discourse Analysis: A Comparative and Critical Introduction*. London: Sage

Wowk, M. T. (2004). *Another Sociological Chimera: Kitzinger's Feminist Conversation Analysis*. Unpublished manuscript

Wowk, M. 1984. Blame allocation, sex and gender in a murder interrogation. *Women's Studies International Forum* 7 (1): 75–82

Yar M. 2002. Recognition and the politics of human(e) desire. In Lash, S. and Featherstone, M. (eds) *Recognition and Difference: Politics, Identity, Multiculture*. London: Sage. 57–76

Zimmerman, D. and West, C. 1975. Sex roles, interruptions, and silences in conversation. In Thorne, B. and Henley, N. (eds) *Language and Sex: Difference and Dominance*. Rowley, MA: Newbury House. 105–29

Zinken, J. 2003. Ideological imagination: Intertextual and correlational metaphors in political discourse. *Discourse and Society* 14 (4): 507–23

Index